PRENTICE HALL MATHEMATICS

GEOMETRY

ALL-IN-ONE
Student Workbook
VERSION B

PEARSON

Prentice
Hall

Boston, Massachusetts
Upper Saddle River, New Jersey

ISBN 0-13-165723-2

2 3 4 5 6 7 8 9 10   10 09 08 07 06

Daily Notetaking Guide

Practice, Guided Problem Solving, Vocabulary

Chapter 1 Tools of Geometry

Chapter 2 Reasoning and Proof

Chapter 3 Parallel and Perpendicular Lines

Chapter 4 Congruent Triangles

Chapter 5 Relationships Within Triangles

Chapter 6 Quadrilaterals

Chapter 7 Similarity

Chapter 8 Right Triangles and Trigonometry

Chapter 9 Transformations

Chapter 10 Area

Chapter 11 Surface Area and Volume

Chapter 12 Circles

A Note to the Student:

This section of your workbook contains notetaking pages for each lesson in your student edition. They are structured to help you take effective notes in class. They will also serve as a study guide as you prepare for tests and quizzes.

Lesson 1-1

Patterns and Inductive Reasoning

Lesson Objective	**NAEP 2005 Strand:** Geometry
▼ Use inductive reasoning to make conjectures	**Topic:** Mathematical Reasoning
	Local Standards: _____

Vocabulary

Inductive reasoning is _____

_____

A _____ is a conclusion you reach using inductive reasoning.

A counterexample is _____

_____

Example

❶ Finding and Using a Pattern Find a pattern for the sequence.
Use the pattern to find the next two terms in the sequence.

384, 192, 96, 48, . . .

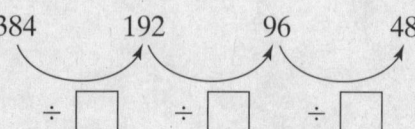

Each term is [   ] the preceding term. The next two

terms are 48 ÷ [   ] = [   ] and 24 ÷ [   ] = [   ].

Quick Check

1. Find the next two terms in each sequence.

a. 1, 2, 4, 7, 11, 16, 22, [   ], [   ], . . .

b. Monday, Tuesday, Wednesday, [   ], [   ], . . .

c.  [   ] , [   ] , . . .

Example

❷ Using Inductive Reasoning Make a conjecture about the sum of the cubes of the first 25 counting numbers.

Find the first few sums. Notice that each sum is a perfect square and that the perfect squares form a pattern.

$$1^3 \qquad\qquad\qquad = \quad 1 = 1^2 = 1^2$$
$$1^3 + 2^3 \qquad\qquad\quad = \quad 9 = 3^2 = (1 + 2)^2$$
$$1^3 + 2^3 + 3^3 \qquad\quad = \quad 36 = 6^2 = (1 + 2 + 3)^2$$
$$1^3 + 2^3 + 3^3 + 4^3 \quad = 100 = 10^2 = (1 + 2 + 3 + 4)^2$$
$$1^3 + 2^3 + 3^3 + 4^3 + 5^3 = 225 = 15^2 = (1 + 2 + 3 + 4 + 5)^2$$

The sum of the first two cubes equals the square of the sum of the first

[_____] counting numbers. The sum of the first three cubes equals the

square of the sum of the first [_____] counting numbers. This pattern

continues for the fourth and fifth rows. So a conjecture might be that

_____

_____

_____

_____

Quick Check

2. Make a conjecture about the sum of the first 35 odd numbers. Use your calculator to verify your conjecture.

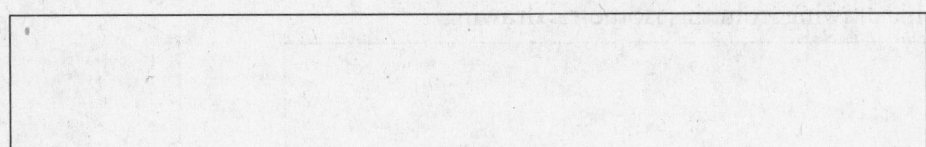

$$1 \qquad\qquad\qquad\qquad = \boxed{} = \boxed{}$$
$$1 + 3 \qquad\qquad\qquad = \boxed{} = \boxed{}$$
$$1 + 3 + \boxed{} \qquad\quad = \boxed{} = \boxed{}$$
$$1 + \boxed{} + \boxed{} + \boxed{} = \boxed{} = \boxed{}$$
$$1 + \boxed{} + \boxed{} + \boxed{} + \boxed{} = \boxed{} = \boxed{}$$

Lesson 1-2

Drawings, Nets, and Other Models

Lesson Objectives	NAEP 2005 Strand: Geometry
☑ Make isometric and orthographic drawings	**Topic:** Dimension and Shape
☑ Draw nets for three-dimensional figures	**Local Standards:** _____

Vocabulary

An isometric drawing of a three-dimensional object shows _____

_____

An _____ is the top view, front view, and right-side view of a three-dimensional figure.

A net is _____

_____

Example

❶ Orthographic Drawing Make an orthographic drawing of the isometric drawing at right.

Orthographic drawings flatten the depth of a figure. An orthographic drawing shows [   ] views. Because no edge of the isometric drawing is hidden in the top, front, and right views, all lines are solid.

Front   Top   Right

Quick Check

1. Make an orthographic drawing from this isometric drawing.

Front   Top   Right

Example

❷ **Drawing a Net** Draw a net for the figure with a square base and four isosceles triangle faces. Label the net with its dimensions.

Think of the sides of the square base as hinges, and "unfold" the figure at these edges to form a net. The base of each of the four isosceles triangle faces is a side of the [   ]. Write in the known dimensions.

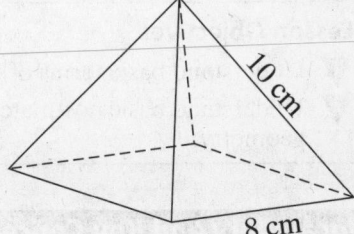

Quick Check

2. The drawing shows one possible net for the Graham Crackers box.

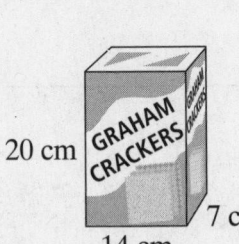 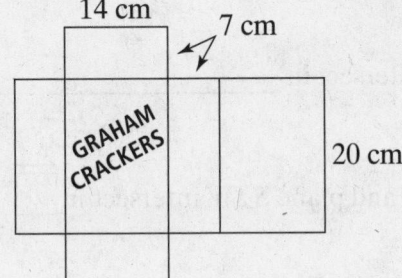

Draw a different net for this box. Show the dimensions in your diagram.

Lesson 1-3

Lesson Objectives	**NAEP 2005 Strand:** Geometry
▼ Understand basic terms of geometry ▼ Understand basic postulates of geometry	**Topic:** Dimension and Shape **Local Standards:** _____

Vocabulary and Key Concepts

Postulate 1-1

Through any two points there is _____

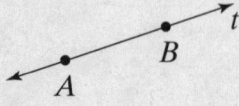 Line t is the only line that passes through points A and ☐.

Postulate 1-2

If two lines intersect, then they intersect in _____

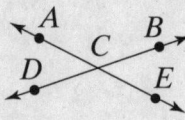 $\overleftrightarrow{AE}$ and $\overleftrightarrow{BD}$ intersect at ☐.

Postulate 1-3

If two planes intersect, then they intersect in _____

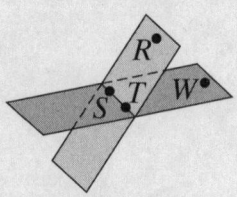 Plane RST and plane STW intersect in $\overset{\leftrightarrow}{\boxed{}}$.

Postulate 1-4

Through any three noncollinear points there is _____

A point is _____

_____ is the set of all points.

A line is _____

_____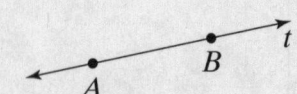

_____ are points that lie on the same line.

Name_____ Class_____ Date _____

A plane is _____

_____

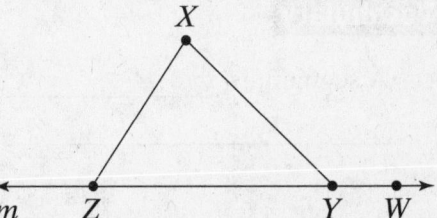
Plane *ABC*

Two points or lines are _____ if they lie on the same plane.

A postulate or axiom is _____

Examples

① **Identifying Collinear Points** In the figure at right, name three points that are collinear and three points that are not collinear.

Points ⬜, ⬜, and ⬜ lie on a line, so they are collinear.

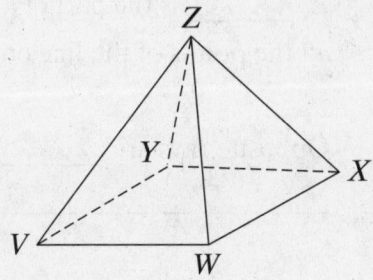

② **Using Postulate 1-4** Shade the plane that contains *X*, *Y*, and *Z*.

Points *X*, *Y*, and *Z* are the vertices of one of the four triangular faces of the pyramid. To shade the plane, shade the interior of the triangle formed by ⬜, ⬜, and ⬜.

Quick Check

1. Use the figure in Example 1.
   a. Are points *W*, *Y*, and *X* collinear?

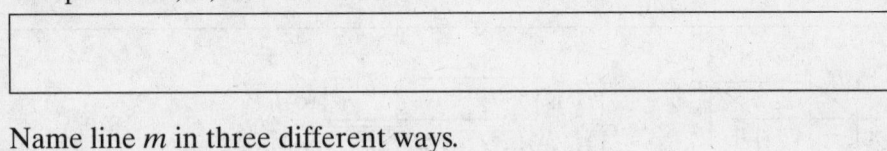

   b. Name line *m* in three different ways.

2. a. Shade plane *VWX*.

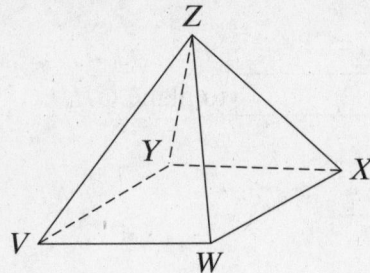

   b. Name a point that is coplanar with points *V*, *W*, and *X*.

Lesson 1-4

Segments, Rays, Parallel Lines and Planes

Lesson Objectives	NAEP 2005 Strand: Geometry
▼ Identify segments and rays ▼ Recognize parallel lines	**Topic:** Relationships Among Geometric Figures **Local Standards:** _____

Vocabulary

A segment is _____

_____

Segment *AB*

$\overline{AB}$ ←•————————•→
  ↗ *A*   *B* ↖
Endpoint [   ]

A _____ is the part of a line consisting of one endpoint and all the points of the line on one side of the endpoint.

Ray *YX*

$\overrightarrow{YX}$ ←————•————————•→
       X   *Y*
            Endpoint

Opposite rays are _____

_____

←——•————————•————————•——→
   Q   *R*   *S*

[   ] and [   ] are opposite rays.

_____ are coplanar lines that do not intersect.

Skew lines are _____

_____

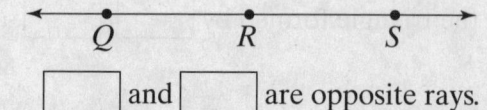

$\overleftrightarrow{AB}$ is [   ] to $\overleftrightarrow{EF}$.
$\overleftrightarrow{AB}$ and $\overleftrightarrow{CG}$ are [   ] lines.

_____ are planes that do not intersect.

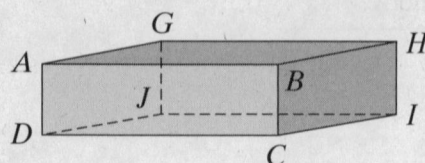

Plane *ABCD* is [   ] to plane *GHIJ*.

Examples

❶ Naming Segments and Rays Name the segments and rays in the figure.

The labeled points in the figure are A, B, and C.

A segment is a part of a line consisting of two endpoints and all points between them. A segment is named by its two endpoints. So the segments are [   ] and [   ].

A ray is a part of a line consisting of one endpoint and all the points of the line on one side of that endpoint. A ray is named by its endpoint first, followed by any other point on the ray. So the rays are [   ] and [   ].

❷ Identifying Parallel Planes Identify a pair of parallel planes in your classroom.

Planes are parallel if they [   ]. If the walls of your classroom are vertical, [   ] walls are parts of parallel planes. If the ceiling and floor of the classroom are level, they are parts of parallel planes.

Quick Check

1. **Critical Thinking** Use the figure in Example 1. $\overrightarrow{CB}$ and $\overrightarrow{BC}$ form a line. Are they opposite rays? Explain.

2. Use the diagram to the right.
   a. Name three pairs of parallel planes.

   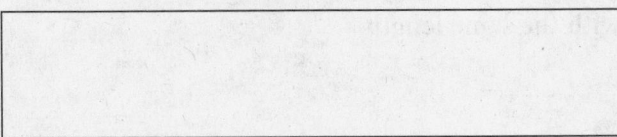

   b. Name a line that is parallel to $\overleftrightarrow{PQ}$.

   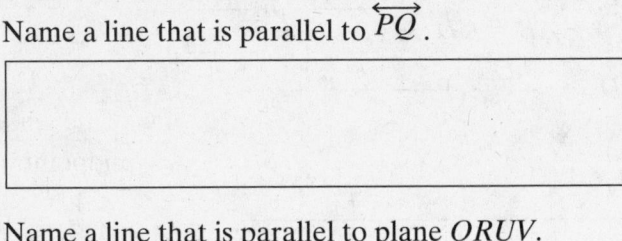

   c. Name a line that is parallel to plane $QRUV$.

   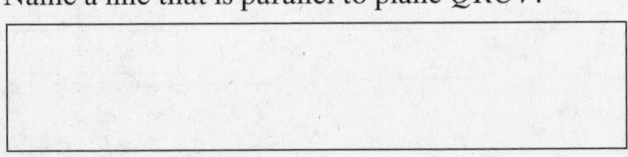

Lesson 1-5

Measuring Segments

Lesson Objectives	NAEP 2005 Strand: Measurement
▼ Find the lengths of segments	Topic: Measuring Physical Attributes
	Local Standards: _____

Vocabulary and Key Concepts

Postulate 1-5: Ruler Postulate

The points of a line can be put into one-to-one
correspondence with the real numbers so
that the distance between any two points is the _____

_____

Postulate 1-6: Segment Addition Postulate

If three points A, B, and C are collinear and B
is between A and C, then _____

A coordinate is _____

_____

the length of $\overline{AB}$

$$AB = | \boxed{} - \boxed{} |$$

coordinate of A coordinate of B

_____ are segments with the same length.

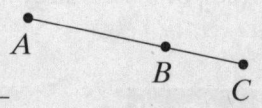

$\rightarrow AB = CD \rightarrow$ $\boxed{}$ $\cong$ $\boxed{}$

A midpoint is _____

_____

midpoint

$\boxed{} \cong \boxed{}$

Name_____ Class_____ Date_____

Examples

① Using the Segment Addition Postulate If $AB = 25$, find the value of x. Then find AN and NB.

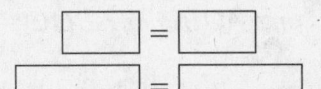

$$2x - 6 \qquad x + 7$$
$$A \qquad\qquad N \qquad\qquad B$$

Use the Segment Addition Postulate (Postulate 1-6) to write an equation.

$\boxed{} + \boxed{} = AB$ $\boxed{}$

$\left(\boxed{}\right) + \left(\boxed{}\right) = 25$ **Substitute.**

$\boxed{} + \boxed{} = 25$ **Simplify the left side.**

$3x = \boxed{}$ **Subtract** $\boxed{}$ **from each side.**

$x = \boxed{}$ **Divide each side by** $\boxed{}$**.**

$AN = 2x - 6 = 2\left(\boxed{}\right) - 6 = \boxed{}$

$NB = x + 7 = \left(\boxed{}\right) + 7 = \boxed{}$ **Substitute** $\boxed{}$ **for** *x***.**

$AN = \boxed{}$ and $NB = \boxed{}$, which checks because the sum equals 25.

② Finding Lengths M is the midpoint of $\overline{RT}$. Find RM, MT, and RT.

$$5x + 9 \qquad 8x - 36$$
$$R \qquad\qquad M \qquad\qquad T$$

Use the definition of midpoint to write an equation.

$\boxed{} = \boxed{}$ **Definition of** $\boxed{}$

$\boxed{} = \boxed{}$ **Substitute.**

$5x + \boxed{} = 8x$ **Add** $\boxed{}$ **to each side.**

$45 = \boxed{}x$ **Subtract** $\boxed{}$ **from each side.**

$\boxed{} = x$ **Divide each side by** $\boxed{}$**.**

$RM = 5x + 9 = 5\left(\boxed{}\right) + 9 = \boxed{}$

$MT = 8x - 36 = 8\left(\boxed{}\right) - 36 = \boxed{}$ **Substitute** $\boxed{}$ **for** *x***.**

$RT = \boxed{} + \boxed{} = \boxed{}$ $\boxed{}$ **Postulate**

RM and MT are each $\boxed{}$, which is half of $\boxed{}$, the length of $\overline{RT}$.

Quick Check

1. $EG = 100$. Find the value of x. Then find EF and FG.

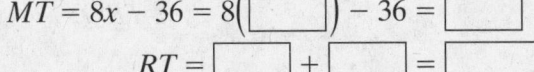

$$4x - 20 \quad 2x + 30$$
$$E \qquad F \qquad G$$

$\boxed{}$

2. Z is the midpoint of $\overline{XY}$, and $XY = 27$. Find XZ.

$\boxed{}$

Name SARAH DUCHARME   Class PERIOD I   Date 4·6

Lesson 1-6   **Measuring Angles**

Lesson Objectives	NAEP 2005 Strand: Measurement
☑ Find the measures of angles	Topic: Measuring Physical Attributes
☑ Identify special angle pairs	Local Standards: _____

Vocabulary and Key Concepts

Postulate 1-7: Protractor Postulate

Let $\overrightarrow{OA}$ and $\overrightarrow{OB}$ be opposite rays in a plane.
$\overrightarrow{OA}$, $\overrightarrow{OB}$, and all the rays with endpoint O that can
be drawn on one side of $\overleftrightarrow{AB}$ can be paired with the
real numbers from 0 to 180 so that

a. $\overrightarrow{OA}$ is paired with $\boxed{0}$ and $\overrightarrow{OB}$ is paired with $\boxed{180}$.

b. If $\overrightarrow{OC}$ is paired with x and $\overrightarrow{OD}$ is paired with y,
then $\boxed{M\angle COD = |x - y|}$.

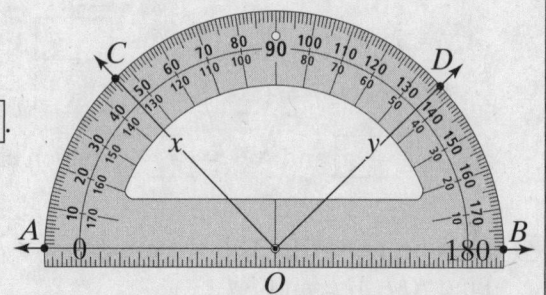

Postulate 1-8: Angle Addition Postulate

If point B is in the interior of $\angle AOC$, then

$m\angle \boxed{AOB} + m\angle \boxed{BOC} = m\angle AOC$.

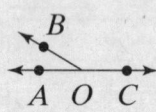

If $\angle AOC$ is a straight angle, then

$m\angle AOB + m\angle BOC = \boxed{180°}$.

An angle ($\angle$) is <u>FORMED BY TWO RAYS WITH THE SAME</u>
<u>ENDPOINT.</u>

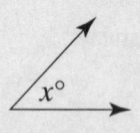  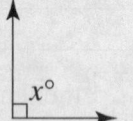 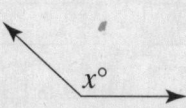 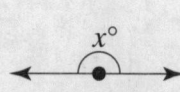

$\angle TBQ$

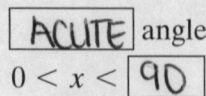 angle   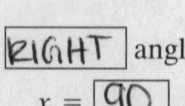 angle   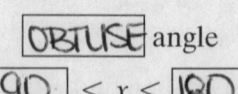 angle   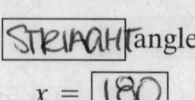angle

$0 < x < \boxed{90}$ $x = \boxed{90}$ $\boxed{90} < x < \boxed{180}$ $x = \boxed{180}$

An <u>ACUTE ANGLE</u> has measurement between 0° and 90°.

A right angle has <u>A MEASUREMENT OF 90° DEGIRES</u>

An <u>OBTUSE ANGLE</u> has measurement between 90° and 180°.

A straight angle has <u>A MEASURE OF 180°</u>

<u>STRAIGHT ANGLE</u> are two angles with the same measure.

Name **SARAH DUCHARME**   Class **PERIOD 1**   Date **4·6·09**

Examples

❶ Naming Angles Name the angle at right in four ways.

The name can be the number between the sides of the angle: **3**.

The name can be the vertex of the angle: **G**.

Finally, the name can be a point on one side, the vertex, and a point on the other side of the angle: **C** or **A**.

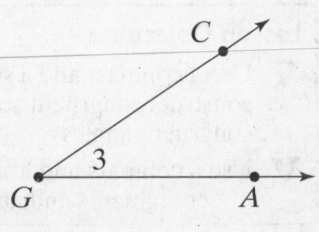

❷ Using the Angle Addition Postulate Suppose that $m\angle 1 = 42$ and $m\angle ABC = 88$. Find $m\angle 2$.

Use the Angle Addition Postulate (Postulate 1-8) to solve.

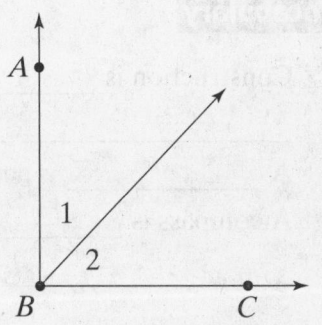

$m\angle \boxed{} + m\angle \boxed{} = m\angle ABC$ $\boxed{}$ **Postulate**

$\boxed{} + m\angle 2 = \boxed{}$ **Substitute** $\boxed{A}$ for $m\angle 1$ and $\boxed{}$ for $m\angle ABC$.

$m\angle 2 = \boxed{}$ **Subtract** $\boxed{}$ from each side.

Quick Check

1. a. Name $\angle CED$ two other ways.

> 1. ∠DEC
> 2. ∠

b. Critical Thinking Would it be correct to name any of the angles $\angle E$? Explain.

2. If $m\angle DEG = 145$, find $m\angle GEF$.

> $180° - 145° = 35°$
> $m\angle GEF = 35°$

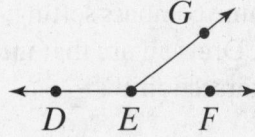

Lesson 1-7

Basic Constructions

Lesson Objectives	NAEP 2005 Strand: Geometry
▼ Use a compass and a straightedge to construct congruent segments and congruent angles	**Topic:** Relationships Among Geometric Figures
▼ Use a compass and a straightedge to bisect segments and angles	**Local Standards:** _____

Vocabulary

Construction is _____

_____

A _____ is a ruler with no markings on it.

A compass is _____

_____

_____ are two lines that intersect to form right angles.

A perpendicular bisector of a segment is _____

_____

_____

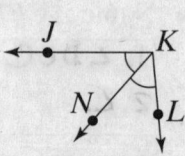

An _____ is a ray that divides an angle into two congruent coplanar angles.

Examples

① Constructing Congruent Segments Construct $\overline{TW}$ congruent to $\overline{KM}$.

Step 1 Draw a ray with endpoint T.

Step 2 Open the compass the length of $\overline{KM}$.

Step 3 With the same compass setting, put the compass point on point T. Draw an arc that intersects the ray. Label the point of intersection W.

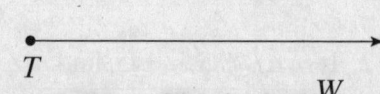

$\overline{KM} \cong \overline{TW}$

❷ Constructing the Perpendicular Bisector

Given: $\overline{AB}$.

Construct: $\overleftrightarrow{XY}$ so that $\overleftrightarrow{XY} \perp \overline{AB}$ at the midpoint M of $\overline{AB}$.

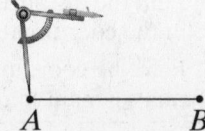

Step 1 Put the compass point on point A and draw a long arc. Be sure that the opening is ⬚⬚⬚⬚⬚⬚ than $\frac{1}{2}AB$.

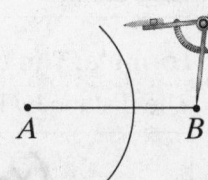

Step 2 With the ⬚⬚⬚⬚⬚ compass setting, put the compass point on point B and draw another long arc. Label the points where the two arcs ⬚⬚⬚⬚⬚⬚ as X and Y.

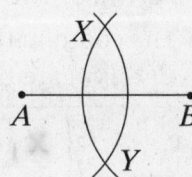

Step 3 Draw $\overleftrightarrow{XY}$. The point of intersection of $\overline{AB}$ and $\overleftrightarrow{XY}$ is M, the ⬚⬚⬚⬚⬚ of $\overline{AB}$.

$\overleftrightarrow{XY} \perp \overline{AB}$ at the midpoint of $\overline{AB}$, so $\overleftrightarrow{XY}$ is the ⬚⬚⬚⬚⬚⬚⬚⬚⬚⬚⬚ of $\overline{AB}$.

Quick Check

1. Use a straightedge to draw $\overline{XY}$. Then construct $\overline{RS}$ so that $RS = 2XY$.

2. Draw $\overline{ST}$. Construct its perpendicular bisector.

Lesson 1-8

The Coordinate Plane

Lesson Objectives	NAEP 2005 Strand: Measurement
▼ Find the distance between two points in the coordinate plane	Topic: Measuring Physical Attributes
▼ Find the coordinates of the midpoint of a segment in the coordinate plane	Local Standards: _____

Key Concepts

Formula: The Distance Formula

The distance d between two points $A(x_1, y_1)$ and $B(x_2, y_2)$ is

$$d = \sqrt{\boxed{(x_2 - x_1)^2} + \boxed{(y_2 - y_1)^2}}.$$

Formula: The Midpoint Formula

The coordinates of the midpoint M of $\overline{AB}$ with endpoints $A(x_1, y_1)$ and $B(x_2, y_2)$ are the following:

$$M\left(\boxed{\frac{x_1 + x_2}{2}}, \boxed{\frac{y_1 + y_2}{2}} \right).$$

Examples

❶ Finding the Midpoint $\overline{AB}$ has endpoints $(8, 9)$ and $(-6, -3)$. Find the coordinates of its midpoint M.

Use the Midpoint Formula. Let (x_1, y_1) be $\boxed{8, 9}$ and (x_2, y_2) be $\boxed{-6, -3}$.

The midpoint has coordinates

$$\left(\frac{\boxed{8} + \boxed{-6}}{\boxed{2}}, \frac{\boxed{-3} + \boxed{9}}{\boxed{2}} \right).$$ **Midpoint Formula**

The x-coordinate is $\dfrac{\boxed{8} + \left(\boxed{-6} \right)}{2} = \dfrac{\boxed{2}}{2} = \boxed{1}$ Substitute $\boxed{8}$ for x_1 and $\boxed{-6}$ for x_2. Simplify.

The y-coordinate is $\dfrac{\boxed{9} + \left(\boxed{-3} \right)}{2} = \dfrac{\boxed{6}}{2} = \boxed{3}$ Substitute $\boxed{9}$ for y_1 and $\boxed{-3}$ for y_2. Simplify.

The coordinates of the midpoint M are $\boxed{1, 3}$.

❷ Finding an Endpoint The midpoint of $\overline{DG}$ is $M(-1, 5)$. One endpoint is $D(1, 4)$. Find the coordinates of the other endpoint G.

Use the Midpoint Formula. Let (x_1, y_1) be $\boxed{1, 4}$ and the midpoint

$\left(\dfrac{x_1 + x_2}{2}, \dfrac{y_1 + y_2}{2} \right)$ be $\boxed{-1, 5}$. Solve for $\boxed{X_2}$ and $\boxed{Y_2}$, the

coordinates of G.

Find the x-coordinate of G.

$\boxed{-1} = \dfrac{\boxed{1} + x_2}{2}$ ← **Use the Midpoint Formula.** → $\boxed{5} = \dfrac{\boxed{4} + y_2}{2}$

$\boxed{-2} = \boxed{1} + x_2$ ← **Multiply each side by** $\boxed{2}$. → $\boxed{10} = \boxed{4} + y_2$

$\boxed{-3} = x_2$ ← **Simplify.** → $\boxed{6} = x_2$

The coordinates of G are $\boxed{-3, 6}$.

Quick Check

1. Find the coordinates of the midpoint of $\overline{XY}$ with endpoints $X(2, -5)$ and $Y(6, 13)$.

STACK
ADD
DIVIDE
$$\begin{array}{l} (2, -5) \\ + (6, 13) \\ \hline \dfrac{8, 8}{2} = (4, 4) \end{array}$$

2. The midpoint of $\overline{XY}$ has coordinates $(4, -6)$. X has coordinates $(2, -3)$. Find the coordinates of Y.

STACK
ADD
DIVIDE
$$\begin{array}{l} (4, -6) \\ + (2, -3) \\ \hline \dfrac{6, -9}{2} = (3, -4.5) \end{array}$$

Name_____ Class_____ Date_____

Lesson 1-9

Perimeter, Circumference, and Area

Lesson Objectives	NAEP 2005 Strand: Measurement
▼ Find perimeters of rectangles and squares, and circumferences of circles	Topic: Measuring Physical Attributes
② Find areas of rectangles, squares, and circles	Local Standards: _____

Key Concepts

Perimeter and Area

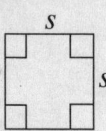

Square with side length *s*.

Perimeter $P =$ $\boxed{4.5}$

Area $A =$ $\boxed{2.5}$

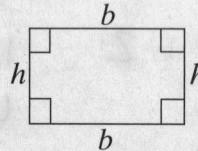

Rectangle with base *b* and height *h*.

Perimeter $P =$ $\boxed{(b+h) \cdot 2}$

Area $A =$ $\boxed{b \cdot h}$

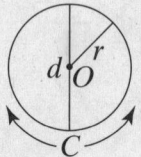

Circle with radius *r* and diameter *d*.

Circumference $C =$ $\boxed{}$

or $C =$ $\boxed{\pi d}$

Area $=$ $\boxed{\pi \cdot r^2}$

Postulate 1-9

If two figures are congruent, then their areas are $\boxed{\text{CONGRUENT}}$

Postulate 1-10

The area of a region is the THE SUM OF THE AREA OF THE

NON OVER LAPPING PARTS

Examples

❶ **Finding Circumference** ⊙*G* has a radius of $\boxed{6.5}$ cm. Find the circumference of ⊙*G* in terms of π. Then find the circumference to the nearest tenth.

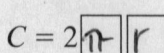

6.5 cm

G

$C = 2$ $\boxed{\pi}$ $\boxed{r}$ Formula for circumference of a circle

$C = 2\pi \left(\boxed{6.5} \right)$ Substitute $\boxed{3.14}$ for *r*.

$C = \boxed{13} \, \pi$ Exact answer

$C = \boxed{13}$ $\boxed{\times}$ $\boxed{\pi}$ $\boxed{=}$ $\boxed{40.82}$ Use a calculator.

The circumference of ⊙*G* is $\boxed{40.82}$, or about $\boxed{40.82}$ cm.

❷ **Finding Area of a Circle** Find the area of ⊙*B* in terms of *π*.

In ⊙*B*, *r* = $\boxed{1.5}$ yd.

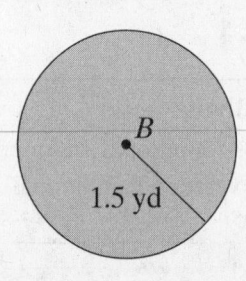

1.5 yd

$A = \pi \boxed{r^2}$ **Formula for the area of a circle**

$A = \pi \left(\boxed{1.5}\right)^2$ **Substitute** $\boxed{1.5}$ **for *r*.**

$A = \boxed{2.25}\ \pi$

The area of ⊙*B* is $\boxed{7.0650}$ yd².

Quick Check

1. a. Find the circumference of a circle with a radius of 18 m in terms of *π*.

$$c = 2\pi \cdot r \qquad c = 2 \cdot 3.14 \cdot 18$$

b. Find the circumference of a circle with a diameter of 18 m to the nearest tenth.

$$c = \pi \cdot d$$

$$c = 56.52$$

2. You are designing a rectangular banner for the front of a museum. The banner will be 4 ft wide and 7 yd high.

How much material do you need in square yards?

$$4FT \times 7yd$$

$$4FT \times 21 FR = 84 FR^2$$

Lesson 2-1

Conditional Statements

Lesson Objectives	NAEP 2005 Strand: Geometry
▼ Recognize conditional statements	**Topic:** Mathematical Reasoning
▼ Write converses of conditional statements	**Local Standards:** _____

Vocabulary and Key Concepts

Conditional Statements and Converses

Statement	Example	Symbolic Form	You read it
Conditional	If an angle is a straight angle, then its measure is 180°.	$p \rightarrow q$	If ☐, then ☐.
Converse	If the measure of an angle is 180°, then it is a straight angle.	$q \rightarrow p$	If ☐, then ☐.

A conditional is _____

_____

The _____ is the part that follows *if* in an *if-then* statement.

_____

The conclusion is _____

_____

The _____ of a statement is "true" or "false" according to whether the

statement is true or false, respectively.

The converse of the conditional "if p, then q" _____

_____

Examples

❶ Identifying the Hypothesis and the Conclusion Identify the hypothesis
and conclusion: If two lines are parallel, then the lines are coplanar.

In a conditional statement, the clause after *if* is the hypothesis and the
clause after *then* is the conclusion.

Hypothesis: _____

_____

Conclusion: _____

_____

Daily Notetaking Guide L1

❷ Writing the Converse of a Conditional Write the converse of the following conditional.

If $x = 9$, then $x + 3 = 12$.

The converse of a conditional exchanges the hypothesis and the conclusion.

Conditional		Converse	
Hypothesis	Conclusion	Hypothesis	Conclusion
$x = 9$	$x + 3 = 12$		

So the converse is: _____

Quick Check

1. Identify the hypothesis and the conclusion of this conditional statement:

   If $y - 3 = 5$, then $y = 8$.

   Hypothesis:

   Conclusion:

2. Write the converse of the following conditional:

   If two lines are not parallel and do not intersect, then they are skew.

Lesson 2-2

Biconditionals and Definitions

Lesson Objectives	NAEP 2005 Strand: Geometry
V Write biconditionals **2** Recognize good definitions	**Topics:** Dimension and Shape; Mathematical Reasoning
	Local Standards: _____

Vocabulary and Key Concepts

Biconditional Statements

A biconditional combines $p \to q$ and $q \to p$ as $p \leftrightarrow q$.

Statement	Example	Symbolic Form	You read it
Biconditional	An angle is a straight angle if and only if its measure is 180°.	$p \leftrightarrow q$	☐ if and only if ☐.

A biconditional statement is _____

A _____ contains the words "if and only if."

Examples

❶ Writing a Biconditional Consider the true conditional statement. Write its converse. If the converse is also true, combine the statements as a biconditional.

Conditional: If $x = 5$, then $x + 15 = 20$.

To write the converse, exchange the hypothesis and conclusion.

Converse: _____

When you subtract 15 from each side to solve the equation, you get $x = 5$. Because

both the conditional and its converse are [_____], you can combine them in

a [_____] using the phrase [_____].

Biconditional: _____

Name_____ Class_____ Date _____

❷ Identifying a Good Definition Is the following statement a good definition? Explain.

An apple is a fruit that contains seeds.

The statement is true as a description of an apple.

Exchange "An apple" and "a fruit that contains seeds." The converse reads:

_____

There are many fruits that contain seeds but are not apples, such as lemons and peaches. These are [＿＿＿＿＿＿＿＿＿＿], so the converse of the statement is [＿＿＿＿＿＿＿] .

The original statement [＿＿＿＿＿＿] a good definition because the statement [＿＿＿＿＿＿] reversible.

Quick Check

1. Consider the true conditional statement. Write its converse. If the converse is also true, combine the statements as a biconditional.

   Conditional: If three points are collinear, then they lie on the same line.

   Converse:

   [＿＿＿＿＿＿＿＿＿＿＿＿＿＿＿＿＿＿＿＿＿＿＿＿＿＿]

   The converse is [＿＿＿＿＿＿＿] .

   Biconditional:

   [＿＿＿＿＿＿＿＿＿＿＿＿＿＿＿＿＿＿＿＿＿＿＿＿＿＿]

2. Is the following statement a good definition? Explain.
   A square is a figure with four right angles.

   [＿＿＿＿＿＿＿＿＿＿＿＿＿＿＿＿＿＿＿＿＿＿＿＿＿＿]

Name_____ Class_____ Date_____

Lesson 2-3   **Deductive Reasoning**

Lesson Objectives	**NAEP 2005 Strand:** Geometry
▼ Use the Law of Detachment	**Topic:** Mathematical Reasoning
▼ Use the Law of Syllogism	**Local Standards:** _____

Vocabulary and Key Concepts

Law of Detachment

If a conditional is true and its hypothesis is true, then its [   ] is true.

In symbolic form:

If $p \rightarrow q$ is a true statement and p is true, then [ ] is true.

Law of Syllogism

If $p \rightarrow q$ and $q \rightarrow r$ are true statements, then [ ] $\rightarrow$ [ ] is a true statement.

Deductive reasoning is _____

_____

Examples

❶ **Using the Law of Detachment** A gardener knows that if it rains, the garden will be watered. It is raining. What conclusion can he make?

The first sentence contains a conditional statement. The hypothesis is

_____

Because the hypothesis is true, the gardener can conclude that

_____

❷ **Using the Law of Detachment** For the given statements, what can you conclude?

Given: If $\angle A$ is acute, then $m\angle A < 90°$. $\angle A$ is acute.

A conditional and its hypothesis are both given as true.

By the [   ], you can conclude that the

conclusion of the conditional, $m\angle A < 90°$, is [   ].

❸ Using the Law of Syllogism Use the Law of Syllogism to draw a conclusion from the following true statements:

If a quadrilateral is a square, then it contains four right angles.

If a quadrilateral contains four right angles, then it is a rectangle.

The conclusion of the first conditional is the hypothesis of the second conditional. This means that you can apply the [_____].

The Law of Syllogism: If [_____] and [_____] are true statements, then [_____] is a true statement.

So you can conclude:

If a quadrilateral is a square, then _____

Quick Check

1. Suppose that a mechanic begins work on a car and finds that the car will not start. Can the mechanic conclude that the car has a dead battery? Explain.

2. If a baseball player is a pitcher, then that player should not pitch a complete game two days in a row. Vladimir Nuñez is a pitcher. On Monday, he pitches a complete game. What can you conclude?

3. If possible, state a conclusion using the Law of Syllogism. If it is not possible to use this law, explain why.

   a. If a number ends in 0, then it is divisible by 10.
      If a number is divisible by 10, then it is divisible by 5.

   b. If a number ends in 6, then it is divisible by 2.
      If a number ends in 4, then it is divisible by 2.

Lesson 2-4

Reasoning in Algebra

Lesson Objective	**NAEP 2005 Strand:** Algebra and Geometry
▼ Connect reasoning in algebra and geometry	**Topics:** Algebraic Representations; Mathematical Reasoning
	Local Standards: _____

Key Concepts

Properties of Equality

Addition Property   If $a = b$, then $a + \boxed{b} = b + \boxed{a}$.

Subtraction Property   If $a = b$, then $a - \boxed{b} = b - \boxed{a}$.

Multiplication Property   If $a = b$, then $a \times \boxed{b} = b \times \boxed{a}$.

Division Property   If $a = b$ and $c \neq 0$, then $\dfrac{a}{\boxed{c}} = \dfrac{b}{\boxed{c}}$.

Reflexive Property $a = \boxed{a}$.

Symmetric Property   If $a = b$, then $b = \boxed{a}$.

Transitive Property   If $a = b$ and $b = c$, then $a = \boxed{c}$.

Substitution Property   If $a = b$, then b can replace $\boxed{a}$ in any expression.

Distributive Property $a(b + c) = \boxed{ab} + \boxed{ac}$.

Properties of Congruence

Reflexive Property $\overline{AB} \cong \boxed{\overline{AB}}$

$\angle A \cong \boxed{\angle A}$

Symmetric Property   If $\overline{AB} \cong \overline{CD}$, then $\overline{CD} \cong \boxed{\overline{AB}}$.

If $\angle A \cong \angle B$, then $\angle B \cong \boxed{\angle A}$.

Transitive Property   If $\overline{AB} \cong \overline{CD}$ and $\overline{CD} \cong \overline{EF}$, then $\overline{AB} \cong \boxed{\overline{EF}}$.

If $\angle A \cong \angle B$ and $\angle B \cong \angle C$, then $\angle A \cong \boxed{\angle C}$.

Name SARAH DUCHARME   Class PERIOD 1   Date 11·18·08

Examples

❶ Justifying Steps in Solving an Equation Justify each step used to solve $5x - 12 = 32 + x$ for x.

Given: $5x - 12 = 32 + x$

$5x = 44 + x$	ADDITION PROPERTY
$4x = 44$	SUBTRACTION PROPERTY
$x = 11$	DIVISION PROPERTY

❷ Using Properties of Equality and Congruence Name the property that justifies each statement.

If $\angle P \cong \angle Q$, $\angle Q \cong \angle R$, and $\angle R \cong \angle S$, then $\angle P \cong \angle S$.

Use the [TRANSITIVE PROPERTY] for

the first two parts of the hypothesis:

If $\angle P \cong \angle Q$ and $\angle Q \cong \angle R$, then [$\angle P \cong \angle R$].

Use the [SYMMETRIC PROPERTY] for

$\angle P \cong \angle R$ and the third part of the hypothesis:

If $\angle P \cong \angle R$ and $\angle R \cong \angle S$, then [$\angle P \cong \angle S$].

Quick Check

1. Fill in each missing reason.

Given: $\overrightarrow{LM}$ bisects $\angle KLN$.

$\overrightarrow{LM}$ bisects $\angle KLN$	GIVEN
$m\angle MLN = m\angle KLM$ Definition of [ANGLE] Bisector	
$4x = 2x + 40$	ADDITION PROPERTY
$2x = 40$	SUBTRACTION PROPERTY
$x = 20$	DIVISION PROPERTY

2. Name the property of equality or congruence illustrated.

a. $\overline{XY} \cong \overline{XY}$

REFLEXIVE

b. If $m\angle A = 45$ and $45 = m\angle B$, then $m\angle A = m\angle B$

TRANSITIVE

Name **SARAH DUCHARME** Class **PERIOD 7** Date **11·20·08**

Lesson 2-5

Proving Angles Congruent

Lesson Objectives	**NAEP 2005 Strand:** Geometry
▽ Prove and apply theorems about angles	**Topic:** Relationships Among Geometric Figures
	Local Standards: _____

Vocabulary and Key Concepts

Theorem 2-1: Vertical Angles Theorem

Vertical angles are ☐ CONGRUENT ☐ .

∠1 ≅ ☐ ∠2 ☐ and ∠3 ≅ ☐ ∠4 ☐

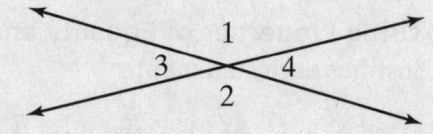

180°

Theorem 2-2: Congruent Supplements Theorem

If two angles are (supplements) of the same angle (or of congruent angles),

then the two angles are ☐ CONGRUENT ☐ .

90°

Theorem 2-3: Congruent Complements Theorem

If two angles are (complements) of the same angle (or of congruent angles),

then the two angles are ☐ CONGRUENT ☐ .

Theorem 2-4

All ☐ RIGHT ☐ angles are congruent.

Theorem 2-5

If two angles are congruent and supplementary, then each is a ☐ RIGHT ☐ angle.

vertical angles

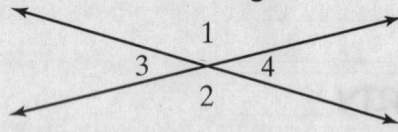

∠1 and ☐ ∠2 ☐ are vertical angles,

as are ∠3 and ☐ ∠4 ☐ .

adjacent angles

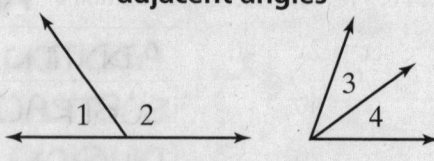

∠1 and ☐ ∠2 ☐ are adjacent angles,

as are ∠3 and ☐ ∠4 ☐ .

Vertical angles **ARE TWO ANGLES WHOSE SIDES FORM OPPOSITE RAYS.**

Adjacent angles **HAVE A COMMON SIDE AND COMMON VERTEX BUT NOT NO COMMON INTERIOR POINTS.**

Geometry Lesson 2-5

Daily Notetaking Guide [L1]

Name SARAH DUCHARME   Class PERIOD 1   Date 11·20·08

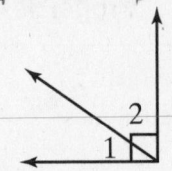

complementary angles

∠1 and ∠2 are complementary angles.

Two angles are complementary angles if
THE SUM OF THEIR MEASURE IS 90°

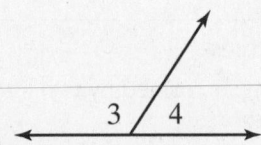

supplementary angles

∠3 and ∠4 are supplementary angles.

Two angles are supplementary angles if
THE SUM OF THEIR MEASURE IS 180°

A theorem A CONJECTOR

A PARAGRAPH PROOF is a convincing argument that uses deductive reasoning in which statements and reasons are connected in sentences.

Examples

❶ **Using the Vertical Angles Theorem** Find the value of x.

The angles with labeled measures are vertical angles. Apply the Vertical Angles Theorem to find x.

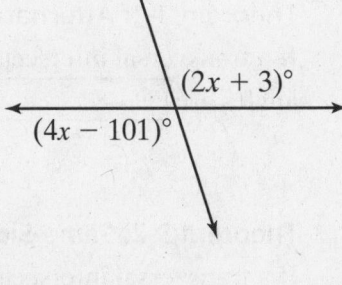

$(2x + 3)°$

$(4x - 101)°$

$4x - 101 = 2x + 3$	VERTICLE ANGLES THEOROM
$4x = 2x + 104$	ADDITION PROPERTY
$2x = 104$	SUBTRACTION PROPERTY
$x = 52$	DIVISION PROPERTY

❷ **Proving Theorem 2-2** Write a paragraph proof of Theorem 2-2 using the diagram at the right.

Start with the given: ∠1 and ∠2 are supplementary, ∠3 and ∠2 are supplementary. By the definition of SUPPLEMENTARY ANGLES

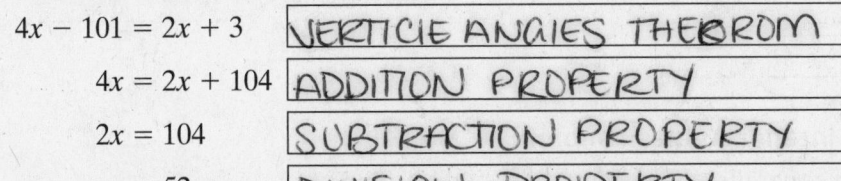

$m\angle 1 + m\angle 2 = 180$ and $m\angle 3 + m\angle 2 = 180$. By substitution, $m\angle 1 + m\angle 2 = \boxed{m\angle 2} + \boxed{m\angle 3}$. Using the SUBTRACTION PROPERTY, subtract $\boxed{m\angle 2}$ from each side. You get $m\angle 1 = \boxed{m\angle 3}$, or $\boxed{\angle 1} \cong \boxed{\angle 3}$.

Quick Check

1. Refer to the diagram for Example 1.
   a. Find the measures of the labeled pair of vertical angles.

   107°

   b. Find the measures of the other pair of vertical angles.

   73°

   c. Check to see that adjacent angles are supplementary.

   107° + 73° = 180°

Lesson 3-1

Properties of Parallel Lines

Lesson Objectives	NAEP 2005 Strand: Measurement
▼ Identify angles formed by two lines and a transversal	**Topic:** Measuring Physical Attributes
❷ Prove and use properties of parallel lines	**Local Standards:** _____

Vocabulary and Key Concepts

Postulate 3-1: Corresponding Angles Postulate

If a transversal intersects two parallel lines, then corresponding

angles are [   ].

[   ] ≅ [   ]

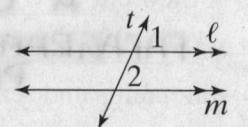

Theorem 3-1: Alternate Interior Angles Theorem

If a transversal intersects two parallel lines, then alternate interior

angles are [   ].

[   ] ≅ [   ]

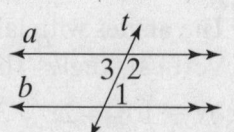

Theorem 3-2: Same-Side Interior Angles Theorem

If a transversal intersects two parallel lines, then same-side interior

angles are [   ].

$m\angle 1 + m\angle 2 =$ [   ]

A transversal is _____

_____

_____ are nonadjacent interior angles that

lie on opposite sides of the transversal.

Same-side interior angles are _____

_____

_____ are angles that lie on the same side

of the transversal and in corresponding positions relative to the

coplanar lines.

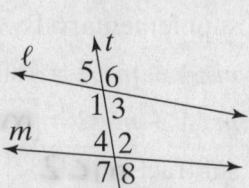

[   ] and [   ] are
alternate interior angles.

[   ] and [   ] are
same-side interior angles.

[   ] and [   ]
corresponding angles.

Examples

❶ Applying Properties of Parallel Lines In the diagram of Lafayette Regional Airport, the black segments are runways and the gray areas are taxiways and terminal buildings.

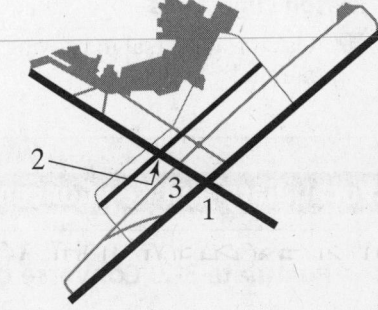

Compare ∠2 and the angle vertical to ∠1. Classify the angles as alternate interior angles, same-side interior angles, or corresponding angles.

The angle vertical to ∠1 is between the runway segments.

∠2 is between the runway segments and on the opposite side of the

transversal runway. Because [ ] are not

adjacent and lie between the lines on opposite sides of the transversal,

∠2 and the angle vertical to ∠1 are [ ].

❷ Finding Measures of Angles

In the diagram at right, $\ell \| m$ and $p \| q$. Find $m\angle 1$ and $m\angle 2$.

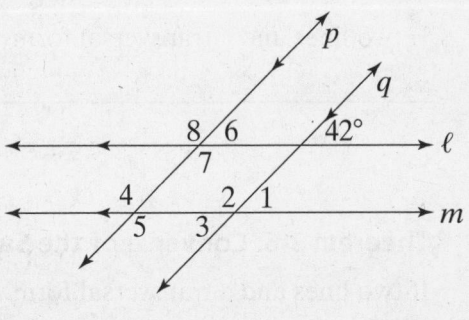

∠1 and the 42° angle are [ ].

Because $\ell \| m, m\angle 1 = $ [ ] by the

[ ].

Because ∠1 and ∠2 are adjacent angles that form a

straight angle, $m\angle 1 + m\angle 2 = $ [ ] by the

[ ]. If you substitute [ ]

for $m\angle 1$, the equation becomes [ ] + [ ] = [ ].

Subtract [ ] from each side to find $m\angle 2 = $ [ ].

Quick Check

1. Use the diagram in Example 1. Classify ∠2 and ∠3 as alternate interior angles, same-side interior angles, or corresponding angles.

[ ]

2. Using the diagram in Example 2 find the measure of each angle. Justify each answer.

   a. ∠3 [ ]

   b. ∠4 [ ]

   c. ∠5 [ ]

Lesson 3-2

Proving Lines Parallel

Lesson Objectives	NAEP 2005 Strand: Measurement
▼ Use a transversal in proving lines parallel	Topic: Measuring Physical Attributes
	Local Standards: _____

Vocabulary and Key Concepts

Postulate 3-2: Converse of the Corresponding Angles Postulate

If two lines and a transversal form _____

_____

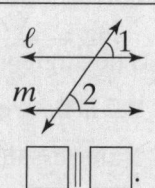

□ ‖ □.

Theorem 3-5: Converse of the Alternate Interior Angles Theorem

If two lines and a transversal form _____

_____

If ∠1 ≅ ∠2, then □ ‖ □.

Theorem 3-6: Converse of the Same-Side Interior Angles Theorem

If two lines and a transversal form _____

_____

If ∠2 and ∠4 are supplementary, then □ ‖ □.

Theorem 3-7: Converse of the Alternate Exterior Angles Theorem

If two lines and a transversal form _____

_____

If ∠3 ≅ ∠5, then □ ‖ □.

Theorem 3-8: Converse of the Same-Side Exterior Angles Theorem

If two lines and a transversal form _____

_____

If ∠3 and ∠6 are supplementary, then □ ‖ □.

A flow proof uses _____

_____

_____ are written below the statements.

Examples

❶ Proving Theorem 3-5 *If two lines and a transversal form alternate interior angles that are congruent, then the two lines are parallel.*

Given: ∠1 ≅ ∠2
Prove: ℓ ∥ m

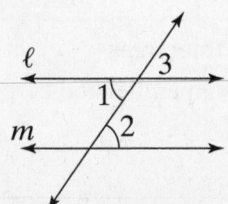

Write the flow proof below of the Alternate Interior Angles Theorem as a paragraph proof.

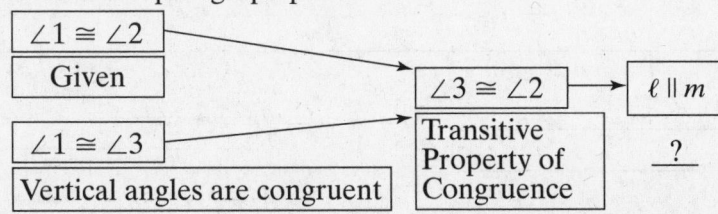

By the Vertical Angles Theorem, ∠3 ≅ ☐ . ∠1 ≅ ∠2, so
∠3 ≅ ☐ by the ☐ Property of Congruence.
Because ☐ and ☐ are corresponding angles, ℓ ∥ m by the
☐ Postulate.

❷ Using Postulate 3-2

Use the diagram at the right. Which lines, if any, must be parallel if ∠3 and ∠2 are supplementary? Justify your answer with a theorem or postulate.

It is given that ∠3 and ∠2 are supplementary. The diagram
shows that ☐ and ☐ are supplementary. Because
supplements of the same angle are ☐
(Congruent Supplements Theorem), ☐ ≅ ☐ . Because ☐
and ☐ are congruent corresponding angles, ☐ ∥ ☐ by the
☐ Postulate.

Quick Check

1. Supply the missing reason in the flow proof from Example 1.

2. Use the diagram from Example 1. Which lines, if any, must be parallel if ∠3 ≅ ∠4? Explain.

Lesson 3-3

Parallel and Perpendicular Lines

Lesson Objectives	**NAEP 2005 Strand:** Geometry
▼ Relate parallel and perpendicular lines	**Topic:** Relationships Among Geometric Figures
	Local Standards: _____

Key Concepts

Theorem 3-9

If two lines are [＿＿＿＿＿＿＿＿＿＿], then

they are [＿＿＿＿] to each other.

Theorem 3-10

In a plane, if two lines are [＿＿＿＿＿＿＿＿＿＿＿],

then they are [＿＿＿＿] to each other.

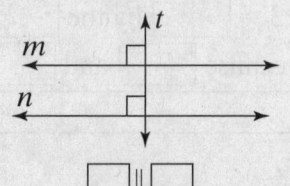

Theorem 3-11

In a plane, if a line is perpendicular to one of two
parallel lines, then it is also perpendicular to the other.

[＿＿] ⊥ [＿＿]

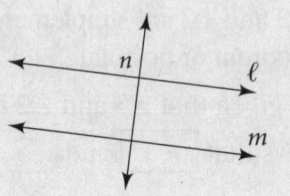

Examples

❶ Proof of Theorem 3-10

Use the diagram at the right. Which angle would you use with ∠1 to prove the theorem *In a plane, if two lines are perpendicular to the same line, then they are parallel to each other* (Theorem 3-10) using the Converse of the Alternate Interior Angles Theorem instead of the Converse of the Corresponding Angles Postulate?

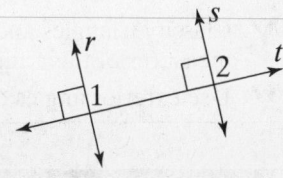

By the Vertical Angles Theorem, ∠1 is [_____] to its vertical angle.

Because ∠1 ≅ [_____], ∠2 is congruent to the vertical angle of [_____] by the

[_____] Property of Congruence. Because alternate interior angles

are congruent, you can use the vertical angle of [_____] and the

[_____] Theorem to prove that

the lines are parallel.

❷ Using Algebra

Find the value of x for which $\ell \| m$.
The labeled angles are [_____].

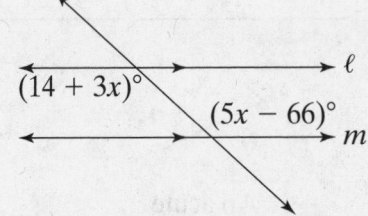

If $\ell \| m$, the alternate interior angles are [_____],

and their measures are [_____]. Write and solve the

equation [_____] − 66 = [_____] + 3x.

[_____] − 66 = [_____] + 3x

[_____] = [_____] + 3x   **Add 66 to each side.**

[_____] = [_____]   **Subtract 3x from each side.**

x = [_____]   **Divide each side by 2.**

Quick Check

1. **Critical Thinking** In a plane, if two lines form congruent angles with a third line, must the lines be parallel? Draw a diagram to support your answer.

[_____]

2. Find the value of x for which $a \| b$. Explain how you can check your answer.

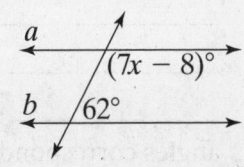

[_____]

Lesson 3-4

Lesson Objectives	NAEP 2005 Strand: Geometry
❶ Classify triangles and find the measures of their angles	Topic: Relationships Among Geometric Figures
❷ Use exterior angles of triangles	Local Standards: _____

Vocabulary and Key Concepts

Theorem 3-12: Triangle Angle-Sum Theorem

The sum of the measures of the angles of a triangle is [   ] .

$m\angle A + m\angle B + m\angle C = 180$

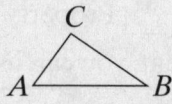

Theorem 3-13: Triangle Exterior Angle Theorem

The measure of each exterior angle of a triangle equals the _____

_____

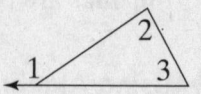

An acute
triangle has

_____

_____

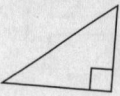

A right
triangle has

_____

_____

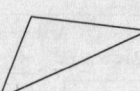

An obtuse
triangle has

_____

_____

An equiangular
triangle has

_____

_____

An equilateral
triangle has

_____

_____

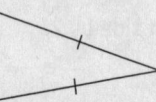

An isosceles
triangle has

_____

_____

A scalene
triangle has

_____

_____

An exterior angle of a polygon is _____

_____

_____

_____ are the two nonadjacent interior
angles corresponding to each exterior angle of a triangle.

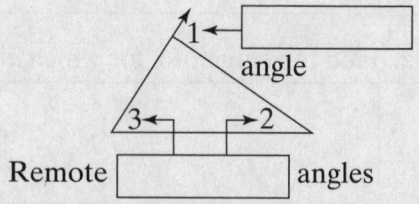

Examples

❶ Applying the Triangle Angle-Sum Theorem Find $m\angle Z$.

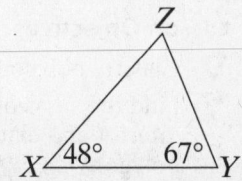

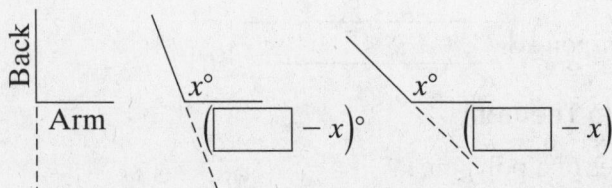

[ ] + [ ] + $m\angle Z =$ [ ]		Triangle Angle-Sum Theorem
[ ] + $m\angle Z = 180$		Simplify.
$m\angle Z =$ [ ]		Subtract 115 from each side.

❷ Applying the Triangle Exterior Angle Theorem Explain what happens to the angle formed by the back of the chair and the armrest as you make a lounge chair recline more.

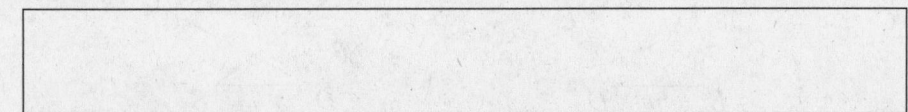

The exterior angle and the angle formed by the back of the chair and

the armrest are [   ], which together form a

[   ]. As one measure increases, the other

measure [   ]. The angle formed by the back of the chair and

the armrest [   ] as you make a lounge chair recline more.

Quick Check

1. a. $\triangle MNP$ is a right triangle. $\angle M$ is a right angle and $m\angle N$ is 58. Find $m\angle P$.

b. Reasoning Explain why this statement must be true:
If a triangle is a right triangle, its acute angles are complementary.

2. a. Find $m\angle 3$.

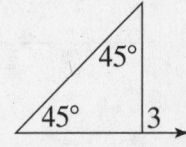

b. Critical Thinking Is it true that if two acute angles of a triangle are complementary, then the triangle must be a right triangle? Explain.

Lesson 3-5

The Polygon Angle-Sum Theorems

Lesson Objectives	NAEP 2005 Strand: Geometry
▼ Classify polygons ▼ Find the sums of the measures of the interior and exterior angles of polygons	**Topic:** Relationships Among Geometric Figures **Local Standards:** _____

Vocabulary and Key Concepts

Theorem 3-14: Polygon Angle-Sum Theorem

The sum of the measures of the angles of an *n*-gon is [   ].

Theorem 3-15: Polygon Exterior Angle-Sum Theorem

The sum of the measures of the exterior angles of a polygon,

one at each vertex, is [   ].

For the pentagon, $m\angle 1 + m\angle 2 + m\angle 3 + m\angle 4 + m\angle 5 =$ [   ].

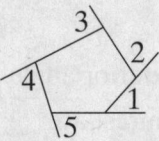

A polygon is _____

_____

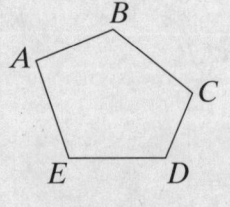

A polygon

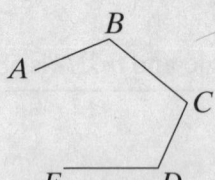

Not a polygon;

not a [   ] figure

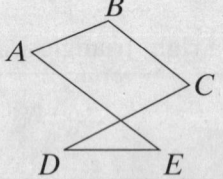

Not a polygon;

two sides [   ]

between endpoints.

A _____ does not have diagonal points

outside of the polygon.

A concave polygon has _____

_____

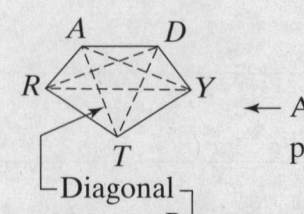

Diagonal

← A [   ] polygon

← A [   ] polygon

An _____ has all sides congruent.

An equiangular polygon has _____.

A _____ is both equilateral and equiangular.

Examples

❶ Classifying Polygons Classify the polygon at the right by its sides. Identify it as convex or concave.

Starting with any side, count the number of sides clockwise around the figure. Because the polygon has [____] sides, it is a dodecagon. Think of the polygon as a star. Draw a diagonal connecting two adjacent points of the star. That diagonal lies [_____] the polygon, so the dodecagon is [_____].

❷ Finding a Polygon Angle Sum Find the sum of the measures of the angles of a decagon.

A decagon has [____] sides, so $n =$ [____].

$$\text{Sum} = (n - 2)(180) \qquad \text{[_____]} \textbf{ Theorem}$$

$$= \left(\boxed{} - 2\right)(180) \qquad \textbf{Substitute } \boxed{} \textbf{ for } n.$$

$$= \boxed{} \cdot 180 \qquad \textbf{Subtract.}$$

$$= \boxed{} \qquad \textbf{Simplify.}$$

Quick Check

1. Classify each polygon by its sides. Identify each as convex or concave.

a.

b.

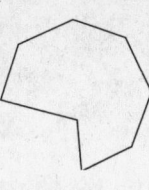

2. Find the sum of the measures of the angles of a 13-gon.

Lesson 3-6

Lines in the Coordinate Plane

Lesson Objectives	NAEP 2005 Strand: Algebra
V1 Graph lines given their equations	**Topics:** Patterns, Relations, and Functions;
V2 Write equations of lines	Algebraic Representations
	Local Standards: _____

Vocabulary

The slope-intercept form of a linear equation is

_____

The _____ form of a linear equation is
$Ax + By = C$.

The point-slope form for a nonvertical line is

_____

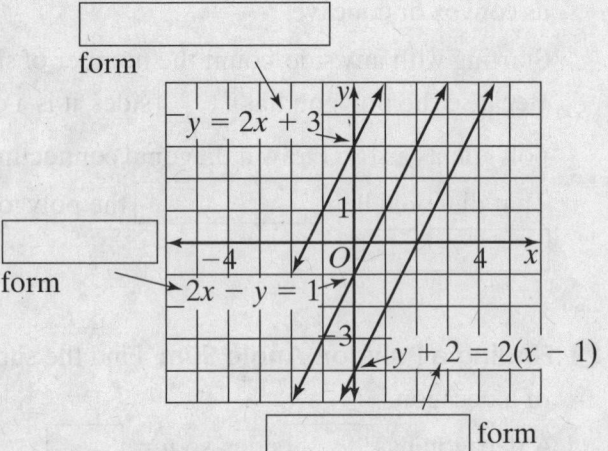

form

form

form

Examples

1 **Graphing Lines Using Intercepts** Use the x-intercept and y-intercept to graph $5x - 6y = 30$.

To find the x-intercept, substitute
0 for y and solve for x.

$$5x - 6y = 30$$
$$5x - 6(\boxed{}) = 30$$
$$5x - \boxed{} = 30$$
$$5x = \boxed{}$$
$$x = \boxed{}$$

The x-intercept is $\boxed{}$.

A point on the line is $(\boxed{}, 0)$.

To find the y-intercept, substitute
0 for x and solve for y.

$$5x - 6y = 30$$
$$5(\boxed{}) - 6y = 30$$
$$\boxed{} - 6y = 30$$
$$-6y = \boxed{}$$
$$y = \boxed{}$$

The y-intercept is $\boxed{}$.

A point on the line is $(0, \boxed{})$.

Plot $(6, 0)$ and $(0, -5)$. Draw the line containing the two points.

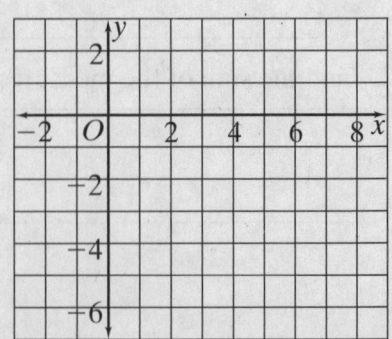

❷ Using Point-Slope Form Write an equation in point-slope form of the line with slope -8 that contains $P(3, -6)$.

$$y - \boxed{} = \boxed{}\left(x - \boxed{}\right)$$ **Use point-slope form.**

$$y - \left(\boxed{}\right) = \boxed{}\left(x - \boxed{}\right)$$ **Substitute -8 for m and $(3, -6)$ for (x_1, y_1).**

$$y + \boxed{} = \boxed{}\left(x - \boxed{}\right)$$ **Simplify.**

Quick Check

1. Graph each equation.

a. $y = -\frac{1}{2}x - 2$ **b.** $-2x + 4y = -8$ **c.** $-5x + y = -3$

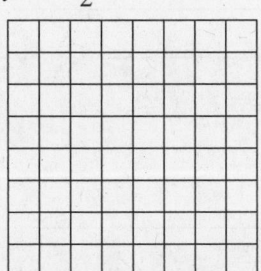 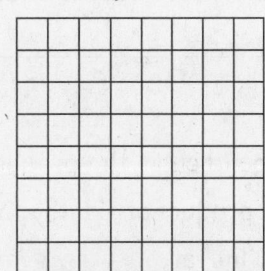 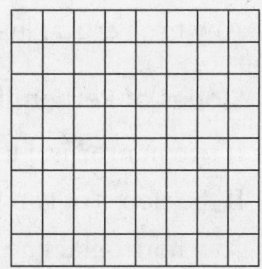

2. Write an equation of the line that contains the points $P(5, 0)$ and $Q(7, -3)$.

Lesson 3-7

Slopes of Parallel and Perpendicular Lines

Lesson Objectives	NAEP 2005 Strand: Measurement
❶ Relate slope and parallel lines	Topic: Measuring Physical Attributes
❷ Relate slope and perpendicular lines	Local Standards: _____

Key Concepts

Slopes of Parallel Lines

If two nonvertical lines are parallel, their slopes are _____

If the slopes of two distinct nonvertical lines are equal, the lines are _____

Any two vertical lines are _____

Slopes of Perpendicular Lines

If two nonvertical lines are perpendicular, the product of their slopes is _____

If the slopes of two lines have a product of -1, the lines are _____

Any horizontal line and vertical line are _____

Examples

❶ **Determining Whether Lines are Parallel** Are the lines $y = -5x + 4$ and $x = -5y + 4$ parallel? Explain.

The equation $y = -5x + 4$ is in [_____]

form. Write the equation $x = -5y + 4$ in slope-intercept form.

$$x = -5y + 4$$

$$x - \boxed{} = -5y \qquad \text{Subtract 4 from each side.}$$

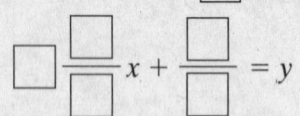 $x + \cfrac{\boxed{}}{\boxed{}} = y \qquad \text{Divide each side by } -5.$

$$y = \boxed{}\cfrac{\boxed{}}{\boxed{}}x + \cfrac{\boxed{}}{\boxed{}}$$

The line $x = -5y + 4$ has slope $\boxed{}$.

The line $y = -5x + 4$ has slope $\boxed{}$.

The lines $\boxed{}$ parallel because their slopes are $\boxed{}$.

❷ Finding Slopes for Perpendicular Lines Find the slope of a line perpendicular to $5x + 2y = 1$.

To find the slope of the given line, rewrite the equation in slope-intercept form.

$5x + 2y = 1$

$2y = \boxed{}x + 1$ **Subtract 5x from each side.**

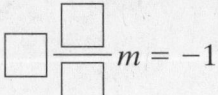 $y = \boxed{}\dfrac{\boxed{}}{\boxed{}}x + \dfrac{\boxed{}}{\boxed{}}$ **Divide each side by 2.**

The line $5x + 2y = 1$ has slope $\boxed{}$.

Find the slope of a line perpendicular to $5x + 2y = 1$. Let m be the slope of the perpendicular line.

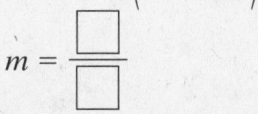 $\boxed{}\dfrac{\boxed{}}{\boxed{}}m = -1$ **The product of the slopes of perpendicular lines is −1.**

$m = -1 \cdot \left(\boxed{}\dfrac{\boxed{}}{\boxed{}} \right)$ **Multiply each side by** $\boxed{}\dfrac{\boxed{}}{\boxed{}}$.

$m = \dfrac{\boxed{}}{\boxed{}}$ **Simplify.**

Quick Check

1. Are the lines $y = -\frac{1}{2}x + 5$ and $2x + 4y = 9$ parallel? Explain.

2. Find the slope of a line perpendicular to $5y - x = 10$.

Lesson 3-8

Constructing Parallel and Perpendicular Lines

Lesson Objectives	NAEP 2005 Strand: Geometry
▼ Construct parallel lines ▼ Construct perpendicular lines	Topic: Relationships Among Geometric Figures Local Standards: _____

Example

1 **Constructing ℓ∥m** Examine the diagram at right. Explain how to construct ∠1 congruent to ∠H. Construct the angle.

Use the method learned for constructing congruent angles.

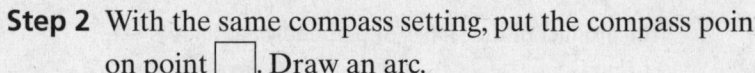

Step 1 With the compass point on point *H*, draw an arc that intersects the sides of [   ].

Step 2 With the same compass setting, put the compass point on point [   ]. Draw an arc.

Step 3 Put the compass point below point *N* where the arc intersects [   ]. Open the compass to the length where the arc intersects line [   ]. Keeping the same compass setting, put the compass point above point *N* where the arc intersects [   ]. Draw an arc to locate a point.

Step 4 Use a straightedge to draw line *m* through the point you located and point *N*.

Quick Check

1. Use Example 1. Explain why lines ℓ and *m* must be parallel.

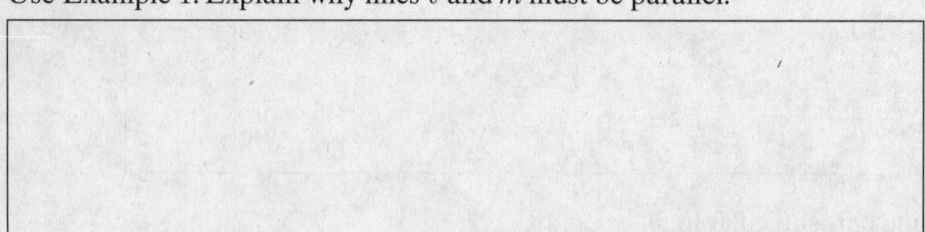

Example

2 **Perpendicular From a Point to a Line** Examine the construction. At what special point does $\overleftrightarrow{RG}$ meet line ℓ?

Point R is the same distance from point ☐ as it is from point ☐ because the arc was made with one compass opening.

Point G is the same distance from point ☐ as it is from point ☐ because both arcs were made with the same compass opening.

This means that $\overleftrightarrow{RG}$ intersects line ℓ at the _____ of $\overline{EF}$, and that $\overleftrightarrow{RG}$ is the _____ of $\overline{EF}$.

Quick Check

2. Use a straightedge to draw $\overleftrightarrow{EF}$. Construct $\overleftrightarrow{FG}$ so that $\overleftrightarrow{FG} \perp \overleftrightarrow{EF}$ at point F.

Lesson 4-1

Congruent Figures

Lesson Objective	NAEP 2005 Strand: Geometry
▼ Recognize congruent figures and their corresponding parts	Topic: Transformation of Shapes and Preservation of Properties
	Local Standards: _____

Vocabulary and Key Concepts

Theorem 4–1

If two angles of one triangle are congruent to two angles of another triangle, then _____

_____

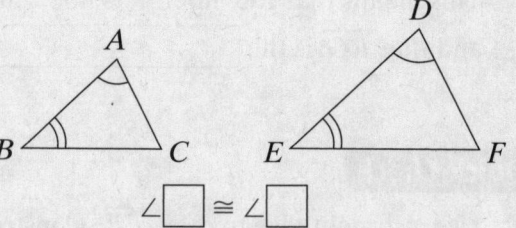

$\angle \boxed{} \cong \angle \boxed{}$

Congruent polygons are _____

_____

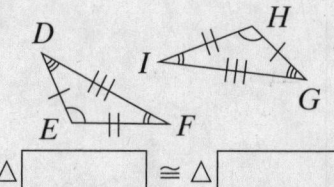

$\triangle \boxed{} \cong \triangle \boxed{}$

Examples

❶ Naming Congruent Parts $\triangle ABC \cong \triangle QTJ$. List the congruent corresponding parts.

List the corresponding sides and angles in the same order.

Angles: $\angle A \cong \angle Q$ $\angle B \cong \angle \boxed{}$ $\angle \boxed{} \cong \angle J$

Sides: $\overline{AB} \cong \overline{QT}$ $\boxed{} \cong \overline{TJ}$ $\overline{AC} \cong \boxed{}$

❷ Using Congruency $\triangle XYZ \cong \triangle KLM, m\angle Y = 67$, and $m\angle M = 48$. Find $m\angle X$.

Use the Triangle Angle-Sum Theorem and the definition of congruent polygons to find $m\angle X$.

$m\angle X + m\angle Y + m\angle Z = \boxed{}$	Triangle Angle-Sum Theorem
$m\angle Z = \boxed{}$	Corresponding angles of congruent triangles are congruent.
$m\angle Z = \boxed{}$	Substitute 48 for $m\angle M$.
$m\angle X + \boxed{} + \boxed{} = 180$	Substitute.
$m\angle X + \boxed{} = 180$	Simplify.
$m\angle X = \boxed{}$	Subtract 115 from each side.

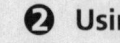

❸ **Finding Congruent Triangles** Can you conclude that △ABC ≅ △CDE?
List corresponding vertices in the same order.

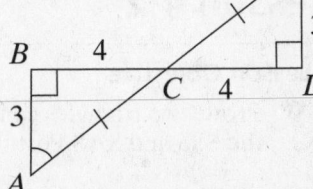

If △ABC ≅ △CDE, then ∠BAC ≅ [ ].

The diagram above shows ∠BAC ≅ [ ], not ∠DCE.

The statement △ABC ≅ △CDE [ ] true.

Notice that $\overline{BC}$ ≅ [ ], $\overline{BA}$ ≅ [ ], and $\overline{AC}$ ≅ [ ].

Also, ∠CBA ≅ [ ] and ∠BAC ≅ [ ].

Using Theorem 4-1, you can conclude that ∠ECD ≅ [ ].

Since all of the corresponding sides and angles are congruent, the triangles
are congruent. The correct way to state this is △ABC ≅ [ ].

Quick Check

1. △WYS ≅ △MKV. List the congruent corresponding parts. Use three letters
for each angle.

Sides: WY ≅ MK [ ]   [ ]

Angles: ∠WSY ≅ ∠MVK [ ]   [ ]

2. It is given that △WYS ≅ △MKV. If m∠Y = 35, what is m∠K? Explain.

m∠K = [ ]

[ ]

3. Can you conclude that △JKL ≅ △MNL? Justify your answer.

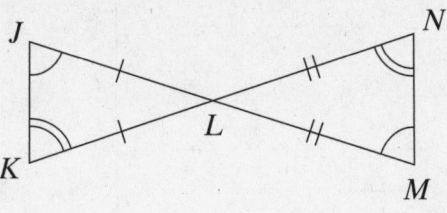

[ ]

Lesson 4-2

Lesson Objective	NAEP 2005 Strand: Geometry
▼ Prove two triangles congruent using the SSS and SAS Postulates	Topic: Transformation of Shapes and Preservation of Properties
	Local Standards: _____

Key Concepts

Postulate 4-1: Side-Side-Side (SSS) Postulate

If the three sides of one triangle are congruent to the three sides of another triangle, then _____

_____

△[_____] ≅ △[_____]

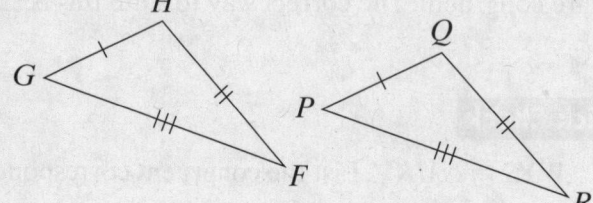

Postulate 4-2: Side-Angle-Side (SAS) Postulate

If two sides and the included angle of one triangle are congruent to two sides and the included angle of another triangle, then _____

_____

△[_____] ≅ △[_____]

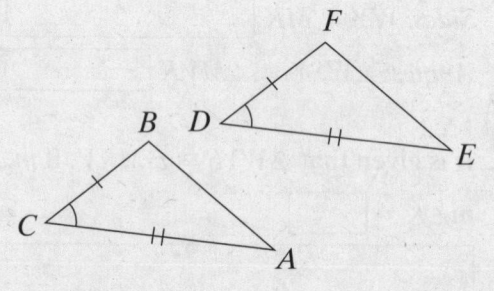

Examples

❶ Proving Triangles Congruent

Given: M is the midpoint of $\overline{XY}$, $\overline{AX} \cong \overline{AY}$
Prove: $\triangle AMX \cong \triangle AMY$

Write a paragraph proof.

You are given that M is the midpoint of [____], and $\overline{AX} \cong$ [____].

Midpoint M implies that $\overline{MX} \cong$ [____]. $\overline{AM} \cong \overline{AM}$ by the

[_____], so

$\triangle AMX \cong \triangle AMY$ by the [_____].

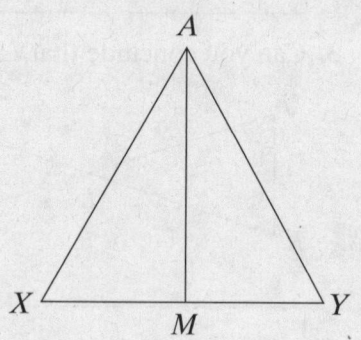

❷ Using SAS $\overline{AD} \cong \overline{BC}$. What other information do you need to prove $\triangle ADC \cong \triangle BCD$ by SAS?

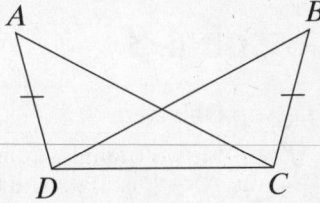

It is given that $\overline{AD} \cong \overline{BC}$. Also, $\overline{DC} \cong \overline{CD}$ by the

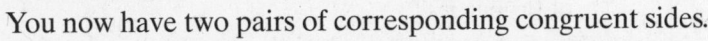 .

You now have two pairs of corresponding congruent sides.

Therefore, if you know ⬚⬚⬚⬚⬚ , you can prove

$\triangle ADC \cong \triangle BCD$ by ⬚⬚⬚ .

Quick Check

1. *Given:* $\overline{HF} \cong \overline{HJ}, \overline{FG} \cong \overline{JK},$
    H is the midpoint of $\overline{GK}.$

Prove: $\triangle FGH \cong \triangle JKH$

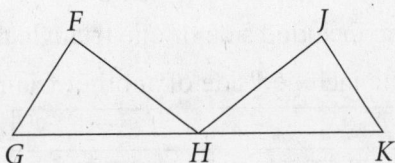

Statements	Reasons
1. $\overline{HF} \cong \overline{HJ}, \overline{FG} \cong \overline{JK}$	**1.**
2. H is the midpoint of $\overline{GK}.$	**2.**
3. $\overline{GH} \cong \overline{HK}$	**3.**
4.	**4.**

2. What other information do you need to prove $\triangle ABC \cong \triangle CDA$ by SAS?

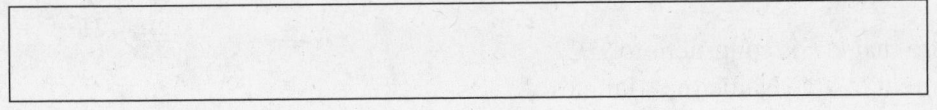

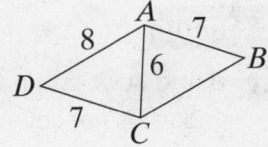

Lesson 4-3

Lesson Objective	NAEP 2005 Strand: Geometry
▼ Prove two triangles congruent using the ASA Postulate and the AAS Theorem	**Topic:** Transformation of Shapes and Preservation of Properties
	Local Standards: _____

Key Concepts

Postulate 4-3: Angle-Side-Angle (ASA) Postulate

If two angles and the included side of one triangle are congruent

to two angles and the included side of another triangle, then

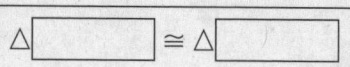

△ [   ] ≅ △ [   ]

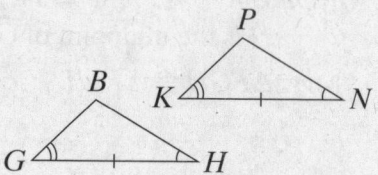

Theorem 4-2: Angle-Angle-Side (AAS) Theorem

If two angles and a nonincluded side of one triangle are congruent

to two angles and the corresponding nonincluded side of another

triangle, then 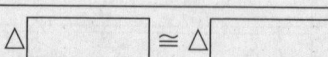.

△ [   ] ≅ △ [   ]

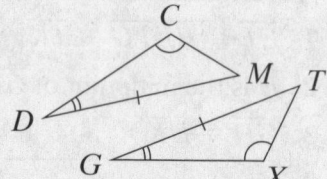

Example

❶ **Using ASA** Suppose that ∠F is congruent to ∠C and ∠I is *not* congruent to ∠C. Name the triangles that are congruent by the ASA Postulate.

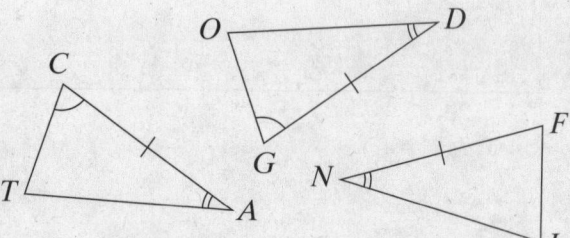

The diagram shows ∠N ≅ ∠A ≅ ∠D and
$\overline{FN} \cong \overline{CA} \cong \overline{GD}$.

If ∠F ≅ ∠C, then ∠F ≅ ∠C ≅ ∠ [   ].

Therefore, △FNI ≅ △CAT ≅ △GDO by [   ].

Quick Check

1. Using only the information in the diagram, can you conclude that △INF is congruent to either of the other two triangles? Explain.

[   ]

Example

② Writing a Proof Write a two-column proof that uses AAS.

Given: $\angle B \cong \angle D, \overline{AB} \| \overline{CD}$
Prove: $\triangle ABC \cong \triangle CDA$

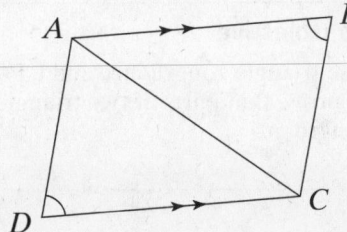

Statements	Reasons
1. $\angle B \cong \angle D, \overline{AB} \| \overline{CD}$	1. [ ]
2. [ ]	2. If lines are parallel, then [ ] angles are congruent.
3. $\overline{AC} \cong \overline{AC}$	3. [ ]
4. $\triangle ABC \cong \triangle CDA$	4. [ ]

Quick Check

2. In Example 2, explain how you could prove $\triangle ABC \cong \triangle CDA$ using ASA.

Name______________________________ Class______________________ Date______________

Lesson 4-4

Using Congruent Triangles: CPCTC

Lesson Objective	NAEP 2005 Strand: Geometry
1 Use triangle congruence and CPCTC to prove that parts of two triangles are congruent	**Topic:** Transformation of Shapes and Preservation of Properties **Local Standards:** ____________________

Vocabulary

CPCTC stands for:

C__________ P__________ of C__________

T__________ are C__________.

Examples

1 **Congruence Statements** The diagram shows the frame of an umbrella. What congruence statements besides $\angle 3 \cong \angle 4$ can you prove from the diagram, in which $\overline{SL} \cong \overline{SR}$ and $\angle 1 \cong \angle 2$ are given?

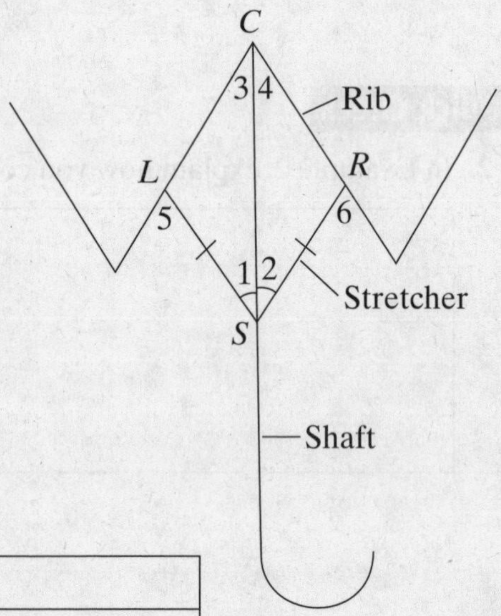

$\overline{SC} \cong$ ______ by the Reflexive Property of Congruence, and $\triangle LSC \cong$ ______ by SAS . $\angle 3 \cong$ ______ because corresponding parts of congruent triangles are congruent.

When two triangles are congruent, you can form congruence statements about three pairs of corresponding angles and three pairs of corresponding sides. List the congruence statements.

Sides:

$\overline{SL} \cong \overline{SR}$	Given
$\overline{SC} \cong$ ______	Reflexive Property of Congruence
$\overline{CL} \cong$ ______	Other congruence statement

Angles:

$\angle 1 \cong \angle 2$	Given
$\angle 3 \cong \angle$ ______	Corresponding Parts of Congruent Triangles
	Other congruence statement

The congruence statements that remain to be proved are

❷ Using Right Triangles According to legend, one of Napoleon's followers used congruent triangles to estimate the width of a river. On the riverbank, the officer stood up straight and lowered the visor of his cap until the farthest thing he could see was the edge of the opposite bank. He then turned and noted the spot on his side of the river that was in line with his eye and the tip of his visor.

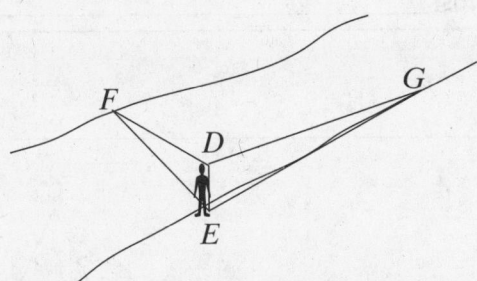

Given: ∠*DEG* and ∠*DEF* are right angles; ∠*EDG* ≅ ∠*EDF*.

The officer then paced off the distance to this spot and declared that distance to be the width of the river!

The given states that ∠*DEG* and ∠*DEF* are [_____].
What conditions must hold for that to be true?

∠*DEG* and ∠*DEF* are the angles that the officer makes with the ground.

So the officer must stand [_____] to the ground, and the

ground must be [_____].

Quick Check

1. In Example 1, what can you say about ∠5 and ∠6? Explain.

[_____]

2. Recall Example 2. About how wide was the river if the officer paced off 20 paces and each pace was about $2\frac{1}{2}$ feet long?

[_____]

Lesson 4-5

Isosceles and Equilateral Triangles

Lesson Objective	NAEP 2005 Strand: Geometry
✔ Use and apply properties of isosceles triangles	Topic: Relationships Among Geometric Figures
	Local Standards: _____

Vocabulary and Key Concepts

Theorem 4-3: Isosceles Triangle Theorem

If two sides of a triangle are congruent, then

_____

∠▢ ≅ ∠▢

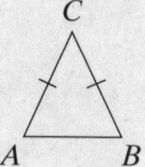

Theorem 4-4: Converse of Isosceles Triangle Theorem

If two angles of a triangle are congruent, then

_____

▢ ≅ ▢

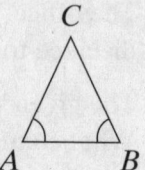

Theorem 4-5

The bisector of the vertex angle of an isosceles triangle is the

[_____] of the base.

$\overline{CD} \perp$ ▢ and ▢ bisects $\overline{AB}$.

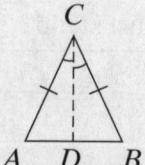

The legs of an isosceles triangle

_____

_____

The _____ of an

isosceles triangle is the third, or

non-congruent, side.

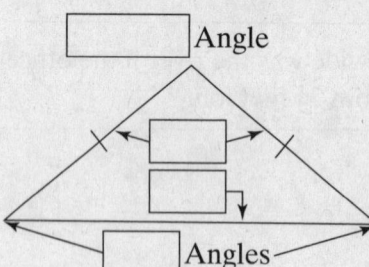

▢ Angle

▢

▢

▢ Angles

The _____ of an

isosceles triangle is formed by

the two congruent sides (legs).

The base angles of an isosceles

triangle _____

_____

Example

Using the Isosceles Triangle Theorems Explain why △ABC is isosceles.

∠ABC and ∠XAB are [   ] angles formed

by $\overleftrightarrow{XA}$, $\overleftrightarrow{BC}$, and the transversal [   ]. Because $\overleftrightarrow{XA} \parallel \overleftrightarrow{BC}$,

∠ABC ≅ ∠[   ].

The diagram shows that ∠XAB ≅ ∠ACB. By

[   ], ∠ABC ≅ ∠[   ].

You can use [   ] to

conclude that $\overline{AB}$ ≅ [   ].

By the definition of an isosceles triangle, △ABC is isosceles.

Quick Check

a. In the figure, suppose $m\angle ACB = 55$. Find $m\angle CBA$ and $m\angle BAC$.

b. In the figure, can you deduce that △ABX is isosceles?

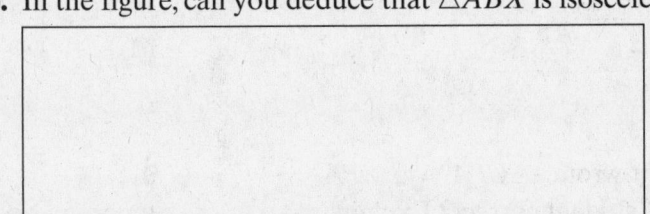

Lesson 4-6

Congruence in Right Triangles

Lesson Objective	NAEP 2005 Strand: Geometry
▼ Prove triangles congruent using the HL Theorem	**Topic:** Transformation of Shapes and Preservation of Properties
	Local Standards: _____

Vocabulary and Key Concepts

Theorem 4-6: Hypotenuse-Leg (HL) Theorem

If the hypotenuse and a leg of one right triangle are congruent to the hypotenuse and leg of another right triangle, then

_____

The hypotenuse of a right triangle is _____

_____

The _____ of a right triangle are the two shortest sides, or the sides that are *not* opposite the right angle.

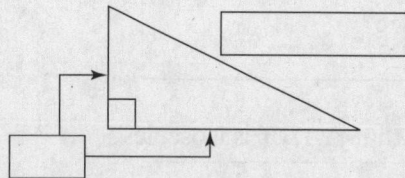

Examples

❶ Proving Triangles Congruent One student wrote "△CPA ≅ △MPA by the HL Theorem" for the diagram. Is the student correct? Explain.

The diagram shows the following congruent parts.

$\overline{CA}$ ≅ [   ]

∠CPA ≅ [   ]

$\overline{PA}$ ≅ [   ]

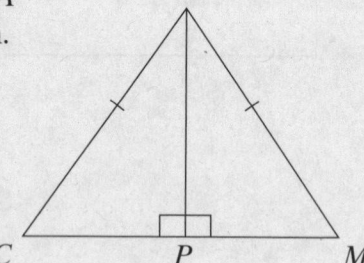

Since $\overline{AC}$ is the [   ] and $\overline{PA}$ is a [   ]

of right triangle CPA, and $\overline{MA}$ is the [   ] and $\overline{PA}$ is a

[   ] of right triangle MPA, the triangles are congruent by

the [   ].

The student [   ] correct.

Name_____ Class_____ Date _____

❷ Two-Column Proof—Using the HL Theorem

Given: $\angle ABC$ and $\angle DCB$ are right angles, $\overline{AC} \cong \overline{DB}$
Prove: $\triangle ABC \cong \triangle DCB$

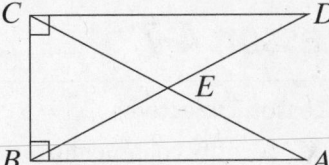

Statements	Reasons
1. $\angle ABC$ and $\angle DCB$ are [ ]	**1.** Given
2. $\triangle ABC$ and $\triangle$ [ ] are right triangles	**2.** Definition of Right Triangle
3. $\overline{AC} \cong$ [ ]	**3.** Given
4. [ ]	**4.** Reflexive Property of Congruence
5. $\triangle ABC \cong \triangle$ [ ]	**5.** [ ]

Quick Check

1.

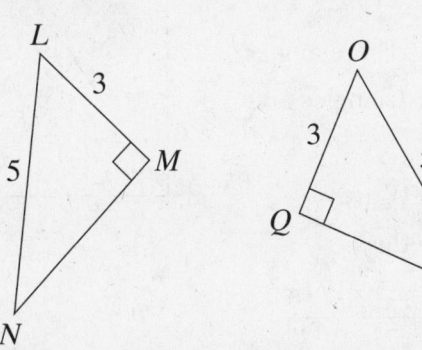 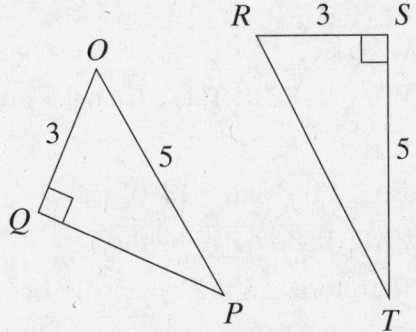

Which two triangles are congruent by the HL Theorem? Write a correct congruence statement.

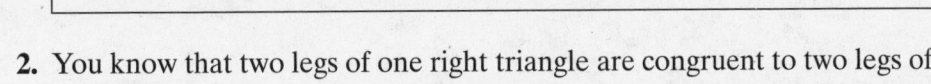

2. You know that two legs of one right triangle are congruent to two legs of another right triangle. Explain how to prove the triangles are congruent.

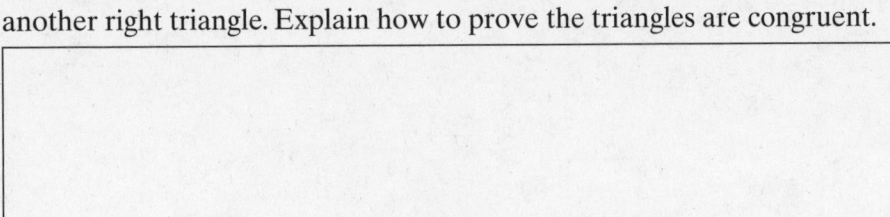

Lesson 4-7

Lesson Objectives	**NAEP 2005 Strand:** Geometry
▼ Identify congruent overlapping triangles	**Topic:** Relationships Among Geometric Figures
▼ Prove two triangles congruent by first proving two other triangles congruent	**Local Standards:** _____

Examples

❶ **Identifying Common Parts** Name the parts of the sides that △*DFG* and △*EHG* share.

Identify the overlapping triangles.

Parts of sides $\overline{DG}$ and ⬚ are shared by △*DFG* and △*EHG*.

These parts are ⬚ and ⬚, respectively.

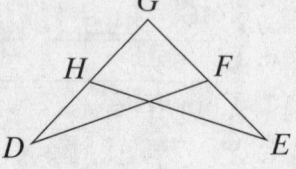

❷ **Using Two Pairs of Triangles** Write a paragraph proof.

Given: $\overline{XW} \cong \overline{YZ}$, ∠*XWZ* and ∠*YZW* are right angles.
Prove: △*XPW* ≅ △*YPZ*

Plan: △*XPW* ≅ △*YPZ* by AAS if ∠*WXZ* ≅ ⬚. These angles

are congruent by ⬚ if △*XWZ* ≅ △*YZW*. These triangles are

congruent by ⬚.

Proof: You are given $\overline{XW} \cong \overline{YZ}$. Because ∠*XWZ* and ∠*YZW* are

⬚, ∠*XWZ* ≅ ∠*YZW*. $\overline{WZ} \cong \overline{ZW}$ by the

⬚. Therefore, △*XWZ* ≅ △*YZW* by

SAS. ∠*WXZ* ≅ ∠ ⬚ by CPCTC, and ∠*XPW* ≅ ∠ ⬚

because ⬚ are congruent. Therefore,

△*XPW* ≅ △*YPZ* by ⬚.

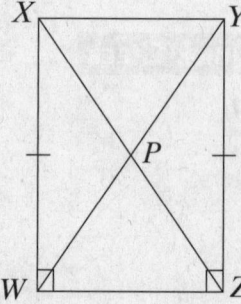

Quick Check

1. The diagram shows triangles from the scaffolding that workers used when they repaired and cleaned the Statue of Liberty.

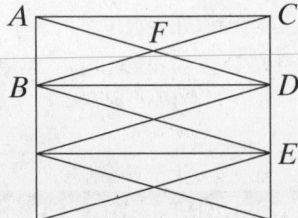

   a. Name the common side in $\triangle ACD$ and $\triangle BCD$.

   [ ]

   b. Name another pair of triangles that share a common side. Name the common side.

   [ ]

2. Write a two-column proof.
   Given: $\overline{PS} \cong \overline{RS}$, $\angle PSQ \cong \angle RSQ$
   Prove: $\triangle QPT \cong \triangle QRT$

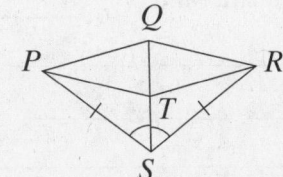

Statements	Reasons
1. [ ]	**1.** Given
2. $\overline{QS} \cong$ [ ]	**2.** Reflexive Property of Congruence
3. $\triangle PSQ \cong$ [ ]	**3.** SAS
4. $\overline{PQ} \cong$ [ ]	**4.** CPCTC
5. $\angle PQT \cong$ [ ]	**5.** CPCTC
6. $\overline{QT} \cong$ [ ]	**6.** Reflexive Property of Congruence
7. $\triangle QPT \cong$ [ ]	**7.** SAS

Lesson 5-1

Midsegments of Triangles

Lesson Objective	NAEP 2005 Strand: Geometry
▼ Use properties of midsegments to solve problems	**Topics:** Relationships Among Geometric Figures
	Local Standards: _____

Vocabulary and Key Concepts

Theorem 5-1: Triangle Midsegment Theorem

If a segment joins the midpoints of two sides of a triangle, then the segment

is [＿＿＿＿＿＿＿＿] to the third side, and is [＿＿＿＿＿] its length.

A midsegment of a triangle is _____

_____

A _____ is a form of proof in which coordinate geometry and algebra are

used to prove a theorem.

Examples

① **Finding Lengths** In $\triangle XYZ$, M, N, and P are midpoints. The perimeter of $\triangle MNP$ is 60. Find NP and YZ.

Because the perimeter of $\triangle MNP$ is 60, you can find NP.

$$NP + MN + MP = 60 \quad \text{Definition of perimeter}$$

$$NP + \boxed{} + \boxed{} = 60 \quad \begin{array}{l}\text{Substitute } \boxed{} \text{ for } \textbf{MN} \text{ and} \\ \boxed{} \text{ for } \textbf{MP.}\end{array}$$

$$NP + \boxed{} = 60 \quad \text{Simplify.}$$

$$NP = \boxed{} \quad \text{Subtract } \boxed{} \text{ from each side.}$$

Use the Triangle Midsegment Theorem to find YZ.

$$MP = \frac{\boxed{}}{\boxed{}} \, YZ \quad \text{Triangle Midsegment Theorem}$$

$$\boxed{} = \boxed{} \, YZ \quad \text{Substitute } \boxed{} \text{ for } \textbf{MP.}$$

$$\boxed{} = YZ \quad \text{Multiply each side by } \boxed{}.$$

❷ **Identifying Parallel Segments** Find $m\angle AMN$ and $m\angle ANM$. $\overline{MN}$ and $\overline{BC}$
are cut by transversal $\overline{AB}$, so $\angle AMN$ and $\angle B$ are [   ]
angles. $\overline{MN} \| \overline{BC}$ by the [   ] Theorem, so
$\angle AMN \cong \angle B$ by the [   ] Postulate.
$m\angle AMN =$ [   ] because congruent angles have the same measure.
In $\triangle AMN$, $AM =$ [   ], so $m\angle ANM =$ [   ] by the
[   ] Theorem. $m\angle ANM =$ [   ]
by substitution.

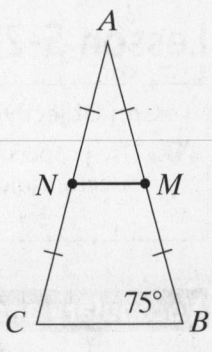

Quick Check

1. $AB = 10$ and $CD = 18$. Find EB, BC, and AC.

2. **Critical Thinking** Find $m\angle VUZ$. Justify your answer.

Lesson 5-2

Bisectors in Triangles

Lesson Objective	**NAEP 2005 Strand:** Geometry
▼ Use properties of perpendicular bisectors and angle bisectors	**Topics:** Relationships Among Geometric Figures
	Local Standards: _____

Vocabulary and Key Concepts

Theorem 5-2: Perpendicular Bisector Theorem

If a point is on the perpendicular bisector of a segment, then it is

_____

Theorem 5-3: Converse of the Perpendicular Bisector Theorem

If a point is equidistant from the endpoints of a segment, then it is

_____

Theorem 5-4: Angle Bisector Theorem

If a point is on the bisector of an angle, then it is

_____

Theorem 5-5: Converse of the Angle Bisector Theorem

If a point in the interior of an angle is equidistant from the sides of the

angle, then it is _____

The distance from a point to a line is _____

_____

_____

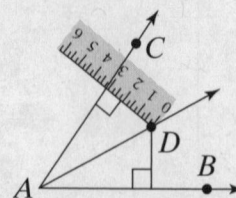 D is 3 in. from $\overleftrightarrow{AB}$ and ☐ .

Example

Using the Angle Bisector Theorem

Find x, FB, and FD in the diagram at right.

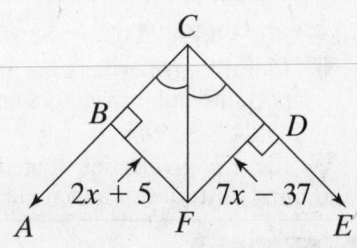

$\boxed{} = \boxed{}$		**Angle Bisector Theorem**
$7x - 37 = 2x + 5$		**Substitute.**
$7x = 2x + \boxed{}$		**Add 37 to each side.**
$\boxed{} = 42$		**Subtract 2x from each side.**
$x = \boxed{}$		**Divide each side by 5.**
$FB = 2(\boxed{}) + 5 = \boxed{}$		**Substitute.**
$FD = 7(\boxed{}) - 37 = \boxed{}$		**Substitute.**

Quick Check

a. According to the diagram, how far is K from $\overrightarrow{EH}$? From $\overrightarrow{ED}$?

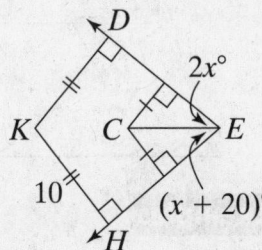

b. What can you conclude about $\overrightarrow{EK}$?

c. Find the value of x.

d. Find $m\angle DEH$.

Name_____ Class_____ Date_____

Lesson 5-3

<table>
<tr><td>**Lesson Objective**
❶ Identify properties of perpendicular bisectors and angle bisectors
❷ Identify properties of medians and altitudes of a triangle</td><td>**NAEP 2005 Strand:** Geometry
Topics: Relationships Among Geometric Figures
Local Standards: _____</td></tr>
</table>

Vocabulary

Concurrent lines are _____

The _____ is the point at which concurrent lines intersect.

A circle is circumscribed about a polygon when _____ ▭circle

_____

The _____ of a triangle is the point of concurrency of the perpendicular bisectors of a triangle.

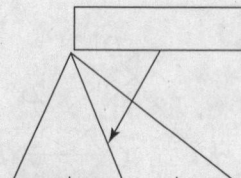 A median of a triangle is _____

_____

_____

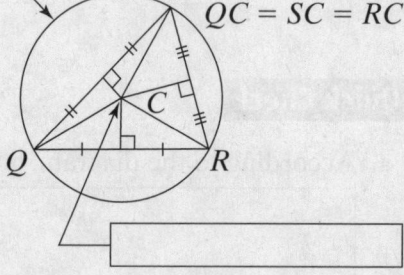

$QC = SC = RC$

Examples

❶ **Finding the Circumcenter** Find the center of the circle that circumscribes △XYZ.

Because X has coordinates ▭ and Y has coordinates ▭, $\overline{XY}$ lies on the vertical line $x =$ ▭. The perpendicular bisector of $\overline{XY}$ is the horizontal line that passes through $(1, \frac{1+7}{2})$ or ▭, so the equation of the perpendicular bisector of $\overline{XY}$ is $y =$ ▭.

Because X has coordinates ▭ and Z has coordinates ▭, $\overline{XZ}$ lies on the horizontal line $y =$ ▭. The perpendicular bisector of $\overline{XZ}$ is the vertical line that passes through ▭ or ▭, so the equation of the perpendicular bisector of $\overline{XZ}$ is $x =$ ▭.

Draw the lines $y =$ ▭ and $x =$ ▭. They intersect at the point ▭. This point is the center of the circle that circumscribes △XYZ.

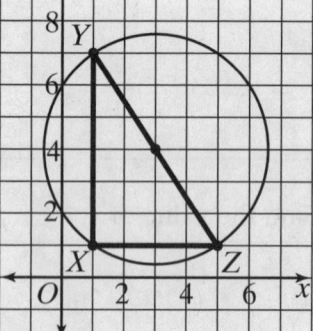

Name_____ Class_____ Date _____

❷ Finding Lengths of Medians *M* is the centroid of △*WOR*, and *WM* = 16. Find *WX*.

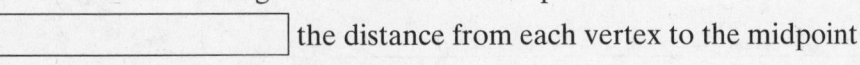

The [＿＿＿＿＿＿＿＿] is the point of concurrency of the medians of a triangle.

The medians of a triangle are concurrent at a point that is

[＿＿＿＿＿＿＿＿] the distance from each vertex to the midpoint

of the opposite side. (Theorem 5-8)

Because *M* is the [＿＿＿＿＿＿＿＿] of △*WOR*, *WM* = [＿＿＿＿＿＿].

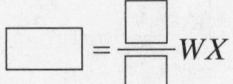

$WM = \dfrac{\square}{\square} WX$ **Theorem** [＿＿＿＿＿]

$\boxed{} = \dfrac{\square}{\square} WX$ **Substitute** [＿＿] **for *WM*.**

$\boxed{} = WX$ **Multiply each side by** [＿＿].

Quick Check

1. a. Find the center of the circle that you can circumscribe about the triangle with vertices $(0,0)$, $(-8,0)$, and $(0,6)$.

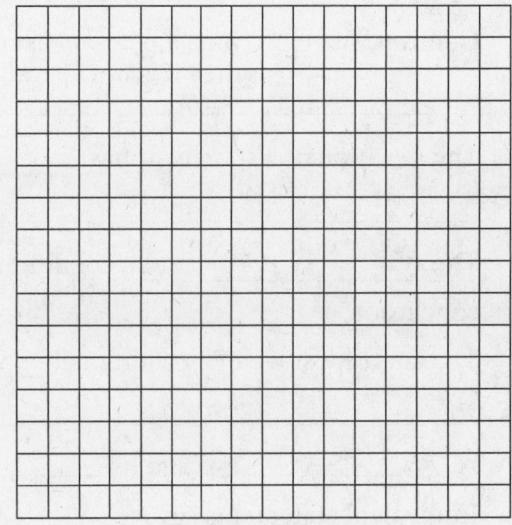

b. Critical Thinking In Example 1, explain why it is not necessary to find the third perpendicular bisector.

2. Using the diagram in Example 2, find *MX*. Check that *WM* + *MX* = *WX*.

All rights reserved.

© Pearson Education, Inc., publishing as Pearson Prentice Hall.

Lesson 5-4

Inverses, Contrapositives, and Indirect Reasoning

Lesson Objectives	**NAEP 2005 Strand:** Geometry
▼ Write the negation of a statement and the inverse and contrapositive of a conditional statement	**Topics:** Mathematical Reasoning
▼ Use indirect reasoning	**Local Standards:** _____

Vocabulary and Key Concepts

Negation, Inverse, and Contrapositive Statements

Statement	Example	Symbolic Form	You Read It
Conditional	If an angle is a straight angle, then its measure is 180.	$p \rightarrow q$	☐ p, ☐ q.
Negation (of p)	An angle is not a straight angle.	$\sim p$	☐ p.
Inverse	If an angle is not a straight angle, then its measure is not 180.	$\sim p \rightarrow \sim q$	☐ p, ☐ q.
Contrapositive	If an angle's measure is not 180, then it is not a straight angle.	$\sim q \rightarrow \sim p$	☐ q, ☐ p.

The negation of a statement has _____

_____

The _____ of a conditional statement negates both the hypothesis and the conclusion.

The contrapositive of a conditional _____

_____

A _____ and its _____ always have the same truth value.

Equivalent statements have _____

Examples

❶ **Writing the Negation of a Statement** Write the negation of "*ABCD* is not a convex polygon."

The negation of a statement has the [   ] truth value. The negation of *is not* in the original statement removes the word [   ].

The negation of "*ABCD* is not a convex polygon" is

_____

Name_____ Class_____ Date _____

❷ **Writing the Inverse and Contrapositive** Write the inverse and contrapositive of the conditional statement "If △ABC is equilateral, then it is isosceles."

To write the inverse of a conditional, negate both the hypothesis and the conclusion.

                                 Hypothesis   **Conclusion**
                                      ↓   ↓
Conditional: If △ABC is equilateral,   then it is isosceles.
                                      ↓   **Negate both.**   ↓
Inverse: If △ABC is [   ],   then it is [   ].

To write the contrapositive of a conditional, switch the hypothesis and conclusion, then negate both.

                                                Hypothesis   **Conclusion**
                                                     ↓   ↓
Conditional: If △ABC is equilateral, then it is isosceles.

                                            Switch and negate both.

Contrapositive: If △ABC is [   ], then it is [   ].

Quick Check

1. Write the negation of each statement.

a. $m\angle XYZ > 70$.

[   ]

b. Today is not Tuesday.

[   ]

2. Write (a) the inverse and (b) the contrapositive of Maya Angelou's statement "If you don't stand for something, you'll fall for anything."

a. [   ]

b. [   ]

Lesson 5-5

Inequalities in Triangles

Lesson Objectives	NAEP 2005 Strand: Geometry
1 Use inequalities involving angles of triangles	**Topics:** Relationships Among Geometric Figures
2 Use inequalities involving sides of triangles	**Local Standards:** _____

Key Concepts

Corollary to the Triangle Exterior Angle Theorem

The measure of an [   ] angle of a triangle is greater than the measure of each of its remote [   ] angles.

[   ] $> m\angle 2$ and [   ] $> m\angle 3$

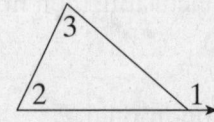

Theorem 5-10

If two sides of a triangle are not congruent, then

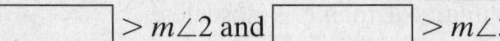

If $XZ > XY$, then $m\angle Y$ [ ] $m\angle Z$.

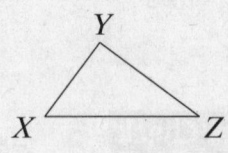

Theorem 5-12: Triangle Inequality Theorem

The sum of the lengths of any two sides of a triangle is

_____

$LM + MN >$ [   ] $MN + LN >$ [   ] $LN + LM >$ [   ]

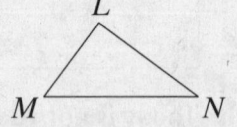

Examples

1 Applying Theorem 5-10 In $\triangle RGY$, $RG = 14$, $GY = 12$, and $RY = 20$.

List the angles from largest to smallest.

No two sides of $\triangle RGY$ are congruent, so the largest angle lies opposite the longest side.

Find the angle opposite each side.

The longest side is [   ]. The opposite angle, [   ], is the largest. The shortest side is [   ]. The opposite angle, [   ], is the smallest. From largest to smallest, the angles are [   ], [   ], [   ].

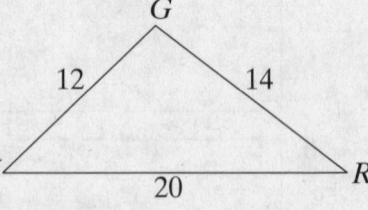

Name_____ Class_____ Date _____

❷ Using the Triangle Inequality Theorem Can a triangle have sides with the given lengths? Explain.

a. 2 cm, 2 cm, 4 cm

According to the [_____] Theorem, the

sum of the lengths of any two sides of a triangle is [_____]

than the length of the third side.

2 + 2 [ ] 4   The sum of 2 and 2 [_____] greater than 4.

[_____], a triangle [_____] have sides with these lengths.

b. 8 in., 15 in., 12 in.

8 + 15 [ ] 12   8 + 12 [ ] 15   15 + 12 [ ] 8

[_____], a triangle [_____] have sides with these lengths.

Quick Check

1. List the angles of △ABC in order from smallest to largest.

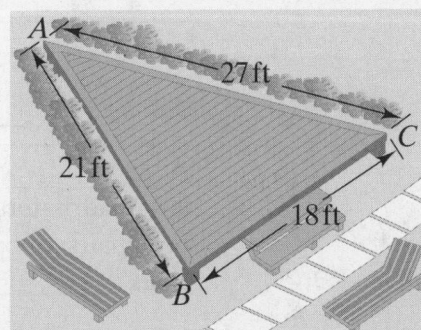

2. Can a triangle have sides with the given lengths? Explain.

a. 2 m, 7 m, and 9 m

b. 4 yd, 6 yd, and 9 yd

Lesson 6-1

Classifying Quadrilaterals

Lesson Objective	NAEP 2005 Strand: Geometry
▼ Define and classify special types of quadrilaterals	**Topic:** Relationships Among Geometric Figures
	Local Standards: _____

Key Concepts

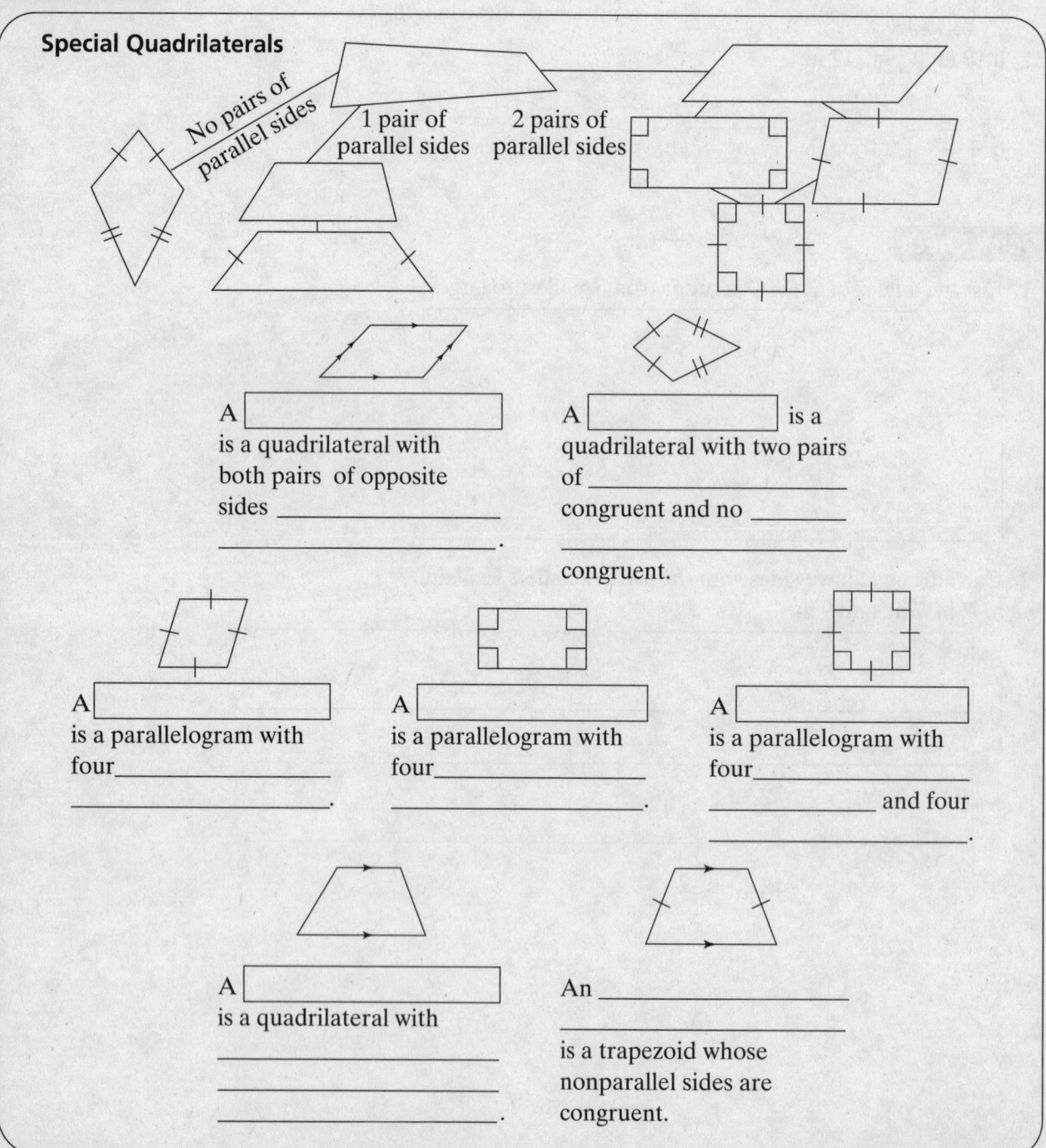

Special Quadrilaterals

No pairs of parallel sides

1 pair of parallel sides

2 pairs of parallel sides

A _____ is a quadrilateral with both pairs of opposite sides _____ _____ .

A _____ is a quadrilateral with two pairs of _____ congruent and no _____ _____ congruent.

A _____ is a parallelogram with four_____ _____ .

A _____ is a parallelogram with four_____ _____ .

A _____ is a parallelogram with four_____ _____ and four _____ .

A _____ is a quadrilateral with _____ _____ _____ .

An _____ _____ is a trapezoid whose nonparallel sides are congruent.

Example

Classifying by Coordinate Methods Determine the most precise name for the quadrilateral with vertices $Q(-4, 4)$, $B(-2, 9)$, $H(8, 9)$, and $A(10, 4)$.

Graph quadrilateral $QBHA$.

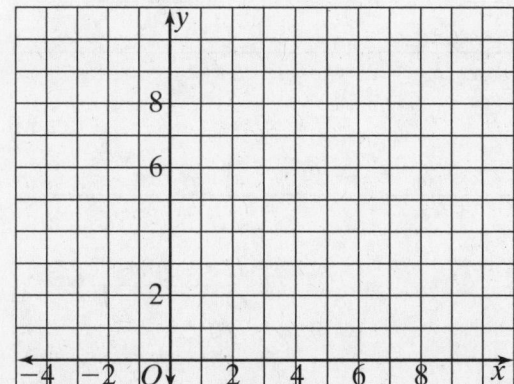

Find the slope of each side.

Slope of $\overline{QB}$ = $\dfrac{9 - 4}{-2 - (-4)}$ = ☐

Slope of $\overline{BH}$ = $\dfrac{9 - 9}{8 - (\boxed{})}$ = ☐

Slope of $\overline{HA}$ = $\dfrac{4 - \square}{10 - \square}$ = ☐

Slope of $\overline{QA}$ = $\dfrac{\square - \square}{\square - \square}$ = ☐

$\overline{BH}$ is parallel to $\overline{QA}$ because their slopes are [   ].

$\overline{HA}$ is not parallel to $\overline{QB}$ because their slopes are [   ].

One pair of opposite sides is parallel, so $QBHA$ is a [   ].

Next, use the distance formula to see whether any pairs of sides are congruent.

$QB = \sqrt{(-2 - (-4))^2 + \left(9 - \square\right)^2} = \sqrt{4 + \boxed{}} = \boxed{}$

$HA = \sqrt{(10 - 8)^2 + \left(\square - \square\right)^2} = \sqrt{4 + \boxed{}} = \boxed{}$

$BH = \sqrt{(8 - (-2))^2 + \left(\square - \square\right)^2} = \sqrt{100 + \square} = \boxed{}$

$QA = \sqrt{\left(-4 - 10\right)^2 + \left(\square - \square\right)^2} = \sqrt{196 + \square} = \boxed{}$

Because $QB = \boxed{}$, $QBHA$ is [   ].

Quick Check

a. Graph quadrilateral $ABCD$ with vertices $A(-3, 3)$, $B(2, 4)$, $C(3, -1)$, and $D(-2, -2)$.

b. Classify $ABCD$ in as many ways as possible.

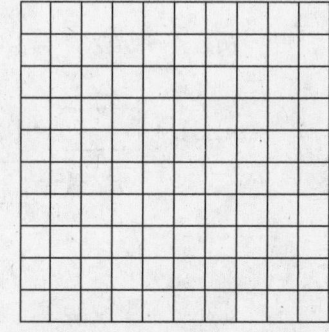

Lesson 6-2

Properties of Parallelograms

Lesson Objectives	NAEP 2005 Strand: Geometry
▼ Use relationships among sides and among angles of parallelograms ▼ Use relationships involving diagonals of parallelograms and transversals	**Topic:** Relationships Among Geometric Figures **Local Standards:** _____

Vocabulary and Key Concepts

Theorem 6-1

[_____] sides of a parallelogram are congruent.

Theorem 6-2

Opposite angles of a parallelogram are [_____].

Theorem 6-3

The diagonals of a parallelogram [_____] each other.

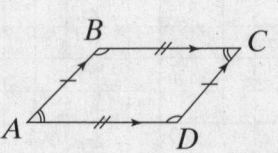

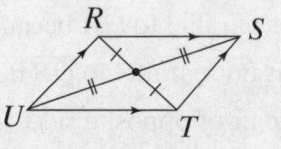

Examples

❶ **Using Algebra** Find the value of *x* in □*ABCD*. Then find *m∠A*.

$x + 15 = 135 - x$ Opposite angles of a parallelogram are [_____].

[____] $+ 15 =$ [____]   Add *x* to each side.

$2x =$ [____]   Subtract 15 from each side.

$x =$ [____]   Divide each side by 2.

$m∠B =$ [____] $+ 15 =$ [____]   Substitute [____] for *x*.

$m∠A + m∠B = 180$ Consecutive angles of a parallelogram are [_____].

$m∠A +$ [____] $= 180$ Substitute [____] for *m∠B*.

$m∠A =$ [____]   Subtract [____] from each side.

❷ **Using Algebra** Find the values of x and y in $\square KLMN$.

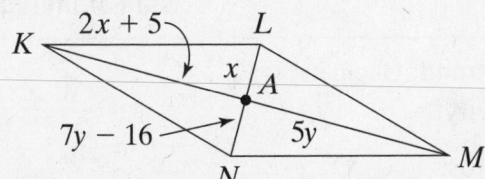

$$x = 7y - 16$$

The diagonals of a parallelogram

[   ] each other.

$$2x + 5 = 5y$$

$$2(7y - 16) + 5 = 5y$$

Substitute $7y - 16$ for x in the second equation to solve for y.

$$\boxed{} - \boxed{} + 5 = 5y$$

Distribute.

$$\boxed{} - \boxed{} = 5y$$

Simplify.

$$-27 = \boxed{}$$

Subtract [   ] from each side.

$$\boxed{} = y$$

Divide each side by [   ].

$$x = 7\left(\boxed{}\right) - 16$$

Substitute [ ] for y in the first equation to solve for x.

$$x = \boxed{}$$

Simplify.

So $x = \boxed{}$ and $y = \boxed{}$.

Quick Check

1. Find the value of y in $\square EFGH$. Then find $m\angle E, m\angle F, m\angle G,$ and $m\angle H$.

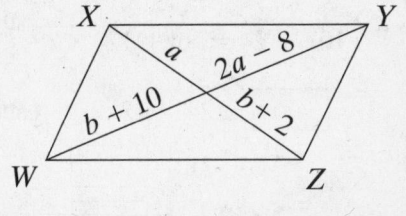

2. Find the values of a and b.

Lesson 6-3

Lesson Objective	NAEP 2005 Strand: Geometry
▼ Determine whether a quadrilateral is a parallelogram	Topic: Geometry
	Local Standards: _____

Key Concepts

Theorem 6-5

If both pairs of opposite sides of a quadrilateral are congruent, then

_____

Theorem 6-6

If both pairs of [   ] of a quadrilateral are congruent,

then the quadrilateral is a parallelogram.

Theorem 6-7

If the diagonals of a quadrilateral [   ] each other,

then the quadrilateral is a parallelogram.

Theorem 6-8

If one pair of opposite sides of a quadrilateral is both [   ]

and [   ], then the quadrilateral is a parallelogram.

Examples

❶ **Finding Values for Parallelograms** Find values for x and y for which $ABCD$ must be a parallelogram.

If the diagonals of quadrilateral $ABCD$ bisect each other, then $ABCD$ is a parallelogram by [   ]. Write and solve two equations to find values of x and y for which the diagonals bisect each other.

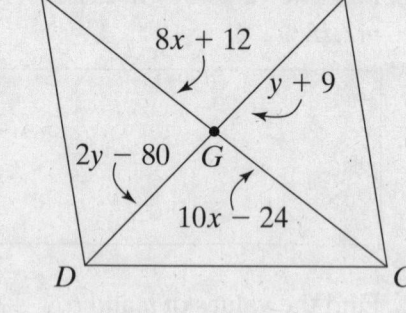

$10x - 24 = 8x + 12$ **Diagonals of parallelograms bisect each other.**

[   ] $- 24 = 12$ **Collect the variables on one side.**

$2x = $ [   ]   **Solve.**

$x = $ [   ]

[   ] $= $ [   ]

[   ] $- 80 = 9$

$y = $ [   ]

If $x = $ [   ] and $y = $ [   ], then $ABCD$ is a parallelogram.

❷ Is the Quadrilateral a Parallelogram? Can you prove the quadrilateral is a parallelogram from what is given? Explain.

Given: $m\angle E = m\angle G = 75°, m\angle F = 105°$
Prove: $EFGH$ is a parallelogram.

The sum of the measures of the angles of a polygon is $(n - 2)180$ where n represents the number of sides, so the sum of the measures of the angles of a quadrilateral is $\left(\boxed{} - 2\right)180 = \boxed{}$.

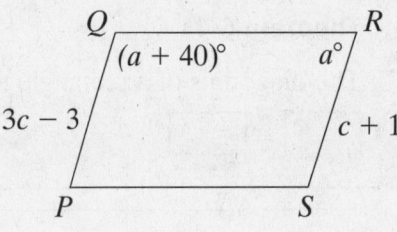

If x represents the measure of the unmarked angle, $x + 75 + 105 + 75 = \boxed{}$, so $x = \boxed{}$.

Theorem 6-6 states _____

_____

_____

Because both pairs of opposite angles are congruent, the quadrilateral is a parallelogram by $\boxed{}$.

Quick Check

1. Find the values of a and c for which $PQRS$ must be a parallelogram.

2. Can you prove the quadrilateral is a parallelogram? Explain.
Given: $\overline{PQ} \cong \overline{SR}, \overline{PQ} \parallel \overline{SR}$
Prove: $PQRS$ is a parallelogram.

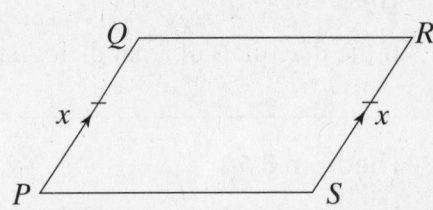

Lesson 6-4

Special Parallelograms

Lesson Objectives	
1 Use properties of diagonals of rhombuses and rectangles	**NAEP 2005 Strand:** Geometry
2 Determine whether a parallelogram is a rhombus or a rectangle	**Topic:** Geometry
	Local Standards: _____

Key Concepts

Rhombuses

Theorem 6-9

Each diagonal of a rhombus _____

$\overline{AC}$ bisects $\angle BAD$, so $\angle\ \boxed{} \cong \angle\boxed{}$

$\boxed{}$ bisects $\angle\ \boxed{}$, so $\angle 3 \cong \angle 4$

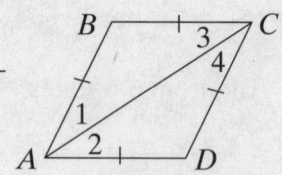

Theorem 6-10

The diagonals of a rhombus are $\boxed{}$.

$\boxed{} \perp \boxed{}$

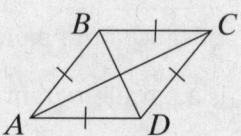

Rectangles

Theorem 6-11

The diagonals of a rectangle are $\boxed{}$.

$\boxed{} \cong \boxed{}$

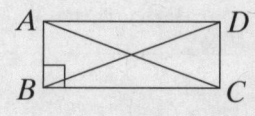

Parallelograms

Theorem 6-12

If one diagonal of a parallelogram bisects two angles of the parallelogram,

_____

Theorem 6-13

If the diagonals of a parallelogram are perpendicular, then

_____

Theorem 6-14

If the diagonals of a parallelogram are congruent, then

_____

Name_____ Class_____ Date _____

Examples

1 **Finding Angle Measures** Find the measures of the numbered angles in the rhombus.

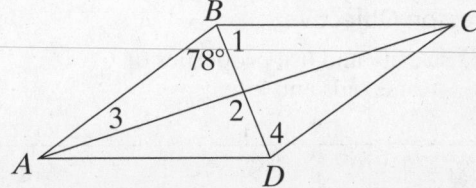

Theorem 6-9 states that each diagonal of a rhombus bisects two angles of the rhombus, so $m\angle 1 = 78$.

Theorem 6-10 states that

[   ],

so $m\angle 2 =$ [   ]. Because the four angles formed by the diagonals

all must have measure 90, $\angle 3$ and $\angle ABD$ must be [   ].

Because $m\angle ABD = 78$, $m\angle 3 = 90 - 78 =$ [   ]. Finally, because $BC = DC$,

the [   ] allows you to conclude that $\angle$ [   ] $\cong \angle 4$.

So $m\angle 4 =$ [   ].

2 **Finding Diagonal Length** One diagonal of a rectangle has length $8x + 2$. The other diagonal has length $5x + 11$. Find the length of each diagonal.

By Theorem 6-11, the diagonals of a rectangle are [   ].

[ ] $=$ [ ]	Diagonals of a rectangle are congruent.		

$11 =$ [   ] $+ 2$ Subtract [   ] from each side.

[   ] $=$ [   ]   Subtract 2 from each side.

[   ] $= x$ Divide each side by [   ].

$8x + 2 = 8\left(\boxed{}\right) + 2 =$ [   ]   Substitute.

$5x + 11 = 5\left(\boxed{}\right) + 11 =$ [   ]   Substitute.

The length of each diagonal is [   ].

Quick Check

1. Find the measures of the numbered angles in the rhombus.

[   ]

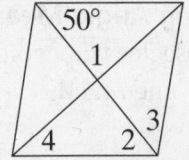

2. Find the length of the diagonals of rectangle *GFED* if $FD = 5y - 9$ and $GE = y + 5$.

[   ]

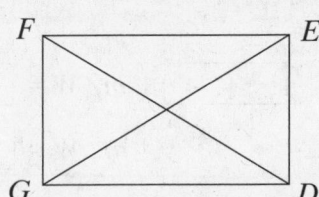

Lesson 6-5

Trapezoids and Kites

Lesson Objective	NAEP 2005 Strand: Geometry
▼ Verify and use properties of trapezoids and kites	Topic: Relationships Among Geometric Figures
	Local Standards: _____

Vocabulary and Key Concepts

Trapezoids

Theorem 6-15

The base angles of an isosceles trapezoid are [ ].

Theorem 6-16

The [ ] of an isosceles trapezoid are congruent.

The base angles of a trapezoid are _____

_____

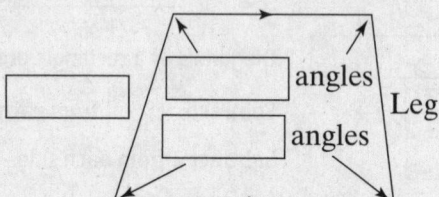

[ ]   [ ] angles   Leg

[ ] angles

Kites

Theorem 6-17

The diagonals of a kite are [ ].

Examples

① **Finding Angle Measures in Trapezoids** $WXYZ$ is an isosceles trapezoid, and $m\angle X = 156$. Find $m\angle Y$, $m\angle Z$, and $m\angle W$.

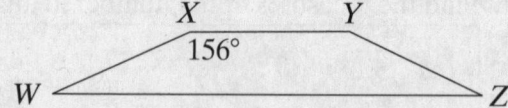

$m\angle X + m\angle W =$ [ ]   Two angles that share
                                   a leg of a trapezoid
                                   are [ ].

[ ] $+ m\angle W =$ [ ]   Substitute.

$m\angle W =$ [ ]   Subtract [ ] from each side.

Because the base angles of an isosceles trapezoid are [ ],
$m\angle Y = m\angle X = 156$ and $m\angle Z =$ [ ] $=$ [ ].

Daily Notetaking Guide   L1

Name_____ Class_____ Date _____

② Finding Angle Measures in Kites Find $m\angle 1, m\angle 2$, and $m\angle 3$ in the kite.

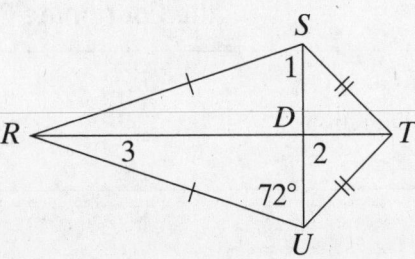

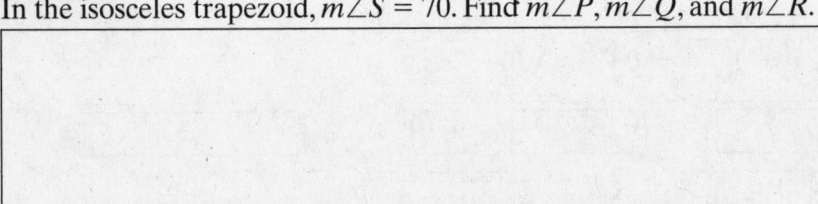

$m\angle 2 = 90$	Diagonals of a kite are ☐.
$RU = $ ☐	Definition of a kite
$m\angle 1 = $ ☐	☐ Triangle Theorem
$m\angle 3 + m\angle RDU + 72 = $ ☐	☐
$m\angle RDU = $ ☐	Diagonals of a kite are perpendicular.
$m\angle 3 + $ ☐ $+ 72 = $ ☐	Substitute.
$m\angle 3 + $ ☐ $= $ ☐	Simplify.
$m\angle 3 = $ ☐	Subtract ☐ from each side.

Quick Check

1. In the isosceles trapezoid, $m\angle S = 70$. Find $m\angle P, m\angle Q$, and $m\angle R$.

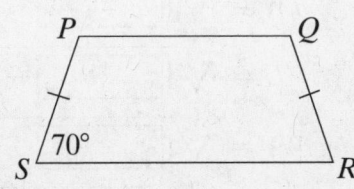

2. Find $m\angle 1, m\angle 2$, and $m\angle 3$ in the kite.

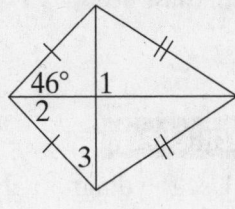

Name_____ Class_____ Date_____

Lesson 6-6

**Placing Figures in
the Coordinate Plane**

Lesson Objective	NAEP 2005 Strand: Geometry
▼ Name coordinates of special figures by using their properties	**Topic:** Position and Direction
	Local Standards: _____

Example

❶ **Proving Congruency** Show that *TWVU* is a parallelogram by proving pairs of opposite sides congruent.

If both pairs of opposite sides of a quadrilateral are

[_____], then the quadrilateral is a

parallelogram by [_____].

You can prove that *TWVU* is a parallelogram by showing that

$TW = VU$ and [____] = [____]. Use the distance formula.

Use the coordinates $T(a, b)$, $W($[____], [____]$)$, $V($[____], [____]$)$, and $U(e, 0)$.

$$TW = \sqrt{(\boxed{} - a)^2 + (\boxed{} - b)^2} = \sqrt{\boxed{}}$$

$$VU = \sqrt{(\boxed{} - e)^2 + (\boxed{} - 0)^2} = \sqrt{\boxed{}}$$

$$WV = \sqrt{(\boxed{} - \boxed{})^2 + (\boxed{} - \boxed{})^2} = \sqrt{\boxed{}}$$

$$TU = \sqrt{(\boxed{} - e)^2 + (\boxed{} - 0)^2} = \sqrt{\boxed{}}$$

Because $TW = VU$ and $WV = TU$, $TWVU$ is a [_____].

Quick Check

1. Use the diagram above. Use a different method: Show that *TWVU* is a parallelogram by finding the midpoints of the diagonals.

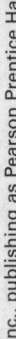

(Diagram at upper right: coordinate plane with points $T(a, b)$, $W(a + c, b + d)$, $V(c + e, d)$, $U(e, 0)$, A, C, O, E, and axes labeled x and y.)

Example

❷ Naming Coordinates Use the properties of parallelogram *OCBA* to find the missing coordinates. Do not use any new variables.

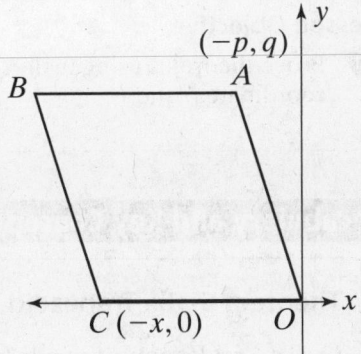

The vertex *O* is the origin with coordinates *O* [____].

Because point *A* is *p* units to the left of point *O*, point *B*

is also [__] units to the left of point [__], because *OCBA* is a

parallelogram. So the first coordinate of point *B* is [____].

Because $\overline{AB} \parallel \overline{CO}$ and $\overline{CO}$ is horizontal, $\overline{AB}$ is also

[_____]. So point *B* has the same second

coordinate, [__], as point *A*.

The missing coordinates are *O* [_____] and *B* [_____].

Quick Check

2. Use the properties of parallelogram *OPQR* to find the missing coordinates. Do not use any new variables.

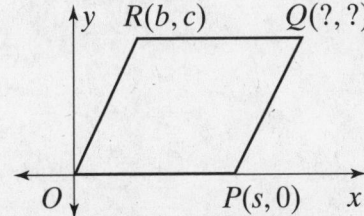

Lesson 6-7

Proofs Using Coordinate Geometry

Lesson Objective	NAEP 2005 Strand: Geometry
▼ Prove theorems using figures in the coordinate plane	**Topics:** Position and Direction; Mathematical Reasoning
	Local Standards: _____

Vocabulary and Key Concepts

Theorem 6-18: Trapezoid Midsegment Theorem

(1) The midsegment of a trapezoid is [   ] to the bases.

(2) The length of the midsegment of a trapezoid is half the sum of the

[   ].

The midsegment of a trapezoid _____

_____

$\overline{MN} \parallel$ [   ], $\overline{MN} \parallel$ [   ], and $MN = \frac{1}{2}($[   ] + [   ]$)$

Example

Using Coordinate Geometry Use coordinate geometry to prove that the quadrilateral formed by connecting the midpoints of rhombus *ABCD* is a rectangle.

Draw quadrilateral *XYZW* by connecting the midpoints of *ABCD*.

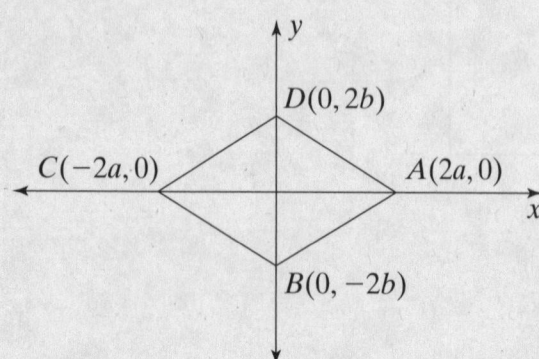

From Lesson 6-6, you know that *XYZW* is a parallelogram.

If the diagonals of a parallelogram are [   ], then the parallelogram is a [   ] from Theorem 6–14.

To show that $XYZW$ is a rectangle, find the lengths of its diagonals, and then compare them to show that they are [   ].

$$XZ = \sqrt{\left(-a - \boxed{}\right)^2 + \left(b - \left(\boxed{}\right)\right)^2}$$
$$= \sqrt{\left(\boxed{}\right)^2 + \left(\boxed{}\right)^2}$$
$$= \sqrt{\boxed{}}$$

$$YW = \sqrt{\left(-a - \boxed{}\right)^2 + \left(-b - \left(\boxed{}\right)\right)^2}$$
$$= \sqrt{\left(\boxed{}\right)^2 + \left(\boxed{}\right)^2}$$
$$= \sqrt{\boxed{}}$$

$XZ \boxed{} YW$

Because the diagonals are congruent, parallelogram $XYZW$ is a [   ].

Quick Check

Use the diagram from the Example on page 82. Explain why the proof using $A(2a, 0), B(0, -2b), C(-2a, 0),$ and $D(0, 2b)$ is easier than the proof using $A(a, 0), B(0, -b), C(-a, 0),$ and $D(0, b)$.

[   ]

Lesson 7-1
Ratios and Proportions

Lesson Objective	NAEP 2005 Strand: Geometry
▼ Write ratios and solve proportions	Topic: Position and Direction
	Local Standards: _____

Vocabulary and Key Concepts

Properties of Proportions

$\frac{a}{b} = \frac{c}{d}$ is equivalent to

(1) $ad =$ ☐   (2) $\frac{b}{a} =$ ☐   (3) $\frac{a}{c} =$ ☐   (4) $\frac{a+b}{b} =$ ☐

A proportion is _____

$\frac{a}{b} = \frac{c}{d}$ and $a:b = c:d$ are examples of proportions.

An _____ is a statement that three or more ratios are equal.

$\frac{6}{24} = \frac{4}{16} = \frac{1}{4}$ is an example of an extended proportion.

The Cross-Product Property states that _____

_____

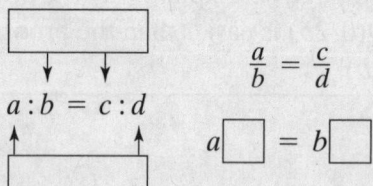

$$a:b = c:d \qquad \frac{a}{b} = \frac{c}{d}$$
$$a\,\square = b\,\square$$

A _____ is a drawing in which all lengths are proportional to corresponding actual lengths.

A scale is _____

_____

Examples

❶ Finding Ratios A scale model of a car is 4 in. long. The actual car is 15 ft long. What is the ratio of the length of the model to the length of the car?

Write both measurements in the same units.

15 ft = 15 × 12 in. = ☐ in.

$\dfrac{\text{length of model}}{\text{length of car}} = \dfrac{4 \text{ in.}}{15 \text{ ft}} = \dfrac{4 \text{ in.}}{180 \text{ in.}} = \dfrac{4}{180} =$ ☐

The ratio of the length of the scale model to the length of the car is ☐ : ☐.

Name_____ Class_____ Date _____

❷ **Solving for a Variable** Solve each proportion.

a. $\frac{2}{5} = \frac{n}{35}$

$5n = \boxed{}\left(\boxed{}\right)$ **Cross-Product Property**

$5n = \boxed{}$ **Simplify.**

$n = \boxed{}$ **Divide each side by** $\boxed{}$.

b. $\frac{x + 1}{3} = \frac{x}{2}$

$3x = \boxed{}\left(\boxed{} + \boxed{}\right)$ **Cross-Product Property**

$3x = \boxed{} + \boxed{}$ **Distributive Property**

$x = \boxed{}$ **Subtract** $\boxed{}$ **from each side.**

Quick Check

1. A photo that is 8 in. wide and $5\frac{1}{3}$ in. high is enlarged to a poster that is 2 ft wide and $1\frac{1}{3}$ ft high. What is the ratio of the height of the photo to the height of the poster?

2. Solve each proportion.

   a. $\frac{5}{z} = \frac{20}{3}$

   b. $\frac{18}{n + 6} = \frac{6}{n}$

Lesson 7-2

Similar Polygons

Lesson Objectives	NAEP 2005 Strand: Geometry and Measurement
▼ Identify similar polygons ▼ Apply similar polygons	**Topics:** Transformation of Shapes and Preservation of Properties; Measuring Physical Attributes **Local Standards:** _____

Vocabulary

Similar figures have _____

_____

_____

The mathematical symbol for _____ is ~.

The similarity ratio is _____

_____

A _____ is a rectangle that can be divided into a square and a

rectangle that is similar to the original rectangle.

The golden ratio is _____

_____

Example

1 Understanding Similarity $\triangle ABC \sim \triangle XYZ$.
Complete each statement.

a. $m\angle B = $ ▇

$\angle B \cong \angle \boxed{}$ and $m\angle Y = 78$, so $m\angle B = \boxed{}$

because congruent angles have the same measure.

b. $\dfrac{BC}{YZ} = \dfrac{▇}{XZ}$

$\boxed{}$ corresponds to $\overline{XZ}$, so $\dfrac{BC}{YZ} = \dfrac{\boxed{}}{XZ}$.

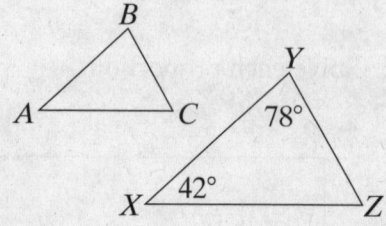

Quick Check

1. Refer to the diagram for Example 1. Complete:

$m\angle A = \boxed{}$ and $\dfrac{BC}{YZ} = \dfrac{\boxed{}}{XY}$

Example

❷ **Using Similar Figures** If $\triangle ABC \sim \triangle YXZ$, find the value of x.

Because $\triangle ABC \sim \triangle YXZ$, you can write and solve a proportion.

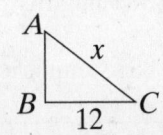 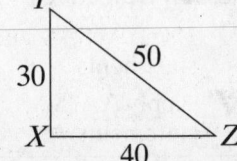

$$\dfrac{AC}{YZ} = \dfrac{\boxed{}}{XZ}$$
   Corresponding sides are
   $\boxed{}$.

$$\dfrac{x}{\boxed{}} = \dfrac{\boxed{}}{40}$$
   Substitute.

$$x = \dfrac{\boxed{}}{\boxed{}} \cdot \boxed{}$$
   Solve for x.

$$x = \boxed{}$$
   Simplify.

Quick Check

2. Refer to the diagram for Example 2. Find AB.

Lesson 7-3

Proving Triangles Similar

Lesson Objectives	NAEP 2005 Strand: Geometry
✔ Use AA, SAS, and SSS similarity statements	**Topic:** Transformation of Shapes and Preservation of Properties
✔ Apply AA, SAS, and SSS similarity statements	**Local Standards:** _____

Vocabulary and Key Concepts

Postulate 7-1: Angle-Angle Similarity (AA~) Postulate

If two angles of one triangle are congruent to two angles of another triangle, then the triangles are similar.

△TRS ~ △ [____]

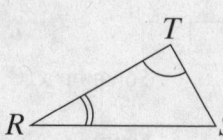 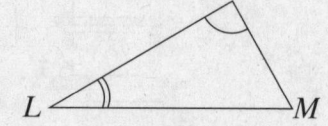

Theorem 7-1: Side-Angle-Side Similarity (SAS~) Theorem

If an angle of one triangle is congruent to an angle of a second triangle, and the sides including the two angles are proportional, then

_____

Theorem 7-2: Side-Side-Side Similarity (SSS~) Theorem

If the corresponding sides of two triangles are proportional, then

_____

Indirect measurement is _____
_____

Examples

1 Using the AA~ Postulate $\overline{MX} \perp \overline{AB}$. Explain why the triangles are similar. Write a similarity statement.

Because $\overline{MX} \perp \overline{AB}$, ∠AXM and ∠BXK are

[_____], so ∠AXM ≅ ∠[_____].

∠A ≅ ∠[__] because their measures are equal.

△AMX ~ △BKX

by the [_____] Postulate.

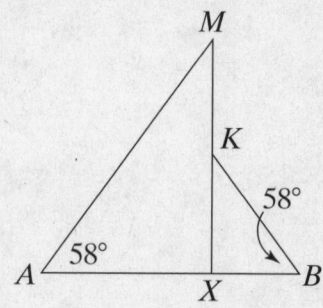

② **Using Similarity Theorems** Explain why the triangles must be similar. Write a similarity statement.

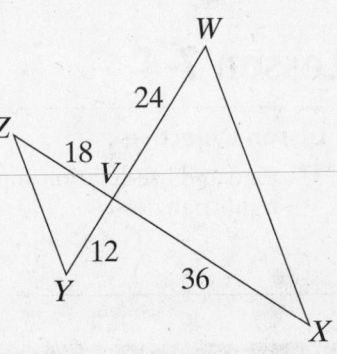

$\angle YVZ \cong \angle WVX$ because _____

$\dfrac{VY}{VW} = \dfrac{12}{24} = \dfrac{\boxed{}}{\boxed{}}$ and $\dfrac{VZ}{VX} = \dfrac{\boxed{}}{\boxed{}} = \dfrac{\boxed{}}{\boxed{}}$,

so corresponding sides are proportional.

Therefore, $\triangle YVZ \sim \triangle WVX$
by the $\boxed{}$ Theorem.

Quick Check

1. In Example 1, you have enough information to write a similarity statement. Do you have enough information to find the similarity ratio? Explain.

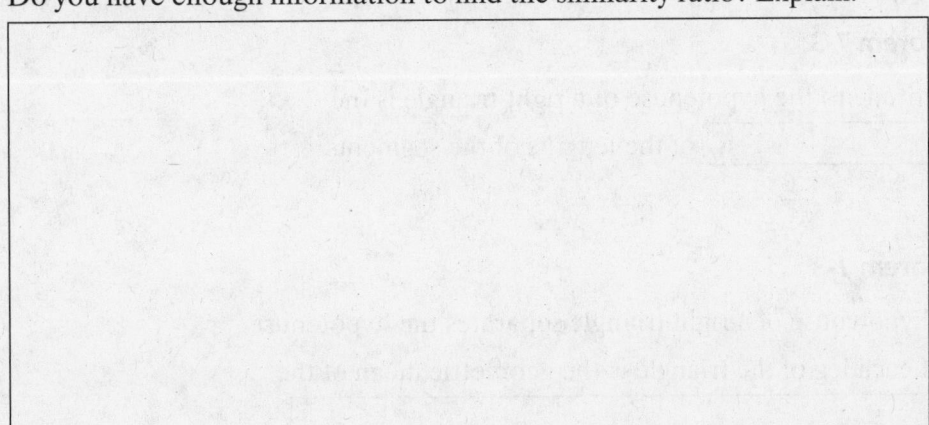

2. Explain why the triangles at the right must be similar. Write a similarity statement.

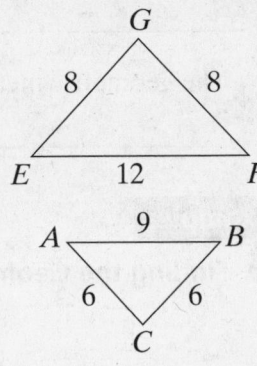

Lesson 7-4

Similarity in Right Triangles

Lesson Objective

▼ Find and use relationships in similar right triangles

NAEP 2005 Strand: Geometry

Topic: Transformation of Shapes and Preservation of Properties

Local Standards: _____

Vocabulary and Key Concepts

Theorem 7-3

The altitude to the hypotenuse of a right triangle divides the triangle into

two triangles that are [   ] to the original triangle and

[   ] to each other.

Corollary 1 to Theorem 7-3

The length of the altitude to the hypotenuse of a right triangle is the

[   ] of the lengths of the segments

of the hypotenuse.

Corollary 2 to Theorem 7-3

The altitude to the hypotenuse of a right triangle separates the hypotenuse

so that the length of each leg of the triangle is the geometric mean of the

length of the [   ]

and the length of the [   ].

The geometric mean of two positive numbers a and b _____

_____

Examples

❶ **Finding the Geometric Mean** Find the geometric mean of 3 and 12.

$\dfrac{3}{x} = \dfrac{\boxed{}}{\boxed{}}$ **Write a proportion.**

$x^2 = \boxed{}$ **Cross-Product Property.**

$x = \boxed{}$ **Find the positive square root.**

$x = \boxed{}$

The geometric mean of 3 and 12 is $\boxed{}$.

❷ **Finding Distance** At a golf course, Maria drove her ball 192 yd straight toward the cup. Her brother Gabriel drove his ball straight 240 yd, but not toward the cup. The diagram shows the results. Find x and y, their remaining distances from the cup.

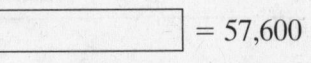

Use Corollary 2 of Theorem 7-3 to solve for x.

$$\frac{x + 192}{240} = \frac{240}{\boxed{}}$$ Write a proportion.

$$\boxed{}(x + 192) = 240^2$$ Cross-Product Property

$$\boxed{} + \boxed{} = 57{,}600$$ Distributive Property

$$\boxed{}x = \boxed{}$$ Solve for x.

$$x = \boxed{}$$

Use Corollary 2 of Theorem 7-3 to solve for y.

$$\frac{\boxed{} + \boxed{}}{y} = \frac{y}{x}$$ Write a proportion.

$$\frac{\boxed{} + 192}{y} = \frac{y}{\boxed{}}$$ Substitute $\boxed{}$ for x.

$$\frac{\boxed{}}{y} = \frac{y}{\boxed{}}$$ Simplify.

$$y^2 = \boxed{}$$ Cross-Product Property

$$y = \boxed{}$$ Find the positive square root.

$$y = \boxed{}$$

Maria's ball is $\boxed{}$ yd from the cup, and Gabriel's ball is $\boxed{}$ yd from the cup.

Quick Check

1. Find the geometric mean of 5 and 20.

2. Recall Example 2. Find the distance between Maria's ball and Gabriel's ball.

Lesson 7-5

Proportions in Triangles

Lesson Objectives	NAEP 2005 Strand: Geometry
▼ 1 Use the Side-Splitter Theorem ▼ 2 Use the Triangle-Angle-Bisector Theorem	Topic: Transformation of Shapes and Preservation of Properties
	Local Standards: _____

Key Concepts

Theorem 7-4: Side-Splitter Theorem

If a line is parallel to one side of a triangle and intersects the other two sides,

then _____

_____

Theorem 7-5: Triangle-Angle-Bisector Theorem

If a ray bisects an angle of a triangle, then _____

_____

Corollary to Theorem 7-4

If three parallel lines intersect two transversals, then _____

_____

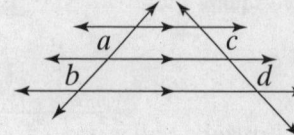

$$\frac{a}{b} = \boxed{}$$

Examples

1 Using the Side-Splitter Theorem Find y.

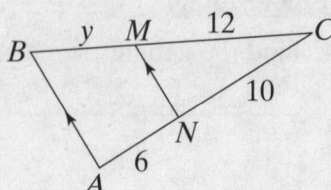

$$\frac{CM}{MB} = \frac{\boxed{}}{\boxed{}}$$ Side-Spitter Theorem

$$\frac{12}{y} = \frac{\boxed{}}{\boxed{}}$$ Substitute.

$$\boxed{} y = \boxed{}$$ Cross-Product Property

$$y = \boxed{}$$ Solve for y.

❷ Using the Triangle-Angle-Bisector Theorem Find the value of *x*.

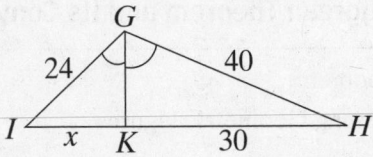

$$\frac{IG}{GH} = \frac{\boxed{}}{\boxed{}}$$ **Triangle-Angle-Bisector Theorem.**

$$\frac{\boxed{}}{\boxed{}} = \frac{x}{\boxed{}}$$ **Substitute.**

$$\frac{\boxed{}}{\boxed{}}\left(\boxed{}\right) = x$$ **Solve for *x*.**

$$x = \boxed{}$$

Quick Check

1. Use the Side-Splitter Theorem to find the value of *x*.

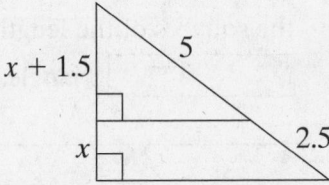

2. Find the value of *y*.

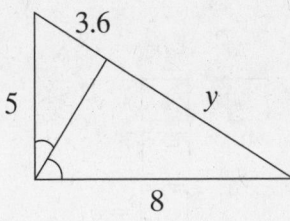

Lesson 8-1

The Pythagorean Theorem and Its Converse

Lesson Objectives	NAEP 2005 Strand: Geometry
▼ 1 Use the Pythagorean Theorem	Topic: Relationships Among Geometric Figures
▼ 2 Use the Converse of the Pythagorean Theorem	Local Standards: _____

Vocabulary and Key Concepts

Theorem 8-5: Pythagorean Theorem

In a right triangle, the sum of the squares of the lengths of the [   ]

is equal to the square of the length of the [   ].

$a^2 + b^2 = \boxed{}^2$

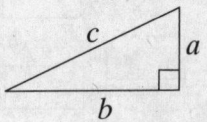

Theorem 8-6: Converse of the Pythagorean Theorem

If the square of the length of one side of a triangle is equal to the sum of

the squares of the lengths of the other two sides, then the triangle is a

[   ] triangle.

A Pythagorean triple is _____

_____

Examples

❶ Pythagorean Triples Find the length of the hypotenuse of $\triangle ABC$.
Do the lengths of the sides of $\triangle ABC$ form a Pythagorean triple?

$a^2 + b^2 = c^2$ Use the [   ] Theorem.

$\boxed{} + \boxed{} = c^2$ Substitute $\boxed{}$ for *a*, and $\boxed{}$ for *b*.

$\boxed{} = c^2$ Simplify.

$\sqrt{\boxed{}} = c$ Take the square root.

$\boxed{} = c$ Simplify.

The length of the hypotenuse is $\boxed{}$. The lengths of the sides, 5, 12, and $\boxed{}$

form a [   ] because they are [   ] numbers that

satisfy $a^2 + b^2 = c^2$.

Name_____ Class_____ Date _____

❷ Is It a Right Triangle? Is this triangle a right triangle?

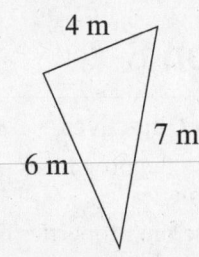

4 m

7 m

6 m

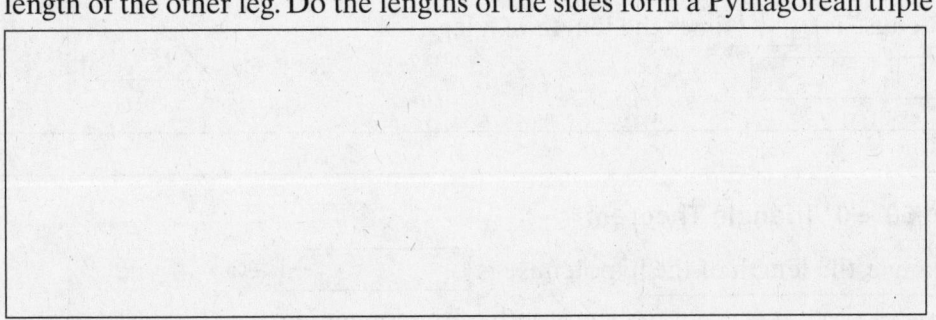

$a^2 + b^2 \stackrel{?}{=} c^2$

[ ] + [ ] $\stackrel{?}{=}$ [ ]   **Substitute** [ ] **for a,** [ ] **for b, and** [ ] **for c.**

[ ] + [ ] $\stackrel{?}{=}$ [ ]   **Simplify.**

[ ] $\neq$ [ ]

Because $a^2 + b^2$ [ ] c^2, the triangle [   ] a right triangle.

Quick Check

1. A right triangle has a hypotenuse of length 25 and a leg of length 10. Find the length of the other leg. Do the lengths of the sides form a Pythagorean triple?

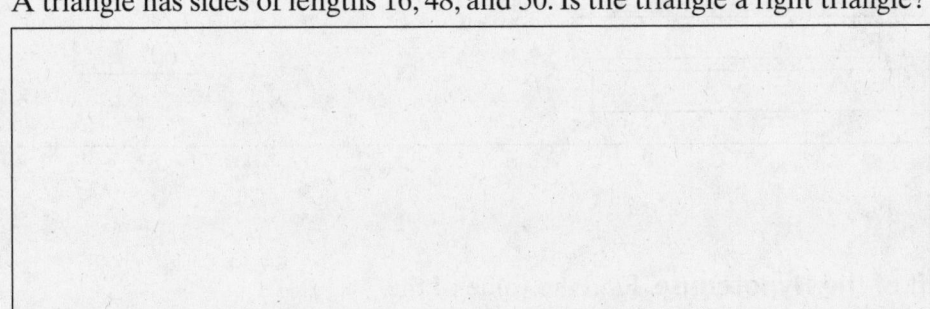

2. A triangle has sides of lengths 16, 48, and 50. Is the triangle a right triangle?

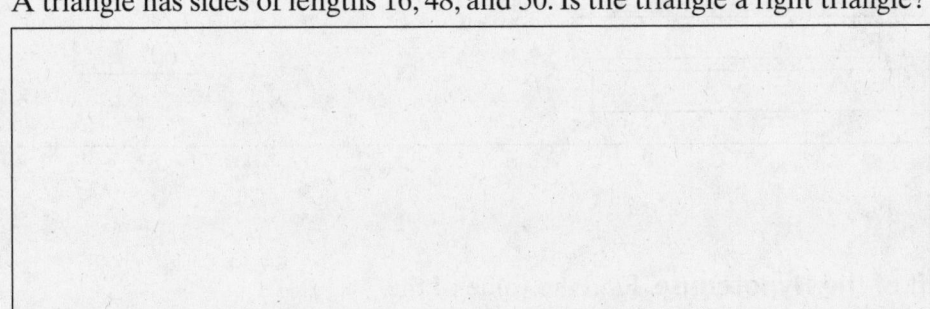

Lesson 8-2

Special Right Triangles

Lesson Objectives	NAEP 2005 Strand: Geometry
▼ Use the properties of 45°-45°-90° triangles	**Topic:** Relationships Among Geometric Figures
❷ Use the properties of 30°-60°-90° triangles	**Local Standards:** _____

Key Concepts

Theorem 8-5: 45°-45°-90° Triangle Theorem

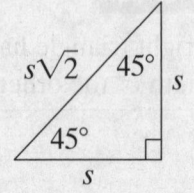

In a 45°-45°-90° triangle, both legs are [   ] and the length of the hypotenuse is [   ] times the length of a leg.

hypotenuse = [   ] · [   ]

Theorem 8-6: 30°-60°-90° Triangle Theorem

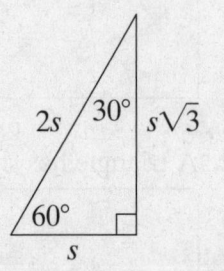

In a 30°-60°-90° triangle, the length of the hypotenuse is [   ] the length of the [   ]. The length of the longer leg is [   ] times the length of the [   ].

hypotenuse = [   ] · [   ]

longer leg = [   ] · [   ]

Examples

❶ **Finding the Length of the Hypotenuse** Find the value of the variable. Use the 45°-45°-90° Triangle Theorem to find the hypotenuse.

$h = $ [   ] $\cdot 5\sqrt{6}$ hypotenuse = [   ] · leg

$h = $ [   ][   ]   **Simplify.**

$h = 5\sqrt{[\ ]([\ ])}$

$h = 5([\ ])\sqrt{[\ ]}$

$h = $ [   ][   ]

The length of the hypotenuse is [   ].

❷ Using the Length of One Side Find the value of each variable.

Use the 30°-60°-90° Triangle Theorem to find the lengths of the legs.

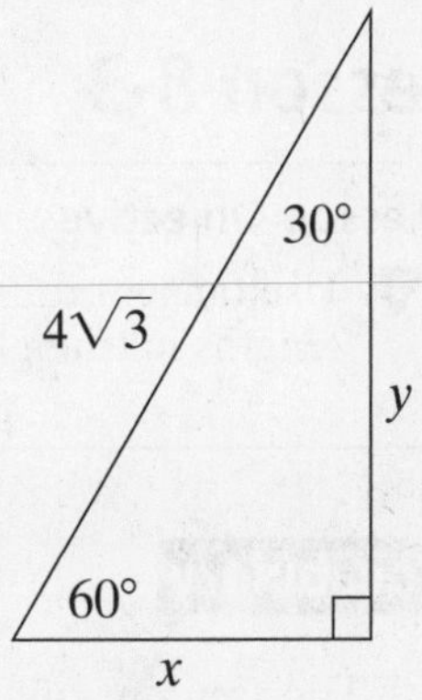

$4\sqrt{3} = \boxed{} \cdot x$ **hypotenuse** = $\boxed{}$ **· shorter leg**

$x = \dfrac{\boxed{}}{\boxed{}}$ **Divide each side by** $\boxed{}$.

$x = \boxed{}\ \boxed{}$ **Simplify.**

$y = \boxed{} \cdot$ shorter leg $\boxed{}$ **Triangle Theorem**

$y = \boxed{} \cdot 2\sqrt{3}$ **Substitute** $\boxed{}$ **for shorter leg.**

$y = 2 \cdot \boxed{} \cdot \boxed{}$ **Simplify.**

$y = \boxed{}$

The length of the shorter leg is $\boxed{}$, and the length of the longer leg is $\boxed{}$.

The triangle figure: 30° at top, 4√3 along the upper hypotenuse side, y on the right vertical side, 60° at bottom left, x along the bottom, right angle at bottom right.

Quick Check

1. Find the length of the hypotenuse of a 45°-45°-90° triangle with legs of length $5\sqrt{3}$.

2. Find the lengths of the legs of a 30°-60°-90° triangle with hypotenuse of length 12.

Lesson 8-3

The Tangent Ratio

Lesson Objective	NAEP 2005 Strand: Measurement
▼ Use tangent ratios to determine side lengths in triangles	**Topic:** Measuring Physical Attributes
	Local Standards: _____

Vocabulary

The tangent of acute $\angle A$ in a right triangle is _____

_____

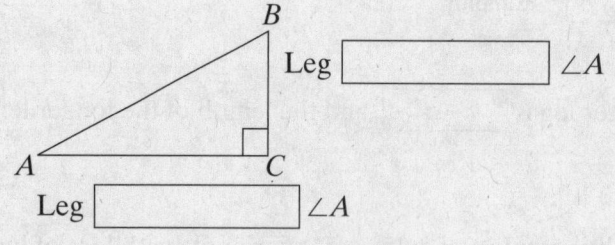

Leg [＿＿＿＿＿] $\angle A$

Leg [＿＿＿＿＿] $\angle A$

tangent of $\angle A$ = [＿＿＿＿＿＿＿＿＿]

You can abbreviate the equation as tan A = [＿＿＿＿＿＿＿] .

Examples

❶ **Writing Tangent Ratios** Write the tangent ratios for $\angle A$ and $\angle B$.

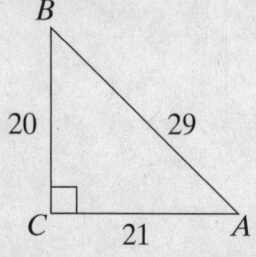

$$\tan A = \frac{\boxed{}}{\boxed{}} = \frac{\boxed{}}{\boxed{}} = \frac{\boxed{}}{\boxed{}}$$

$$\tan B = \frac{\boxed{}}{\boxed{}} = \frac{\boxed{}}{\boxed{}} = \frac{\boxed{}}{\boxed{}}$$

Name_____ Class_____ Date_____

❷ Using a Tangent Ratio To measure the height of a tree, Alma walked 125 ft from the tree and measured a 32° angle from the ground to the top of the tree. Estimate the height of the tree.

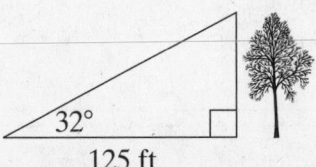

The tree forms a [   ] angle with the ground, so you can use the tangent ratio to estimate the height of the tree.

$$\tan 32° = \frac{\boxed{}}{\boxed{}}$$ **Use the tangent ratio.**

$\text{height} = \boxed{}\left(\boxed{}\right)$ **Solve for height.**

125 **TAN** 32 **ENTER** *78.108669*   **Use a calculator.**

The tree is about [   ] feet tall.

Quick Check

1. Write the tangent ratios for ∠K and ∠J.

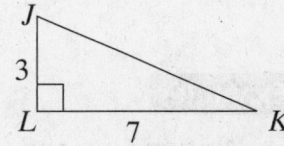

2. Find the value of *w* to the nearest tenth.

a.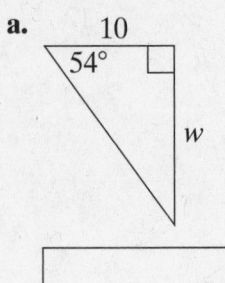

b.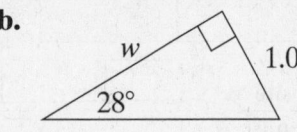

Lesson 8-4

Sine and Cosine Ratios

Lesson Objective	NAEP 2005 Strand: Measurement
▼ Use sine and cosine to determine side lengths in triangles	Topic: Measuring Physical Attributes
	Local Standards: _____

Vocabulary

The sine of ∠A is _____

_____

The _____ of ∠A is the ratio of the length of the leg adjacent to ∠A to the

hypotenuse.

sine of ∠A = [   ]

This can be abbreviated sin A = [   ].

_____ = leg adjacent to ∠A / hypotenuse

This can be abbreviated _____ = adjacent / hypotenuse.

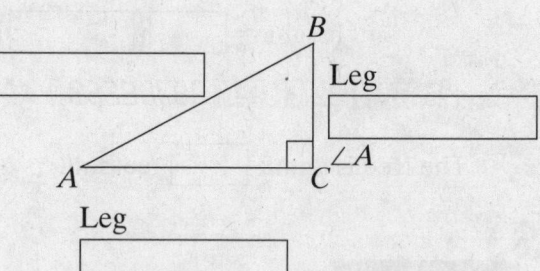

Leg
∠A

Leg
∠A

Examples

1 **Writing Sine and Cosine Ratios** Use the triangle to find sin *T*, cos *T*, sin *G*, and cos *G*. Write your answers in simplest terms.

sin *T* = [   ] / [   ] = [   ] / [   ] = [   ] / [   ]

cos *T* = [   ] / [   ] = [   ] / [   ] = [   ] / [   ]

[   ] *G* = opposite / hypotenuse = [   ] / [   ] = [   ] / [   ]

[   ] *G* = adjacent / hypotenuse = [   ] / [   ] = [   ] / [   ]

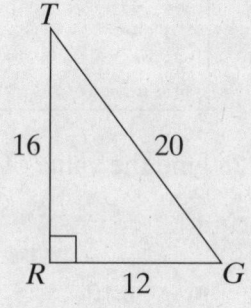

❷ Using the Cosine Ratio A 20-ft wire supporting a flagpole forms a 35° angle with the flagpole. To the nearest foot, how high is the flagpole?

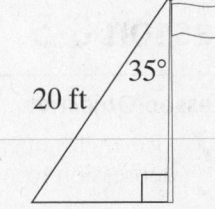

The flagpole, wire, and ground form a [＿＿＿＿＿＿] with the

wire as the [＿＿＿＿＿＿]. Because you know an angle and the

measure of its hypotenuse, you can use the [＿＿＿＿＿] ratio

to find the height of the flagpole.

$$\cos 35° = \frac{\boxed{}}{\boxed{}}$$ **Use the cosine ratio.**

height = $\boxed{}$ · $\boxed{}$ **Solve for height.**

20 **COS** 35 **ENTER** *16.383041*   **Use a calculator.**

The flagpole is about $\boxed{}$ feet tall.

Quick Check

1. Write the sine and cosine ratios for ∠X and ∠Y.

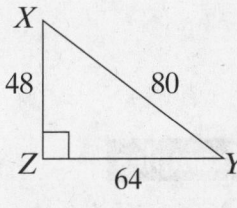

2. In Example 2, suppose that the angle the wire makes with the ground is 50°. What is the height of the flagpole to the nearest foot?

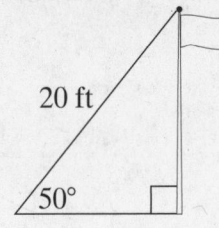

Lesson 8-5

Lesson Objective	NAEP 2005 Strand: Measurement
▼ Use angles of elevation and depression to solve problems	**Topic:** Measuring Physical Attributes **Local Standards:** _____

`Vocabulary

An angle of elevation _____

_____

An _____ is the angle formed by a horizontal line and the line of

sight to an object below the horizontal line.

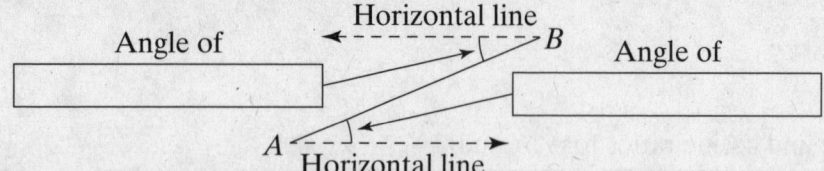

Examples

❶ Identifying Angles of Elevation and Depression Describe ∠1 and ∠2
as they relate to the situation shown.

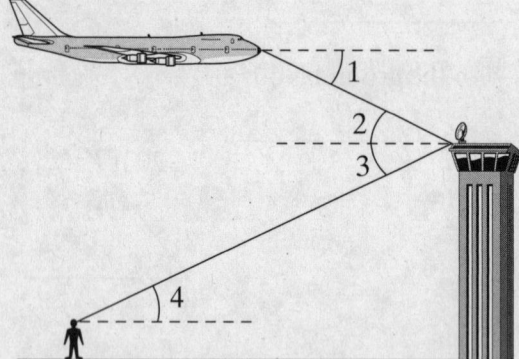

One side of the angle of depression is a horizontal line. ∠1 is the angle of

[   ] from the [   ] to the [   ].

One side of the angle of elevation is a horizontal line. ∠2 is the angle of

[   ] from the [   ] to the [   ].

❷ Aviation An airplane flying 3500 ft above the ground begins a 2° descent to land at the airport. How many miles from the airport is the airplane when it starts its descent? (Note: The angle is not drawn to scale.)

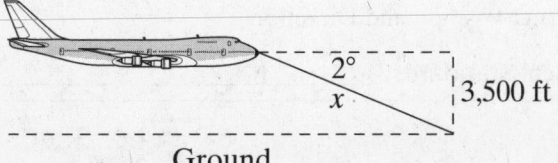

Ground

$$\boxed{} = \frac{3,500}{x}$$ Use the $\boxed{}$ ratio.

$$x = \frac{\boxed{}}{\boxed{}}$$ Solve for *x*.

   Use a calculator.

   Divide by $\boxed{}$ to convert feet to miles.

The airplane is about $\boxed{}$ miles from the airport when it starts its descent.

Quick Check

1. Describe each angle as it relates to the situation in Example 1.

   a. ∠3

   b. ∠4

2. An airplane pilot sees a life raft at a 26° angle of depression. The airplane's altitude is 3 km. What is the airplane's surface distance *d* from the raft?

Lesson 8-6

Vectors

Lesson Objectives	NAEP 2005 Strand: Geometry
▼ Describe vectors	**Topic:** Position and Direction
▼ Solve problems that involve vector addition	**Local Standards:** _____

Vocabulary and Key Concepts

Adding Vectors

For $\vec{a} = \langle x_1, y_1 \rangle$ and $\vec{c} = \langle x_2, y_2 \rangle, \vec{a} + \vec{c} = $ [   ].

A vector is _____

_____

A _____ can be represented with an arrow.

The magnitude of a vector is _____

_____

The _____ of a vector is the point at which it starts.

The terminal point of a vector is _____

_____

A _____ is the sum of other vectors.

Examples

❶ **Describing a Vector** Describe $\overrightarrow{OM}$ as an ordered pair.

Give coordinates to the nearest tenth.
Use the sine and cosine ratios to find the values of x and y.

$\cos 40° = \dfrac{\boxed{}}{\boxed{}}$ **Use sine and cosine.** $\sin 40° = \dfrac{\boxed{}}{\boxed{}}$

$x = 80 \left(\boxed{}\right)$ **Solve for the variable.** $y = 80\left(\boxed{}\right)$

$x \approx \boxed{}$ **Use a calculator.** $y \approx \boxed{}$

Because point M is in the $\boxed{}$ quadrant, both coordinates are

$\boxed{}$. To the nearest tenth, $\overrightarrow{OM} \approx \boxed{}$.

Name_____ Class_____ Date _____

❷ Adding Vectors Vectors $\vec{v}\,\langle 4,3\rangle$ and $\vec{w}\,\langle 4,-3\rangle$ are shown at the right. Write the sum of the two vectors as an ordered pair. Then draw $\vec{s}$, the sum of $\vec{v}$ and $\vec{w}$.

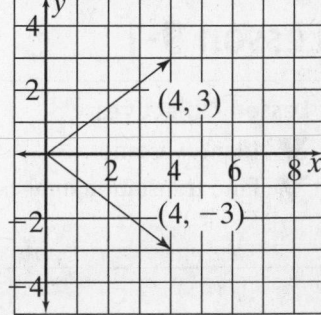

To find the first coordinate of $\vec{s}$, add the [   ] coordinates of $\vec{v}$ and $\vec{w}$.

To find the second coordinate of $\vec{s}$, add the [   ] coordinates of $\vec{v}$ and $\vec{w}$.

$\vec{s} = \langle 4,3\rangle + \langle 4,-3\rangle$

$= \langle\ \boxed{\quad}\ ,\ \boxed{\quad}\ \rangle$ **Add the coordinates.**

$= \langle\ \boxed{\ }\ ,\ \boxed{\ }\ \rangle$ **Simplify.**

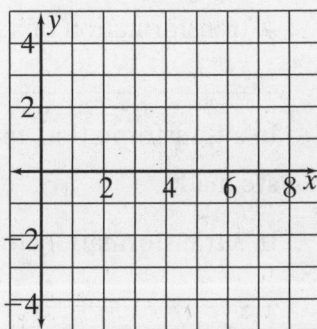

Draw vector $\vec{v}$ using the origin as the initial point. Draw vector $\vec{w}$ using the terminal point of $\vec{v}$, $(4,3)$, as the initial point. Draw the resultant vector $\vec{s}$ from the [   ] of $\vec{v}$ to the [   ] of $\vec{w}$.

Quick Check

1. Describe the vector at the right as an ordered pair. Give the coordinates to the nearest tenth.

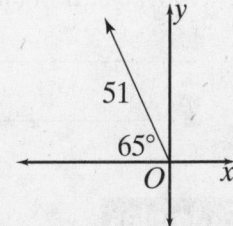

[   ]

2. Write the sum of the two vectors $\langle 2,3\rangle$ and $\langle -4,-2\rangle$ as an ordered pair.

[   ]

All rights reserved.

© Pearson Education, Inc., publishing as Pearson Prentice Hall.

L1 Daily Notetaking Guide   *Geometry* Lesson 8-6 **105**

Name_____ Class_____ Date_____

Lesson 9-1   **Translations**

Lesson Objectives Identify isometries Find translation images of figures	**NAEP 2005 Strand:** Geometry **Topic:** Transformation of Shapes and Preservation of Properties; Position and Direction **Local Standards:** _____

Vocabulary

A transformation of a geometric figure is _____

_____

In a transformation, the _____ is the original image before changes
are made.

In a transformation, the image is _____

_____

An _____ is a transformation in which the preimage and the image
are congruent.

A translation (slide) is _____

_____

A _____ is a combination of two or more transformations.

Examples

❶ Identifying Isometries Does the transformation appear to be an
isometry?

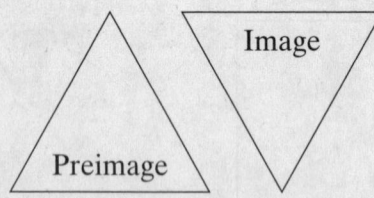

The image appears to be the same as the preimage, but ⬚⬚⬚⬚⬚⬚⬚⬚.
Because the figures appear to be ⬚⬚⬚⬚⬚⬚⬚⬚, the transformation
appears to be an isometry.

Name_____ Class_____ Date _____

❷ Finding a Translation Image Find the image of $\triangle ABC$ under the translation $(x, y) \rightarrow (x + 2, y - 3)$.

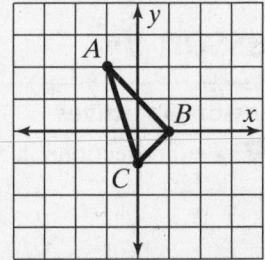

$A(-1, 2) \rightarrow A'(\boxed{}, \boxed{} - 3)$ **Use the rule $(x, y) \rightarrow (x + 2, y - 3)$**

$B(1, 0) \rightarrow B'(\boxed{} + 2, \boxed{})$

$C(0, -1) \rightarrow C'(\boxed{}, \boxed{})$

The image of $\triangle ABC$ is $\triangle A'B'C'$ with $A'(\boxed{}, \boxed{})$, $B'(\boxed{}, \boxed{})$,

and $C'(\boxed{}, \boxed{})$.

Quick Check

1. Does the transformation appear to be an isometry? Explain.

a.

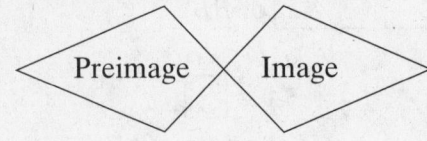

b.

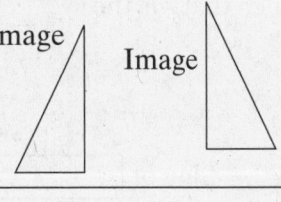

2. Find the image of $\triangle ABC$ for the translation $(x - 2, y + 1)$.

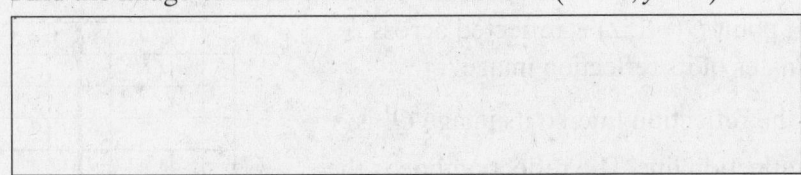

Lesson 9-2

Reflections

Lesson Objectives	NAEP 2005 Strand: Geometry
▼ Find reflection images of figures	**Topics:** Transformation of Shapes and Preservation of Properties
	Local Standards: _____

Vocabulary

A reflection in line r is a transformation such that if a point A is on line r, then the image of A is [   ], and if a point B is not on line r, then its image B' is the point such that r is the [   ] of $\overline{BB'}$.

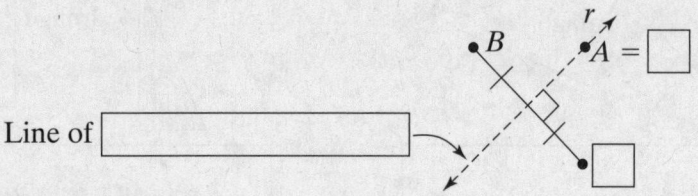

Line of [   ]

Example

① Finding Reflection Images If point $Q(-1, 2)$ is reflected across line $x = 1$, what are the coordinates of its reflection image?

Q is [ ] units to the [   ] of the reflection line, so its image Q' is [ ] units to the [   ] of the reflection line. The reflection line is the perpendicular bisector of $\overline{QQ'}$ if Q' is at [   ].

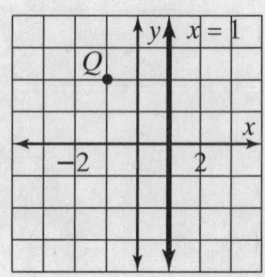

Quick Check

1. What are the coordinates of the image of Q if the reflection line is $y = -1$?

Examples

❷ Drawing Reflection Images △*XYZ* has vertices *X*(0, 3), *Y*(2, 0), and *Z*(4, 2). Draw △*XYZ* and its reflection image in the line *x* = 4.

First locate vertices *X*, *Y*, and *Z* and draw △*XYZ* in a coordinate plane.

Locate points *X′*, *Y′*, and *Z′* such that the line of reflection *x* = 4

is the [ ] of $\overline{XX'}$, $\overline{YY'}$, and $\overline{ZZ'}$.

Draw the reflection image *X′Y′Z′*.

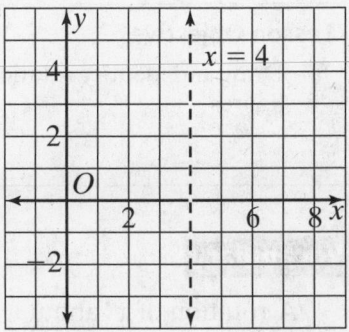

❸ Congruent Angles *D′* is the reflection of *D* across ℓ. Show that $\overline{PD}$ and $\overline{PW}$ form congruent angles with line ℓ.

Because a reflection is an [ ], $\overline{PD}$ and

$\overline{PD'}$ form congruent angles with line ℓ.

$\overline{PD'}$ and $\overline{PW}$ also form congruent angles with line ℓ

because [ ] angles are congruent.

Therefore, $\overline{PD}$ and $\overline{PW}$ form congruent angles with line ℓ

by the [ ] Property.

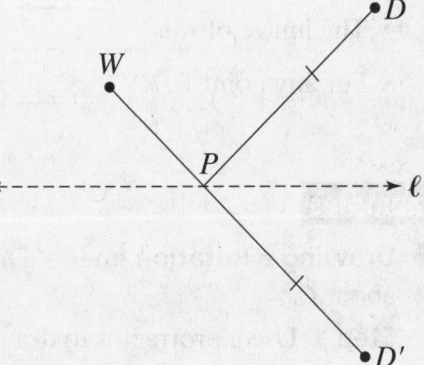

Quick Check

2. △*ABC* has vertices *A*(−3, 4), *B*(0, 1), and *C*(2, 3). Draw △*ABC* and its reflection image in the line *x* = 3.

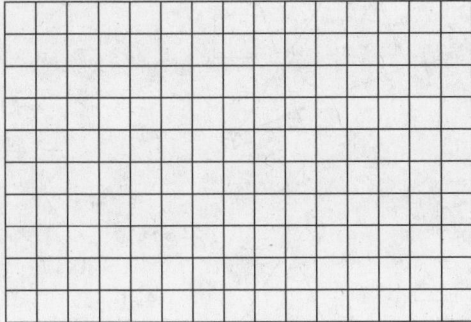

3. In Example 3, what kind of triangle is △*DPD′*? Imagine the image of point *W* reflected across line ℓ. What can you say about △*WPW′* and △*DPD′*?

Lesson 9-3

Rotations

Lesson Objective	NAEP 2005 Strand: Geometry
▼ Draw and identify rotation images of figures	Topic: Transformation of Shapes and Preservation of Properties
	Local Standards: _____

Vocabulary

A rotation of $x°$ about a point R is a transformation for which the following are true:

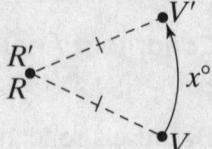

- The image of R is [＿＿＿＿＿＿] (that is, $R' =$ [＿＿]).
- For any point V, $RV' =$ [＿＿] and $m\angle VRV' =$ [＿＿].

Examples

❶ Drawing a Rotation Image Draw the image of $\triangle LOB$ under a 60° rotation about C.

Step 1 Use a protractor to draw a 60° angle at vertex C with one side $\overline{CO}$.

Step 2 Use a compass to construct $\overline{CO'} \cong \overline{CO}$.

Step 3 Locate L' and B' in a similar manner. Then draw $\triangle L'O'B'$.

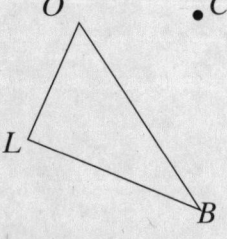
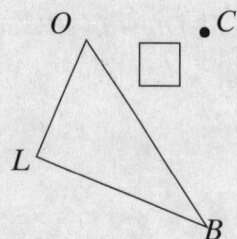
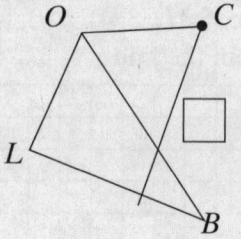

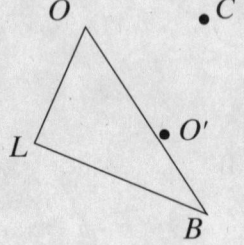
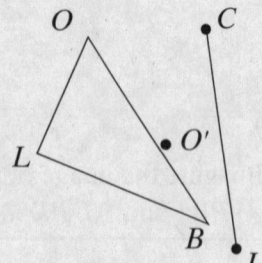
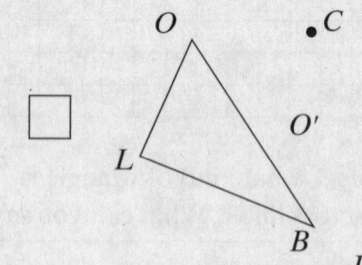

Name_____ Class_____ Date _____

2 Identifying a Rotation Image Regular hexagon *ABCDEF* is divided into six equilateral triangles.

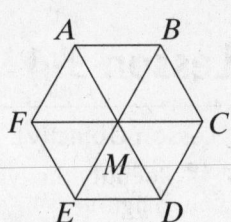

   a. Name the image of *B* for a 240° rotation about *M*.

   Because 360 ÷ 6 = ☐ , each central angle of *ABCDEF* measures ☐ . A 240° counterclockwise rotation about center *M* moves point *B* across ☐ triangles. The image of point *B* is point ☐ .

   b. Name the image of *M* for a 60° rotation about *F*.

   △*AMF* is equilateral, so ∠*AFM* has measure 180 ÷ 3 = ☐ . A 60° rotation of △*AMF* about point *F* would superimpose $\overline{FM}$ on $\overline{FA}$, so the image of *M* under a 60° rotation about point *F* is point ☐ .

Quick Check

   1. Draw the image of *LOB* for a 50° rotation about point *B*. Label the vertices of the image.

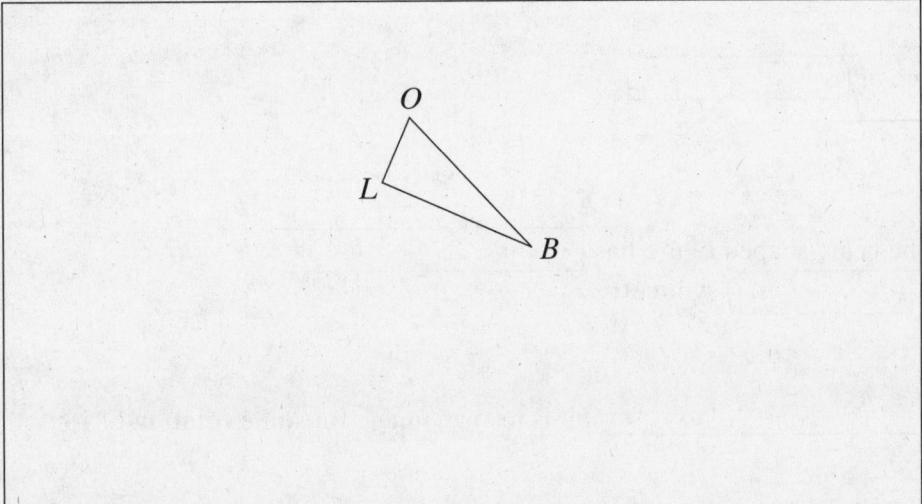

   2. Regular pentagon *PENTA* is divided into 5 congruent triangles. Name the image of *T* for a 144° rotation about point *X*.

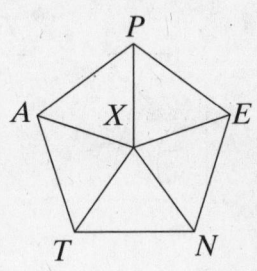

Lesson 9-4

Symmetry

Lesson Objective	NAEP 2005 Strand: Geometry
▼ Identify the type of symmetry in a figure	Topic: Transformation of Shapes and Preservation of Properties
	Local Standards: _____

Vocabulary

A figure has symmetry if _____

_____

A figure has _____ if there is symmetry that maps the figure onto itself.

Line symmetry is the same as _____

_____

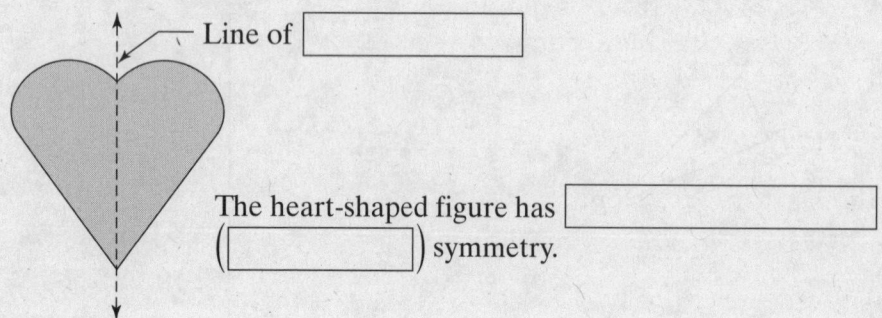

Line of [_____]

The heart-shaped figure has [_____] ([_____]) symmetry.

A figure has _____ if it is its own image for some rotation of 180° or less.

A figure has point symmetry if _____

_____

The figure is its own image after one half-turn, so it has rotational symmetry with a [_____]° angle of rotation.

The figure also has [_____] symmetry.

Name_____ Class_____ Date _____

Examples

❶ **Identifying Lines of Symmetry** Draw all lines of symmetry for the isosceles trapezoid.

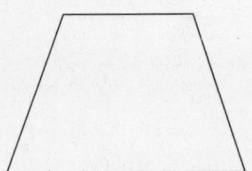

Draw any lines that divide the isosceles trapezoid so that half of the figure is a mirror image of the other half.

There is [   ] line of symmetry.

❷ **Identifying Rotational Symmetry** Judging from appearance, do the letters V and H have rotational symmetry? If so, give an angle of rotation.

The letter V does not have rotational symmetry because it must be rotated

[   ]° before it is its own image.

The letter H is its own image after one half-turn, so it has rotational

symmetry with a [   ]° angle of rotation.

Quick Check

1. Draw a rectangle and all of its lines of symmetry.

2. a. Judging from appearance, tell whether the figure at the right has rotational symmetry. If so, give the angle of rotation.

[   ]

b. Does the figure have point symmetry?

[   ]

Lesson 9-5

Dilations

Lesson Objective	NAEP 2005 Strand: Geometry
▼ Locate dilation images of figures	**Topic:** Geometry
	Local Standards: _____

Vocabulary

A dilation is a transformation with center C and scale factor n for which the following are true:

- The image of C is [_____] (that is, $C' =$ [___]).

- For any point R, R' is on $\overrightarrow{CR}$ and $CR' =$ [___] $\times$ [___].

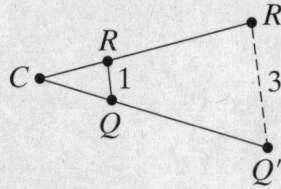 $\overline{R'Q'}$ is the image of $\overline{RQ}$ under a [_____]
with center [___] and scale factor [___].

An enlargement is _____

_____

A _____ is a dilation with a scale factor less than 1.

Examples

❶ Finding a Scale Factor Circle A with 3-cm diameter and center C is a dilation of concentric circle B with 8-cm diameter. Describe the dilation.

The circles are concentric, so the dilation has center [___].

Because the diameter of the dilation image is smaller, the dilation is a

[_____].

Scale factor: $\dfrac{\text{diameter of dilation image}}{\text{diameter of preimage}} =$ [_____]

The dilation is a reduction with center [___] and scale factor [_____].

❷ **Scale Drawings** The scale factor on a museum's floor plan is 1 : 200. The length and width of one wing on the drawing are 8 in. and 6 in. Find the actual dimensions of the wing in feet and inches.

The floor plan is a reduction of the actual dimensions by a scale factor of ⬚.

Multiply each dimension on the drawing by 200 to find the actual dimensions. Then write the dimensions in feet and inches.

8 in. × 200 = ⬚ in. = ⬚ ft, ⬚ in.

6 in. × 200 = ⬚ in. = ⬚ ft

The museum wing measures ⬚ by ⬚.

Quick Check

1. Quadrilateral $J'K'L'M'$ is a dilation image of quadrilateral $JKLM$. Describe the dilation.

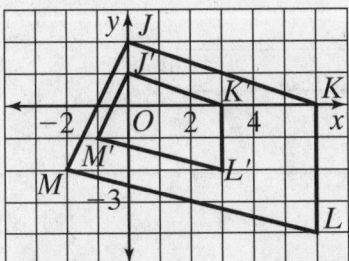

⬚

2. The height of a tractor-trailer truck is 4.2 m. The scale factor for a model truck is $\frac{1}{54}$. Find the height of the model to the nearest centimeter.

Lesson 9-6

Compositions of Reflections

Lesson Objectives	NAEP 2005 Strand: Geometry
1 Use a composition of reflections	**Topic:** Transformation of Shapes and Preservation of Properties
2 Identify glide reflections	**Local Standards:** _____

Vocabulary and Key Concepts

Theorem 9-1

A translation or rotation is a composition of two [   ] .

Theorem 9-2

A composition of reflections across two parallel lines is a [   ] .

Theorem 9-3

A composition of reflections across two intersecting lines is a [   ] .

Theorem 9-4: Fundamental Theorem of Isometries

In a plane, one of two congruent figures can be mapped onto the other by a composition of at most three [   ] .

Theorem 9-5: Isometry Classification Theorem

There are only four isometries. They are the following:

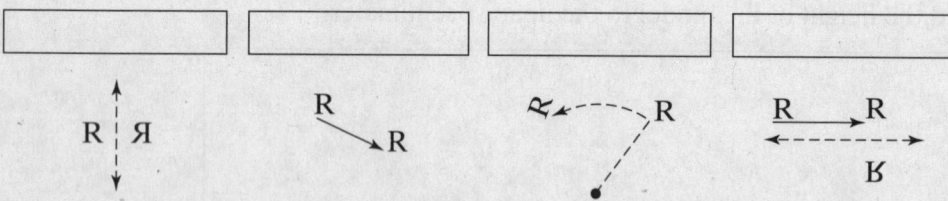

A glide reflection _____
_____

Example

Composition of Reflections in Intersecting Lines The letter D is reflected in line *x* and then in line *y*. Describe the resulting rotation.

Find the image of D through a reflection across line *x*.

Find the image of the reflection through another reflection across line *y*.

The composition of two reflections across intersecting lines is a [_____].

The center of rotation is [_____], and the angle

is [_____]. So, the letter D

is rotated [_____]° clockwise, or [_____]° counterclockwise, with the center of

rotation at point [___].

Quick Check

a. Reflect the letter R across *a* and then *b*. Describe the resulting rotation.

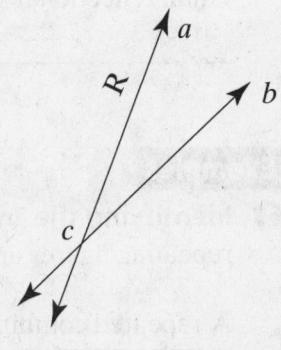

b. Use parallel lines ℓ and *m*. Draw R between ℓ and *m*. Find the image of R for a reflection across line ℓ and then across line *M*. Describe the resulting translation.

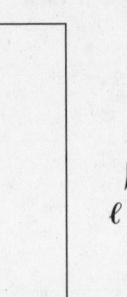

Lesson 9-7

Tessellations

Lesson Objectives	NAEP 2005 Strand: Geometry
✓ Identify transformation in tessellations, and figures that will tessellate	**Topic:** Geometry
✓ Identify symmetries in tessellations	**Local Standards:** _____

Vocabulary and Key Concepts

Theorem 9-6

Every triangle tessellates.

Theorem 9-7

Every quadrilateral tessellates.

A tessellation, or tiling, is _____

_____

_____ is the type of symmetry for which there is a translation that

maps a figure onto itself.

Glide reflectional symmetry is _____

_____

Examples

❶ **Identifying the Transformation in a Tessellation** Identify the repeating figures and a transformation in the tessellation.

A repeated combination of an [   ] and one adjoining

[   ] will completely cover the plane without gaps or

overlaps. Use arrows to show a translation.

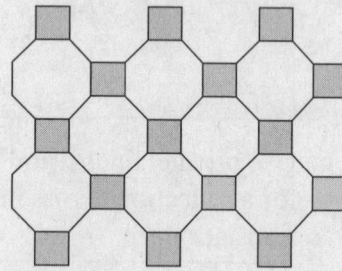

❷ Identifying Symmetries in Tessellations List the
symmetries in the tessellation.

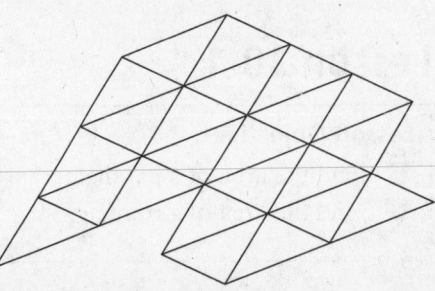

Starting at any vertex, the tessellation can be mapped

onto itself using a [   ] rotation, so the tessellation

has [   ] symmetry centered at any vertex.

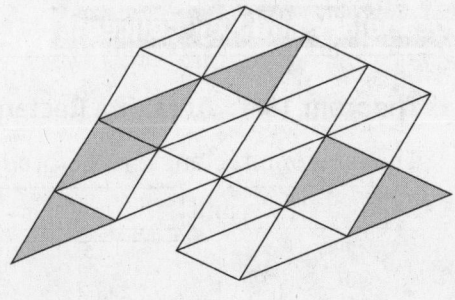

The tessellation also has [   ]

symmetry, as can be seen by sliding any triangle

onto a copy of itself along any of the lines.

Quick Check

1. Identify a transformation and outline the smallest repeating figure in the
   tessellation below.

[   ]

2. List the symmetries in the tessellation.

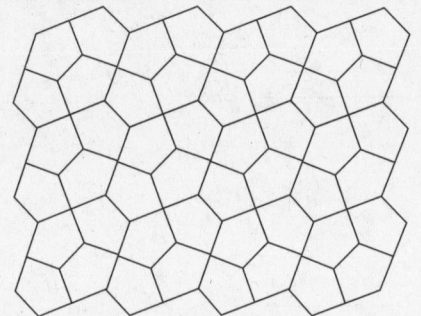

Name_____ Class_____ Date_____

Lesson 10-1

Areas of Parallelograms and Triangles

Lesson Objectives	NAEP 2005 Strand: Measurement
❶ Find the area of a parallelogram ❷ Find the area of a triangle	**Topic:** Measuring Physical Attributes **Local Standards:** _____

Vocabulary and Key Concepts

Theorem 10-1: Area of a Rectangle

The area of a rectangle is the product of

its [_____] and [_____].

$A =$ [_____]

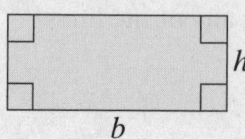

Theorem 10-2: Area of a Parallelogram

The area of a parallelogram is the product of a

[_____] and the corresponding [_____].

$A =$ [_____]

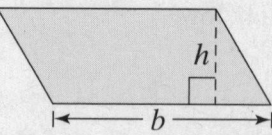

Theorem 10-3: Area of a Triangle

The area of a triangle is [_____] the product of

a [_____] and the corresponding [_____].

$A =$ [_____]

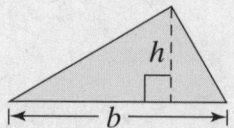

A base of a parallelogram is _____

The _____ of a parallelogram corresponding

to a given base is the segment perpendicular to the line

containing that base drawn from the side opposite the base.

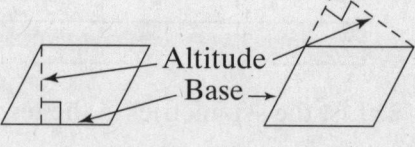

The height of a parallelogram is _____

A _____ of a triangle is any of its sides.

The height of a triangle is _____

_____

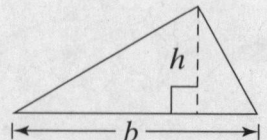

Daily Notetaking Guide   L1

Name_____ Class_____ Date _____

Examples

❶ Finding the Area of a Parallelogram A parallelogram has 9-in. and 18-in. sides. The height corresponding to the 9-in. base is 15 in. Find the area of the parallelogram.

$A = bh$ **Area of a parallelogram**

$A = \boxed{}(\boxed{})$ **Substitute** $\boxed{}$ **for** *b* **and** $\boxed{}$ **for** *h*.

$A = \boxed{}$ **Simplify.**

The area of the parallelogram is $\boxed{}$ in.^{2}

❷ Finding the Area of a Triangle Find the area of $\triangle XYZ$.

$A = \frac{1}{2}bh$ **Area of a** $\boxed{}$

$A = \frac{1}{2}(\boxed{})(\boxed{})$ **Substitute** $\boxed{}$ **for** *b* **and** $\boxed{}$ **for** *h*.

$A = \boxed{}$ **Simplify.**

$\triangle XYZ$ has area $\boxed{}$ cm^2.

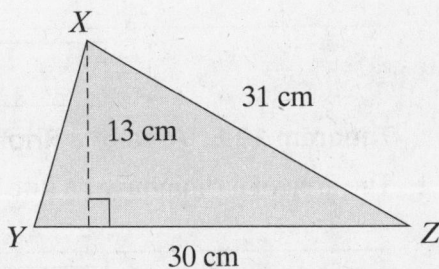

Quick Check

1. A parallelogram has sides 15 cm and 18 cm. The height corresponding to a 15-cm base is 9 cm. Find the area of the parallelogram.

2. Find the area of the triangle.

Lesson 10-2

Areas of Trapezoids, Rhombuses, and Kites

Lesson Objectives	NAEP 2005 Strand: Measurement
❶ Find the area of a trapezoid ❷ Find the area of a rhombus or a kite	Topic: Measuring Physical Attributes Local Standards: _____

Vocabulary and Key Concepts

Theorem 10-4: Area of a Trapezoid

The area of a trapezoid is _____

_____

$A =$ [_____]

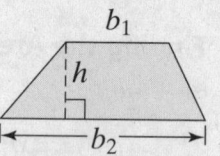

Theorem 10-5: Area of a Rhombus or a Kite

The area of a rhombus or a kite is _____

_____

$A =$ [_____]

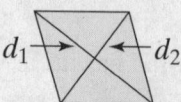

The height of a trapezoid is _____

_____

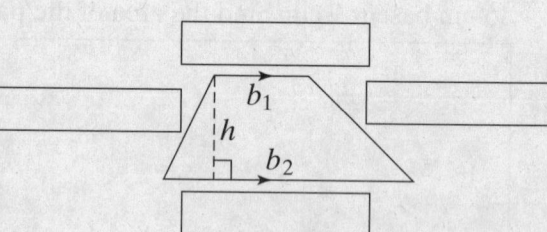

Examples

❶ **Applying the Area of a Trapezoid** A car window is shaped like the trapezoid shown. Find the area of the window.

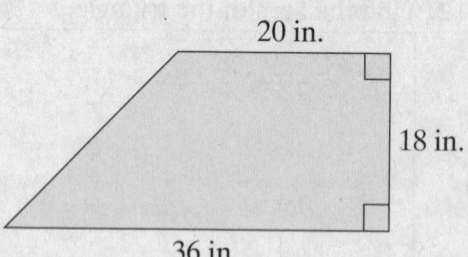

20 in.

18 in.

36 in.

$A = \frac{1}{2}h\left(\boxed{} + \boxed{}\right)$ Area of a trapezoid

$A = \frac{1}{2}\left(\boxed{}\right)\left(\boxed{} + \boxed{}\right)$ Substitute $\boxed{}$ for h, $\boxed{}$ for b_1, and $\boxed{}$ for b_2.

$A = \boxed{}$ Simplify.

The area of the car window is $\boxed{}$ in.^{2}.

❷ Finding the Area of a Rhombus Find the area of rhombus $RSTU$.
To find the area, you need to know the lengths of both diagonals.
Draw diagonal $\overline{SU}$, and label the intersection of the diagonals point X.

$\triangle SXT$ is a [_____] triangle because the diagonals of a rhombus
are perpendicular.

The diagonals of a rhombus bisect each other, so $TX =$ [_____] ft.

You can use the Pythagorean triple 5, 12, 13 or the Pythagorean Theorem
to conclude that $SX =$ [_____] ft.

$SU =$ [_____] ft because the diagonals of a rhombus bisect each other.

$A = \frac{1}{2}$ [_____] [_____]   **Area of a rhombus**

$A = \frac{1}{2}\left(\boxed{}\right)\left(\boxed{}\right)$ **Substitute** [_____] **for** d_1 **and** [_____] **for** d_2.

$A =$ [_____]   **Simplify.**

The area of rhombus $RSTU$ is [_____] ft^2.

R   S

24 ft   13 ft

U   T

Quick Check

1. Find the area of a trapezoid with height 7 cm and bases 12 cm and 15 cm.

2. **Critical Thinking** In Example 2, explain how you can use a Pythagorean
   triple to conclude that $XU = 5$ ft.

Lesson 10-3

Areas of Regular Polygons

Lesson Objective	NAEP 2005 Strand: Measurement
▼ Find the area of a regular polygon	Topic: Measuring Physical Attributes
	Local Standards: _____

Vocabulary and Key Concepts

Theorem 10-6: Area of a Regular Polygon

The area of a regular polygon is _____

_____

$$A = \boxed{}$$

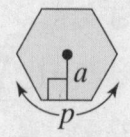

The center of a regular polygon is _____

The _____ of a regular polygon is the distance from the center to a vertex.

The apothem of a regular polygon is _____

_____

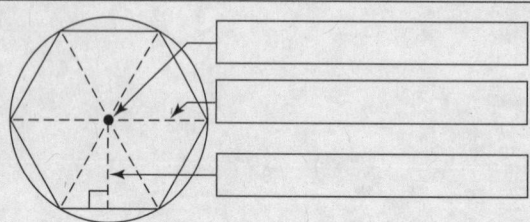

Examples

❶ Finding Angle Measures This regular hexagon has an apothem and radii drawn. Find the measure of each numbered angle.

$m\angle 1 = \dfrac{360}{\boxed{}} = \boxed{}$ Divide 360 by the number of sides.

$m\angle 2 = \dfrac{\boxed{}}{\boxed{}} m\angle 1$ The apothem bisects the vertex angle of

the $\boxed{}$ triangle formed by

the radii.

$m\angle 2 = \dfrac{\boxed{}}{\boxed{}}\left(\boxed{}\right) = \boxed{}$ Substitute $\boxed{}$ for $m\angle 1$.

$m\angle 3 = 180 - \left(\boxed{} + \boxed{}\right) = \boxed{}$ The sum of the measures of the angles of a triangle is 180.

$m\angle 1 = \boxed{}$, $m\angle 2 = \boxed{}$, and $m\angle 3 = \boxed{}$

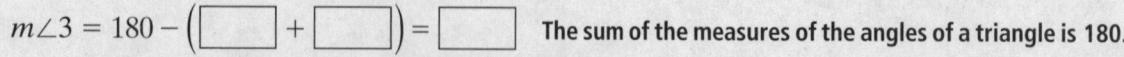

Daily Notetaking Guide   L1

Name_____ Class_____ Date _____

❷ Finding the Area of a Regular Polygon A library is in the shape of a regular octagon. Each side is 18.0 ft. The radius of the octagon is 23.5 ft. Find the area of the library to the nearest 10 ft^2.

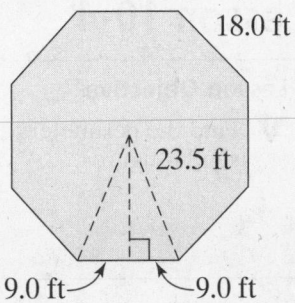

18.0 ft

23.5 ft

9.0 ft— —9.0 ft

Consecutive radii form an isosceles triangle, so an apothem bisects the side of the octagon.

To apply the area formula $A = \frac{1}{2}ap$, you need to find a and p.

Step 1 Find the apothem a.

$a^2 + \left(\boxed{}\right)^2 = \left(\boxed{}\right)^2$ **Pythagorean Theorem**

$a^2 + \boxed{} = \boxed{}$ **Solve for a.**

$a^2 = \boxed{}$

$a \approx \boxed{}$

Step 2 Find the perimeter p.

$p = ns$ **Find the perimeter, where n = the number of sides of a regular polygon.**

$p = (8)\left(\boxed{}\right) = \boxed{}$ **Substitute** $\boxed{}$ **for n and** $\boxed{}$ **for s, and simplify.**

Step 3 Find the area A.

$A = \frac{1}{2}ap$ **Area of a** $\boxed{}$ **polygon**

$A \approx \frac{1}{2}\left(\boxed{}\right)\left(\boxed{}\right)$ **Substitute** $\boxed{}$ **for a and** $\boxed{}$ **for p.**

$A \approx \boxed{}$ **Simplify.**

To the nearest 10 ft^2, the area is $\boxed{}$ ft^2.

Quick Check

1. At the right, a portion of a regular octagon has radii and an apothem drawn. Find the measure of each numbered angle.

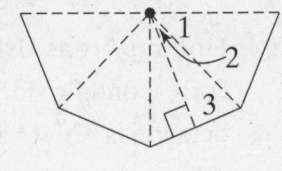

2. Find the area of a regular pentagon with 11.6-cm sides and an 8-cm apothem.

Name_____ Class_____ Date_____

Lesson 10-4

Perimeters and Areas of Similar Figures

Lesson Objective	NAEP 2005 Strand: Measurement and Number Properties and Operations
▼ Find the perimeters and areas of similar figures	Topics: Systems of Measurement; Ratios and Proportional Reasoning
	Local Standards: _____

Key Concepts

Theorem 10-7: Perimeters and Areas of Similar Figures

If the similarity ratio of two similar figures is $\frac{a}{b}$, then

(1) the ratio of their perimeters is ⬜ and

(2) the ratio of their areas is ⬜ .

Examples

❶ Finding Ratios in Similar Figures The triangles at the right are similar. Find the ratio (larger to smaller) of their perimeters and of their areas.

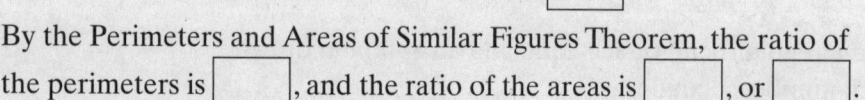

The shortest side of the left-hand triangle has length ⬜ , and

the shortest side of the right-hand triangle has length ⬜ .

From larger to smaller, the similarity ratio is ⬜ .

By the Perimeters and Areas of Similar Figures Theorem, the ratio of

the perimeters is ⬜ , and the ratio of the areas is ⬜ , or ⬜ .

❷ Finding Areas Using Similar Figures The ratio of the length of the corresponding sides of two regular octagons is $\frac{8}{3}$. The area of the larger octagon is 320 ft^2. Find the area of the smaller octagon.

All regular octagons are similar.

Because the ratio of the lengths of the corresponding sides of the regular

octagons is $\frac{8}{3}$, the ratio of their areas is ⬜ , or ⬜ .

$$\frac{\boxed{}}{\boxed{}} = \frac{320}{A}$$ **Write a proportion.**

$A = $ ⬜   **Use the Cross-Product Property.**

$A = $ ⬜   **Divide each side by** ⬜ .

The area of the smaller octagon is ⬜ ft^2.

Daily Notetaking Guide   L1

❸ Using Similarity Ratios Benita plants the same crop in two rectangular fields. Each dimension of the larger field is $3\frac{1}{2}$ times the dimension of the smaller field. Seeding the smaller field costs $8. How much money does seeding the larger field cost?

The similarity ratio of the fields is 3.5 : 1, so the ratio of the areas of the fields is $(3.5)^2 : (1)^2$, or [   ].

Because seeding the smaller field costs $8, seeding 12.25 times as much land costs [   ] × [   ].

Seeding the larger field costs [   ].

Quick Check

1. Two similar polygons have corresponding sides in the ratio 5 : 7.

    a. Find the ratio of their perimeters.   **b.** Find the ratio of their areas.

2. The corresponding sides of two similar parallelograms are in the ratio $\frac{3}{4}$. The area of the smaller parallelogram is 54 in.^{2}. Find the area of the larger parallelogram.

3. The similarity ratio of the dimensions of two similar pieces of window glass is 3 : 5. The smaller piece costs $2.50. What should be the cost of the larger piece?

Lesson 10-5

Trigonometry and Area

Lesson Objectives	NAEP 2005 Strand: Measurement
▼ Find the area of a regular polygon using trigonometry	**Topic:** Measuring Physical Attributes
▼ Find the area of a triangle using trigonometry	**Local Standards:** _____

Key Concepts

Theorem 10-8: Area of a Triangle Given SAS

The area of a triangle is one half the product of

[   ] and

[   ].

Area of $\triangle ABC$ = [   ]

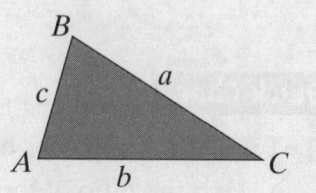

Examples

1 **Finding Area** The radius of a garden in the shape of a regular pentagon is 18 feet. Find the area of the garden.

Find the perimeter p and apothem a, and then find the area using the

formula $A = \frac{1}{2} ap$.

Because a pentagon has five sides, $m\angle ACB = \dfrac{\boxed{}}{5} = \boxed{}$.

$\overline{CA}$ and $\overline{CB}$ are radii, so $CA = \boxed{}$. Therefore, $\triangle ACM \cong \triangle BCM$ by the

HL Theorem, so $m\angle ACM = \frac{1}{2} m\angle ACB = \boxed{}$.

Use the cosine ratio to find a.   Use the sine ratio to find AM.

$\boxed{}\,36° = \dfrac{a}{18}$ **Use the ratio.** $\boxed{}\,36° = \dfrac{AM}{18}$

$a = \boxed{}$ **Solve.** $AM = \boxed{}$

Use AM to find p. Because $\triangle ACM \cong \triangle BCM$, $AB = 2 \cdot \boxed{}$. Because

the pentagon is regular, $p = 5 \cdot \boxed{}$.

So $p = 5(2 \cdot \boxed{}) = \boxed{} \cdot \boxed{} = \boxed{} \cdot \boxed{} = \boxed{}$.

Finally, substitute into the area formula $A = \frac{1}{2} ap$.

$A = \frac{1}{2} \cdot$ [ ] $\cdot$ [ ]   **Substitute for *a* and *p*.**

$A =$ [ ] $(\cos 36°) \cdot (\sin 36°)$ **Simplify.**

$A \approx$ [ ]   **Use a calculator.**

The area is about [ ] ft².

❷ **Surveying** A triangular park has two sides that measure 200 ft and 300 ft and form a 65° angle. Find the area of the park to the nearest hundred square feet.

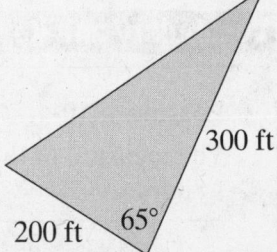

Use Theorem 10-8: The area of a triangle is [ ] the product of the lengths of two sides and the [ ] of the included angle.

Area = $\frac{1}{2} \cdot$ side length $\cdot$ side length $\cdot$ sine of included angle   **Theorem 10-8**

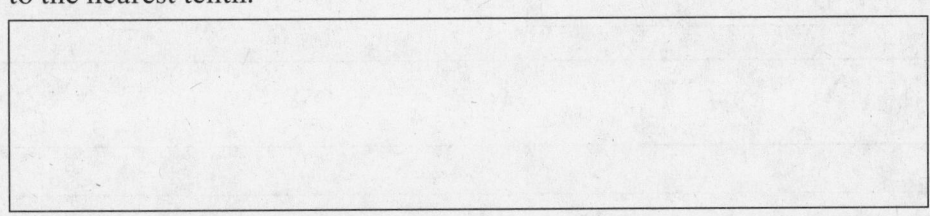

Area = $\frac{1}{2} \cdot$ [ ] $\cdot$ [ ] $\cdot$ [ ]   **Substitute.**

Area = [ ] [ ]   **Substitute.**

$\approx$ [ ]   **Use a calculator.**

The area of the park is approximately [ ] ft².

Quick Check

1. Find the area of a regular octagon with a perimeter of 80 in. Give the area to the nearest tenth.

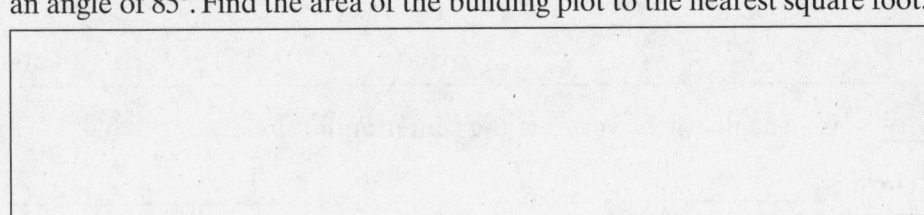

2. Two sides of a triangular building plot are 120 ft and 85 ft long. They include an angle of 85°. Find the area of the building plot to the nearest square foot.

Lesson 10-6

Circles and Arcs

Lesson Objectives	NAEP 2005 Strand: Measurement
1 Find the measures of central angles and arcs	**Topic:** Measuring Physical Attributes
2 Find circumference and arc length	**Local Standards:** _____

Vocabulary and Key Concepts

Postulate 10-1: Arc Addition Postulate

The measure of the arc formed by two adjacent arcs is _____

_____

$m\overarc{ABC} =$ [   ]

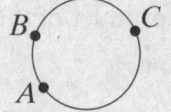

Theorem 10-9: Circumference of a Circle

The circumference of a circle is [   ].

$C =$ [   ] or $C =$ [   ]

Theorem 10-10: Arc Length

The length of an arc of a circle is the product of the ratio

[   ] and the [   ].

[   ]

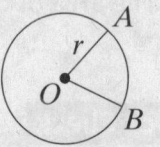

length of $\overarc{AB} =$ [   ]

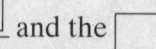

A circle is _____

_____

A _____ of a circle is the point from which all points are equidistant.

A radius is _____

_____

A _____ is an angle whose vertex is the center of the circle.

Circumference of a circle is _____

_____ is the ratio of the circumference of a circle to its diameter.

Examples

❶ Finding the Measures of Arcs Find $m\widehat{XY}$ and $m\widehat{DXM}$ in circle C.

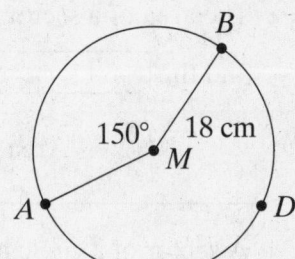

$m\widehat{XY} = \boxed{} + m\widehat{DY}$ **Arc Addition Postulate**

$m\widehat{XY} = m\angle\boxed{} + m\widehat{DY}$ **The measure of a minor arc is the measure of its corresponding central angle.**

$m\widehat{XY} = \boxed{} + \boxed{}$ **Substitute.**

$m\widehat{XY} = \boxed{}$ **Simplify.**

$m\widehat{DXM} = m\widehat{DX} + \boxed{}$ **Arc Addition Postulate**

$m\widehat{DXM} = \boxed{} + 180$ **Substitute.**

$m\widehat{DXM} = \boxed{}$ **Simplify.**

❷ Finding Arc Length Find the length of $\widehat{ADB}$ in circle M in terms of π.

Because $m\widehat{AB} = 150$,

$m\widehat{ADB} = \boxed{} - \boxed{} = \boxed{}$.   **Arc Addition Postulate**

length of $\widehat{ADB} = \dfrac{m\widehat{ADB}}{360} \cdot 2\boxed{}$ **Arc Length Postulate**

$ = \dfrac{\boxed{}}{360} \cdot 2\pi\left(\boxed{}\right)$ **Substitute.**

$ = \boxed{}\pi$

The length of $\widehat{ADB}$ is 21π cm.

Quick Check

1. Use the diagram in Example 1. Find $m\angle YCD$, $m\widehat{YMW}$, $m\widehat{MW}$, and $m\widehat{XMY}$.

2. Find the length of a semicircle with radius 1.3 m in terms of π.

Name_____ Class_____ Date_____

Lesson 10-7

Areas of Circles and Sectors

Lesson Objective	NAEP 2005 Strand: Measurement
▼ Find the areas of circles, sectors, and segments of circles	**Topic:** Measuring Physical Attributes
	Local Standards: _____

Vocabulary and Key Concepts

Theorem 10-11: Area of a Circle

The area of a circle is [_____].

$A = $ [_____]

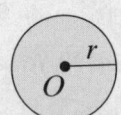

Theorem 10-12: Area of a Sector of a Circle

The area of a sector of a circle is the product of the ratio $\dfrac{\text{measure of the arc}}{[\quad]}$

and the [_____].

Area of sector $AOB = $ [_____]

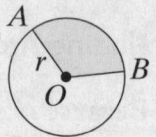

A sector of a circle is _____

_____

A _____ of a circle is the part bounded by an arc and
the segment joining its endpoints.

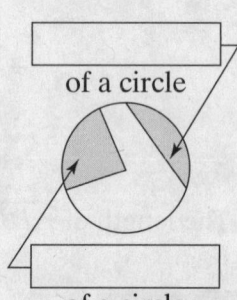

[_____] of a circle

[_____] of a circle

Examples

❶ **Applying the Area of a Circle** A circular archery target has a 2-ft diameter.
It is yellow except for a red bull's-eye at the center with a 6-in. diameter.
Find the area of the yellow region to the nearest whole number.

First find the areas of the archery target and the red bull's-eye.

The radius of the archery target is $\frac{1}{2}\left([\quad] \text{ ft}\right) = [\quad]$ ft = 12 in.

The area of the archery target is $\pi r^2 = \pi\left([\quad]\right)^2 = [\quad\quad]$ in.^{2}

The radius of the red bull's-eye region is $\frac{1}{2}\left([\quad] \text{ in.}\right) = [\quad]$ in.

The area of the red region is $\pi r^2 = \pi\left([\quad]\right)^2 = [\quad]$ in.^{2}

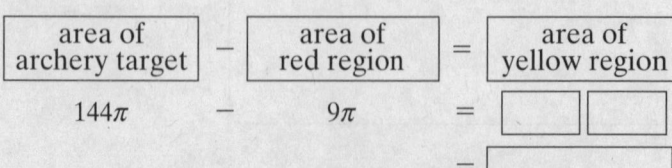

144π − 9π = [____][____]

= [_____] **Simplify.**

The area of the yellow region is about [____] in.^{2}

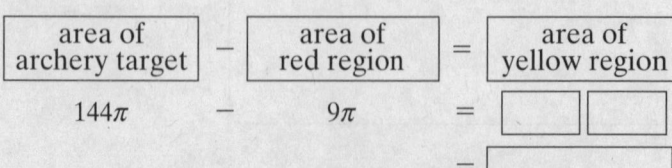 (table: area of archery target − area of red region = area of yellow region)

❷ Finding the Area of a Sector of a Circle Find the area of sector *ACB*.
Leave your answer in terms of π.

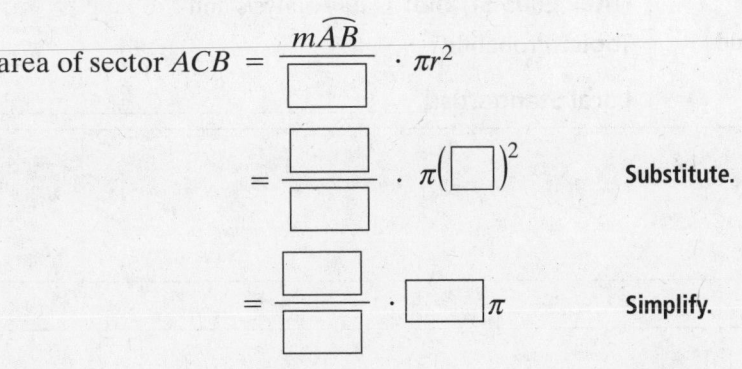

area of sector $ACB = \dfrac{m\widehat{AB}}{\boxed{}} \cdot \pi r^2$

$= \dfrac{\boxed{}}{\boxed{}} \cdot \pi\left(\boxed{}\right)^2$ **Substitute.**

$= \dfrac{\boxed{}}{\boxed{}} \cdot \boxed{}\,\pi$ **Simplify.**

$= \boxed{}\,\pi$ **Simplify.**

The area of sector *ACB* is $\boxed{}$ m^2.

Quick Check

1. How much more pizza is in a 14-in.-diameter pizza than in a 12-in. pizza?

2. **Critical Thinking** A circle has a diameter of 20 cm. What is the area of a sector bounded by a 208° major arc? Round your answer to the nearest tenth.

Lesson 10-8

Geometric Probability

Lesson Objective	NAEP 2005 Strand: Data Analysis and Probability
▼ Use segment and area models to find the probabilities of events	Topic: Probability Local Standards: _____

Vocabulary

Geometric probability is _____

_____

Example

❶ **Finding Probability Using Segments** A gnat lands at random on the edge of the ruler below. Find the probability that the gnat lands on a point between 2 and 10.

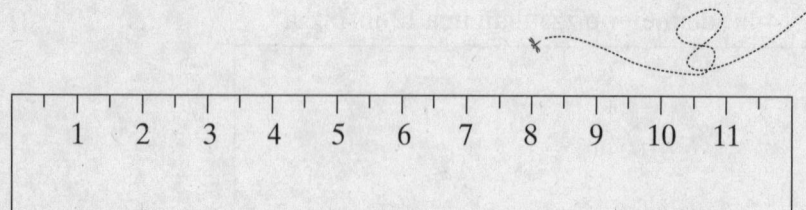

The length of the segment between 2 and 10 is $\boxed{} - \boxed{} = \boxed{}$.

The length of the ruler is $\boxed{}$.

P(landing between 2 and 10)

$$= \frac{\text{length of } \boxed{} \text{ segment}}{\text{length of } \boxed{} \text{ segment}} = \frac{\boxed{}}{\boxed{}} = \frac{2}{3}$$

Quick Check

1. A point on $\overline{AB}$ is selected at random. What is the probability that it is a point on $\overline{CD}$?

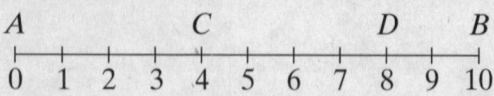

Daily Notetaking Guide   L1

Name_____ Class_____ Date _____

Example

❷ **Finding Probability Using Area** A circle is inscribed in a square target with 20-cm sides. Find the probability that a dart landing randomly within the square does not land within the circle.

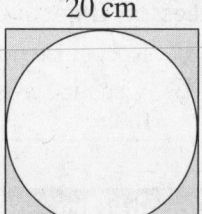

20 cm

Find the area of the square.

$$A = s^2 = \boxed{} = \boxed{} \; cm^2$$

Find the area of the circle. Because the square has sides of length 20 cm, the circle's diameter is $\boxed{}$ cm, so its radius is $\boxed{}$ cm.

$$A = \pi r^2 = \pi \left(\boxed{}\right)^2 = \boxed{} \; cm^2$$

Find the area of the region between the square and the circle.

$$A = \left(400 - \boxed{}\right) cm^2$$

Use areas to calculate the probability that a dart landing randomly in the square does not land within the circle. Use a calculator. Round to the nearest thousandth.

$P(\text{between square and circle}) = \dfrac{\text{area between square and circle}}{\text{area of square}}$

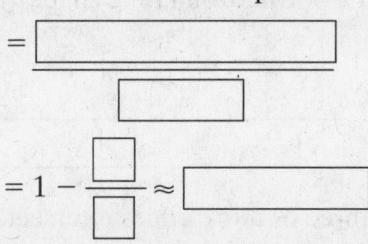

$$= \dfrac{\boxed{}}{\boxed{}}$$

$$= 1 - \dfrac{\boxed{}}{\boxed{}} \approx \boxed{}$$

The probability that a dart landing randomly in the square does not land within the circle is about $\boxed{}$ %.

Quick Check

2. Use the diagram in Example 2. If you change the radius of the circle as indicated, what then is the probability of hitting outside the circle?

   a. Divide the radius by 2.

   b. Divide the radius by 5.

   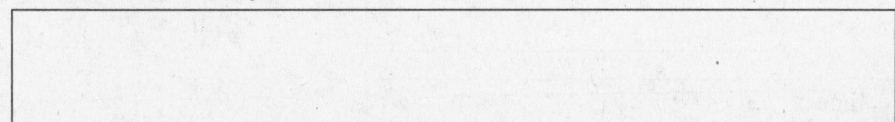

Lesson 11-1

Space Figures and Cross Sections

Lesson Objective	NAEP 2005 Strand: Geometry
❶ Recognize polyhedra and their parts ❷ Visualize cross sections of space figures	Topic: Dimension and Shape Local Standards: _____

Vocabulary and Key Concepts

Euler's Formula

The numbers of faces (F), vertices (V), and edges (E) of a polyhedron are related by the formula [_____].

A polyhedron is _____

_____

A _____ is a flat surface of a polyhedron in the shape of a polygon.

An edge is _____

_____

A _____ is a point where three or more edges intersect.

A cross section is _____

_____

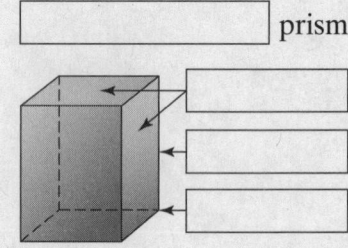

[_____] prism

Examples

❶ **Identifying Vertices, Edges, and Faces** How many vertices, edges, and faces are there in the polyhedron shown? Give a list of each.

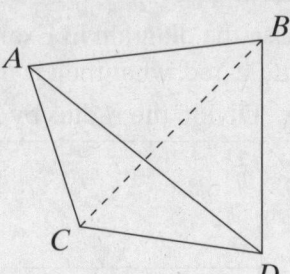

There are [_____] vertices: [_____].

There are [_____] edges: [_____].

There are [_____] faces: [_____].

Name_____ Class_____ Date _____

❷ **Using Euler's Formula** Use Euler's Formula to find the number of edges on a solid with 6 faces and 8 vertices.

$F + V = E + 2$ **Euler's Formula**

   **Substitute the number of faces and vertices.**

☐ = E   **Simplify.**

A solid with 6 faces and 8 vertices has ☐ edges.

Quick Check

1. List the vertices, edges, and faces of the polyhedron.

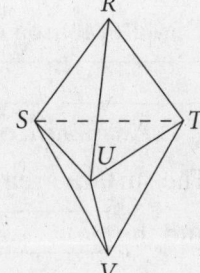

2. Use Euler's Formula to find the number of edges on a polyhedron with eight triangular faces.

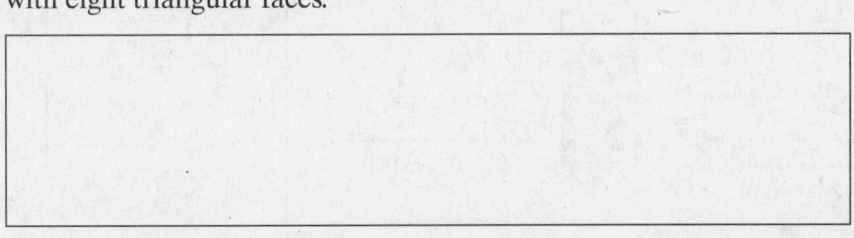

Lesson 11-2   **Surface Areas of Prisms and Cylinders**

Lesson Objectives	**NAEP 2005 Strand:** Measurement
▼ Find the surface area of a prism	**Topic:** Measuring Physical Attributes
▼ Find the surface area of a cylinder	**Local Standards:** _____

Vocabulary and Key Concepts

Theorem 11-1: Lateral and Surface Area of a Cylinder

The lateral area of a right cylinder is the product of the

[_____] and the [_____].

   L.A. = $2\pi rh$, or L.A. = πdh

The surface area of a right cylinder is the sum of the [_____]

and the [_____].

   S.A. = L.A. + 2B, or S.A. = $2\pi rh + 2\pi r^2$

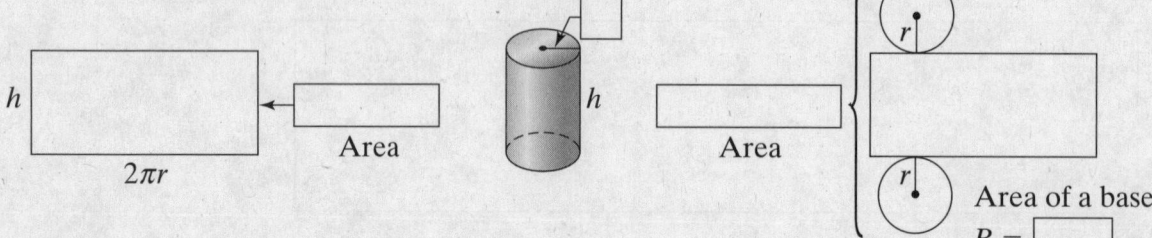

h $2\pi r$ Area h Area r r Area of a base   B = [_____]

A prism is _____

_____

[_____] prism

The _____ of a polyhedron are the parallel

faces.

Lateral faces are _____

The _____ of a prism is the sum of the areas

of the lateral faces.

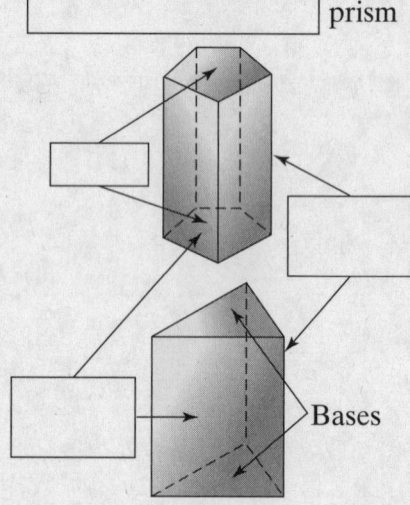

Bases

The surface area of a prism or a cylinder is _____

_____

[_____] prism

Name_____ Class_____ Date_____

A _____ is a three-dimensional figure with two congruent circular bases that lie in parallel planes.

In a cylinder, the bases are _____

_____

The _____ of a cylinder is the area of the curved surface.

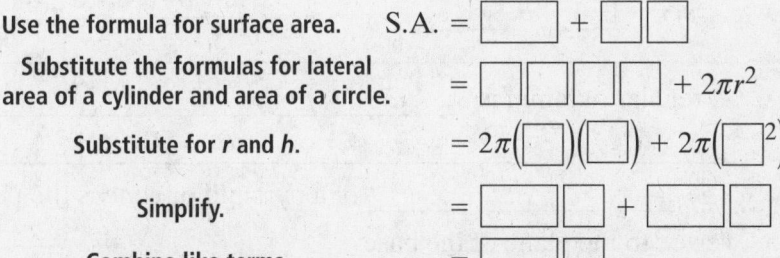

cylinders

Example

Finding Surface Area of Cylinders A company sells cornmeal and barley in cylindrical containers. The diameter of the base of the 6-in.-high cornmeal container is 4 in. The diameter of the base of the 4-in.-high barley container is 6 in. Which container has the greater surface area?

Find the surface area of each container. Remember that $r = \frac{d}{2}$.

Cornmeal Container

S.A. = ▢ + ▢▢

= $2\pi rh$ + ▢▢▢

= $2\pi(▢)(▢) + 2\pi(▢^2)$

= ▢▢ + ▢▢

= ▢▢

Use the formula for surface area.

Substitute the formulas for lateral area of a cylinder and area of a circle.

Substitute for *r* and *h*.

Simplify.

Combine like terms.

Barley Container

S.A. = ▢ + ▢▢

= ▢▢▢▢ + $2\pi r^2$

= $2\pi(▢)(▢) + 2\pi(▢^2)$

= ▢▢ + ▢▢

= ▢▢

Because 42π in.^{2} ▢ 32π in.^{2}, the [_____] container has the greater surface area.

Quick Check

a. Find the surface area of a cylinder with height 10 cm and radius 10 cm in terms of π.

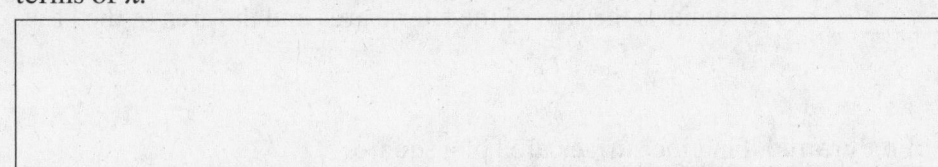

b. The company in the Example wants to make a label to cover the cornmeal container. The label will cover the container all the way around, but will not cover any part of the top or bottom. What is the area of the label to the nearest tenth of a square inch?

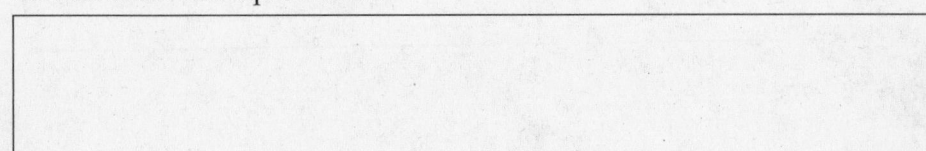

Lesson 11-3

Surface Areas of Pyramids and Cones

Lesson Objectives	**NAEP 2005 Strand:** Measurement
▼ Find the surface area of a pyramid	**Topic:** Measuring Physical Attributes
② Find the surface area of a cone	**Local Standards:** _____

Vocabulary and Key Concepts

Theorem 11-3: Lateral and Surface Area of a Regular Pyramid

The lateral area of a regular pyramid is half the product of the

[   ] and the [   ].

L.A. = [   ]

The surface area of a regular pyramid is the sum of the

[   ] and the [   ].

S.A. = [   ] + [   ]

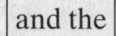

A regular pyramid is _____

_____

The _____ of a pyramid or cone is the perpendicular segment from the

vertex to the plane of the base.

The height of a pyramid or a cone is _____

_____

The _____ of a regular pyramid

is the length of the altitude of a lateral face.

The lateral area of a pyramid is _____

_____

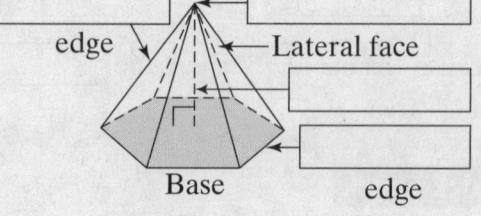
edge — Lateral face
Base   edge
Regular Pyramid

The _____ of a pyramid is the sum of the lateral area and the area of the base.

Example

Finding Surface Area of a Pyramid Find the surface area of a square
pyramid with base edges 7.5 ft and slant height 12 ft.

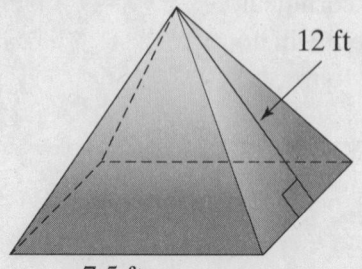
12 ft
7.5 ft

The perimeter p of the square base is $4 \times$ [ ] ft, or [ ] ft.

You are given $\ell =$ [ ] ft and you found that $p =$ [ ] ft, so you can find the lateral area.

L.A. = $\dfrac{\Box}{\Box}$ $\Box$ $\Box$ **Use the formula for lateral area of a pyramid.**

$= \frac{1}{2}\left(\right)\left(\right)$ **Substitute.**

$=$ [ ]   **Simplify.**

Find the area of the square base.

Because the base is a square with side length 7.5 ft,

$B = s^2 =$ [ ]$^2 =$ [ ].

S.A. = [ ] + [ ]   **Use the formula for surface area of a pyramid.**

$=$ [ ] + [ ]   **Substitute.**

$=$ [ ]   **Simplify.**

The surface area of the square pyramid is [ ] ft^2.

Quick Check

Find the surface area of a square pyramid with base edges 5 m and slant height 3 m.

Lesson 11-4

Volumes of Prisms and Cylinders

Lesson Objectives	NAEP 2005 Strand: Measurement
✔ Find the volume of a prism ✔ Find the volume of a cylinder	**Topic:** Measuring Physical Attributes **Local Standards:** _____

Vocabulary and Key Concepts

Theorem 11-5: Cavalieri's Principle

If two space figures have the same height and the same cross sectional area

at every level, then they have the same [_____].

Theorem 11-6: Volume of a Prism

The volume of a prism is the product of the [_____]

and the [_____].

$V = $ [_____]

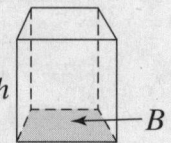

Theorem 11-7: Volume of a Cylinder

The volume of a cylinder is the product of the [_____]

and the [_____].

$V = Bh$, or $V = $ [_____]

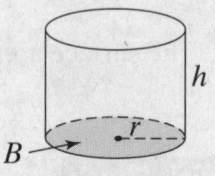

Volume is _____

A _____ space figure is a three-dimensional figure that is the combination

of two or more simpler figures.

Examples

❶ **Finding Volume of a Cylinder** Find the volume of the cylinder.
Leave your answer in terms of π.

The formula for the volume of a cylinder is [_____].

The diagram shows h and d, but you must find r.

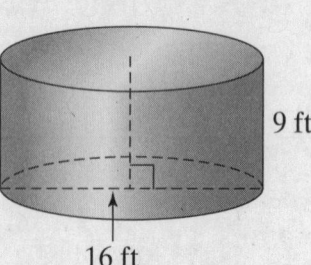

9 ft

16 ft

$r = \frac{1}{2}d = $ [____]

$V = $ [____][____][____]   **Use the formula for the volume of a cylinder.**

$= \pi \cdot$ [____] $\cdot$ [____]   **Substitute.**

$= $ [____][____]   **Simplify.**

The volume of the cylinder is [_____] ft^3.

Name_____ Class_____ Date_____

❷ Finding Volume of a Triangular Prism Find the volume of the prism.

The prism is a [_____] with triangular bases. The

base of the triangular prism is a [_____] where one leg

is the [_____] and the other leg is the [_____]. Use the

Pythagorean Theorem to calculate the length of the other leg.

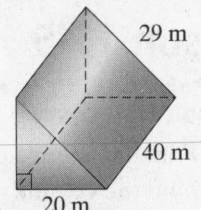
29 m
40 m
20 m

$$\sqrt{\boxed{}^2 - \boxed{}^2} = \sqrt{\boxed{} - \boxed{}} = \sqrt{\boxed{}} = \boxed{}$$

The area B of the base is $\frac{1}{2}bh = \frac{1}{2}\left(\boxed{}\right)\left(\boxed{}\right) = \boxed{}$. Use the

area of the base to find the volume of the prism.

$V = \boxed{}\boxed{}$ **Use the formula for the volume of a prism.**

$= \boxed{} \cdot \boxed{}$ **Substitute.**

$= \boxed{}$ **Simplify.**

The volume of the triangular prism is $\boxed{}$ m^3.

Quick Check

1. The cylinder shown is oblique.
   a. Find its volume in terms of π.

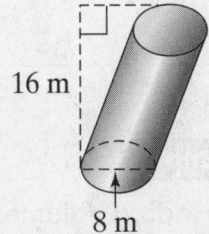
16 m
8 m

   b. Find its volume to the nearest tenth of a cubic meter.

2. Find the volume of the triangular prism.

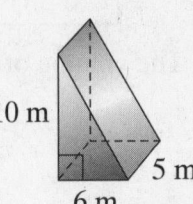
10 m
5 m
6 m

Lesson 11-5

Volumes of Pyramids and Cones

Lesson Objectives	NAEP 2005 Strand: Measurement
▼ Find the volume of a pyramid	**Topic:** Measuring Physical Attributes
▼ Find the volume of the cone	**Local Standards:** _____

Key Concepts

Theorem 11-8: Volume of a Pyramid

The volume of a pyramid is one third the product of the

[   ] and the [   ].

$V = $ [   ]

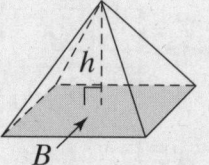

Theorem 11-9: Volume of a Cone

The volume of a cone is one third the product of the

[   ] and the [   ].

$V = \frac{1}{3}Bh$, or $V = $ [   ]

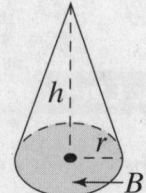

Examples

❶ **Finding Volume of a Pyramid** Find the volume of a square pyramid with base edges 15 cm and height 22 cm.

Because the base is a square, $B = $ [   ] · [   ] = [   ].

$V = \frac{1}{3}$[   ][   ]   **Use the formula for volume of a pyramid.**

$= \frac{1}{3}($[   ]$)($[   ]$)$ **Substitute** [   ] **for** *B* **and** [   ] **for** *h*.

$= $ [   ]   **Simplify.**

The volume of the square pyramid is [   ] cm³.

Daily Notetaking Guide [L1]

❷ **Finding Volume of an Oblique Cone** Find the volume of the oblique cone in terms of π.

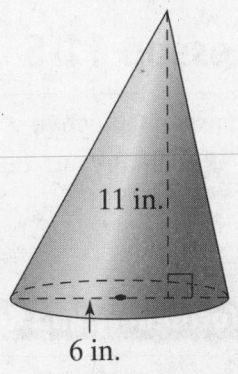

11 in.

6 in.

$r = \dfrac{\boxed{}}{\boxed{}}\boxed{} = \boxed{}$ in.

$V = \frac{1}{3}\pi\,\boxed{}\,\boxed{}$ **Use the formula for the volume of a cone.**

$= \frac{1}{3}\pi(\boxed{}^2)(\boxed{})$ **Substitute** $\boxed{}$ **for** *r* **and** $\boxed{}$ **for** *h*.

$= \boxed{}\boxed{}$ **Simplify.**

The volume of the cone is $\boxed{}$ in.^{3}.

Quick Check

1. Find the volume of a square pyramid with base edges 24 m and slant height 13 m.

2. A small child's teepee is in the shape of a cone 6 ft tall and 7 ft in diameter. Find the volume of the teepee to the nearest cubic foot.

Lesson 11-6

Surface Areas and Volumes of Spheres

Lesson Objective	NAEP 2005 Strand: Measurement
▼ Find the surface area and volume of a sphere	Topic: Measuring Physical Attributes
	Local Standards: _____

Vocabulary and Key Concepts

Theorem 11-10: Surface Area of a Sphere

The surface area of a sphere is four times the product of [ ] and

the [_____] of the [_____] of the sphere.

S.A. = [_____]

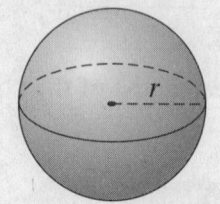

Theorem 11-11: Volume of a Sphere

The volume of a sphere is four thirds the product of [ ] and

the [_____] of the [_____] of the sphere.

S.A. = [_____]

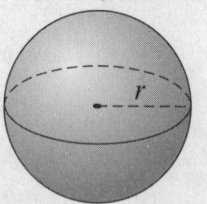

A sphere is _____

_____

The _____ of a sphere is the given point

from which all points on the sphere are equidistant.

The radius of a sphere is _____

_____

The _____ of a sphere is a segment passing

through the center with endpoints on the sphere.

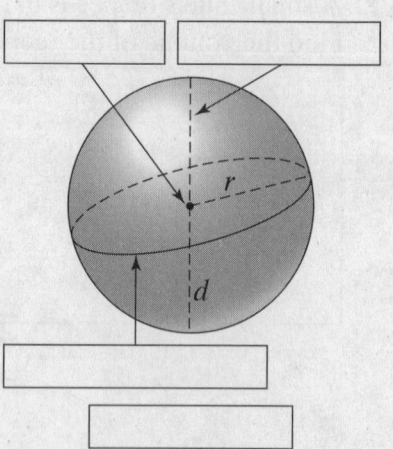

A great circle is _____

_____

The _____ divides a sphere into two

congruent hemispheres.

The circumference of a sphere is _____

_____

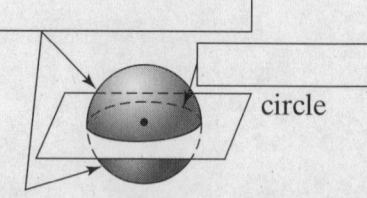
circle

Daily Notetaking Guide [L1]

Examples

❶ Finding Surface Area The circumference of a rubber ball is 13 cm.
Calculate its surface area to the nearest whole number.

Step 1 First, find the radius.

$$C = 2\pi r$$ **Use the formula for circumference.**

$$\boxed{} = 2\pi r$$ **Substitute** $\boxed{}$ **for C.**

$$\dfrac{\boxed{}}{2\pi} = r$$ **Solve for** *r*.

Step 2 Use the radius to find the surface area.

$$S.A. = 4\pi r^2$$ **Use the formula for surface area of a sphere.**

$$= 4\pi \cdot \left(\dfrac{\boxed{}}{2\pi}\right)^2$$ **Substitute** $\dfrac{\boxed{}}{2\pi}$ **for** *r*.

$$= \dfrac{\boxed{}}{\pi}$$ **Simplify.**

$$\approx \boxed{}$$ **Use a calculator.**

To the nearest whole number, the surface area of the rubber ball is $\boxed{}$ cm².

❷ Finding Volume Find the volume of the sphere.
Leave your answer in terms of π.

30 cm

$$V = \dfrac{4}{3}\boxed{}\boxed{}$$ **Use the formula for volume of a sphere.**

$$= \dfrac{4}{3}\pi \cdot \boxed{}^3$$ **Substitute** $r = \dfrac{30}{2} = \boxed{}$.

$$= \boxed{}\,\pi$$ **Simplify.**

The volume of the sphere is $\boxed{}$ cm³.

Quick Check

1. Find the surface area of a sphere with $d = 14$ in. Give your answer in two
ways, in terms of π and rounded to the nearest square inch.

2. Find the volume to the nearest cubic inch of a sphere with diameter 60 in.

Lesson 11-7

Areas and Volumes of Similar Solids

Lesson Objective	NAEP 2005 Strand: Measurement
▼ Find relationships between the ratios of the areas and volumes of similar solids	**Topic:** Systems of Measurement
	Local Standards: _____

Vocabulary and Key Concepts

Theorem 11-12: Areas and Volumes of Similar Solids

If the similarity ratio of two similar solids is $a : b$, then

(1) the ratio of their corresponding areas is ☐ : ☐ , and

(2) the ratio of their volumes is ☐ : ☐ .

Similar solids have _____

_____

The _____ of two similar objects is the ratio of their corresponding linear dimensions.

Examples

① **Identifying Similar Solids** Are the two solids similar? If so, give the similarity ratio.

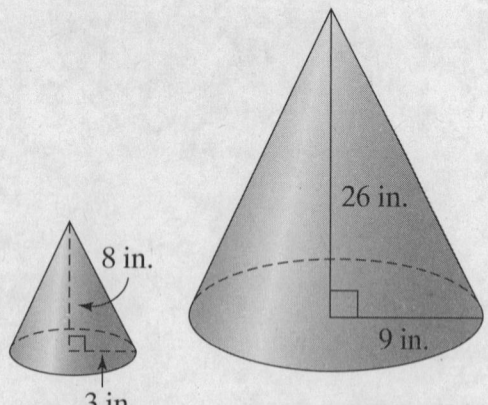

26 in.

8 in.

9 in.

3 in.

Both figures have the same shape. Check that the ratios of the corresponding dimensions are equal.

The ratio of the radii is ☐ , and the ratio of the heights is ☐ .

The cones are ☐ because ☐ .

❷ Finding the Similarity Ratio Find the similarity ratio of two similar cylinders with surface areas of 98π ft^2 and 2π ft^2.

Use the ratio of the surface areas to find the similarity ratios.

$\dfrac{a^2}{b^2} = \dfrac{\boxed{}}{\boxed{}}$ **The ratio of the surface areas is** $\boxed{}$ **:** $\boxed{}$.

$\dfrac{a^2}{b^2} = \dfrac{\boxed{}}{\boxed{}}$ **Simplify.**

$\dfrac{a}{b} = \dfrac{\boxed{}}{\boxed{}}$ **Take the** $\boxed{}$ **of each side.**

The similarity ratio is $\boxed{}$: $\boxed{}$.

Quick Check

1. Are the two cylinders similar? If so, give the similarity ratio.

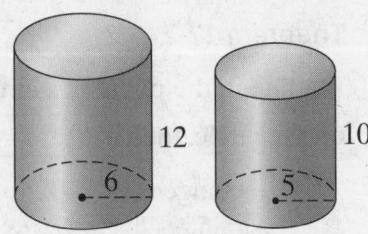

2. Find the similarity ratio of two similar prisms with surface areas 144 m^2 and 324 m^2.

Lesson 12-1

Tangent Lines

Lesson Objectives	NAEP 2005 Strand: Geometry
1 Use the relationship between a radius and a tangent	**Topic:** Relationships Among Geometric Figures
2 Use the relationship between two tangents from one point	**Local Standards:** _____

Vocabulary and Key Concepts

Theorem 12-1

If a line is tangent to a circle, then _____

_____

$\overleftrightarrow{AB} \perp \overline{OP}$

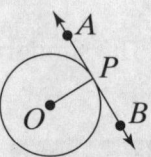

Theorem 12-2

If a line in the plane of a circle is perpendicular to a radius at its endpoint

on the circle, then [　　　　　　　　　　].

$\overleftrightarrow{AB}$ is tangent to $\odot O$.

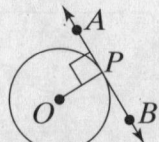

Theorem 12-3

The two segments tangent to a circle from a point outside the circle

are [　　　　　　　　　].

$\overline{AB} \cong \overline{CB}$

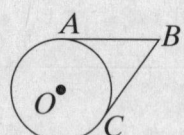

A tangent to a circle is _____

_____

The _____ is the point where a circle and a tangent intersect.

A triangle is inscribed in a circle if _____

_____

A triangle is _____ a circle if each side of the triangle is tangent

to the circle.

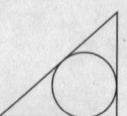

Example

Applying Tangent Lines A belt fits tightly around two circular pulleys, as shown. Find the distance between the centers of the pulleys. Round your answer to the nearest tenth.

Draw $\overline{OP}$. Then draw $\overline{OD}$ parallel to $\overline{ZW}$ to form rectangle $ODWZ$. Because $\overline{OZ}$ is a radius of $\odot O$, $OZ =$ ☐ cm.

Because opposite sides of a rectangle have the same measure,

$DW =$ ☐ cm and $OD =$ ☐ cm.

Because $\angle ODP$ is the [_____] of a [_____] angle,

$\angle ODP$ is also a right angle, and $\triangle OPD$ is a [_____] triangle.

Because the radius of $\odot P$ is 7 cm, $PD =$ [_____] cm.

$OD^2 + PD^2 = OP^2$	**Pythagorean Theorem**
☐$^2 +$ ☐$^2 = OP^2$	**Substitute.**
[____] $= OP^2$	**Simplify.**
$OP \approx$ [_____]	**Use a calculator to find the square root.**

The distance between the centers of the pulleys is about [_____] cm.

Quick Check

A belt fits tightly around two circular pulleys, as shown. Find the distance between the centers of the pulleys.

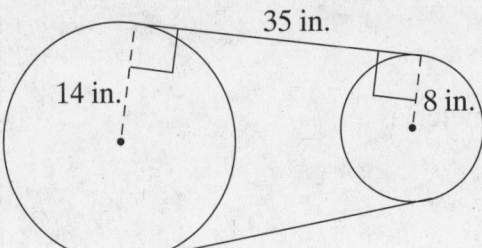

Lesson 12-2

Chords and Arcs

Lesson Objectives	**NAEP 2005 Strand:** Geometry
▼ Use congruent chords, arcs, and central angles	**Topic:** Relationships Among Geometric Figures
▼ Recognize properties of lines through the center of a circle	**Local Standards:** _____

Vocabulary and Key Concepts

Theorem 12-4

Within a circle or in congruent circles

(1) Congruent central angles have [_____] chords.

(2) Congruent chords have [_____] arcs.

(3) Congruent arcs have [_____] central angles.

Theorem 12-5

Within a circle or in congruent circles

(1) Chords equidistant from the center are [_____].

(2) Congruent chords are [_____] from the center.

Theorem 12-6

In a circle, a diameter that is perpendicular to a chord bisects the

[_____] and its [_____].

Theorem 12-7

In a circle, a diameter that bisects a chord (that is not a diameter) is

[_____] to the chord.

Theorem 12-8

In a circle, the perpendicular bisector of a chord contains the [_____] of the circle.

A chord is _____

_____

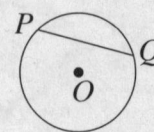

··········

Examples

❶ Using Theorem 12-4 In the diagram, radius $\overline{OX}$ bisects $\angle AOB$. What can you conclude?

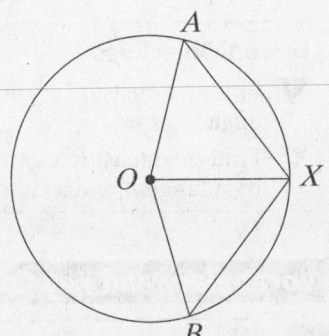

$\angle AOX \cong$ [____] by the definition of an angle bisector.

$\overline{AX} \cong$ [____] because [_____] central angles have

[_____] chords.

$\overline{AX} \cong$ [____] because [_____] chords have

[_____] arcs.

❷ Using Theorem 12-5 Find AB.

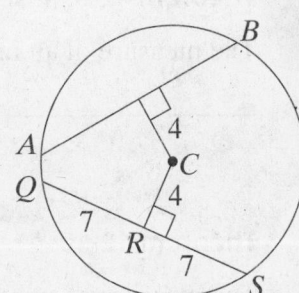

$QS = QR + RS$	**Segment Addition Postulate**
$QS = $ [__] $+$ [__]	**Substitute.**
$QS = $ [__]	**Simplify.**
$AB = $ [__]	**Chords that are equidistant from the center of a circle are congruent.**
$AB = $ [__]	**Substitute** [__] **for QS.**

Quick Check

1. If you are given that $\overline{BC} \cong \overline{DF}$ in the circles, what can you conclude?

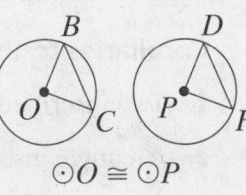

$\odot O \cong \odot P$

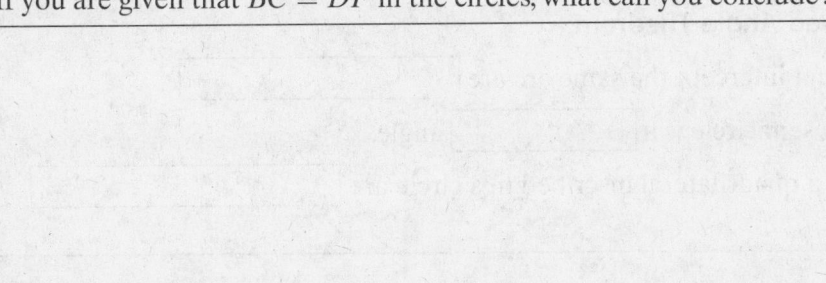

2. Find the value of x in the circle at the right.

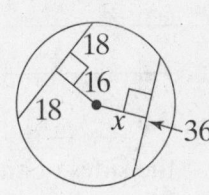

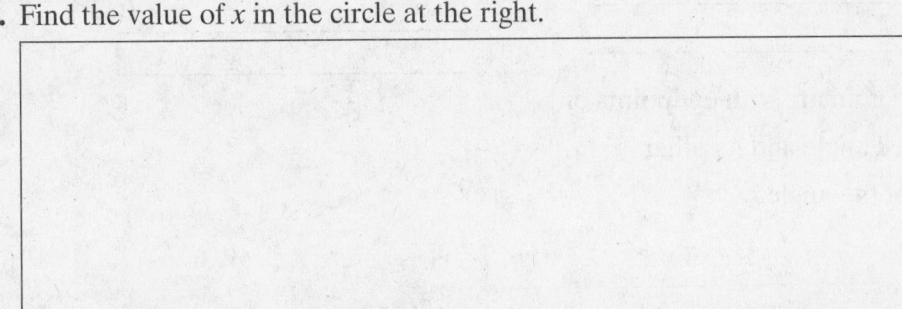

Lesson 12-3

Inscribed Angles

All rights reserved.

Lesson Objectives	NAEP 2005 Strand: Geometry
▼ Find the measure of an inscribed angle	Topic: Relationships Among Geometric Figures
② Find the measure of an angle formed by a tangent and a chord	Local Standards: _____

Vocabulary and Key Concepts

Theorem 12-9: Inscribed Angle Theorem

The measure of an inscribed angle is

_____

$$m\angle B = \boxed{}$$

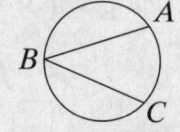

Theorem 12-10

The measure of an angle formed by a tangent and a chord is

_____

$$m\angle C = \boxed{}$$

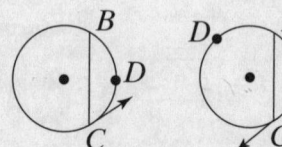

Corollaries to the Inscribed Angle Theorem

1. Two inscribed angles that intercept the same arc are $\boxed{}$.

2. An angle inscribed in a semicircle is a $\boxed{}$ angle.

3. The opposite angles of a quadrilateral inscribed in a circle are $\boxed{}$.

An inscribed angle has _____

_____

_____

An _____ is an arc with endpoints on

the sides of an inscribed angle and its other

points in the interior of the angle.

© Pearson Education, Inc., publishing as Pearson Prentice Hall.

Example

Using the Inscribed Angle Theorem Find the values of *x* and *y*.

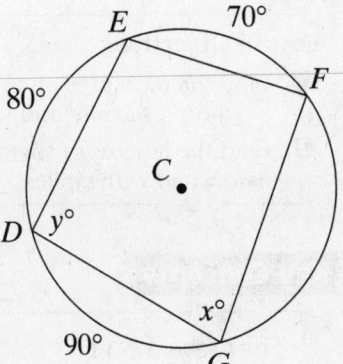

$x = \frac{1}{2}m\widehat{DEF}$ **Inscribed Angle Theorem**

$x = \frac{1}{2}\left(m\boxed{} + m\boxed{}\right)$ **Arc Addition Postulate**

$x = \frac{1}{2}\left(\boxed{} + \boxed{}\right)$ **Substitute.**

$x = \boxed{}$ **Simplify.**

Because $\widehat{EFG}$ is the intercepted arc of $\angle D$, you need to find $m\widehat{FG}$ in order to find $m\widehat{EFG}$. The arc measure of a circle is 360°, so

$m\widehat{FG} = 360 - \boxed{} - \boxed{} - \boxed{} = \boxed{}$.

$y = \frac{1}{2}m\widehat{EFG}$ **Inscribed Angle Theorem**

$y = \frac{1}{2}\left(m\boxed{} + m\boxed{}\right)$ **Arc Addition Postulate**

$y = \frac{1}{2}\left(\boxed{} + \boxed{}\right)$ **Substitute.**

$y = \boxed{}$ **Simplify.**

Quick Check

In the Example, find $m\angle DEF$.

Lesson 12-4

Lesson Objectives	NAEP 2005 Strand: Geometry
❶ Find the measures of angles formed by chords, secants, and tangents	**Topic:** Relationships Among Geometric Figures
❷ Find the lengths of segments associated with circles	**Local Standards:** _____

Key Concepts

Theorem 12-11

The measure of an angle formed by two lines that

(1) intersect inside a circle is half the _____

_____

$m\angle 1 = $ [   ]

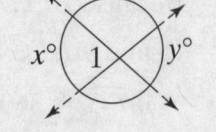

(2) intersect outside a circle is half the

_____

_____

$m\angle 1 = $ [   ]

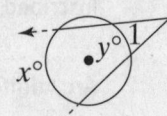 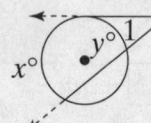 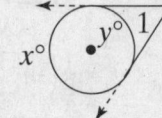

Theorem 12-12

For a given point and circle, the product of the lengths of the two segments from the point to the circle is _____

_____

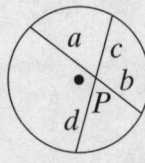
I.

$a \cdot b = c \cdot d$

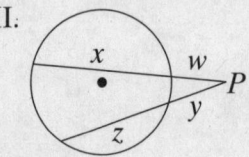
II.

$(w + x)w = (y + z)y$

 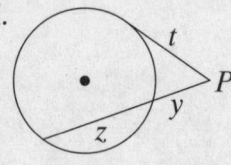
III.

$(y + z)y = t^2$

Examples

❶ **Finding Arc Measures** An advertising agency wants a frontal photo of a "flying saucer" ride at an amusement park. The photographer stands at the vertex of the angle formed by tangents to the "flying saucer." What is the measure of the arc that will be in the photograph? In the diagram, the photographer stands at point T. $\overrightarrow{TX}$ and $\overrightarrow{TY}$ intercept minor arc $\overarc{XY}$ and major arc $\overarc{XAY}$.

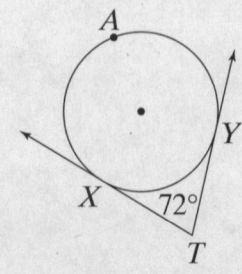

Let $m\widehat{XY} = x$.

Then $m\widehat{XAY} = \boxed{} - x$.

$m\angle T = \frac{1}{2}(m\widehat{XAY} - m\widehat{XY})$ **Theorem 12-11(2)**

$\boxed{} = \frac{1}{2}\left[\left(\boxed{}\right) - \boxed{}\right]$ **Substitute.**

$\boxed{} = \frac{1}{2}\left(\boxed{} - 2x\right)$ **Simplify.**

$\boxed{} = \boxed{} - x$ **Distributive Property.**

$x + \boxed{} = \boxed{}$ **Add x to both sides.**

$x = \boxed{}$ **Solve for x.**

A $\boxed{}$ arc will be in the advertising agency's photo.

❷ **Finding Segment Lengths** A tram travels from point A to point B along the arc of a circle with a radius of 125 ft. Find the shortest distance from point A to point B.

The perpendicular bisector of the chord $\overline{AB}$ contains the center of the circle. Because the radius is 125 ft, the diameter is $\boxed{} \cdot \boxed{} = \boxed{}$ ft. The length of the other segment along the diameter is $\boxed{}$ ft $- \boxed{}$ ft, or $\boxed{}$ ft.

$x \cdot x = \boxed{} \cdot \boxed{}$ **Theorem 12-12(1)**

$x^2 = \boxed{}$ **Multiply.**

$x = \boxed{}$ **Solve for x.**

The shortest distance from point A to point B is $2x$ or $\boxed{}$ ft.

Quick Check

1. Find the value of w.

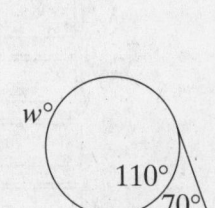

2. Find the value of x to the nearest tenth.

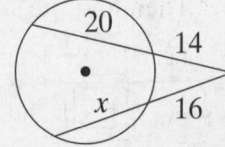

Lesson 12-5

**Circles in the
Coordinate Plane**

Lesson Objectives	**NAEP 2005 Strand:** Geometry
▼ Write an equation of a circle	**Topic:** Position and Direction
▼ Find the center and radius of a circle	**Local Standards:** _____

Key Concepts

Theorem 12-13

The standard form of an equation of a circle with center ☐☐☐

and radius ☐ is $(x - h)^2 + (y - k)^2 = r^2$.

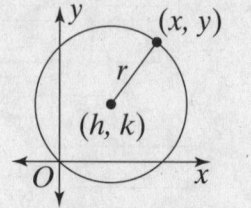

Examples

❶ Writing the Equation of a Circle Write the standard equation of a circle
with center $(-8, 0)$ and radius $\sqrt{5}$.

$(x - \boxed{})^2 + (y - \boxed{})^2 = \boxed{}^2$ **Standard form**

$[x - (\boxed{})]^2 + (y - \boxed{})^2 = (\boxed{})^2$ **Substitute $(-8, 0)$ for (h, k) and**

                                     $\sqrt{5}$ for r.

$\left(x + \boxed{}\right)^2 + y^2 = \boxed{}$ **Simplify.**

❷ Using the Center and a Point on a Circle Write the standard equation of
a circle with center $(5, 8)$ that passes through the point $(-15, -13)$.

First find the radius.

$r = \sqrt{(x - \boxed{})^2 + (y - \boxed{})^2}$ **Use the Distance Formula to find r.**

$= \sqrt{(\boxed{} - \boxed{})^2 + (\boxed{} - \boxed{})^2}$ **Substitute $(5, 8)$ for (h, k) and $(-15, -13)$ for (x, y).**

$= \sqrt{(\boxed{})^2 + (\boxed{})^2}$ **Simplify.**

$= \sqrt{\boxed{} + \boxed{}}$

$= \sqrt{\boxed{}} = \boxed{}$

Then find the standard equation of the circle with center $(5, 8)$ and radius $\boxed{}$.

$(x - \boxed{})^2 + (y - \boxed{})^2 = \boxed{}^2$ **Standard form**

$(x - \boxed{})^2 + (y - \boxed{})^2 = (\boxed{})^2$ **Substitute $(5, 8)$ for (h, k) and $\boxed{}$ for r.**

$(x - \boxed{})^2 + (y - \boxed{})^2 = \boxed{}$ **Simplify.**

❸ Graphing a Circle Given Its Equation Find the center and radius of the circle with equation $(x + 4)^2 + (y - 1)^2 = 25$. Then graph the circle.

$$(x + 4)^2 + (y - 1)^2 = 25$$
$$(x - {-4})^2 + (y - 1)^2 = (5)^2$$

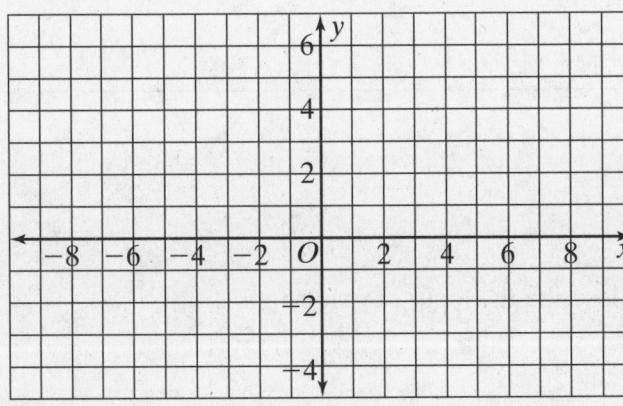

Relate the equation to the standard form
$(x - h)^2 + (y - k)^2 = r^2$.

The center is ⬚ and the radius is ⬚.

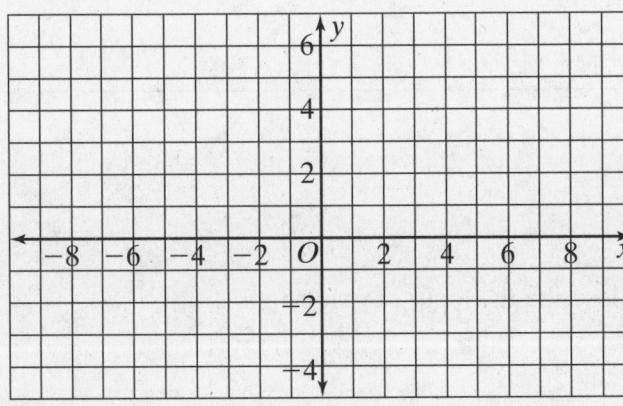

Quick Check

1. Write the standard equation of the circle with center $(-2, -1)$ and radius $\sqrt{2}$.

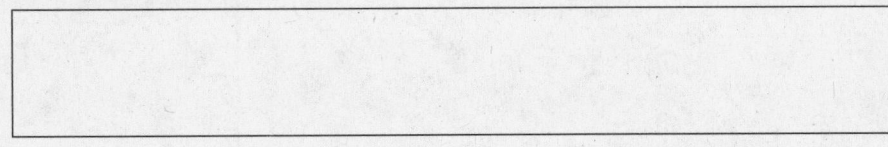

2. Write the standard equation of the circle with center $(2, 3)$ that passes through the point $(-1, 1)$.

3. Find the center and radius of the circle with equation $(x - 2)^2 + (y - 3)^2 = 100$. Then graph the circle.

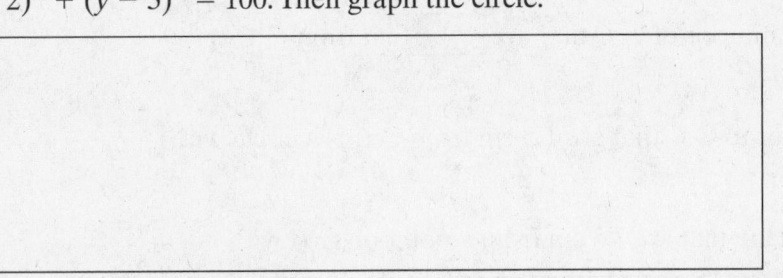

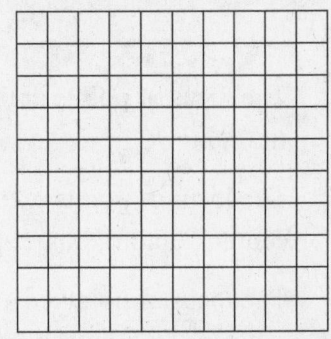

Name_____ Class_____ Date_____

Lesson 12-6

Locus: A Set of Points

Lesson Objective	NAEP 2005 Strand: Geometry
▼ Draw and describe a locus	Topic: Dimension and Shape
	Local Standards: _____

Vocabulary

A locus is _____

_____

Examples

1 Describing a Locus in a Plane Draw and describe the locus of points in a plane that are 1.5 cm from ⊙ C with radius 1.5 cm.

Use a compass to draw ⊙ C with radius 1.5 cm.

The locus of points in the interior of ⊙ C that are ☐ cm from ⊙ C is the center C.

The locus of points exterior to ⊙ C that are 1.5 cm from ⊙ C is a circle with center C and radius ☐ cm.

The locus of points in a plane that are 1.5 cm from a point on ⊙ C with radius ☐ cm is point C and a circle with radius ☐ cm and center C.

Daily Notetaking Guide

② **Describing a Locus in Space** Describe the locus of points in space that are 4 cm from a plane M.

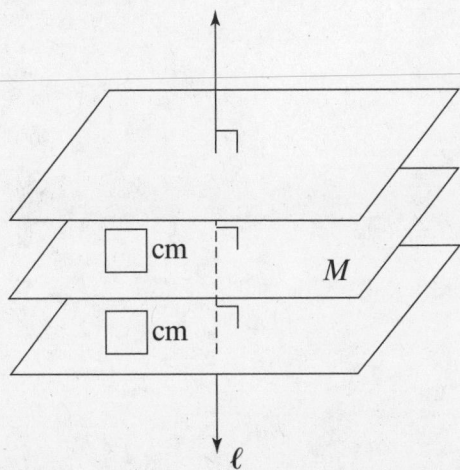

Imagine plane M as a horizontal plane. Because distance is measured along a perpendicular segment from a point to a plane, the locus of points in space that are 4 cm from a plane M are a plane ☐ cm above and parallel to plane M and another plane ☐ cm below and parallel to plane M.

Quick Check

1. Draw and describe the locus: In a plane, the points 2 cm from line $\overleftrightarrow{XY}$.

2. Draw and describe the locus of points in space that are equidistant from two parallel planes.

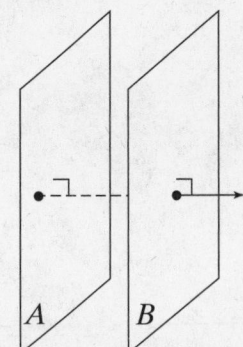

A Note to the Student:

This section of your workbook contains a series of pages that support your mathematics understandings for each chapter and lesson presented in your student edition.

- Practice pages provide additional practice for every lesson.

- Guided Problem Solving pages lead you through a step-by-step solution to an application problem in each lesson.

- Vocabulary pages contain a variety of activities to increase your reading and math understanding, ranging from graphic organizers to vocabulary review puzzles.

Practice • Guided Problem Solving • Vocabulary

Name_____ Class_____ Date_____

Practice 1-1   Patterns and Inductive Reasoning
. . . .

Find a pattern for each sequence. Use the pattern to show the next two terms.

1. 17, 23, 29, 35, 41, _____   **2.** 12, 14, 18, 24, 32, _____   **3.** 2, −4, 8, −16, 32, _____

Name two different ways to continue each pattern.

4. 1, 1, 2, _____   **5.** 2, 4, _____   **6.** A, Z, B, _____

Draw the next figure in each sequence.

7. 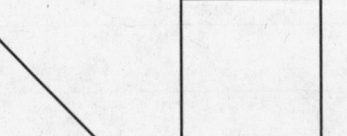  _____

8. 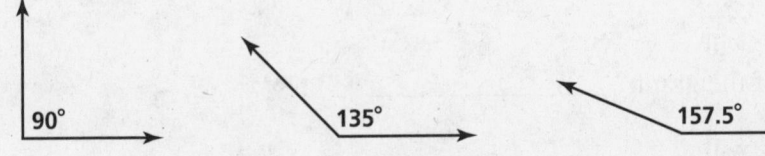 _____

The Fibonacci sequence consists of the pattern 1, 1, 2, 3, 5, 8, 13, . . .

9. What is the ninth term in the pattern?_____

10. Using your calculator, look at the successive ratios of one term to the next.
Make a conjecture.

_____

_____

_____

11. List the first eight terms of the sequence formed by finding the differences of
successive terms in the Fibonacci sequence.

_____

. . . .
L1 Practice   *Geometry* Lesson 1-1   **165**

1-1 • Guided Problem Solving

GPS **Student Page 8, Exercise 48**

Communications The table shows the number of commercial radio stations in the United States for a 50-year period.

a. Make a line graph of the data.

b. Use the graph and inductive reasoning to make a conjecture about the number of radio stations in the United States in the year 2010.

c. How confident are you about your conjecture? Explain.

Number of Radio Stations

1950	2,835
1960	4,224
1970	6,519
1980	7,871
1990	9,379
2000	10,577

SOURCE: Federal Communications Commission

Read and Understand

1. Describe why a line graph might be helpful for making a conjecture about the number of radio stations in 2010. _____

2. Do you think the graph will go up or down as time increases? _____

Plan and Solve

3. What information from the table will you use for the horizontal axis of the graph? _____

4. What information from the table will you use for the vertical axis of the graph? _____

5. Are the number of radio stations steadily increasing or decreasing with time? _____

6. Based on the answer you found in Step 5, do you think the number of stations in the year 2010 will be greater or less than the number of stations in 2000? _____

7. Is the pattern from the years 1950 through 2000 consistent enough to make a conjecture about the number of stations in 2010? _____ Why? _____

Look Back and Check

8. Write a sentence to explain why patterns are important for making a conjecture.

_____

Solve Another Problem

9. List a set of numbers that could not be used to make a conjecture confidently. _____

Practice 1-2

Drawings, Nets, and Other Models

Make an isometric drawing of each cube structure.

1.

2.
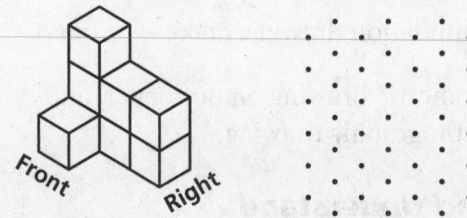

For each figure, (a) make a foundation drawing, and (b) make an orthographic drawing.

3.
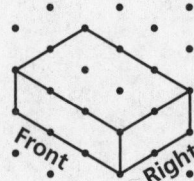

4.
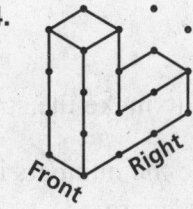

5. Choose the nets that will fold to make a cube.

A.
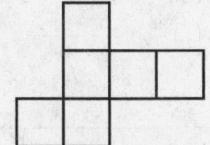

B.

C.
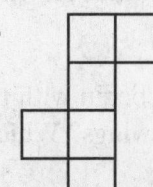

D.
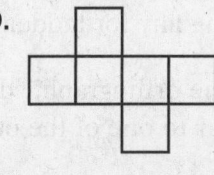

Match each three-dimensional figure with its net.

6.
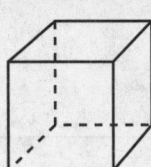

7.
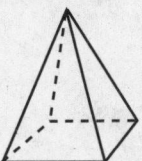

8.
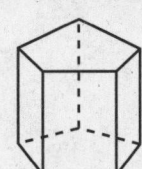

9.
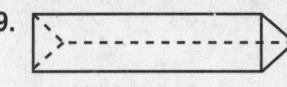

A.
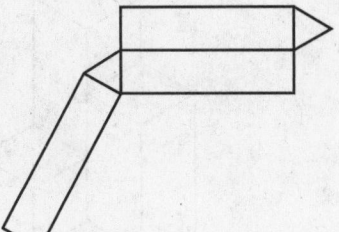

B.
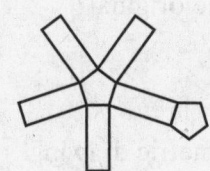

C.
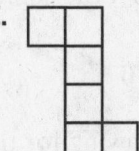

D.
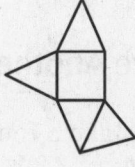

1-2 • Guided Problem Solving

•••

GPS **Student Page 14, Exercise 18**

For the foundation drawing, make

a. an isometric drawing on dot paper, and
b. an orthographic drawing.

3	3
2	1

Right

Front

Read and Understand

1. How do isometric, orthographic, and foundation drawings represent three-dimensional objects? _____

Plan and Solve

2. How many cubes are needed to make the structure in the figure?

3. For the isometric drawing: use the numbers in the Front boxes to sketch the front part of the figure.

4. Sketch the back part of the figure and complete the drawing by adding any missing connecting lines for visible edges and erasing any for hidden edges.

5. For the orthographic drawing: begin with the Top view. Is this similar to one of the other drawings? Which one?

6. Make the Front view. Are there any hidden edges to add to the front view? _____

7. Complete the drawing by making the Right view.

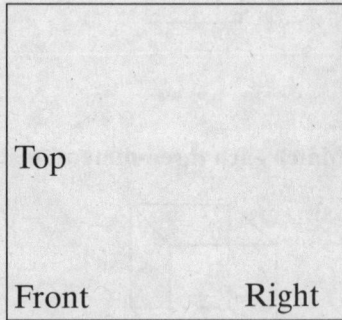

Top

Front   Right

Look Back and Check

8. From your isometric drawing, make a foundation drawing. Is it the same as the original?

Solve Another Problem

9. Make a foundation drawing for the isometric drawing.

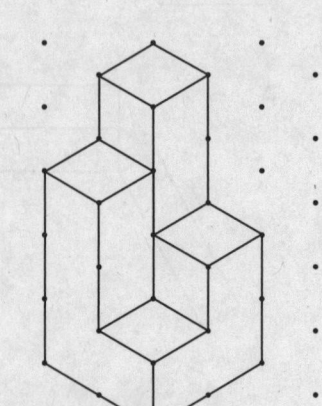

Practice 1-3

Refer to the diagram at the right for Exercises 1–8.

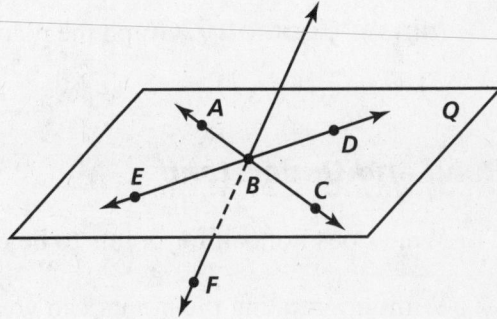

1. Name $\overleftrightarrow{AB}$ in another way. _____

2. Give two other names for plane Q. _____

Are the following sets of points collinear?

3. $\overleftrightarrow{AB}$ and C _____

4. $\overleftrightarrow{EB}$ and A _____

Are the following sets of points coplanar?

5. E, B, and F _____

6. $\overleftrightarrow{AC}$ and $\overleftrightarrow{ED}$ _____

7. F, A, B, and C _____

8. plane Q and $\overleftrightarrow{EC}$ _____

Find the intersection of the following lines and planes in the figure at the right.

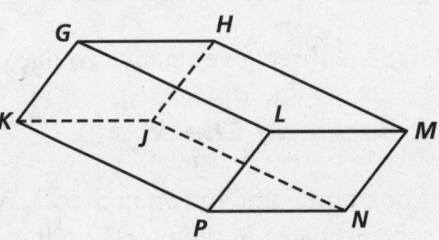

9. $\overleftrightarrow{GK}$ and $\overleftrightarrow{LG}$ _____

10. planes GLM and LPN _____

11. planes HJN and GKL _____

12. $\overleftrightarrow{KP}$ and plane KJN _____

Refer to the diagram at the right.

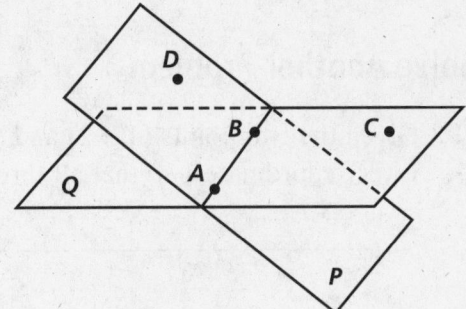

13. Name plane P in another way. _____

14. What is the intersection of planes P and Q? _____

15. Are D, A, B, and C coplanar? _____

16. Are D and C collinear? _____

17. What is the intersection of $\overleftrightarrow{AB}$ and $\overleftrightarrow{DC}$? _____

18. Are planes P and Q coplanar? _____

19. Are $\overleftrightarrow{AB}$ and plane Q coplanar? _____

20. Are B and C collinear? _____

1-3 • Guided Problem Solving

GPS **Student Page 20, Exercise 50**

Coordinate Geometry Graph the points and state whether they are collinear.

$(3, -3), (2, -3), (-3, 1)$

Read and Understand

1. What does it mean for points to be collinear? _____

2. Without graphing the points, can you tell whether or not they are collinear? _____ If so, how?

   _____

Plan and Solve

3. Graph the first two points, $(3, -3)$ and $(2, -3)$, and draw the line through the points. What kind of line is it? _____

4. Plot the third point, $(-3, 1)$.
   Is it on the line found in Step 3? _____

5. Are the three given points collinear? _____

Look Back and Check

6. Look at the line drawn in Step 3. What is unique about the y-coordinates of the points on this line?

   _____

7. Does the third point, $(-3, 1)$, share the property found in Step 6? _____

Solve Another Problem

8. Given the two points $(4, -2)$ and $(-2, 1)$, find a third point with x-coordinate 1 so that all three points are collinear.

   _____

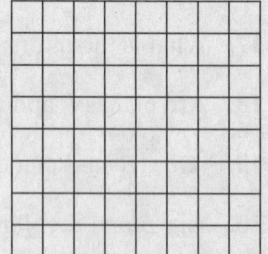

Practice 1-4

Segments, Rays, Parallel Lines and Planes

Write *true* or *false*.

1. $\overleftrightarrow{XY}$ is the same as $\overleftrightarrow{YX}$. _____

2. $\overrightarrow{XY}$ is the same as $\overrightarrow{YX}$. _____

3. If two rays have the same endpoint, then they form a line. _____

4. If the union of two rays is a line, then the rays are opposite rays. _____

Refer to the diagram at the right.

5. Name all segments parallel to $\overline{EF}$. _____

6. Name three pairs of skew lines. _____

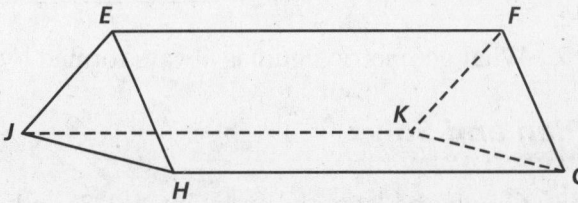

Refer to the diagram at the right.

7. Which pair(s) of planes is (are) parallel? _____

8. Which planes intersect in $\overleftrightarrow{MN}$? _____

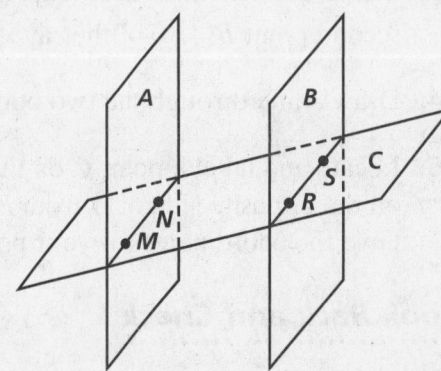

Refer to the diagram at the right.

9. Name $\overrightarrow{EF}$ in another way. _____

10. Name a pair of opposite rays with E as an endpoint. _____

11. Name in two different ways the ray opposite $\overrightarrow{FG}$. _____

12. Are $\overline{EG}$ and $\overline{GE}$ the same segment? _____

Draw each of the following.

13. parallel planes S, T, and U

14. planes R and W intersecting in $\overleftrightarrow{PQ}$

Name _____ Class _____ Date _____

1-4 • Guided Problem Solving

GPS **Student Page 26, Exercise 35**

Coordinate Geometry $\overrightarrow{AB}$ has endpoint $A(2, 3)$ and contains $B(4, 6)$.
Give possible coordinates for point C so that $\overrightarrow{AB}$ and $\overrightarrow{AC}$ are opposite rays.
Graph your answer.

Read and Understand

1. What are opposite rays? _____

2. What geometric figure is always formed by opposite rays? _____

Plan and Solve

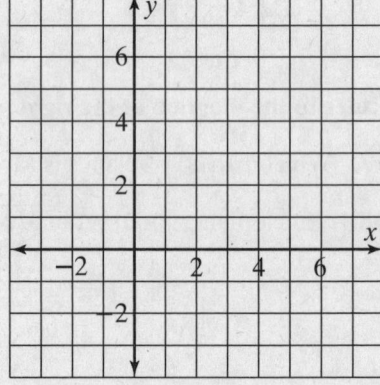

3. Graph and label the endpoint $A(2, 3)$ and
   second point $B(4, 6)$ of the ray $\overrightarrow{AB}$.

4. Draw a line through the two points graphed in Step 3.

5. Locate and label a point C on the line,
   on the opposite side of A from B.
   Give the coordinates for your point C. _____

Look Back and Check

6. Graph the ray $\overrightarrow{CA}$ with endpoint C found in Step 5. Does the ray $\overrightarrow{CA}$ pass through $B(4, 6)$?

_____

Solve Another Problem

7. Graph the line containing the points $J(6, 3)$
   and $K(2, 1)$. Give the coordinates for the point L
   on the line such that $\overrightarrow{LJ}$ and $\overrightarrow{LK}$ are opposite rays. _____

Guided Problem Solving

Practice 1-5

Measuring Segments

If _GJ_ = 32, find the value of each of the following.

1. _x_ _____

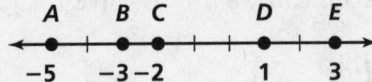

2. _GH_ _____

3. _HJ_ _____

4. Find _PD_ if the coordinate of _P_ is −7 and the coordinate of _D_ is −1.

5. Find _SK_ if the coordinate of _S_ is 17 and the coordinate of _K_ is −5.

6. Find the lengths of $\overline{AC}$ and $\overline{BD}$. _____

7. Are $\overline{AC}$ and $\overline{BD}$ congruent? _____

8. Find the midpoint of $\overline{AD}$. _____

If _AC_ = 58, find the value of each of the following.

9. _x_ _____

10. _AB_ _____

11. _BC_ _____

1-5 • Guided Problem Solving

GPS **Student Page 34, Exercise 34**

Algebra Use the diagram at the right.

If $AD = 12$ and $AC = 4y - 36$, find the value of y. Then find AC and DC.

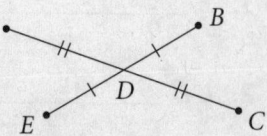

Read and Understand

1. The segments $\overline{AD}$ and $\overline{DC}$ are marked alike. What does that indicate?

   _____

2. Based on your answer to Step 1, how are the lengths of $\overline{AD}$ and $\overline{DC}$ related? _____

3. What postulate can we use to solve for y? _____

Plan and Solve

4. Based on your answer to Step 2, how are AC and AD related? _____

5. What is AC? _____

6. Use your results from Steps 4 and 5 to solve for y. _____

7. Based on your answer to Step 1, what is DC? _____

Look Back and Check

8. Write a sentence describing how the Segment Addition Postulate has been used.

   _____

   _____

Solve Another Problem

9. Use the diagram at the top of the page.
   If $EB = 5x - 3$ and $DB = x + 6$, find ED, DB, and EB. _____

Practice 1-6

1. Name the angle at the right in three different ways. _____

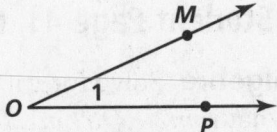

Name an angle or angles in the diagram described by each of the following.

2. complementary to ∠BOC _____

3. supplementary to ∠BOC _____

4. adjacent and congruent to ∠AOC _____

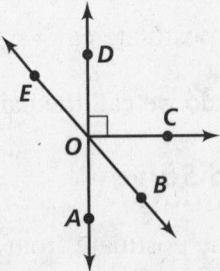

Find the measure of each angle.

5. ∠EBF _____

6. ∠EBA _____

7. ∠ABF _____

8. ∠DBF _____

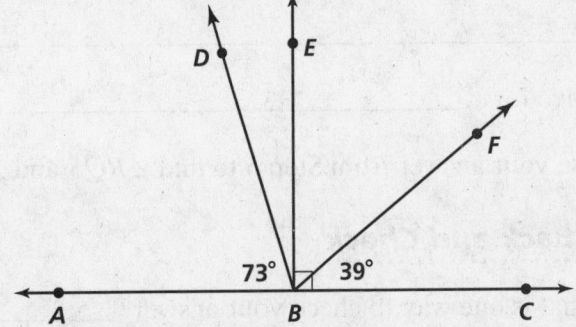

9. Name all acute angles in the figure. _____

10. Name all obtuse angles in the figure. _____

11. Name all right angles in the figure. _____

1-6 • Guided Problem Solving

a. **Algebra** Solve for x if $m\angle RQS = 2x + 4$ and $m\angle TQS = 6x + 20$.
b. What is $m\angle RQS$? $m\angle TQS$?
c. Show how you can check your answer.

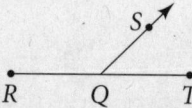

Read and Understand

1. What postulate can we use to solve the problem? _____

2. What do we call the pair of angles $\angle RQS$ and $\angle TQS$? _____

Plan and Solve

3. Use the postulate from Step 1 to write an equation using the angles in the diagram.

   _____

4. Next, make substitutions in this equation, using the information given.

   _____

5. Solve for x. _____

6. Use your answer from Step 5 to find $\angle RQS$ and $\angle TQS$. _____

Look Back and Check

7. What is one way to check your answer? _____

Solve Another Problem

8. a. **Algebra** Solve for x if $m\angle AOB = 2x - 5$ and
   $m\angle COB = 6x + 7$. _____

   b. What is $m\angle AOB$? $m\angle COB$?

   _____

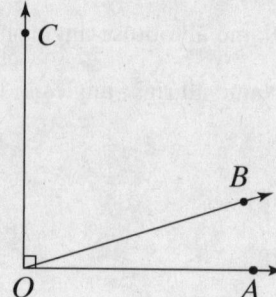

Practice 1-7

Basic Constructions

Construct each figure as directed.

1. Construct $\overline{AB}$ congruent to $\overline{XY}$. Check your work with a ruler.

2. Construct the perpendicular bisector of $\overline{XY}$.

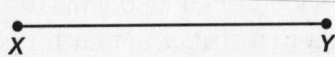

3. Construct a triangle whose sides are all the same length as $\overline{XY}$.

Check your work with a protractor.

4. **a.** Construct a 90° angle.

   b. Construct a 45° angle.

5. Construct $\angle A$ so that $m\angle A = m\angle 1 + m\angle 2$.

6. Construct $\angle C$ so that $m\angle C = 2m\angle 2$.

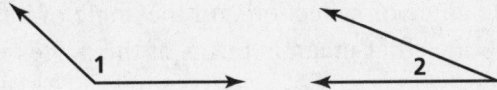

7. Construct the angle bisector of $\angle X$.

8. Construct $\angle W$ so that $m\angle W = 2m\angle X$.

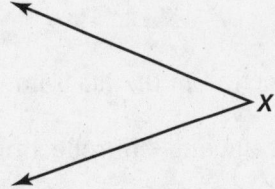

Write *true* or *false*.

9. $\overline{AB} \cong \overline{XY}$ _____

10. $m\angle 1 = 40$ _____

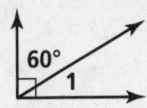

11. If $m\angle A = 80$, then $\angle A$ is obtuse. _____

12. The perpendicular bisector of a line segment creates four 90° angles. _____

1-7 • Guided Problem Solving

GPS **Student Page 48, Exercise 18**

Optics A beam of light and a mirror can be used to study the behavior of light. Light that strikes the mirror is reflected so that the angle of reflection and the angle of incidence are congruent. In the diagram, $\overline{BC}$ is perpendicular to the mirror, and $\angle ABC$ has a measure of 41°.

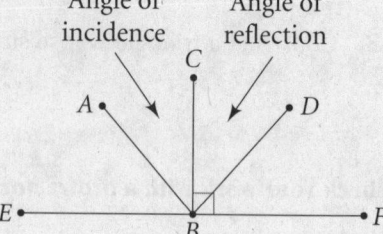

a. Name the angle of reflection and find its measure.
b. Find $m\angle ABD$.
c. Find $m\angle ABE$ and $m\angle DBF$.

Read and Understand

1. If the angle of reflection and the angle of incidence are congruent, what does that mean in terms of the angles in the diagram? _____

2. What kind of angles are the pair $\angle ABC$ and $\angle ABE$? _____

Plan and Solve

3. Name the angle of reflection in the diagram. _____

4. What is the measure of the angle of reflection? _____

5. Use the Angle Addition Postulate to find $m\angle ABD$. _____

6. Use the Angle Addition Postulate to find $m\angle ABE$. _____

7. What is $m\angle DBF$? _____

Look Back and Check

8. Write a sentence describing how complementary or supplementary angles can be used to check the answers.

_____

_____

Solve Another Problem

9. Refer to the diagram above. If $m\angle CBD = x - 4$ and $m\angle FBD = 3x - 6$, find $m\angle CBD, m\angle FBD, m\angle CBA,$ and $m\angle EBA.$ _____

Guided Problem Solving

Practice 1-8

Graph each point in the coordinate plane.

1. $A(-2, 5)$ 2. $B(5, -2)$ 3. $C(0, 6)$

4. $D(-4, 0)$ 5. $E(-4, -2)$

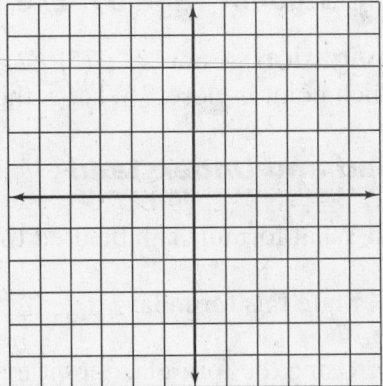

Find the distance between the points.

6. $Q(10, 10), R(10, -2)$ _____

7. $U(11, -2), V(-1, 3)$ _____

Find the coordinates of the midpoint of each segment. The coordinates of the endpoints are given.

8. $A(6, 7), B(4, 3)$ _____

9. $O(0, 0), G(-5, 12)$ _____

10. $H(2.8, 1.1), I(-3.4, 5.7)$ _____

11. The midpoint of $\overline{AB}$ is $(1, 2)$. The coordinates of A are $(-3, 6)$. Find the coordinates of B. _____

12. Graph the points $A(2, 1), B(2, -5), C(-4, -5)$, and $D(-4, 1)$. Draw the segments connecting A, B, C, and D in order. Are the lengths of the sides of $ABCD$ the same? _____

   Explain. _____

13. A crow flies to a point that is 1 mile east and 20 miles south of its starting point. How far does the crow fly? _____

Quadrilateral $PQSR$ has coordinates as follows: $P(0, 0), Q(-1, 4), R(8, 2)$, and $S(7, 6)$.

14. Graph quadrilateral $PQSR$.

15. What is the perimeter of $PQSR$? _____

16. What is the midpoint of $\overline{QR}$? _____

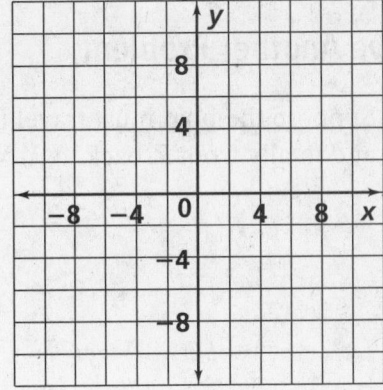

1-8 • Guided Problem Solving

GPS **Student Page 57, Exercise 48**

Navigation A boat at $X(5, -2)$ needs to travel to $Y(-6, 9)$ or $Z(17, -3)$. Which point is closer? What is the distance to the closer point?

Read and Understand

1. What formula can be used to solve the problem? _____

2. State this formula. _____

3. Using the formula, does it matter which order we assign the points? _____

   Why? _____

Plan and Solve

4. To find the distance from X to Y, use the formula and make substitutions using the coordinates of $X(5, -2)$ and $Y(-6, 9)$. _____

5. What is the distance from X to Y? _____

6. Find the distance from X to Z in a similar manner. What is the distance from X to Z?

   _____

7. Which point is closer to X—Y or Z? _____

Look Back and Check

8. To check the distances, reverse the order of the points and use the formula to re-calculate the distances. Are your results the same? _____

Solve Another Problem

9. Suppose the boat must travel from X to Y, then from Y to Z, and finally from Z back to X. What is the total distance traveled? _____

Practice 1-9

Perimeter, Circumference, and Area

Find the area of each rectangle with the given base and height.

1. base: 3 ft
height: 22 in. _____

2. base: 2 m
height: 120 cm _____

Find the circumference of each circle in terms of π.

3. _____

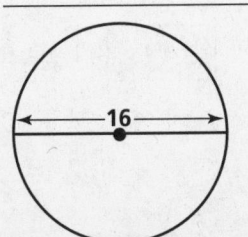

4. _____

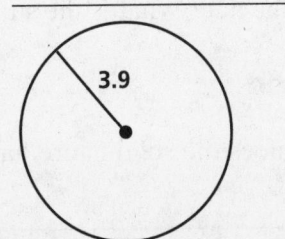

Find the perimeter and area of each rectangle with the given base and height.

5. $b = 7$ cm, $h = 6$ cm _____

6. $b = 4$ in., $h = 10.5$ in. _____

7. $b = 11$ m, $h = 9$ m _____

Find the perimeter and area of each figure. All angles in the figures are right angles.

8. _____

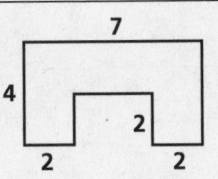

9. _____

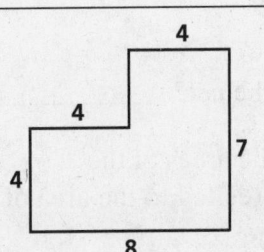

Find the area of each circle in terms of π.

10. _____

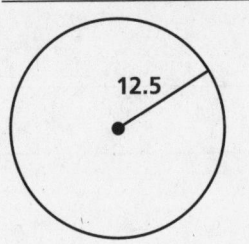

11. _____

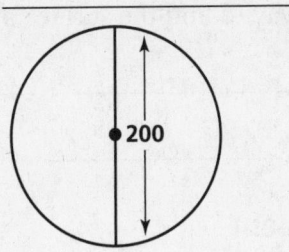

12. Find the perimeter of $\triangle PQR$ with vertices $P(-2, 9)$, $Q(7, -3)$, and $R(-2, -3)$.

13. The circumference of a circle is 26π. Find the diameter and the radius.

1-9 • Guided Problem Solving

GPS **Student Page 66, Exercise 51**

The surface area of a three-dimensional figure is the sum of the areas of all of its surfaces. You can find the surface area by finding the area of a net for the figure.

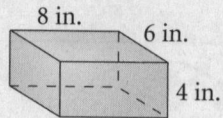

  a. Draw a net for the solid shown. Label the dimensions.
  b. What is the area of the net? What is the surface area of the solid?

Read and Understand

  1. How many surfaces does the solid figure have? _____

  2. What is a net? _____

Plan and Solve

  3. What kind of figures are the sides of the solid? _____

  4. Draw a net for the solid. Label all the dimensions.

  5. What is the area of the net? _____

  6. How is the total of the areas of the
    surfaces of the solid related to the area of the net?_____

  7. What is the surface area of the solid? _____

Look Back and Check

  8. Describe another way to find the surface area.

    _____

    _____

Solve Another Problem

  9. Find the surface area of a rectangular solid if all the dimensions are 7 in.

    _____

Guided Problem Solving

1A: Graphic Organizer

For use before Lesson 1-1

Study Skill Always write down your assignments. Do not rely on your memory to recall all assignments from all your classes.

Write your answers.

1. What is the chapter title? _____

2. Find the Table of Contents page for this chapter at the front of the book. Name four topics you will study in this chapter.

   _____   _____

   _____   _____

3. Complete the graphic organizer as you work through the chapter.
   1. Write the title of the chapter in the center oval.
   2. When you begin a lesson, write the name of the lesson in a rectangle.
   3. When you complete that lesson, write a skill or key concept from that lesson in the outer oval linked to that rectangle.
   Continue with steps 2 and 3 clockwise around the graphic organizer.

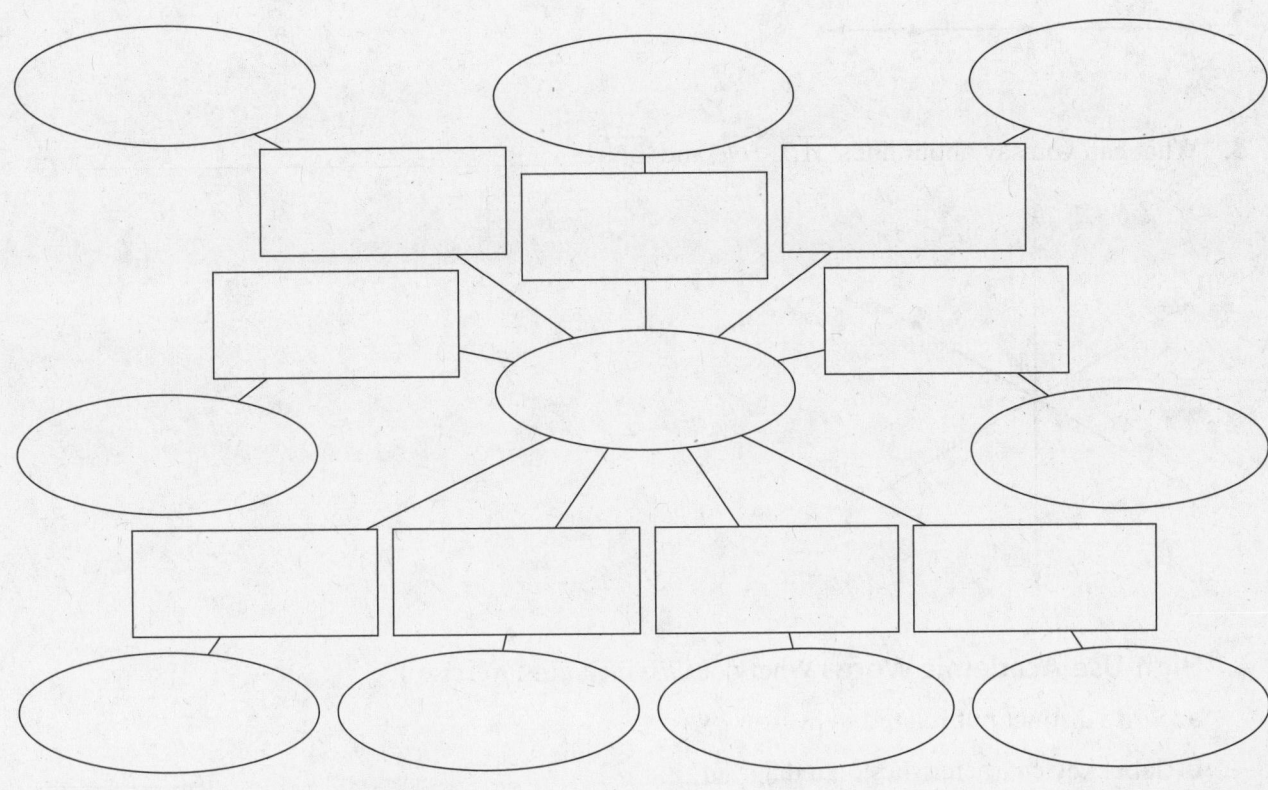

Name_____ Class_____ Date_____

1B: Reading Comprehension

For use after Lesson 1-8

Study Skill One key skill in the study of geometry is reading and interpreting diagrams. These diagrams will include points, lines, planes, angles, triangles, and other figures. You will often be asked to read and interpret mathematical relationships from these diagrams.

1. The diagram suggests many mathematical relationships among lines, segments, angles, etc. List at least seven mathematical statements that can be made by reading the diagram and interpreting the diagram.

_____

_____

_____

_____

_____

_____

_____

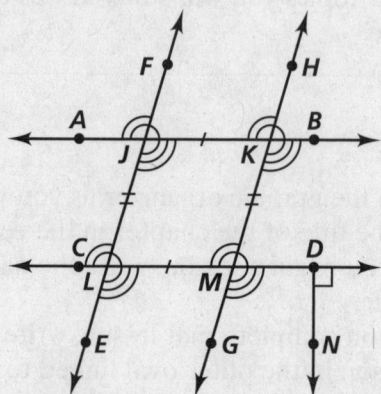

2. What can you say about the points in this diagram? _____

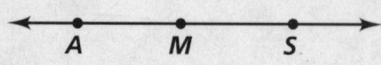

3. What can you say about lines $\overleftrightarrow{AB}$, $\overrightarrow{HI}$, and $\overleftrightarrow{LN}$? _____

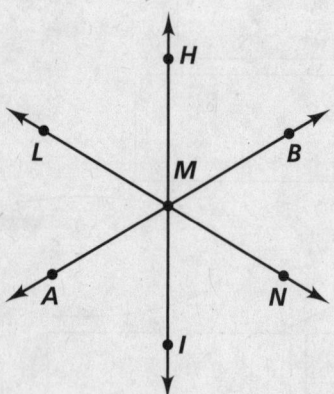

4. **High-Use Academic Words** What does *list* mean in Exercise 1?

   a. write distinct but related items row by row

   b. label key characteristics on a diagram

1C: Reading/Writing Math Symbols For use after Lesson 1-4

Study Skill When you take good notes in class, you must use the appropriate mathematical symbols. Some of the symbols you will use in geometry are segment, line, ray, angle, triangle, parallel, perpendicular, etc. Many of these symbols are very similar to others, so it is important that you write symbols clearly enough for you to understand when you review your notes at a later time.

Explain the meaning of each math expression or statement.

1. $\overleftrightarrow{BC} \parallel \overleftrightarrow{MN}$ _____

2. $\overleftrightarrow{CD}$ _____

3. $\overline{GH}$ _____

4. $\overrightarrow{AB}$ _____

5. $XY > ST$ _____

Write each statement using math symbols.

6. Segment MN and segment XY are equal in length. _____

7. The length of segment GH is twice the length of segment KL. _____

8. Segment ST is perpendicular to segment UV. _____

9. A plane containing points A, B, and C is parallel to a plane containing points X, Y, and Z. _____

10. Segment AB is parallel to segment DE. _____

1D: Visual Vocabulary Practice

For use after Lesson 1-6

Study Skill The Glossary contains the key vocabulary for this course.

Concept List

congruent sides	foundation drawing	isometric drawing
opposite rays	parallel planes	perpendicular lines
right angle	Segment Addition Postulate	supplementary angles

**Write the concept that best describes each exercise.
Choose from the concept list above.**

1. 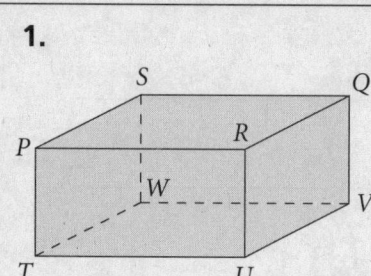 $PSQR \parallel TWVU$ _____	**2.**  $AB + BC = AC$ _____	**3.** $m\angle ABC + m\angle DBC = 180$ _____
4. 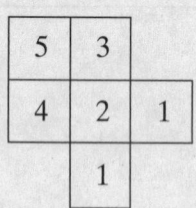 $\overrightarrow{RQ}$ and $\overrightarrow{RS}$ _____	**5.** 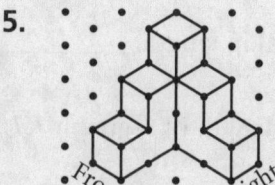 _____	**6.** $\overleftrightarrow{AB} \perp \overleftrightarrow{CD}$ _____
7.	5	3		4	2	1			1		_____	**8.** 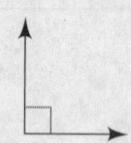 _____	**9.** 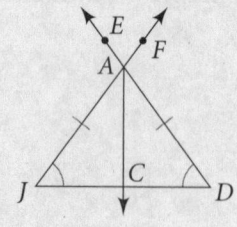 $\overline{AJ} \cong \overline{AD}$ _____

Name ____________________ Class ____________ Date ____________

1E: Vocabulary Check

For use after Lesson 1-5

Study Skill Strengthen your vocabulary. Use these pages and add cues and summaries by applying the Cornell Notetaking style.

Write the definition for each word at the right. To check your work, fold the paper back along the dotted line to see the correct answers.

____________________	Net
____________________	Conjecture
____________________	Collinear points
____________________	Midpoint
____________________	Postulate

Name_____ Class_____ Date_____

1E: Vocabulary Check (continued)   For use after Lesson 1-5

Write the vocabulary word for each definition. To check your work, fold the
paper forward along the dotted line to see the correct answers.

A two-dimensional pattern
that you can fold to form
a three-dimensional figure.   _____

A conclusion reached
using inductive reasoning.   _____

Points that lie on the
same line.   _____

A point that divides a line
segment into two
congruent segments.   _____

An accepted statement
of fact.   _____

1F: Vocabulary Review Puzzle

For use with Chapter Review

Study Skill When you have to identify words in a word search, read the list of words carefully and completely so you can find the words in the puzzle. Remember to cross out words as you find them.

Complete the word search.

acute angle   congruent   conjecture
collinear   counterexample   inductive reasoning
construction   midpoint   obtuse angle
parallel   perpendicular   right angle
segment   skew lines   straight angle

```
C O L L I N E A R P P D C L Z J P S
Y J E Z C C C E O R H L O E G E L K
C A F R T S V I L A B B N L I L A E
A O R E U N N X W L T Z S L B G N W
I N N Y L T I Y Y U R G T A C N E L
F Q G G D P C O S C S B R R K A C I
E N I L R D M E P I D O U A X T F N
R V P V E U A A J D V K C P Y H U E
D I C V D N E H X N I I T X S G M S
L X S E G M E N T E O M I A V I X K
F L P L S D K V T P R C O F J R N E
B L E V D V J S S R R E N L W F Q H
G N I N O S A E R E V I T C U D N I
R O T C E S I B L P J A E N R U K R
S T R A I G H T A N G L E W U Q A P
E L G N A E T U C A W K M F B O Z N
T U B A R N K I W T K Q R U I V C F
```

Name _____ Class _____ Date _____

Practice 2-1

Conditional Statements

Show that each conditional is false by finding a counterexample.

1. If it is 12:00 noon, then the sun is shining. _____

2. If a number is divisible by 3, then it is odd. _____

Write the converse of each conditional.

3. If you drink milk, then you will be strong. _____

_____

4. If a rectangle has four sides the same length, then it is a square. _____

_____

Write the converse of each statement. If the converse is true, write *true;* **if it is not true, provide a counterexample.**

5. If $x - 4 = 22$, then $x = 26$. _____

6. If m^2 is positive, then m is positive. _____

7. If two lines have equal slopes, then the lines are parallel. _____

_____

Answer the following questions about the given quote.

"If you like to shop, then visit the Pigeon Forge outlets in Tennessee."

8. Identify the hypothesis and the conclusion. _____

9. Write the converse of the conditional. _____

_____

Answer the following questions about the billboard advertisement shown.

10. What does the billboard imply? _____

_____

11. Write the advertisement slogan as a conditional statement.

_____

12. Write the converse of the conditional statement from Exercise 11.

_____

Train **harder,**
run **faster**
with
SUSTAIN

L1 Practice

Geometry Lesson 2-1   **191**

2-1 • Guided Problem Solving

GPS **Student Page 84, Exercise 36**

Error Analysis Ellen claims that both this conditional and its converse are true.
If x is an integer divisible by 3, then x^2 is an integer divisible by 3.

  a. Write the converse of the conditional.

  b. Only one of the statements is true. Determine which statement is false
     and provide a counterexample to support your answer.

Read and Understand

  1. What is the hypothesis of Ellen's statement? _____

  2. What is the conclusion of Ellen's statement? _____

Plan and Solve

  3. Is it true that if x is an integer divisible by 3, then x^2 is an integer divisible by 3?_____

    Explain your reasoning. _____

  4. Write the converse of Ellen's statement. _____

  5. Which statement is false? Give a counterexample.

    _____

Look Back and Check

  6. Check the reasonableness of your answers. Is it possible to find a counterexample to prove that
    Ellen's original statement is false? _____

    Explain. _____

  7. Is it possible for the converse to be true if you can find a counterexample? Explain.

    _____

Solve Another Problem

  8. Write the converse of the following conditional statement.
    If $x = 4$, then $5x + 3 = 23$.
    Determine the truth value of the statement and its converse.

    _____

    _____

Practice 2-2

Each conditional statement is true. Consider each converse. If the converse is true, combine the statements and write them as a biconditional.

1. If two angles have the same measure, then they are congruent. _____

_____

2. If $n = 17$, then $|n| = 17$. _____

Write the two conditional statements that make up each biconditional.

3. A whole number is a multiple of 5 if and only if its last digit is either a 0 or a 5.

_____

4. Two lines are perpendicular if and only if they intersect to form four right angles.

_____

Explain why each of the following is not an acceptable definition.

5. An automobile is a motorized vehicle with four wheels. _____

6. Cricket is a game played on a large field with a ball and a bat. _____

7. A rectangle is a very pleasing shape with smooth sides and very rigid corners. _____

Some figures that are _piggles_ are shown below, as are some _nonpiggles_.

piggles

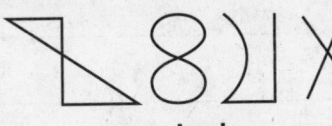

nonpiggles

Tell whether each of the following is a _piggle_.

8. ⬭

9. ⬭

10.

_____   _____   _____

2-2 • Guided Problem Solving

GPS **Student Page 91, Exercise 27**

Use the figures below to write a good definition of *linear pair*.

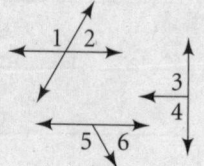

Linear pairs   Not linear pairs

Read and Understand

1. A good definition has several important components. List three of them.

   _____

Plan and Solve

2. It appears that a linear pair shares a common side. Which of the not-linear-pairs angles do not share a common side? _____

3. It also appears that a linear pair has a common vertex. Does this seem to be true for all of the not linear pairs? _____

4. The not-linear-pairs figure that contains angles 1 and 2 includes a common vertex and a common side. Why are they not a linear pair? _____

5. Based on these results, write a good definition of a *linear pair*.

   _____

   _____

Look Back and Check

6. Does your definition have the qualities of a good definition found in Steps 1–3? _____

7. Is your definition reasonable? Do the three given examples of linear pairs satisfy the definition?

   _____

Solve Another Problem

8. In the figure at right, there are six different pairs of angles. Which of them are linear pairs? _____

   Which of them are not linear pairs? _____

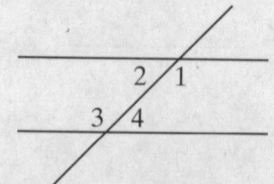

Practice 2-3

Use the Law of Detachment to draw a conclusion.

1. If the football team wins on Friday night, then practice is canceled for Monday.

   The football team won by 7 points on Friday night.

   _____

2. If a triangle has one 90° angle, then the triangle is a right triangle.

   In $\triangle DEF$, $m\angle E = 90$.

   _____

Use the Law of Syllogism to draw a conclusion.

3. If two lines are not parallel, then they intersect.

   If two lines intersect, then they intersect at a point.

   _____

4. If you vacation at the beach, then you must like the ocean.

   If you like the ocean, then you will like Florida.

   _____

If possible, use the Law of Detachment to draw a conclusion. If not possible, write *not possible*.

5. If a person lives in Omaha, then he or she lives in Nebraska.

   Tamika lives in Omaha.

   _____

6. If two figures are congruent, their areas are equal.

   The area of *ABCD* equals the area of *PQRS*.

   _____

Use the Law of Detachment and the Law of Syllogism to draw conclusions from the following statements.

7. If it is raining, the temperature is greater than 32°F.

   If the temperature is greater than 32°F, then it is not freezing outside.

   It is raining.

   _____

8. If you live in Providence, then you live in Rhode Island.

   If you live in Rhode Island, then you live in the smallest state in the United States.

   Shannon lives in Providence.

   _____

2-3 • Guided Problem Solving

GPS **Student Page 98, Exercise 32**

Reasoning Assume that the following statements are true.

If Anita goes to the concert, Beth will go.
If Beth goes to the concert, Aisha will go.
If Aisha goes to the concert, Ramon will go.

Only two of the four students went to the concert. Who were they?

Read and Understand

1. The Law of Detachment requires a _____ statement with a true

   _____.

2. Is it appropriate to use the Law of Detachment to solve this problem? _____.

Plan and Solve

3. In fact, it is appropriate to use the Law of Detachment several times.
   Let "Anita goes to the concert" be the true hypothesis, and apply the Law
   to the first conditional. What is the true conclusion?

   _____

4. Continue applying the Law, using your answer from part 3 as a new true
   hypothesis. If Anita went to the concert, of the four students, who went to
   the concert?

   _____

5. According to the problem statement, is this what happened? _____ Why?_____

6. Assume that Anita did not go but that Beth went to the concert. Under these assumptions,
   which of the four students went to the concert? Is this what happened?

   _____

7. Which two of the four students went to the concert? _____

Look Back and Check

8. Does your answer seem reasonable? _____ For instance,

   is it possible for another pair of these four students to go to the concert? _____

Solve Another Problem

9. Suppose only one student went to the concert. Which student was that? _____

Guided Problem Solving

Practice 2-4

Use the given property to complete each statement.

1. Symmetric Property of Equality

   If $MN = UT$, then _____.

2. Addition Property of Equality

   If $y - 15 = 36$, then _____.

3. Reflexive Property of Congruence

   $\overline{JL} \cong$ _____.

Give a reason for each step.

4. $0.25x + 2x + 12 = 39$

   $2.25x + 12 = 39$ _____

   $2.25x = 27$ _____

   $225x = 2700$ _____

   $x = 12$ _____

Name the property that justifies each statement.

5. If $m\angle G = 35$ and $m\angle S = 35$, then $m\angle G = m\angle S$. _____

6. If $10x + 6y = 14$ and $x = 2y$, then $10(2y) + 6y = 14$. _____

7. If $\overline{JK} \cong \overline{LM}$, then $\overline{LM} \cong \overline{JK}$. _____

Fill in the missing information. Solve for x, and justify each step.

8.

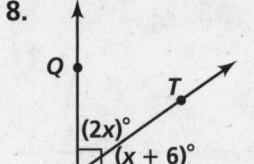

   $m\angle QWT + m\angle TWX = 90$

   $2x + (x + 6) =$ _____   _____

   _____ $+ 6 = 90$ _____

   _____ $=$ _____   _____

   $x =$ _____   _____

2-4 • Guided Problem Solving

GPS **Student Page 107, Exercise 29**

Algebra In the figure at the right, $m\angle GFI = 128$.

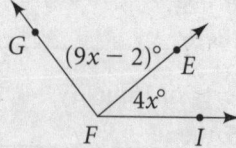

  a. Solve for x. Justify each step.
  b. Find $m\angle EFI$.

Read and Understand

1. You are given two angles in terms of x and the sum of the two angles.
What property or postulate can you use to solve this exercise?

_____

Plan and Solve

2. Justify each step in the solution by citing the appropriate property of equality.

  $4x + (9x - 2) = 128$ _____

  $13x - 2 = 128$ _____

  $13x = 130$ _____

  $x = 10$ _____

3. If $x = 10$, what is $m\angle EFI$? _____

Look Back and Check

4. Do your answers seem reasonable? _____

  Does $\angle EFI + \angle GFE$ equal 128? _____

Solve Another Problem

5. Change $m\angle EFI$ from $4x°$ to $x°$. Solve for x and $m\angle EFI$.

_____

Practice 2-5

Proving Angles Congruent

Find the values of the variables.

1. _____

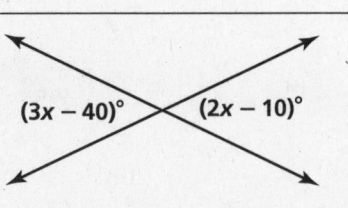

$(3x - 40)°$ $(2x - 10)°$

2. _____

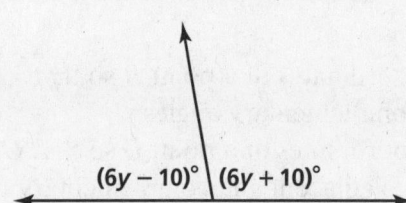

$(6y - 10)°$ $(6y + 10)°$

3. _____

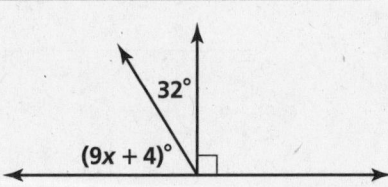

$32°$

$(9x + 4)°$

Find the measure of each angle.

4. $\angle A$ is three times as large as its supplement, $\angle B$. _____

5. $\angle A$ is one eighth as large as its complement, $\angle B$. _____

Write three conclusions that can be drawn from each figure.

6. _____

_____

_____

_____

P   *O*

125°

M   *N*

Q

7. _____

_____

_____

_____

B

A   *W*   *C*

D

2-5 • Guided Problem Solving

GPS **Student Page 114, Exercise 20**

Coordinate Geometry $\angle AOX$ contains points $A(1, 3)$, $O(0, 0)$, and $X(4, 0)$.

a. Find the coordinates of a point B so that $\angle BOA$ and $\angle AOX$ are adjacent complementary angles.

b. Find the coordinates of a point C so that $\overrightarrow{OC}$ is a side of a different angle that is adjacent and complementary to $\angle AOX$.

Read and Understand

1. If $\angle AOX$ and $\angle BOA$ are complementary, then $m\angle AOX + m\angle BOA =$ _____.

Plan and Solve

2. Graph the points $A(1, 3)$, $O(0, 0)$, and $X(4, 0)$. Draw $\angle AOX$.

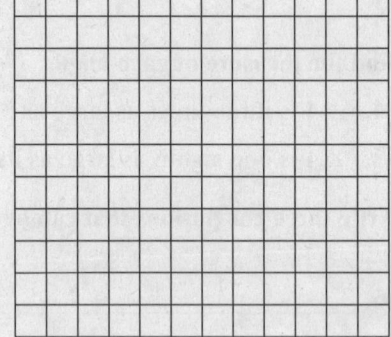

3. Where must a point B lie so that $\angle BOA$ and $\angle AOX$ are adjacent and complementary? _____

4. Give the coordinates of a point B. _____

5. If $\angle BOA$ and $\angle COX$ are both adjacent and complementary to $\angle AOX$, then $\angle COX \cong \angle BOA$. Draw $\angle COX$ such that $\angle COX \cong \angle BOA$.

6. How do $\angle COX$ and $\angle AOX$ relate? _____

7. What are the coordinates of a point C so that $\overrightarrow{OC}$ is adjacent and complementary to $\angle AOX$? _____

Look Back and Check

8. If $\angle AOX$ and $\angle BOA$ are complementary angles, what kind of angle is formed by their sum? _____

9. Do $\angle AOX$ and $\angle BOA$ from the angle in Step 8? _____ How can you tell? _____

Solve Another Problem

10. Find the coordinates of a point D so that $\angle DOA$ and $\angle AOX$ are adjacent supplementary angles. _____

2A: Graphic Organizer

For use before Lesson 2-1

Study Skill Keep notes as you work through each chapter to help you organize your thinking and to make it easier to review the material when you complete the chapter.

Write your answers.

1. What is the chapter title? _____

2. Find the Table of Contents page for this chapter at the front of the book. Name four topics you will study in this chapter.

   _____   _____

   _____   _____

3. Complete the graphic organizer as you work through the chapter.
   1. Write the title of the chapter in the center oval.
   2. When you begin a lesson, write the name of the lesson in a rectangle.
   3. When you complete that lesson, write a skill or key concept from that lesson in the outer oval linked to that rectangle.
   Continue with steps 2 and 3 clockwise around the graphic organizer.

Name_____ Class_____ Date_____

2B: Reading Comprehension

Study Skill When a diagram is shown, read the information about the diagram with care. Look at the diagram to decide what conclusions can be drawn from the figure.

Read the problem and follow along with the thought process and the written steps to solve the problem. Check your understanding by completing the exercises at the bottom of the page.

Find the measure of the obtuse angle in the figure at the right. Justify each step.

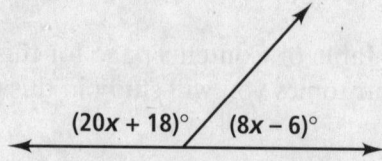

$(20x + 18)°$ $(8x - 6)°$

Thought Process	Written Steps	
What information am I given?	The two angles form a straight angle.	
The two angles are supplementary. The Angle Addition Postulate can be used to write an equation.	$20x + 18 + 8x - 6 = 180$	Angle Addition Postulate
The equation can be solved for x.	$28x + 12 = 180$ $28x = 168$ $x = 6$	Simplify. Subtraction Property of Equality Division Property of Equality
Does $x = 6$ give a sum of 180 for the two angles?	$20(6) + 18 + 8(6) - 6 = 180$ $120 + 18 + 48 - 6 = 180$ $180 = 180$	Substitution. Simplify.
Which angle is the obtuse angle? The diagram shows $20x + 18$ as the obtuse angle. I know $x = 6$, so I will substitute to find the measure.	$20(6) + 18 = 138$	
Now, I write my final answer.	The measure of the obtuse angle is 138°.	

1. In the example above, what is the measure of the acute angle?

2. Angle *NRO* is a right angle. *T* is a point in the interior of $\angle NRO$. $m\angle NRT = 11x - 3$ and $m\angle TRO = 7x + 3$. Find the measure of the smaller angle.

3. **High-Use Academic Words** What does *justify* mean in the direction line to the example?

   a. show

   b. give a reason for

Vocabulary and Study Skills

2C: Reading/Writing Math Symbols

For use after Lesson 2-2

Vocabulary and Study Skills

Study Skill When you take notes in any subject, it helps if you learn to use abbreviations and symbols. In geometry there are many symbols that are commonly used to abbreviate the names of points, lines, planes, angles, and other figures.

Explain the meaning of each math statement.

1. $\overline{MN} \cong \overline{PQ}$ _____

2. $p \rightarrow q$ _____

3. $MN = PQ$ _____

4. $\angle XQV \cong \angle RDC$ _____

5. $q \rightarrow p$ _____

6. $m\angle XQV = m\angle RDC$ _____

7. $p \leftrightarrow q$ _____

Write each statement using math symbols.

8. b is true if a is true. _____

9. Segment AB is equal in length to segment MN. _____

10. The measures of angles XYZ and RPS are equal. _____

11. If b is true, then a is true. _____

12. Segment AB is congruent to segment MN. _____

13. a is true if and only if b is true. _____

14. Angle XYZ is congruent to angle RPS. _____

2D: Visual Vocabulary Practice

For use after Lesson 2-4

Study Skill Mathematics builds on itself, so build a strong foundation. The vocabulary is a key part of the foundation.

Concept List

biconditional	conclusion	Distributive Property
good definition	hypothesis	Law of Detachment
Law of Syllogism	Reflexive Property	Symmetric Property

Write the concept that best describes each exercise.
Choose from the concept list above.

1. If it snows, I won't go skiing. It is snowing. So, I won't go skiing.	**2.** p in $p \rightarrow q$	**3.** $2(x + 5) = 2x + 2(5)$
4. $m\angle ABC = m\angle ABC$	**5.** If $p \rightarrow q$ and $q \rightarrow r$ are true, then $p \rightarrow r$ is true.	**6.** Two angles are complementary if and only if the sum of their measures is 90.
7. q in $p \rightarrow q$	**8.** clearly understood, precise, and reversible	**9.** If $-3 = y$, then $y = -3$.

2E: Vocabulary Check

Study Skill Strengthen your vocabulary. Use these pages and add cues and summaries by applying the Cornell Notetaking style.

Write the definition for each word at the right. To check your work, fold the paper back along the dotted line to see the correct answers.

_____

_____

_____

Truth value

_____

_____

Hypothesis

_____

_____

_____

Biconditional

_____

_____

_____

Conclusion

_____

_____

Conditional

Name ______________________ Class ______________ Date ______________

2E: Vocabulary Check (continued)

For use after Lesson 2-3

Write the vocabulary word for each definition. To check your work, fold the paper forward along the dotted line to see the correct answers.

"True" or "false" according to whether the statement is true or false, respectively. ______________________

The part that follows *if* in an *if-then* statement. ______________________

The combination of a conditional statement and its converse; it contains the words "if and only if." ______________________

The part of an *if-then* statement that follows *then*. ______________________

An *if-then* statement. ______________________

Name _____ Class _____ Date _____

2F: Vocabulary Review Puzzle   For use with the Chapter Review

Study Skill One of the hardest things about reading a mathematics textbook is the new vocabulary you will encounter. Many times you will encounter numerous new terms in just one section. Mathematics is a series of concepts you need to learn and remember. It is important to learn the definitions of new terms as soon as they are introduced. Read aloud or recite the new terms as you read them. Reciting a rule, definition, or formula can help you to remember and recall it.

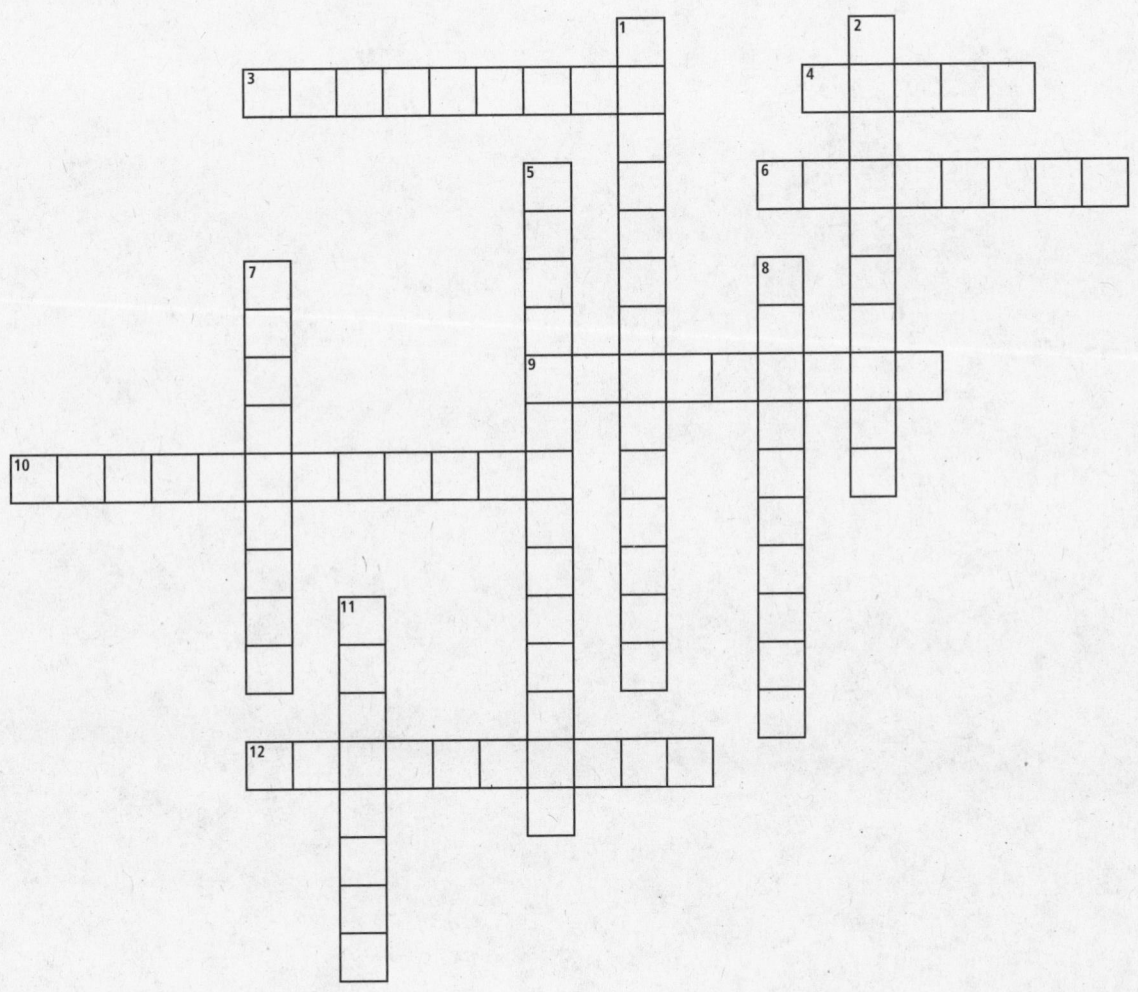

ACROSS	**DOWN**
3. Statement accepted as true	**1.** Two nonadjacent angles formed by two intersecting lines.
4. Has no size and dimension, merely position	**2.** One of the numbers that describe the position of a point on a plane.
6. Two lines that lie in the same plane and are always the same distance apart	**5.** Two coplanar angles with a common side, a common vertex, and no common interior points
9. Points that lie on the same line	**7.** Two segments that have the same length
10. Using a straightedge and compass to make geometric figures	**8.** Describes a conclusion reached from observations
12. *If* part of a conditional statement	**11.** The point of a segment that divides the segment into two congruent segments

Practice 3-1

Classify each pair of angles as *alternate interior angles, same-side interior angles,* or *corresponding angles.*

1._____

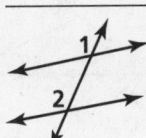

2._____

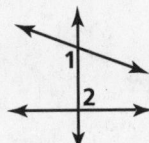

3._____

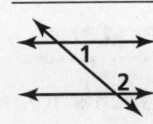

Use the figure on the right to answer Exercises 4–6.

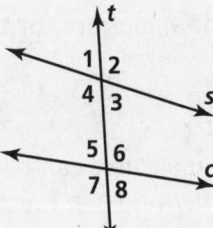

4. Name two pairs of corresponding angles formed by the transversal *t* and lines *s* and *c*. _____

5. Name two pairs of alternate interior angles formed by the transversal *t* and lines *s* and *c*. _____

6. Name two pairs of same-side interior angles formed by the transversal *t* and lines *s* and *c*. _____

Find $m\angle 1$ and then $m\angle 2$. Justify each answer.

7._____

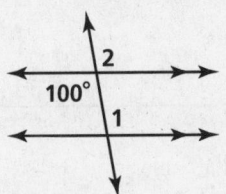

8._____

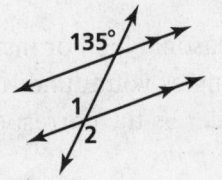

Algebra **Find the value of *x*. Then find the measure of each angle.**

9._____

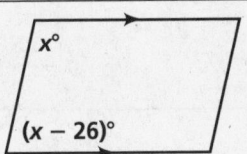

10._____

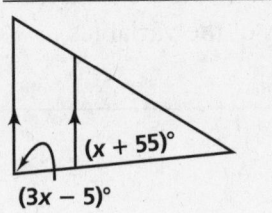

Name _____ Class _____ Date _____

3-1 • Guided Problem Solving

GPS **Student Page 132, Exercise 24**

Algebra Find the values of the variables.

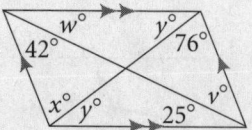

Read and Understand

1. Which line segments are parallel?

   _____

2. Which line segments are transversals? _____

3. What types of angles are formed by parallel lines and transversals? _____

Plan and Solve

4. Which angle measures can be found directly using known
   angles and Theorem 3-1, the Alternate Interior Angles Theorem? _____
   Give those angle measures.

   _____

5. Find the remaining angle measure(s) using
   Theorem 3-2, the Same-Side Interior Angles Theorem. _____

Look Back and Check

6. Do your answers seem reasonable? For instance,
   list the measures of the angles you found from smallest to largest. _____
   Are these in the same order as the corresponding angles in the illustration?

   _____

Solve Another Problem

7. Suppose that the 25 in the figure is instead 35, and the 76 is instead 57.
   Again find the values of the variables.

   _____

Guided Problem Solving

Practice 3-2

Which lines or segments are parallel? Justify your answer with a theorem or postulate.

1. _____

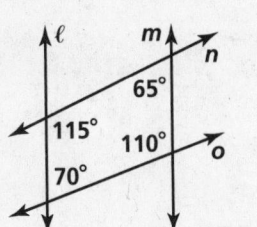

2. _____

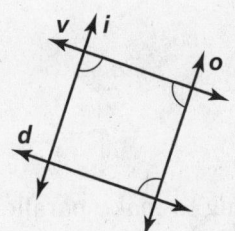

3. _____

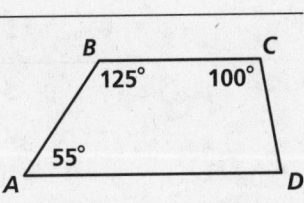

4. _____

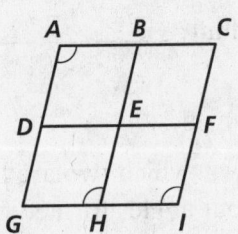

Algebra **Find the value of *x* for which *a* ∥ *t*.**

5. _____

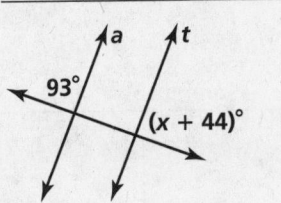

6. _____

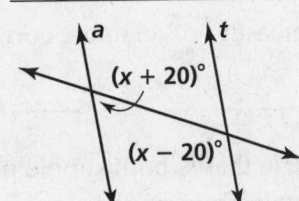

7. _____

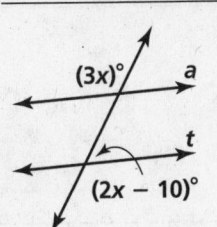

8. _____

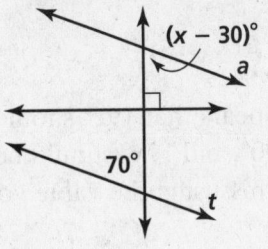

3-2 • Guided Problem Solving

GPS **Student Page 138, Exercise 24**

Find the value of x for which $\ell \parallel m$.

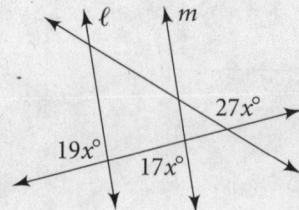

Read and Understand

1. Which lines are you trying to make parallel? _____

2. In relation to lines ℓ and m, what do you call the other two lines? _____

3. What are you asked to find? _____

Plan and Solve

4. Of the three angles shown, which two are likely to be
   related by theorems about angles formed by parallel
   lines and a transversal, given that you want to have $\ell \parallel m$? _____

5. What must be the sum of the two angles in Step 4?

   _____

6. What must be the measure of an angle corresponding to the $17x°$ angle?

   _____

7. Since there is an angle that is both supplementary to
   the $19x°$ angle and corresponding to the $17x°$ angle,
   what can be said about the quantities in Steps 5 and 6? _____

8. Find x. _____

Look Back and Check

9. From the figure, it appears that $19x°$ should be
   a little greater than 90°, and $17x°$ should be a little
   less than 90°. Verify this, using the value you found for x. _____

Solve Another Problem

10. Repeat the above steps to find x, using $11x°$ instead of $17x°$ for the one angle. _____

Name _____ Class _____ Date _____

Practice 3-3

Parallel and Perpendicular Lines

· ·

In a soon-to-be-built town, all streets will be designated either as avenues or as boulevards. The avenues will all be parallel to one another, the boulevards will all be parallel to one another, and in the middle of town, Center City Boulevard will intersect Founders Avenue at right angles. Is each of the following statements true or false? Justify your answer in each case.

1. Every avenue will be perpendicular to every boulevard. _____

   _____

2. All city blocks will be rectangular. _____

   _____

3. All city blocks will be bordered on one side by either
   Center City Boulevard or Founders Avenue. _____

a, *b*, *c*, *d*, and *e* **are distinct lines in the same plane. For each combination of relationships between** *a* **and** *b*, *b* **and** *c*, *c* **and** *d*, **and** *d* **and** *e*, **how are** *a* **and** *e* **related?**

4. $a \parallel b, b \parallel c, c \perp d, d \parallel e$ _____

5. $a \perp b, b \parallel c, c \parallel d, d \perp e$ _____

6. $a \parallel b, b \parallel c, c \perp d, d \perp e$ _____

7. $a \perp b, b \perp c, c \perp d, d \perp e$ _____

8. Suppose you are given information about a sequence of lines,
   ℓ_1 through ℓ_n, in the following form:

   $$\ell_1 \square \ell_2, \ell_2 \square \ell_3, \ell_3 \square \ell_4, \ldots, \ell_{n-2} \square \ell_{n-1}, \text{ and } \ell_{n-1} \square \ell_n,$$

   where each $\square$ is either a $\parallel$ or a $\perp$. Now you are asked whether
   $\ell_1 \parallel \ell_n$ or $\ell_1 \perp \ell_n$. How can you decide by simply counting the
   number of $\perp$ statements in the given information?

   _____

   _____

   _____

   _____

   _____

· ·

3-3 • Guided Problem Solving

GPS **Student Page 143, Exercise 11**

Prove Theorem 3-11: In a plane, if a line is perpendicular to one
of two parallel lines, then it is also perpendicular to the other.

Given: In a plane, $a \perp b$, and $b \parallel c$.

Prove: $a \perp c$

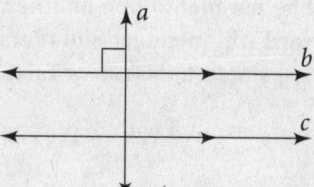

Read and Understand

1. Choose any pair of adjacent angles formed by the
   intersection of a and b. What do we call this pair? _____

2. If one of the two angles in Step 1 is
   a right angle, what must the other angle be? _____

Plan and Solve

3. Which postulates and/or theorems from
   Lesson 3-1 would enable you to complete the proof? _____

4. Choose any angle formed by the intersection of
   a and b. Since $a \perp b$ is given, the measure of this angle is _____.

5. Locate the corresponding angle formed by the intersection
   of a and c. How is this angle related to the angle in Step 4? _____

   Why is this so? _____

6. The measure of this angle is _____.

7. Therefore, how are lines a and c related? _____.

Look Back and Check

8. Is the result true for any line parallel to b or true only for the given line c?

   _____

Solve Another Problem

9. Is it also true that if a transversal is not perpendicular to one of two
   parallel lines, then it is not perpendicular to the other one either? Explain. _____

   _____

Name _____ Class _____ Date _____

Practice 3-4

Parallel Lines and the Triangle Angle-Sum Theorem

Find the value of each variable.

1. _____

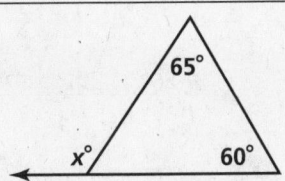

2. _____

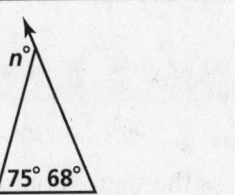

3. _____

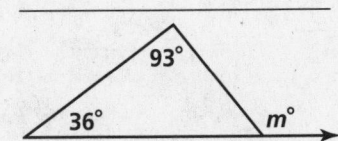

4. _____

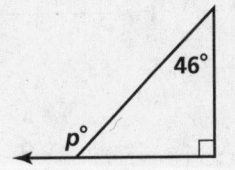

5.

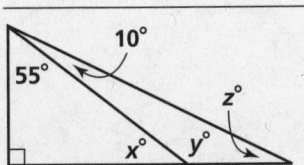

6.

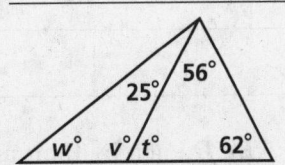

Find the measure of each numbered angle.

7. _____

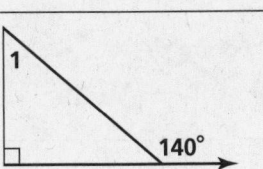

8. _____

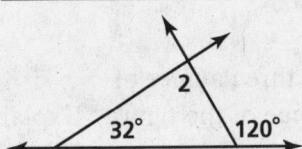

9. _____

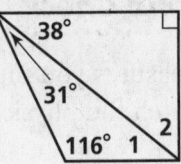

Use a protractor and a centimeter ruler to measure the angles and the sides of each triangle. Classify each triangle by its angles and sides.

10. _____

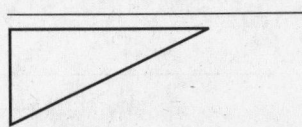

11. _____

12. _____

3-4 • Guided Problem Solving

GPS Student Page 151, Exercise 25

Algebra Find the values of the variables and then the measures of the angles. Classify each triangle in the figure by its angles.

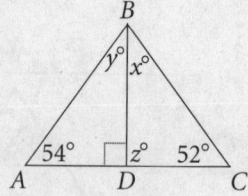

Read and Understand

1. How many triangles does the figure contain? _____

2. The sum of the measures in any triangle is _____.

3. What kind of triangle is $\triangle ABD$? _____

Plan and Solve

4. What is the value of z? _____ Explain. _____

5. What postulate or theorem can be used to find x and y,
   now that the other angles in $\triangle ABD$ and $\triangle CBD$ are known? _____

6. Find x. _____

7. Find y. _____

8. Classify $\triangle ABD$ and $\triangle BCD$ each by their angles. _____

9. Add x and y to find $m\angle ABC$. _____

10. Classify $\triangle ABC$ by its angles. _____

Look Back and Check

11. Do the measures you found for the three angles of
    $\triangle ABC$ match the physical appearance of the figure? Explain. _____

    _____

Solve Another Problem

12. Suppose that $m\angle ABD$ and $m\angle CBD$ are both $y°$.
    What other angle in the figure would have to change
    in order for the triangles to each have angle sum of 180°? _____

Practice 3-5

The Polygon Angle-Sum Theorems

Find the values of the variables for each polygon. Each is a regular polygon.

1. $x =$ _____, $y =$ _____

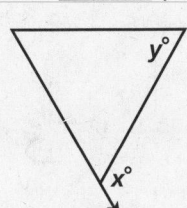

2. $n =$ _____

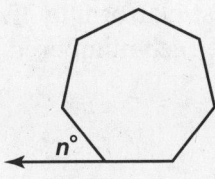

3. $a =$ _____, $b =$ _____

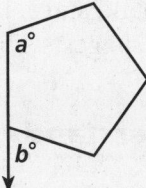

Find the missing angle measures.

4. _____

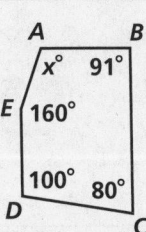

5. _____

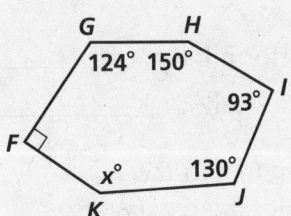

6. _____

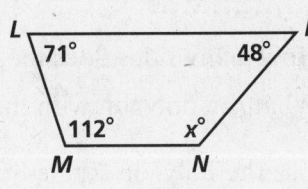

For a regular 12-sided polygon, find each of the following.

7. the measure of an exterior angle _____

8. the measure of an interior angle _____

The measure of an interior angle of a regular polygon is given. Find the number of sides.

9. 120 _____

10. 108 _____

Identify each item in Exercises 11–14 in the figure.

11. quadrilateral _____

12. exterior angle _____

13. pair of supplementary angles _____

14. pentagon _____

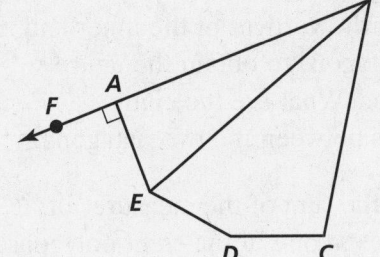

3-5 • Guided Problem Solving

GPS **Student Page 162, Exercise 37**

Stage Design The diagram at the right shows platforms constructed for a theater-in-the-round stage. Describe the largest platform by the type of regular polygon it suggests. Find the measure of each numbered angle.

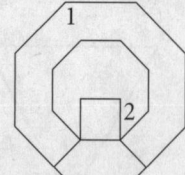

Read and Understand

1. What does the figure show? _____

2. What are you being asked to find? _____

Plan and Solve

3. How many sides does the largest platform have? _____

   What is a polygon with that many sides called? _____

4. Use the Polygon Angle-Sum Theorem to find the
   sum of the measures of the eight angles in an octagon. _____

5. In a regular octagon, each of the eight
   angles has the same measure. What is $m\angle 1$? _____

6. The measure of angle 1 equals the sum of the measures of
   angle 2 and the adjacent angle inside the square. What is $m\angle 2$? _____

Look Back and Check

7. In the figure, $\angle 1$ appears to be an obtuse angle
   and $\angle 2$ is acute. Do your answers agree with this? _____

Solve Another Problem

8. Connect the vertices of the inner and
   outer octagons to obtain the figure
   illustrated. What are the eight
   polygons between the two octagons? _____

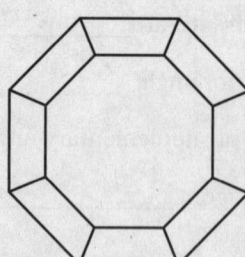

9. What is the sum of the measures of
   the angles in one of the eight polygons? _____

Practice 3-6

Write an equation of the line with the given slope that contains the given point.

1. $F(3, -6)$, slope $\frac{1}{3}$ _____

2. $Q(5, 2)$, slope -2 _____

3. $R(15, 10)$, slope $\frac{4}{5}$ _____

4. $D(1, -9)$, slope 4 _____

Graph each line.

5. $y = -2x$

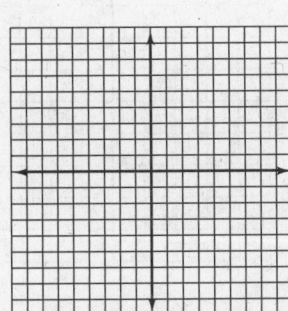

6. $y = 5x + 4$

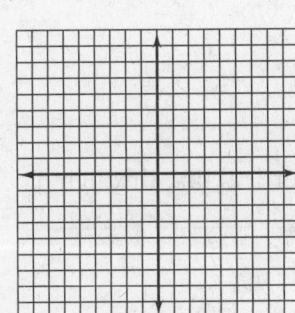

7. $2y = 8x - 2$

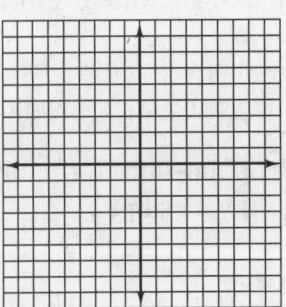

Write an equation of the line containing the given points.

8. $P(-1, 3)$, $Q(0, 4)$ _____

9. $S(10, 2)$, $T(2, -2)$ _____

10. $D(7, -4)$, $E(-5, 2)$ _____

11. $M(8, -3)$, $N(7, 3)$ _____

Write equations for (a) the horizontal line and (b) the vertical line that contain the given point.

12. $Z(2, -11)$ _____

13. $D(0, 2)$ _____

Graph each line using intercepts.

14. $2x + 4y = -4$

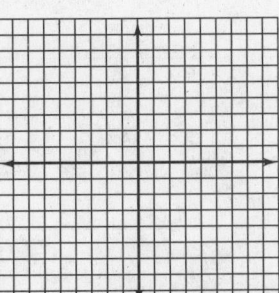

15. $3x + 3y = 18$

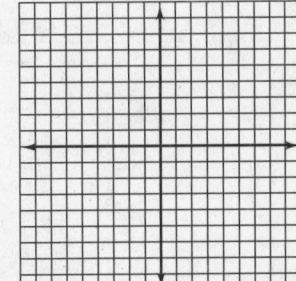

16. $2x - 2y = 8$

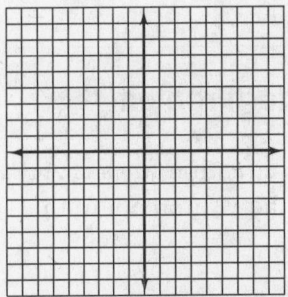

3-6 • Guided Problem Solving

GPS **Student Page 170, Exercise 56**

The vertices of a triangle are $A(0, 0)$, $B(2, 5)$, $C(4, 0)$.

a. Write an equation for the line through A and B.
b. Write an equation for the line through B and C.
c. Compare the slopes and y-intercepts of the two lines.

Read and Understand

1. Graph the triangle whose vertices are given.

2. What is the slope m of the line through the points (x_1, y_1) and (x_2, y_2)? _____

3. What is the point-slope form for a nonvertical line through point (x_1, y_1) with slope m? _____

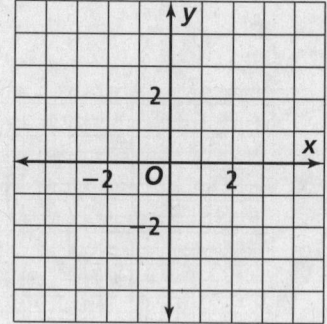

Plan and Solve

4. What is the slope of line $\overleftrightarrow{AB}$? Of line $\overleftrightarrow{BC}$? What do you notice? _____

_____

5. Write the equation for line $\overleftrightarrow{AB}$ in point-slope form, then convert it to slope-intercept form.

_____

6. Write the equation for line $\overleftrightarrow{BC}$, first in point-slope form and then in slope-intercept form.

_____

7. What is the y-intercept of each line? _____

Look Back and Check

8. Do the results match the appearance of $\triangle ABC$ as graphed in Step 1? Explain.

_____

Solve Another Problem

9. Write the equation for line $\overleftrightarrow{AC}$ and compare the y-intercept to that of line $\overleftrightarrow{AB}$. _____

_____

Practice 3-7

Slopes of Parallel and Perpendicular Lines

Are the lines parallel, perpendicular, or neither? Explain.

1. _____

$y = 3x - 2$

$y = \frac{1}{3}x + 2$

2. _____

$y = \frac{1}{2}x + 1$

$-4y = 8x + 3$

3. _____

$\frac{2}{3}x + y = 4$

$y = -\frac{2}{3}x + 8$

4. _____

$y = 2$

$x = 0$

Are lines l_1 and l_2 parallel, perpendicular, or neither? Explain.

5. _____

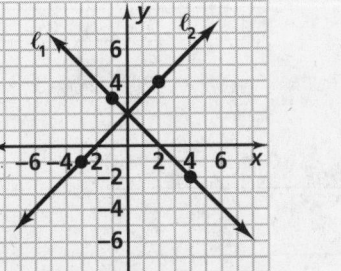

6. _____

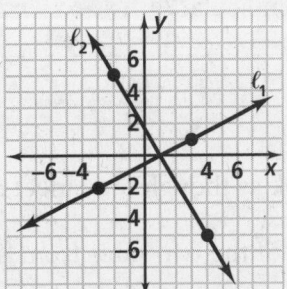

7. _____

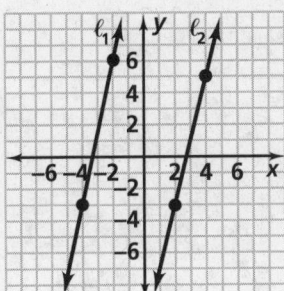

8. _____

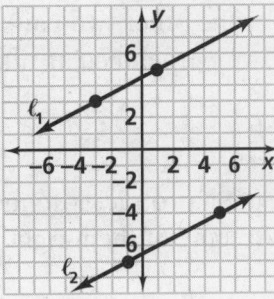

Write an equation for the line perpendicular to $\overleftrightarrow{XY}$ that contains point Z.

9. $\overleftrightarrow{XY}: 3x + 2y = -6, Z(3, 2)$ _____

Write an equation for the line parallel to $\overleftrightarrow{XY}$ that contains point Z.

10. $\overleftrightarrow{XY}: x = \frac{1}{2}y + 1, Z(1, -2)$ _____

3-7 • Guided Problem Solving

GPS **Student Page 179, Exercise 36**

Use slope to determine whether a triangle with
vertices $G(3, 2)$, $H(8, 5)$, and $K(0, 10)$ is a right triangle.
Explain.

Read and Understand

1. Graph the triangle whose vertices are given.

2. What is the most important feature of a right triangle?
_____

3. Given two lines with slopes m_1 and m_2, how can we tell
if the lines are perpendicular?
_____

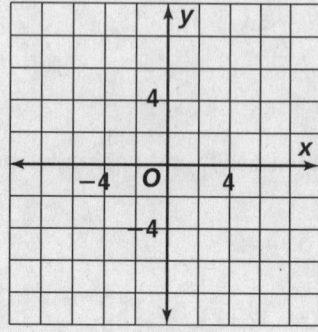

Plan and Solve

4. Which two sides look as though they meet at right angles? _____

5. What are the slopes of the two sides from Step 4? _____

6. Find the product of the two slopes from Step 5. Does it equal -1? _____
Interpret the result. _____

7. Repeat the analysis for the other two pairs of sides, to determine
whether $\triangle GHK$ has two perpendicular sides. Is it a right triangle? _____

Look Back and Check

8. To check your result, use a protractor to measure
the angles in Step 1. Are any of them right angles? _____

9. Which is the largest angle? _____ What is its measure? _____

Solve Another Problem

10. Explain why a triangle with vertices $L(4, 1)$, $M(6, 8)$, $N(-3, 3)$ is a right triangle.

_____

_____

Practice 3-8

Constructing Parallel and Perpendicular Lines

Construct a line perpendicular to line *l* through point *Q*.

1.

Construct a line perpendicular to line *l* at point *T*.

2.

Construct a line parallel to line *l* and through point *K*.

3.

For Exercises 4–6, use the segments at the right.

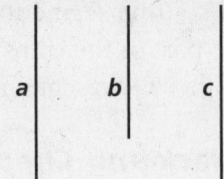

4. Construct a quadrilateral with one pair of parallel sides of lengths *a* and *b*.

5. Construct a square with side lengths of *b*.

6. Construct a right triangle with leg lengths of *a* and *c*.

Name _____ Class _____ Date _____

3-8 • Guided Problem Solving

Student Page 185, Exercise 21

a. Construct a quadrilateral with a pair of parallel sides of length c.

b. **Make a Conjecture** What appears to be true about the other pair of sides in the quadrilateral you constructed?

c. Use a protractor, a ruler, or both to check the conjecture you made in part (b).

c

Read and Understand

1. What are you given? _____

2. What are you asked to do? _____

Plan and Solve

3. Construct two parallel lines and a transversal, using a straightedge and a compass. Call the lines ℓ and m.

4. Set the compass to mark off a distance equal to the length c as given above.

5. With the compass, mark a point on line ℓ that lies a distance c from the intersection with the transversal. Do the same on line m, on the same side of the transversal.

6. Draw a line segment between the two marked points. You have now constructed the quadrilateral.

7. Look at the segment you drew in Step 6, and the segment opposite (the part of the transversal that lies between the parallel lines). Do those two segments appear congruent? Do they appear parallel? _____

Look Back and Check

8. Check your answers to Step 7 by measuring the length of each segment and by measuring a pair of alternate interior angles. _____

Solve Another Problem

9. Repeat Steps 3 through 6, but this time ignore the transversal and mark two segments of length c, one positioned arbitrarily on line ℓ and the other arbitrarily on line m. Connect adjacent ends of those two segments with two more segments. Are opposite sides of the resulting quadrilateral congruent and parallel? What is this type of figure called?

_____

Guided Problem Solving

3A: Graphic Organizer

For use before Lesson 3-1

Study Skill Before you start your new chapter, read the major headings and summaries. This will give you a good idea of what the entire chapter will be about.

Write your answers.

1. What is the chapter title? _____

2. Find the Table of Contents page for this chapter at the front of the book. Name four topics you will study in this chapter.

_____   _____

_____   _____

3. Complete the graphic organizer as you work through the chapter.
  1. Write the title of the chapter in the center oval.
  2. When you begin a lesson, write the name of the lesson in a rectangle.
  3. When you complete that lesson, write a skill or key concept from
     that lesson in the outer oval linked to that rectangle.
  Continue with steps 2 and 3 clockwise around the graphic organizer.

3B: Reading Comprehension

Study Skill Word problems require you to extract the necessary information. When you find values that may be important, write them on a separate sheet of paper. Cross out values that are not needed for solving the problem.

Read through the problem and answer the questions below.

The owners of a local bakery want to redesign their parking lot to accommodate more cars. The old and new designs are shown in the diagram. The parking lot is 50 ft by 70 ft. Black top costs $2 per square foot. The parking lot spaces are 20 ft deep and 10 ft wide. The paint used to stripe the stalls costs $1.50 per linear ft. A parking stall is defined to be the space between two lines.

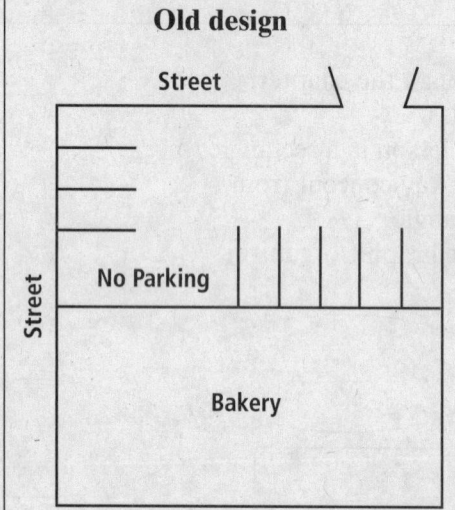

Old design

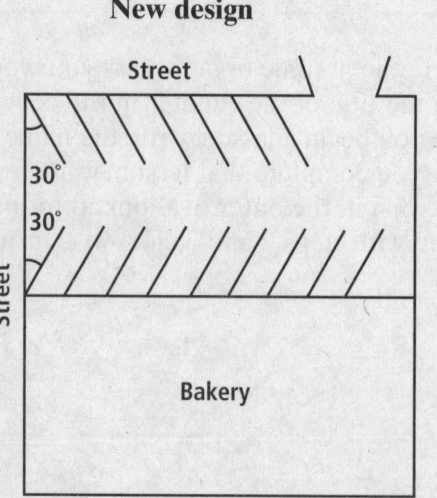

New design

1. How many parking spaces are in the new parking lot layout? _____

2. The new design increases the available parking by how many spaces? _____

3. If the parking stripes are parallel with each other in the new design, then the angles formed by the transversal and the stripes are _____ angles.

4. What is the cost of paving the entire lot? _____
   What is the cost of the stripes? _____

5. What quantity given in the problem is unnecessary for answering questions 1 through 4? _____

6. **High-Use Academic Words** What does *extract* mean in the Study Skill?

   a. fill in   **b.** pull out

3C: Reading/Writing Math Symbols

For use after Lesson 3-3

Vocabulary and Study Skills

Study Skill Often when you take notes, it helps to illustrate concepts with simple drawings. For example, if you write that line *XY* is parallel to line *ST*, make a quick sketch of two parallel lines with those labels.

Write each statement using math symbols.

1. Line *m* is perpendicular to line *n*. _____

2. Angle 1 is supplementary to angle 2. _____

3. Line *AB* is parallel to line *CD*. _____

4. Angle *MNP* is complementary to angle *MNQ*. _____

5. Angle 3 and angle *EFD* are congruent. _____

Explain the meaning of each math statement.

6. $l_1 \parallel l_2$ _____

7. $m\angle ABC = m\angle XYZ$ _____

8. $\overleftrightarrow{AB} \perp \overleftrightarrow{DF}$ _____

9. $m\angle ABC + m\angle ABD = 90°$ _____

10. $m\angle 2 = 90°$ _____

11. Use math symbols to write two math statements that describe the figure.

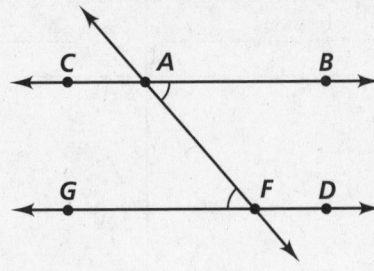

3D: Visual Vocabulary Practice
High-Use Academic Words

For use after Lesson 3-6

....

Study Skill If a word is not in the Glossary, use a dictionary to find its meaning.

Concept List

approximate	compare	conclusion
contradiction	describe	formula
measure	pattern	property

Write the concept that best describes each exercise. Choose from the concept list above.

1. 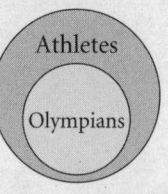 All Olympians are athletes. _____	**2.** If $a = b$ and $b = c$, then $a = c$. _____	**3.** 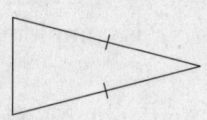 acute isosceles triangle _____
4. $d = \sqrt{(x_2 - x_1)^2 + (y_2 - y_1)^2}$ _____	**5.** 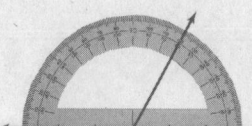 _____	**6.** $\frac{22}{7}$ for π _____
7. 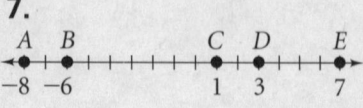 $BD > CD$ _____	**8.** $1 = 4$ _____	**9.**  A B C D _____

....

Name ____________________ Class ____________ Date ____________

3E: Vocabulary Check

For use after Lesson 3-4

Study Skill Strengthen your vocabulary. Use these pages and add cues and summaries by applying the Cornell Notetaking style.

Write the definition for each word at the right. To check your work, fold the paper back along the dotted line to see the correct answers.

____________________ ____________________ ____________________	Transversal
____________________ ____________________ ____________________	Alternate interior angles
____________________ ____________________ ____________________	Same-side interior angles
____________________ ____________________ ____________________	Corresponding angles
____________________ ____________________ ____________________	Flow proof

Vocabulary and Study Skills

3E: Vocabulary Check (continued)

Write the vocabulary word for each definition. To check your work, fold the paper forward along the dotted line to see the correct answers.

A line that intersects two coplanar lines in two points.

_____

Nonadjacent interior angles that lie on opposite sides of the transversal.

_____

Interior angles that lie on the same side of a transversal between two lines.

_____

Angles that lie on the same side of a transversal between two lines, in corresponding positions.

_____

A convincing argument that uses deductive reasoning, in which arrows show the logical connections between the statements.

_____

3F: Vocabulary Review

For use with Chapter Review

Study Skill You can use mnemonic devices to help you remember new vocabulary words. A mnemonic device is a phrase that reminds you of the meaning of a word.

Match the key concept in Column A with its description in Column B by drawing a line between them.

Column A

1.	acute angle
2.	corresponding angles
3.	equilateral
4.	exterior angle
5.	isosceles
6.	standard form

Column B

A.	at least two sides congruent
B.	angle formed by a side of a polygon and an extension of an adjacent side
C.	an angle whose measure is between 0° and 90°
D.	all sides congruent
E.	angles that are in a similar position on the same side of the transversal
F.	$7x + 5y = 35$

Match the key concept in Column C with its description in Column D by drawing a line between them.

Column C

7.	regular polygon
8.	scalene
9.	transversal
10.	same-side interior angles
11.	slope-intercept form
12.	perpendicular

Column D

G.	two angles that must be supplementary if the lines are parallel
H.	no sides congruent
I.	$y = 7x + 9$
J.	two lines that intersect at 90°
K.	a figure that is equiangular and equilateral
L.	a line that intersects two coplanar lines at two distinct points

Practice 4-1

Each pair of polygons is congruent. Find the measures of the numbered angles.

1. $m\angle 1 =$ _____, $m\angle 2 =$ _____

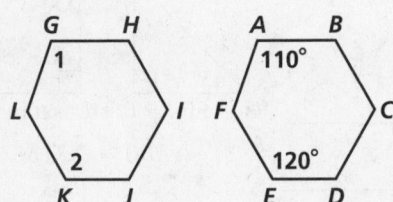

2. $m\angle 3 =$ _____, $m\angle 4 =$ _____

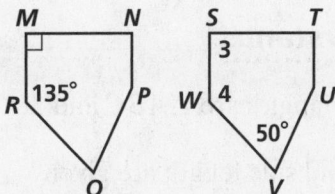

$\triangle CAT \cong \triangle JSD$. **List each of the following.**

3. three pairs of congruent sides _____

_____

4. three pairs of congruent angles _____

_____

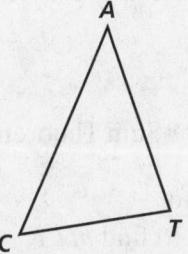
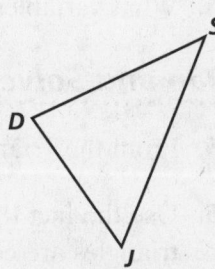

State whether the pairs of figures are congruent. Explain.

5. $\triangle GHJ$ and $\triangle IHJ$ _____

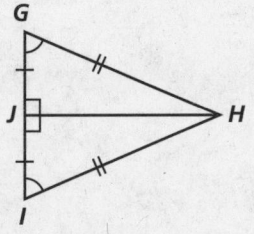

6. $\triangle QRS$ and $\triangle TVS$ _____

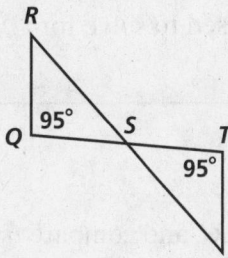

7. Developing Proof Use the information given in the figure.
Give a reason that each statement is true.

a. $\angle L \cong \angle Q$ _____

b. $\angle LNM \cong \angle PNQ$ _____

c. $\angle M \cong \angle P$ _____

d. $\overline{LM} \cong \overline{QP}, \overline{LN} \cong \overline{QN}, \overline{MN} \cong \overline{PN}$ _____

e. $\triangle LNM \cong \triangle QNP$ _____

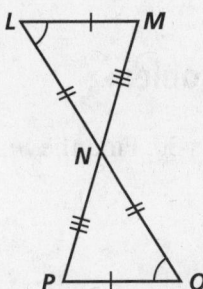

4-1 • Guided Problem Solving

Student Page 201, Exercise 30

Algebra Find the values of the variables.

Read and Understand

1. What kind of triangles are △ABC and △KLM? _____

2. Which angles and side length are given? _____

3. What does the statement △ABC ≅ △KLM mean? _____

4. What variables are used in this problem? _____

$\triangle ABC \cong \triangle KLM$

Plan and Solve

5. From the Triangle Angle-Sum Theorem, what is $m\angle C$? _____

6. Use the fact that the two
   triangles are congruent to find $m\angle K$ _____ and $m\angle M$. _____

7. What equation can be used to solve for x? _____

8. What is the value of x? _____

9. Use the fact that the two triangles are congruent to find LK. _____

10. What equation can be used to solve for t? _____

11. What is the value of t? _____

Look Back and Check

12. Compare $m\angle A$ and $m\angle C$, and compare $m\angle K$ and $m\angle M$. Do
    your findings match the physical appearance of the figure? Explain. _____

    _____

Solve Another Problem

13. Suppose $m\angle A$ is 30. Find the $m\angle M$. _____

Practice 4-2

Triangle Congruence by SSS and SAS

Decide whether you can use the SSS or SAS Postulate to prove the triangles congruent. If so, write the congruence statement, and identify the postulate. If not, write *not possible*.

1. _____

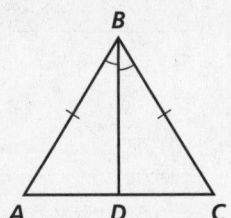

2. _____

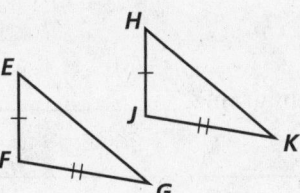

3. _____

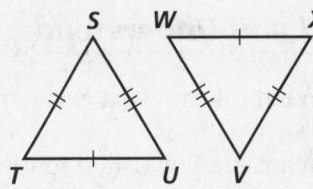

4. _____

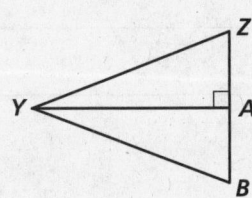

5. _____

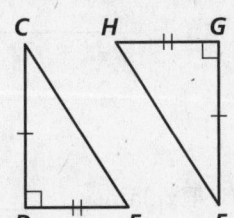

6. _____

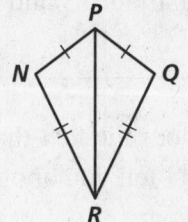

Draw a triangle. Label the vertices *A*, *B*, and *C*.

7. What angle is between $\overline{BC}$ and $\overline{AC}$?

8. What sides include $\angle B$?

9. What angles include $\overline{AB}$?

10. What side is included between $\angle A$ and $\angle C$?

11. Developing Proof Supply the reasons in this proof.

Given: $\overline{AB} \cong \overline{DC}$, $\angle BAC \cong \angle DCA$

Prove: $\triangle ABC \cong \triangle CDA$

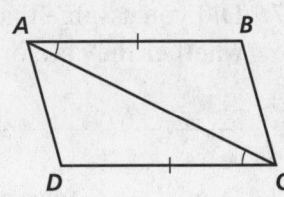

Statements	*Reasons*
1. $\overline{AB} \cong \overline{DC}$, $\angle BAC \cong \angle DCA$	**a.** _____
2. $\overline{AC} \cong \overline{CA}$	**b.** _____
3. $\triangle ABC \cong \triangle CDA$	**c.** _____

4-2 • Guided Problem Solving

GPS **Student Page 210, Exercise 34**

What can you prove about $\triangle ISP$ and $\triangle OSP$ given the information in the diagram and the fact that $\overline{SP}$ is the bisector of $\angle ISO$?

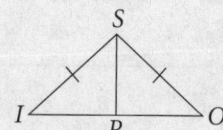

Read and Understand

1. What information is given in the diagram? _____

2. What are you asked to identify? _____

Plan and Solve

3. What does the information given in the diagram
   tell you about $\overline{IS}$ and $\overline{OS}$? Justify your answer. _____

   _____

4. What does the fact that $\overline{SP}$ is the bisector
   of $\angle ISO$ tell you about $\angle ISP$ and $\angle OSP$? Explain. _____

   _____

5. What side is common to both $\triangle ISP$ and $\triangle OSP$? _____

6. What can you conclude about $\triangle ISP$ and $\angle OSP$? Justify your answer. _____

   _____

Look Back and Check

7. Did you assume that points I, P, and O were collinear? Does it matter
   whether they are or not? Explain.

   _____

Solve Another Problem

8. From the information given, does it follow that $\overline{IP} \cong \overline{OP}$? Why or why not?

   _____

   _____

Practice 4-3

Triangle Congruence by ASA and AAS

• •

**Tell whether the ASA Postulate or the AAS Theorem can be applied
directly to prove the triangles congruent. If the triangles cannot be
proved congruent, write *not possible*.**

1. _____

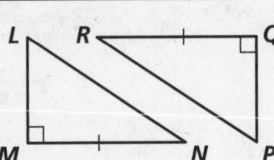

2. _____

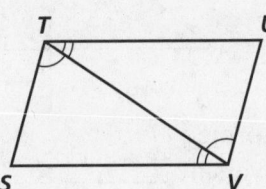

3. _____

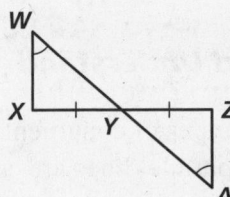

4. _____

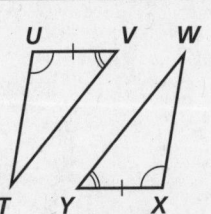

5. _____

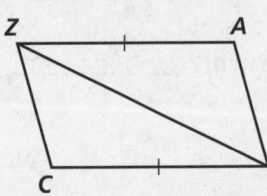

6. _____

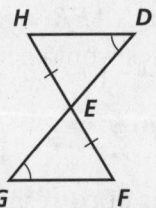

7. Write a two-column proof.
  Given: $\angle K \cong \angle M, \overline{KL} \cong \overline{ML}$
  Prove: $\triangle JKL \cong \triangle PML$

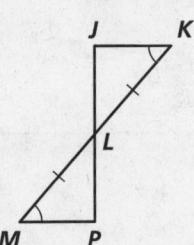

**What else must you know to prove the triangles congruent for the
reason shown?**

8. _____

ASA

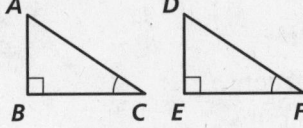

9. _____

AAS

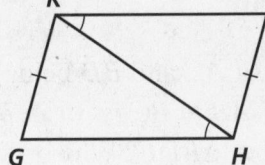

4-3 • Guided Problem Solving

GPS **Student Page 217, Exercise 22**

Given: $\overline{AE} \| \overline{BD}, \overline{AE} \cong \overline{BD}, \angle E \cong \angle D$

Prove: $\triangle AEB \cong \triangle BDC$

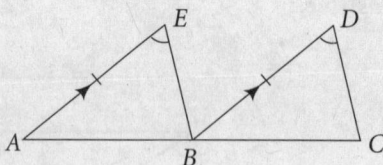

Read and Understand

1. What types of congruent angles are formed
   when parallel lines are cut by a transversal? _____

2. In order for $\triangle AEB \cong \triangle BDC$ by ASA, what
   pair of angles would need to be congruent? _____

3. In order for $\triangle AEB \cong \triangle BDC$ by AAS, what
   pair of angles would need to be congruent? _____

Plan and Solve

4. Name a pair of corresponding angles that
   are formed by $\overline{AC}$ intersecting $\overline{AE}$ and $\overline{BD}$. _____

5. What parts of $\triangle AEB$ and $\triangle BDC$
   are now known to be congruent? _____

6. Why can you conclude that $\triangle AEB \cong \triangle BDC$?

   _____

Look Back and Check

7. Can $\triangle AEB$ and $\triangle BDC$ be shown to be congruent
   using a method different than the one you used? _____

   What postulate or theorem would you use? _____

   What additional information would you need? _____

Solve Another Problem

8. Suppose that instead of $\overline{AE}$ and $\overline{BD}$ being given as parallel and congruent,
   it is simply given that $\overline{AB} \cong \overline{BC}$ (with A, B, and C collinear). Can you
   conclude that $\triangle AEB \cong \triangle BDC$? Why or why not?

   _____

Practice 4-4

Explain how you can use SSS, SAS, ASA, or AAS with CPCTC to prove each statement true.

1. $\angle A \cong \angle C$

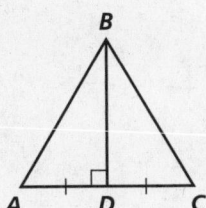

2. $\overline{HE} \cong \overline{FG}$

3. $\angle QST \cong \angle SQR$

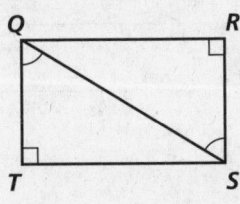

4. $\overline{ZA} \cong \overline{AC}$

5. $\overline{JK} \cong \overline{KL}$

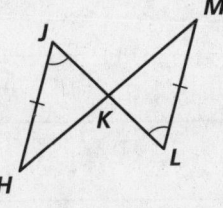

6. $\angle N \cong \angle Q$

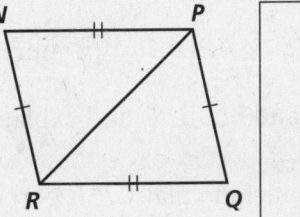

Write a Plan for Proof.

7. Given: $\overline{BD} \perp \overline{AB}$, $\overline{BD} \perp \overline{DE}$, $\overline{BC} \cong \overline{CD}$

Prove: $\angle A \cong \angle E$

4-4 • Guided Problem Solving

GPS **Student Page 224, Exercise 13**

Constructions The construction of a line perpendicular to line ℓ through point P on ℓ is shown here.

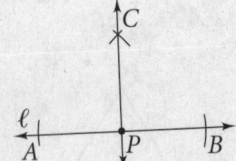

a. Which lengths or distances are equal by construction?

b. Explain why you can conclude that $\overleftrightarrow{CP}$ is perpendicular to ℓ.

(*Hint:* Do the construction. Then draw $\overline{CA}$ and $\overline{CB}$.)

Read and Understand

1. What steps were involved in the construction? _____

_____

2. What are you asked to do? _____

Plan and Solve

3. Draw $\overline{CA}$ and $\overline{CB}$. What two triangles are formed? _____

4. Which lengths or distances are equal by construction? _____

5. What can you conclude about $\triangle APC$ and $\triangle BPC$? _____ Why? _____

6. Why is $\angle APC \cong \angle BPC$? Justify your answer. _____

7. Find $m\angle APC$ and $m\angle BPC$ and explain how you did it. _____

8. Why can you conclude that $\overleftrightarrow{CP}$ is perpendicular to ℓ? _____

Look Back and Check

9. Does it matter what the distance is from P to A and from P to B? Why or why not? How about the distance from A to C and from B to C? _____

_____

Solve Another Problem

10. How could you use construction techniques similar to those used in this problem to construct two parallel lines?

_____

_____

Practice 4-5

Isosceles and Equilateral Triangles

Find the values of the variables.

1. $x =$ _____, $y =$ _____

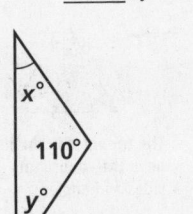

2. $x =$ _____, $y =$ _____

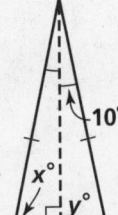

3. $t =$ _____

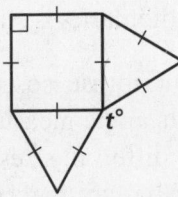

4. $x =$ _____, $y =$ _____, $z =$ _____

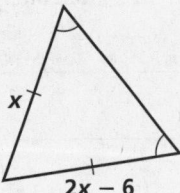

5. $x =$ _____

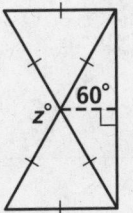

6. $z =$ _____

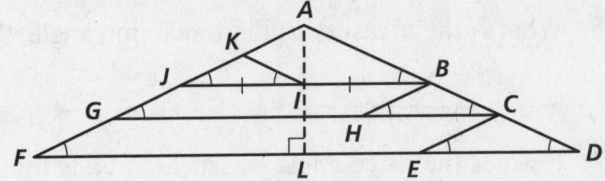

Complete each statement. Explain why it is true.

7. $\overline{AF} \cong$ _____, _____

8. $\overline{KI} \cong$ _____, _____

9. $\overline{JA} \cong$ _____, _____

Given $m\angle D = 25$, find the measure of each angle.

10. $\angle JAB =$ _____

11. $\angle JKI =$ _____

12. Find the values of x and y. $x =$ _____, $y =$ _____

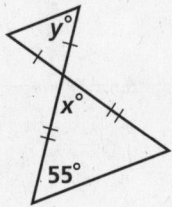

4-5 • Guided Problem Solving

GPS Student Page 231, Exercise 17

Graphic Arts A former logo for the National Council of Teachers of Mathematics is shown at the right.

a. Highlight an obtuse isosceles triangle in the design. Then find its angle measures.

b. How many different sizes of angles can you find in the logo? What are their measures?

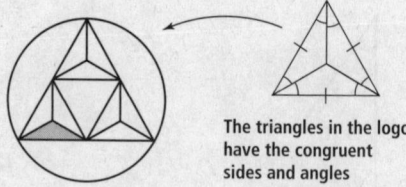

The triangles in the logo have the congruent sides and angles

Read and Understand

1. Describe the angles of an obtuse isosceles triangle. _____

_____

2. What are you asked to do? _____

Plan and Solve

3. Find an obtuse isosceles triangle in the figure and highlight it.

4. The highlighted triangle and its two identical neighbors together form an equilateral triangle. What is the measure of each angle of the equilateral triangle? _____

5. What is the measure of a base angle of the highlighted triangle? Explain. _____

_____

6. What is the measure of the remaining angle, the obtuse angle? Why? _____

_____

7. Besides the three angle measures already found (30°, 60°, and 120°), there are two others. Identify one of each in the figure. _____

Look Back and Check

8. The obtuse angle of the highlighted triangle adjoins two other angles just like it. Together, they cover a full 360°. Does this match your finding for the measure of the obtuse angle? Explain.

_____

Solve Another Problem

9. Design a logo that contains several angles each of measures 45°, 90°, and 135°.

Practice 4-6

Congruence in Right Triangles

Write a two-column proof.

1. Given: $\overline{AB} \perp \overline{BC}$, $\overline{ED} \perp \overline{FE}$, $\overline{AB} \cong \overline{ED}$, $\overline{AC} \cong \overline{FD}$

   Prove: $\triangle ABC \cong \triangle DEF$

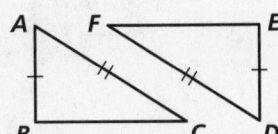

Write a flow proof.

2. Given: $\overline{MJ} \perp \overline{NK}$, $\overline{MN} \cong \overline{MK}$

   Prove: $\triangle MJN \cong \triangle MJK$

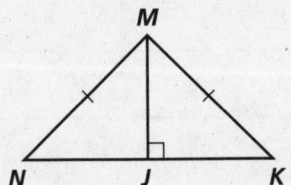

What additional information do you need to prove each pair of triangles congruent by the HL Theorem?

3. _____

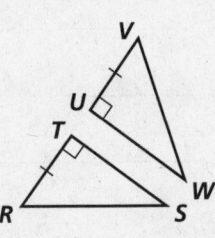

4. _____

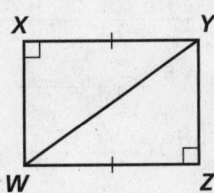

5. _____

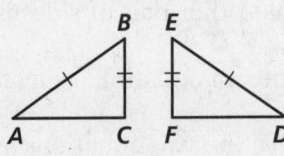

6. _____

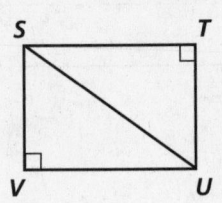

7. _____

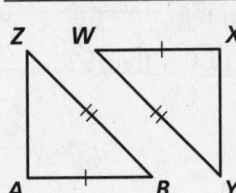

8. _____

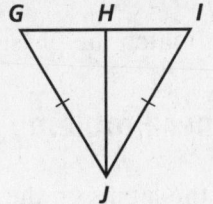

4-6 • Guided Problem Solving

GPS Student Page 238, Exercise 10

Algebra For what values of x and y are the triangles congruent by HL?

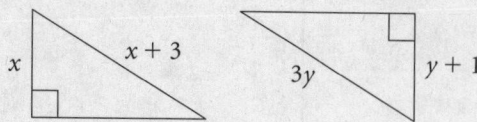

Read and Understand

1. What are you given? _____

_____

2. What are you asked to find? _____

Plan and Solve

3. If the triangles are congruent, which leg on the triangle on
   the left is congruent to which leg on the triangle on the right? _____

4. Write an equation, using the result from Step 3. _____

5. What other pair of sides is congruent? _____

6. Write an equation, using the result from Step 5._____

7. Solve the two equations as a system, for x and y. _____

Look Back and Check

8. For each triangle, what is the ratio $\dfrac{\text{hypotenuse}}{\text{shorter leg}}$? _____

   Does this match the physical appearance of the figure? _____

Solve Another Problem

9. Suppose the labels on the two hypotenuses ($x + 3$ and $3y$) are swapped
   but the labels on the legs remain where they are. How does this affect
   the solution for x and y? Explain.

_____

_____

Practice 4-7

Using Corresponding Parts of Congruent Triangles

Name a pair of overlapping congruent triangles in each diagram. State whether the triangles are congruent by SSS, SAS, ASA, AAS, or HL.

1. _____

Given: $\overline{ZW} \cong \overline{XY}$, $\angle YXW$
and $\angle ZWX$ are right $\angle$s

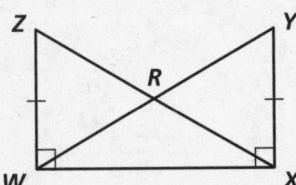

2. _____

Given: $\overline{LP} \cong \overline{LO}$,
$\overline{PM} \cong \overline{ON}$

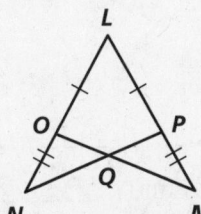

3. _____

Given: $\overline{DE} \cong \overline{FG}$,
$\overline{AC} \cong \overline{CB}$, $\overline{EC} \cong \overline{FC}$

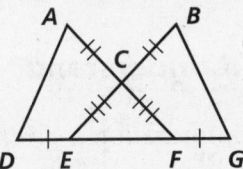

Separate and redraw the indicated triangles. Identify any common angles or sides.

4. △EFG and △HGF

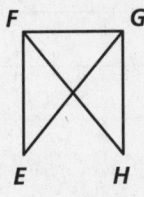

5. △JML and △NKL

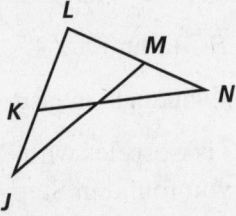

6. Write a two-column proof.

Given: $\overline{AX} \cong \overline{AY}$, $\overline{CX} \perp \overline{AB}$, $\overline{BY} \perp \overline{AC}$

Prove: △BYA ≅ △CXA

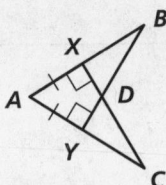

4-7 • Guided Problem Solving

Student Page 245, Exercise 19

The figure at the right is part of a clothing design pattern. In the figure, $\overline{AB} \| \overline{DE} \| \overline{FG}$, $\overline{AB} \perp \overline{BC}$, and $\overline{GC} \perp \overline{AC}$. $\triangle DEC$ is isosceles with base $\overline{DC}$, and $m\angle A = 56$. Find the measures of all the numbered angles in the figure.

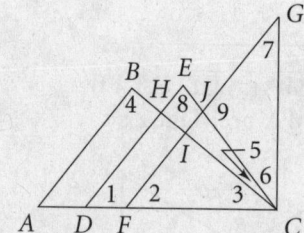

Read and Understand

1. What information is given? _____

2. How many angle measures are you asked to find? _____

3. What is true about the base angles of an isosceles triangle? _____

Plan and Solve

4. Since $\overline{AB} \| \overline{DE} \| \overline{FG}$, the corresponding angles $\angle A$, $\angle 1$, and $\angle 2$ are congruent. What is their measure? _____

5. Use the fact that $\overline{AB} \perp \overline{BC}$ to find $m\angle 4$. _____

6. Find $m\angle 3$, the last unknown angle measure of $\triangle ABC$. _____

7. Use the fact that $\triangle DEC$ is isosceles with base $\overline{DC}$ and $m\angle 1$ that you found in Step 4 to find $m\angle DCE$. _____

8. Use $m\angle 3$ that you found in Step 6 with $m\angle DCE$ you found in Step 7 to find $m\angle 5$. _____

9. Use the fact that $\overline{GC} \perp \overline{AC}$ to find $m\angle FCG$. _____

10. Use the angle measures you found in Steps 6, 8, and 9 to find $m\angle 6$. _____

11. Use the results from Steps 3–6 together with Theorem 3-12, the Triangle Angle-Sum Theorem, to find $m\angle 7$, $m\angle 8$, and $m\angle 9$. _____

Look Back and Check

12. $\angle 9$ is related to $\angle 2$ and $\angle FCE$ (= $\angle DCE$) by Theorem 3-13, the Triangle Exterior Angle Theorem. Use this relationship to verify $m\angle 9$.

Solve Another Problem

13. Name four additional angles in the figure and find their measures. Justify your answers.

_____

_____

_____

4A: Graphic Organizer

For use before Lesson 4-1

Study Skill As you read over the material in the chapter, take notes and write questions that you have. You should read the material before the teacher presents it. This will help you understand some of the material better.

Write your answers.

1. What is the chapter title? _____

2. Find the Table of Contents page for this chapter at the front of the book. Name four topics you will study in this chapter.

   _____   _____

   _____   _____

3. Complete the graphic organizer as you work through the chapter.
   1. Write the title of the chapter in the center oval.
   2. When you begin a lesson, write the name of the lesson in a rectangle.
   3. When you complete that lesson, write a skill or key concept from that lesson in the outer oval linked to that rectangle.
   Continue with steps 2 and 3 clockwise around the graphic organizer.

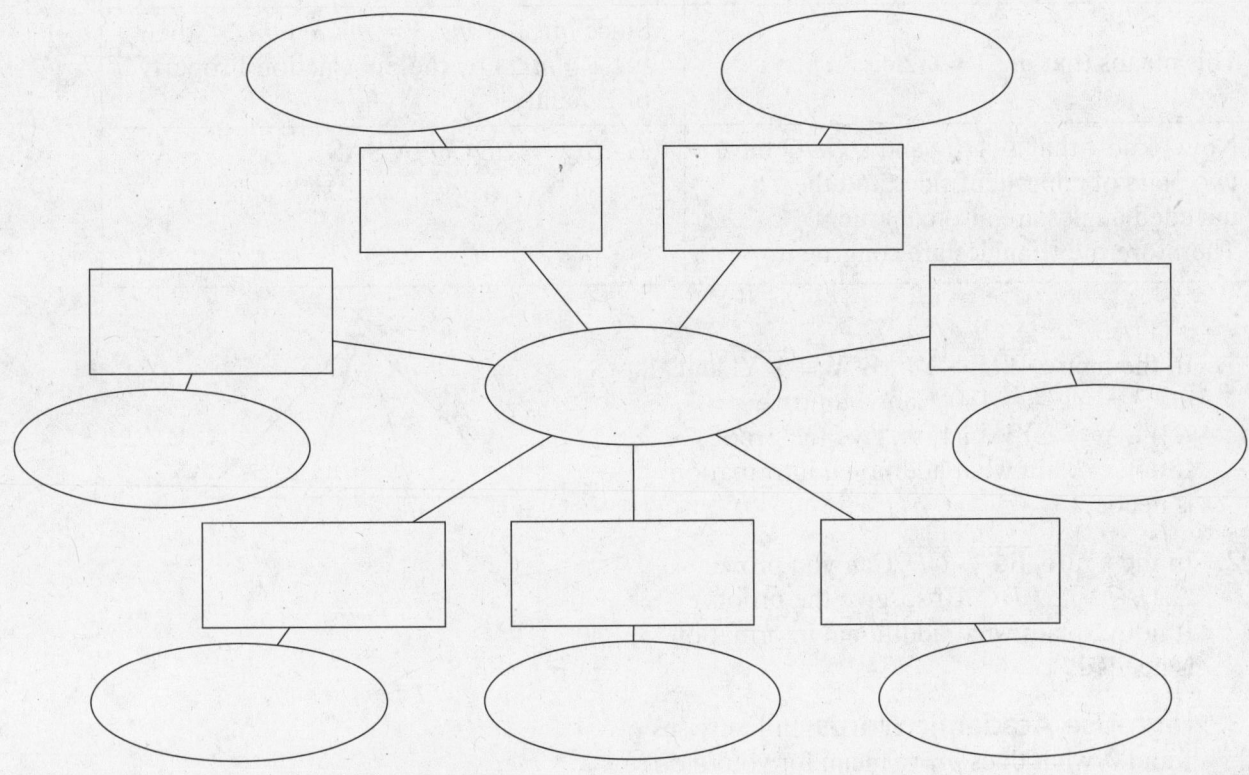

4B: Reading Comprehension

For use after Lesson 4-6

Study Skill When an informal proof is presented, read the given and prove statements with care. Look at the diagram to decide what conclusions can be drawn from the figure.

Read the problem and follow along with the written steps to solve the problem. Check your understanding by solving the exercises at the bottom of the page.

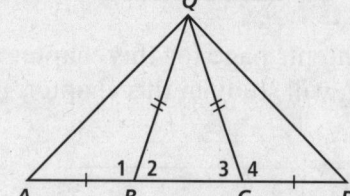

Given: $\overline{AB} \cong \overline{DC}, \overline{QB} \cong \overline{QC}$
$\quad\quad m\angle 1 + m\angle 3 = 180$

Prove: $\triangle ABQ \cong \triangle DCQ$

Thought Process	Informal Proof
It is given that there are two pairs of congruent sides in $\triangle ABQ$ and $\triangle CDQ$. This means the triangles must be proven to be congruent using either SAS or SSS.	$\overline{AB} \cong \overline{DC}$ and $\overline{QB} \cong \overline{QC}$ This is given information.
Also given is the fact that $m\angle 1 + m\angle 3 = 180$. Furthermore, I can say that $m\angle 3 + m\angle 4 = 180$.	$m\angle 1 + m\angle 3 = 180$ Given $m\angle 3 + m\angle 4 = 180$ by the Angle Addition Postulate.
This means that $m\angle 1 = m\angle 4$.	Since $m\angle 1 + m\angle 3 = m\angle 3 + m\angle 4$, then $m\angle 1 = m\angle 4$ by the Subtraction Property of Equality.
Now I know that $\triangle ABQ$ and $\triangle CDQ$ have two pairs of congruent sides and the included angles are also congruent. Therefore the triangles are congruent.	$\triangle ABQ \cong \triangle DCQ$ by SAS

1. In the figure, $\overline{WU} \cong \overline{YV}, \overline{WX} \cong \overline{YX}$, and $m\angle 3 + m\angle 4 = 180$. Can you prove $\triangle WUX \cong \triangle YVX$? If so, give the proof. If not, explain what additional information is needed.

2. In the figure, $\overline{BC} \cong \overline{CD}$. Can you prove $\triangle ABC \cong \triangle EDC$? If so, give the proof. If not, explain what additional information is needed.

3. **High-Use Academic Words** In Exercises 1 and 2, what does *prove* mean for you to do?

   a. show a statement is true in all cases
   b. find at least one case that makes the statement true

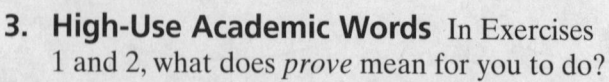

Vocabulary and Study Skills

4C: Reading/Writing Math Symbols

For use after Lesson 4-3

Study Skill Abbreviations or certain combinations and arrangements of letters (sometimes Greek) take on universally accepted meanings. For example, in geometry, the letters *SSS* are accepted shorthand for the Side-Side-Side congruence postulate. This "symbolism" can be a timesaving device if you can recognize some of the more popular arrangements.

Write the meaning for each abbreviation or math expression.

1. AAS _____

2. $\triangle XYZ$ _____

3. $\angle PQR$ _____

4. $\overline{BD}$ _____

5. $\overleftrightarrow{ST}$ _____

6. $\overrightarrow{WX}$ _____

7. HL _____

8. l_3 _____

9. $\angle 6$ _____

10. ASA _____

Name_____ Class_____ Date_____

4D: Visual Vocabulary Practice

For use after Lesson 4-5

Study Skill When a math exercise is difficult, try to determine what makes it difficult. Is it a word that you don't understand? Are the numbers difficult to use?

Concept List

base angle of an isoceles triangle	corollary	congruent polygons
base of an isosceles triangle	CPCTC	legs of an isosceles triangle
postulate	theorem	vertex angle of an isosceles triangle

Write the concept that best describes each exercise.
Choose from the concept list above.

1. A statement that can be proven by using postulates, definitions and properties. _____	**2.** 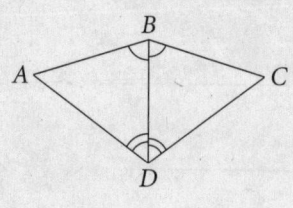 C corresponds to R. ∠B corresponds to ∠Q. $\overline{AX}$ corresponds to $\overline{PY}$. ACBX ≅ PRQY _____	**3.** 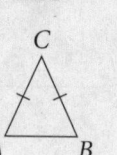 _____
4. ∠A ≅ ∠C _____	**5.** A self-evident truth _____	**6.** ∠C 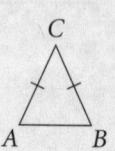 _____
7. A statement that follows directly from a theorem. _____	**8.** $\overline{AB}$  _____	**9.** $\overline{AC}$ and $\overline{AB}$  _____

Vocabulary and Study Skills

4E: Vocabulary Check

For use after Lesson 4-4

Study Skill Strengthen your vocabulary. Use these pages and add cues and summaries by applying the Cornell Notetaking style.

Write the definition for each word at the right. To check your work, fold the paper back along the dotted line to see the correct answers.

_____

_____

_____   Angle

_____

_____

_____   Congruent angles

_____

_____

_____   Congruent segments

_____

_____

_____   Congruent polygons

_____

_____

_____   CPCTC

_____

4E: Vocabulary Check (continued)

Write the vocabulary word for each definition. To check your work, fold the paper forward along the dotted line to see the correct answers.

Formed by two rays with the same endpoint.

_____

Angles that have the same measure.

_____

Segments that have the same length.

_____

Polygons that have corresponding sides congruent and corresponding angles congruent.

_____

An abbreviation for "corresponding parts of congruent triangles are congruent."

_____

4F: Vocabulary Review Puzzle

For use with Chapter Review

Study Skill Math vocabulary may seem less important than being able to solve problems, but without knowing the vocabulary words from previous lessons or chapters, you may have trouble understanding new concepts as they are introduced.

Fill in the boxes in each sentence.

1. A ☐☐☐☐☐☐☐☐ is an accepted statement of fact.

2. The longest side of a right triangle is the ☐☐☐☐☐☐☐☐☐☐ .

3. An ☐☐☐☐☐ is formed by two rays with a common endpoint.

4. A point where two sides of a figure meet is a ☐☐☐☐☐☐ .

5. A segment that connects two vertices of a triangle is known as a ☐☐☐☐ .

6. A ☐☐ is one of the two shorter sides of a right triangle.

7. Two lines are ☐☐☐☐☐☐☐☐☐☐☐☐☐ if they form a right angle when they intersect.

8. A ☐☐☐☐☐☐☐ is a closed figure with at least three sides.

9. ☐☐☐☐☐☐☐☐☐☐☐ angles sum to 180°.

10. Lines that are ☐☐☐☐☐☐☐☐ never intersect.

11. ☐☐☐☐☐☐☐☐☐☐☐☐ angles are in similar positions on the same side of a transversal.

Practice 5-1

Use the diagrams at the right to complete the exercises.

1. In △MNO, the points C, D, and E are midpoints. CD = 4 cm, CE = 8 cm, and DE = 7 cm.

   a. Find MO. _____

   b. Find NO. _____

   c. Find MN. _____

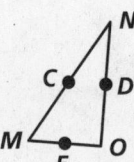

2. In △LOB, the points A, R, and T are midpoints. LB = 19 cm, LO = 35 cm, and OB = 29 cm.

   a. Find RT. _____

   b. Find AT. _____

   c. Find AR. _____

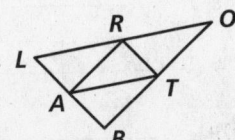

Find the value of the variable.

3. _____

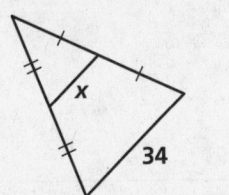

4. _____

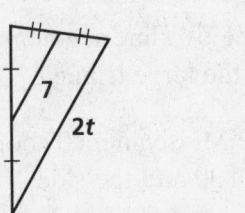

5. _____

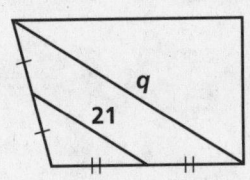

6. _____

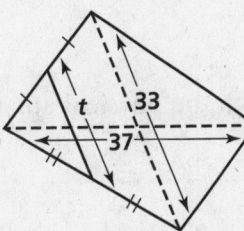

7. $\overline{QR}$ is a midsegment of △LMN.

   a. QR = 9. Find NM. _____

   b. LN = 12 and LM = 31. Find the perimeter of △LMN. _____

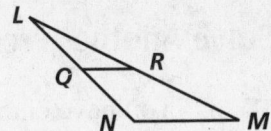

Use the given measures to identify three pairs of parallel segments in each diagram.

8. _____

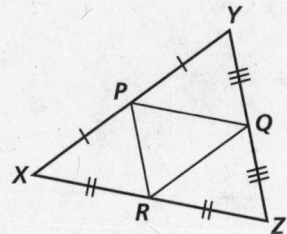

5-1 • Guided Problem Solving

Student Page 263, Exercise 30

Algebra Find the value of x.

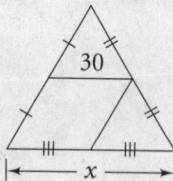

Read and Understand

1. Which segment length is given? _____

2. What other information is given? _____

3. What are you asked to find? _____

Plan and Solve

4. What term describes the two line segments
lying in the interior of the large triangle? _____

5. What does the Triangle Midsegment Theorem imply
about the side of length 30 and the side of length x? _____

6. What is the value of x? _____

Look Back and Check

7. Does your finding match the physical appearance of the figure? Explain.

_____

_____

Solve Another Problem

8. Do you have enough information to find the lengths of the
other midsegment and the side it is parallel to? Why or why not? _____

_____

Practice 5-2

Bisectors in Triangles

Use the figure at the right for Exercises 1–4.

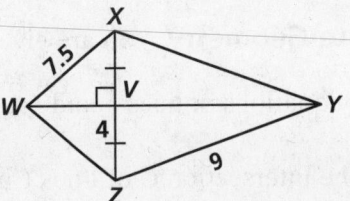

1. How is $\overline{WY}$ related to $\overline{XZ}$? _____

2. Find XV. _____

3. Find XY. _____

4. What kind of triangle is $\triangle WXV$? _____

Use the figure at the right for Exercises 5–7.

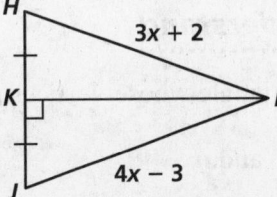

5. Find the value of x. _____

6. Find HI. _____

7. What kind of triangle is $\triangle HIJ$? _____

Use the figure at the right for Exercises 8–10.

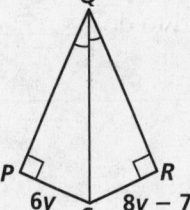

8. Find the value of y. _____

9. Find PS. _____

10. What kind of triangle is $\triangle PQS$? _____

Use the figure at the right for Exercises 11–15.

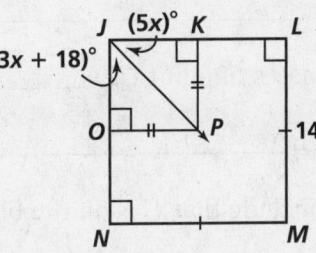

11. How is $\overrightarrow{JP}$ related to $\angle LJN$? _____

12. Find the value of x. _____

13. Find $m\angle KJP$. _____

14. Find NM. _____

15. What kind of triangle is $\triangle JOP$? _____

5-2 • Guided Problem Solving

GPS **Student Page 269, Exercise 42**

Coordinate Geometry You are given points $A(6, 8)$, $O(0, 0)$, and $B(10, 0)$.

a. Write equations of lines ℓ and m such that $\ell \perp \overleftrightarrow{OA}$ at A and $m \perp \overleftrightarrow{OB}$ at B.

b. Find the intersection C of lines ℓ and m.

c. Show that $CA = CB$.

d. Explain why C is on the bisector of $\angle AOB$.

Read and Understand

1. Graph the triangle whose vertices are given.

2. Draw lines ℓ and m.

3. Label the point of intersection of lines ℓ and m as point C.

4. What are you asked to do? _____

_____

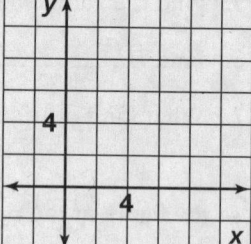

Plan and Solve

5. Write equations in slope-intercept form for lines ℓ and m.

_____

6. Find the coordinates of point C. _____

7. Find CA and CB. _____ Are they equal? _____

8. Why can you conclude that C is on the bisector of $\angle AOB$? _____

_____

Look Back and Check

9. Draw $\overleftrightarrow{OC}$ and use a protractor to measure $\angle AOC$ and $\angle BOC$. Do they appear to be equal? _____

Solve Another Problem

10. How could you have done parts (c) and (d) without writing equations for lines ℓ and m?

_____

Guided Problem Solving

Practice 5-3

Concurrent Lines, Medians, and Altitudes

Find the center of the circle that circumscribes △LMN.

1. _____

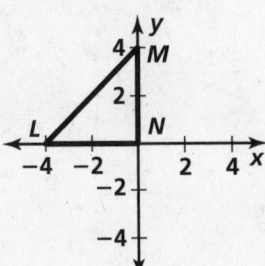

2. _____

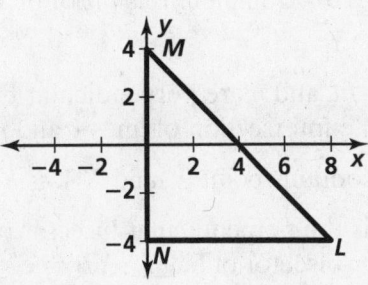

Is $\overline{AB}$ a perpendicular bisector, an angle bisector, an altitude, a median, or none of these?

3.

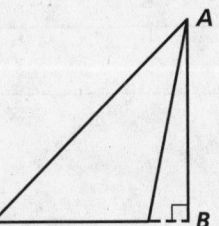

4.

5.

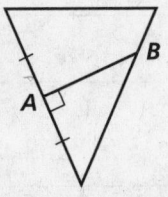

6.

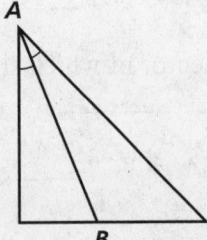

For each triangle, give the coordinates of the point of concurrency of (a) the perpendicular bisectors of the sides and (b) the altitudes.

7a. _____

7b. _____

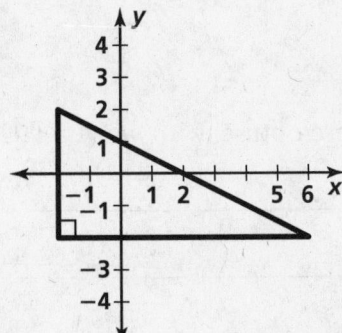

8a. _____

8b. _____

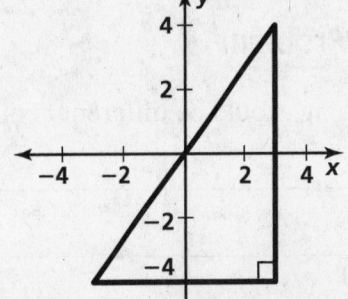

Name _____ Class _____ Date _____

5-3 • Guided Problem Solving

Developing Proof Complete this proof of Theorem 5-6 by filling in the blanks.

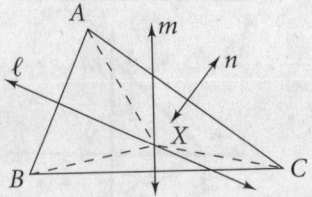

Given: Lines ℓ, m, and n are perpendicular bisectors of the sides of $\triangle ABC$. X is the intersection of lines ℓ and m.

Prove: Line n contains point X, and $XA = XB = XC$.

Proof: Since ℓ is the perpendicular bisector of **a.** _?_ , $XA = XB$. Since m is the perpendicular bisector of **b.** _?_ , $XB = $ **c.** _?_ . Thus $XA = XB = XC$. Since $XA = XC$, X is on line n by the Converse of the **d.** _?_ Theorem.

Read and Understand

1. What is given? _____

2. What are you asked to do? _____

Plan and Solve

3. ℓ is the perpendicular bisector of which side of $\triangle ABC$? Fill in blank **a.** _____.

4. Why does it follow that $XA = XB$? _____

5. m is the perpendicular bisector of which side of $\triangle ABC$? Fill in blank **b.** _____ and blank **c.** _____.

6. Why does it follow that $XA = XC$? _____

7. Fill in blank **d.** _____.

Look Back and Check

8. Why was n drawn the way it was, not showing whether it ran through point X?

_____

Solve Another Problem

9. What, if anything, would be different about the proof if $\triangle ABC$ were obtuse, with $m\angle A > 90$?

_____

_____

Practice 5-4

Inverses, Contrapositives, and Indirect Reasoning

Identify the two statements that contradict each other.

1. _____

    I. $ABCD$ is a trapezoid with base $\overline{CD}$.
    II. $\overline{AB} \parallel \overline{CD}$
    III. $\overline{BC} \parallel \overline{AD}$

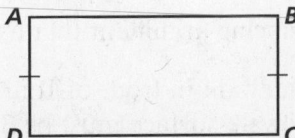

2. _____

    I. $\overline{AB} \cong \overline{BC}$
    II. $m\angle A + m\angle B = 80$
    III. $\triangle ABC$ is isosceles.

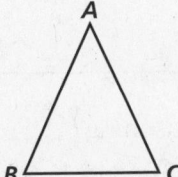

Write the negation of each statement.

3. The angle measure is 65. _____

4. Tina has her driver's license. _____

5. The figure has eight sides. _____

6. $\triangle ABC$ is not congruent to $\triangle XYZ$. _____

Write (a) the inverse and (b) the contrapositive of the statement. Give the truth value of each.

7. If you live in Toronto, then you live in Canada.

7a. _____
_____

7b. _____
_____

Write the first step of an indirect proof.

8. $m\angle A = m\angle B$ _____

9. $\overline{LM}$ intersects $\overline{NO}$. _____

10. It is sunny outside. _____

11. Write an indirect proof that $m\angle A < 90$.

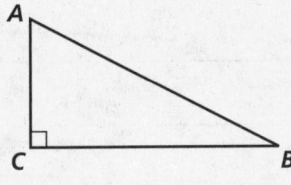

5-4 • Guided Problem Solving

Student Page 284, Exercise 31

Writing Write a convincing argument that uses indirect reasoning.

Ice is forming on the sidewalk in front of Toni's house. Show that the temperature of the sidewalk surface must be 32°F or lower.

Read and Understand

1. What fact is given? _____

2. How do you use indirect reasoning? _____

Plan and Solve

3. What assumption should you use to begin your argument? _____

4. What fact about the freezing point of water is relevant to this problem?

_____

5. What is implied by the answers to Steps 3 and 4?

_____

6. How has a contradiction been obtained? _____

7. Finish the argument by drawing a conclusion that is the opposite of the assumption made in Step 3.

_____

Look Back and Check

8. Write the fact found in Step 4 as an *if-then* statement.
   How true is this statement? What about its converse? Explain. _____

Solve Another Problem

9. Use indirect reasoning to show that the title "World's Tallest Person" cannot be held by two people at the same time.

_____

_____

_____

Practice 5-5

Inequalities in Triangles

....

Determine the two largest angles in each triangle.

1. _____

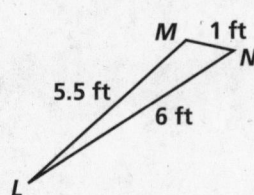

2. _____

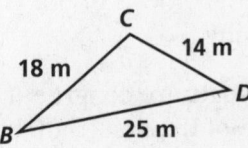

3. _____

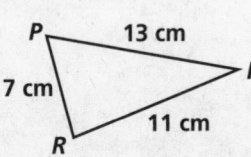

4. _____

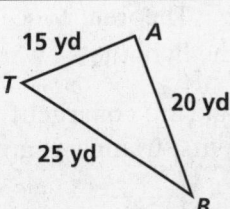

Can a triangle have sides with the given lengths? Explain.

5. 4 m, 7 m, and 8 m _____

6. 6 m, 10 m, and 17 m _____

7. 4 in., 4 in., and 4 in. _____

8. 11 m, 12 m, and 13 m _____

9. 18 ft, 20 ft, and 40 ft _____

10. 1.2 cm, 2.6 cm, and 4.9 cm _____

List the sides of each triangle in order from shortest to longest.

11. _____

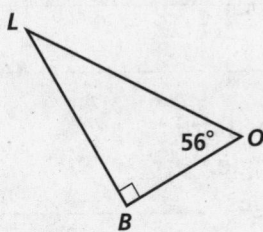

12. _____

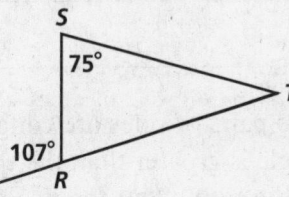

List the angles of each triangle in order from largest to smallest.

13. _____

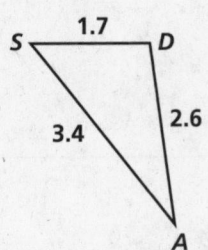

14. _____

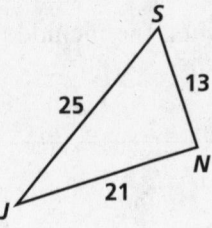

The lengths of two sides of a triangle are given. Describe the lengths possible for the third side.

15. 4 in., 7 in. _____

16. 9 cm, 17 cm _____

17. 5 ft, 5 ft _____

18. 11 m, 20 m _____

....

5-5 • Guided Problem Solving

GPS Student Page 293, Exercise 30

The Hinge Theorem The hypothesis of the Hinge Theorem is stated below. The conclusion is missing.

Suppose two sides of one triangle are congruent to two sides of another triangle. If the included angle of the first triangle is larger than the included angle of the second triangle, then __?__.

a. Draw a diagram to illustrate the hypothesis.
b. The conclusion of the Hinge Theorem concerns the sides opposite the two angles mentioned in the hypothesis. Write the conclusion.

Suppose two sides of one triangle are congruent to two sides of another triangle. If the third side of the first triangle is greater than the third side of the second triangle, then __?__.

Read and Understand

1. Draw a diagram showing two sides of one triangle congruent to two sides of another triangle, but with different-sized included angles.

Plan and Solve

2. What appears to be the case about the two sides opposite the included angles?

_____

_____

3. Now suppose the two pairs of sides are congruent as before. Assume the third side of the first triangle is greater than the third side of the second triangle. What appears to be the case about the two angles opposite the third sides? _____

_____

Look Back and Check

4. What happens in part (a) when the included angles are both drawn with a measure of nearly 180?

_____

Solve Another Problem

5. When triangles with two congruent sides are drawn so that the included angles are the same size, what happens to the opposite sides? _____

Why does this make sense? _____

_____

5A: Graphic Organizer

For use before Lesson 5-1

Study Skill Develop and use a consistent method of note-taking, including punctuation and abbreviations. Take and keep your notes in a large notebook. A large notebook allows you to take notes without running out of paper or space.

Write your answers.

1. What is the chapter title? _____

2. Find the Table of Contents page for this chapter at the front of the book. Name four topics you will study in this chapter.

_____   _____

_____   _____

3. Complete the graphic organizer as you work through the chapter.
   1. Write the title of the chapter in the center oval.
   2. When you begin a lesson, write the name of the lesson in a rectangle.
   3. When you complete that lesson, write a skill or key concept from that lesson in the outer oval linked to that rectangle.
   Continue with steps 2 and 3 clockwise around the graphic organizer.

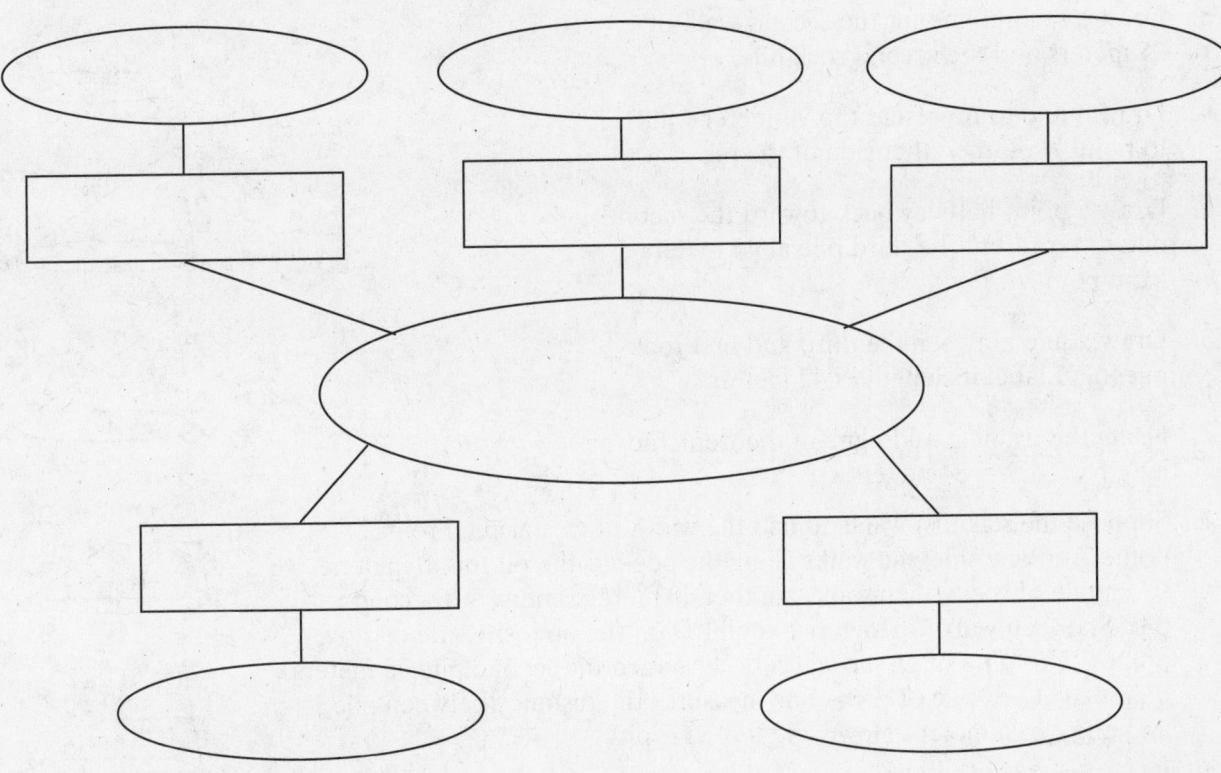

5B: Reading Comprehension

Study Skill It is often important in mathematics to be able to draw a diagram. Read the problem thoroughly. Then draw your diagram and label it to show all the known information.

Read through the following word problem and the steps to draw the diagram and solve the problem. Then solve the word problem at the bottom of the page.

A scientist has discovered an ancient tar pit, oval in shape. To calculate the length, she starts at one end of the pit at point *A*, walks a distance of 25 meters, and sets up a pile of rocks. She then continues in the same direction for another 25 meters and sets a second pile of rocks. Then, she walks directly to point *B* at the other end of the pit. The distance from the second pile to point *B* is 90 meters. She then turns around and walks back toward the second rock pile for 45 meters and sets a third rock pile. The distance from pile 3 to pile 1 is 42 meters. What is the length of the tar pit?

Follow these steps to create a diagram of the tar pit.

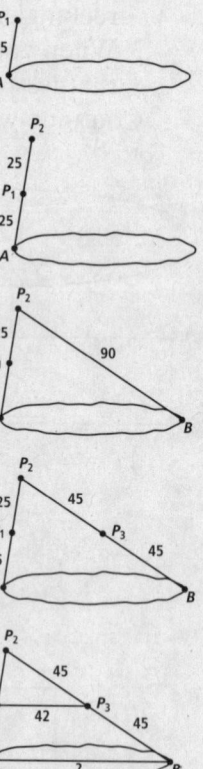

1. Draw an oval-shaped crater.

2. Draw a line to represent the first walk of 25 meters and the first pile of rocks.

3. Draw a second line for the second walk of 25 meters and the second rock pile.

4. Draw a line to represent the 90-meter walk to point *B* on the other side of the pit.

5. Draw a point halfway back toward the second pile to represent the third pile at 45 meters from point *B*.

6. Draw a line between the third and first rock piles, and label its length as 42 meters.

7. Using the triangle midsegment theorem, the length of $\overline{AB}$ = 84 meters.

1. Suppose the scientist wants to find the width of the tar pit. From point *C* on one side, she walks along the edge of the pit for 40 meters, sets a pile of rocks, then walks another 40 meters, and sets a second pile. She then walks 70 meters to point *D* on the opposite side of point *C*. From point *D*, she walks back toward the second pile 35 meters and sets a third pile of rocks. She measures the distance between pile 1 and pile 3 as 5 meters. How wide is the tar pit?

2. **High-Use Academic Words** In the word problem at the top of the page, what does *discovered* mean?

   a. invented   **b.** found

5C: Reading/Writing Math Symbols

For use after Lesson 5-2

Study Skill Many symbols look like the word or meaning they represent. The percent sign, %, for example, looks like a fraction, because percent is often written as a fraction with a denominator of 100.

Match the expression from the left hand column to its equivalent meaning in the right-hand column by drawing a line between them.

1. $p \rightarrow q$

2. $\overleftrightarrow{XY}$

3. $\triangle ABC$

4. $\overline{AB} \cong \overline{MN}$

5. $AB = MN$

6. $\overrightarrow{XY}$

7. $\angle ABC$

8. $\overline{XY}$

9. $\overleftrightarrow{AB} \parallel \overleftrightarrow{MN}$

10. $AB < MN$

11. $p \rightarrow \sim q$

12. $\overleftrightarrow{AB} \perp \overleftrightarrow{MN}$

13. $\frac{1}{2}XY$

14. $\angle ABC \cong \angle XYZ$

15. $m\angle ABC + m\angle XYZ = 180°$

A. The length of segment AB equals the length of segment MN.

B. if p then not q

C. $\angle ABC$ is supplementary to $\angle XYZ$.

D. Line AB is perpendicular to line MN.

E. Line AB is parallel to line MN.

F. line XY

G. Segment AB is congruent to segment MN.

H. segment XY

I. ray XY

J. Angle ABC is congruent to angle XYZ.

K. The length of segment AB is less than the length of segment MN.

L. if p then q

M. angle ABC

N. one half the length of segment XY

O. triangle ABC

Vocabulary and Study Skills

5D: Visual Vocabulary Practice

For use after Lesson 5-4

Study Skill When you come across something you don't understand, view it as an opportunity to increase your brainpower.

Concept List

altitude	centroid	circumcente
contrapositive	equivalent statements	incenter
inverse	median	negation

Write the concept that best describes each exercise. Choose from the concept list above.

1. 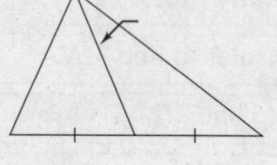	**2.** For p, it is $\sim p$.	**3.** 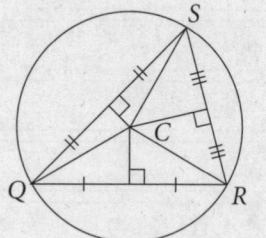
_____	_____	_____
4. For $p \rightarrow q$, it is $\sim q \rightarrow \sim p$.	**5.** 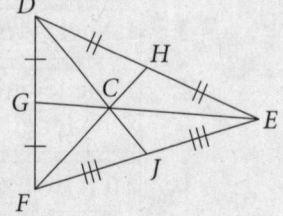	**6.** p and $\sim\sim p$
_____	_____	_____
7. 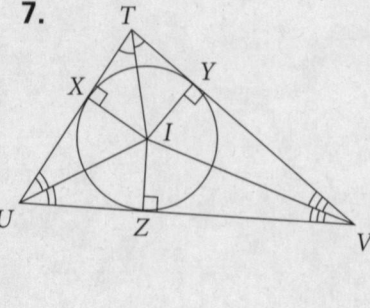	**8.** For $p \rightarrow q$, it is $\sim p \rightarrow \sim q$.	**9.** 
_____	_____	_____

Name ______________________ Class ______________ Date ______________

5E: Vocabulary Check

For use after Lesson 5-3

Study Skill Strengthen your vocabulary. Use these pages and add cues and summaries by applying the Cornell Notetaking style.

Write the definition for each word at the right. To check your work, fold the paper back along the dotted line to see the correct answers.

______________________ ______________________ ______________________	Midpoint
______________________ ______________________ ______________________	Midsegment of a triangle
______________________ ______________________ ______________________	Proof
______________________ ______________________ ______________________	Coordinate proof
______________________ ______________________ ______________________	Distance from a point to a line

Vocabulary and Study Skills

5E: Vocabulary Check (continued)

For use after Lesson 5-3

Write the vocabulary word for each definition. To check your work, fold the paper forward along the dotted line to see the correct answers.

A point that divides a line segment into two congruent segments.

_____

The segment that joins the midpoints of two sides of a triangle.

_____

A convincing argument that uses deductive reasoning.

_____

A proof in which a figure is drawn on a coordinate plane and the formulas for slope, midpoint, and distance are used to prove properties of the figure.

_____

The length of the perpendicular segment from the point to the line.

_____

5F: Vocabulary Review

Study Skill Whenever possible, try to draw a sketch of the object being described by a vocabulary word. It is often easier to remember the meaning of a word when you can associate the word with a drawing or sketch.

Fill in the blanks with the appropriate word.

1. A(n) _____ of a triangle is a perpendicular segment from the vertex to the line containing the side opposite the vertex.

2. A(n) _____ is a series of points that extends in two opposite directions without end.

3. A(n) _____ of a triangle is a segment joining a vertex and the midpoint of the side opposite the vertex.

4. The _____ of a statement has the opposite truth value.

5. A(n) _____ is the negation and interchanging of the hypothesis and conclusion.

6. The bisectors of the angles of a triangle are concurrent at a point known as the _____.

7. The lines containing the altitudes of a triangle are concurrent at a point known as the _____.

8. When an equation is in _____ form, the slope and *y*-intercept are easily identified.

9. The measure of each _____ angle of a triangle equals the sum of the measures of its two remote interior angles.

10. A(n) _____ angle has a measure between 90° and 180°.

11. When two coplanar lines are cut by a transversal, the angles between the two lines on opposite sides of the transversal are called _____ angles.

12. The medians of a triangle are concurrent at a point known as the _____.

13. Statements that always have the same truth-value are _____.

14. A(n) _____ triangle has one angle formed by perpendicular lines.

15. Coplanar lines that do not intersect are _____ lines.

Practice 6-1

Determine the most precise name for each quadrilateral.

1. _____

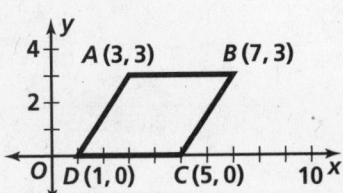

2. _____

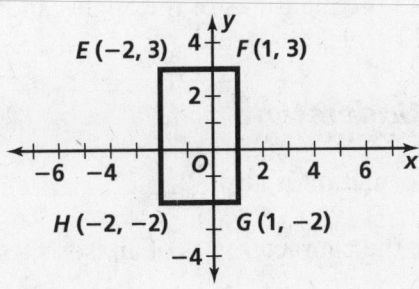

Judging by appearance, classify each quadrilateral in as many ways as possible.

3. _____

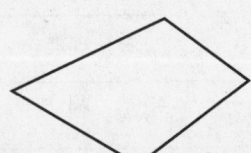

4. _____

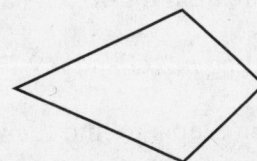

5. _____

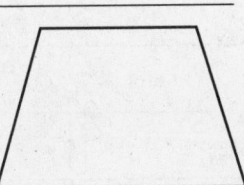

6. _____

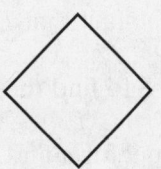

Algebra **Find the values of the variables. Then find the lengths of the sides of each quadrilateral.**

7. _____

rhombus *ABDC*

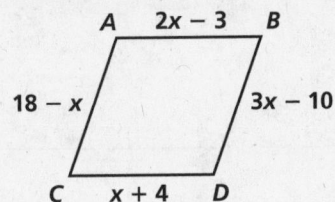

8. _____

square *FGHI*

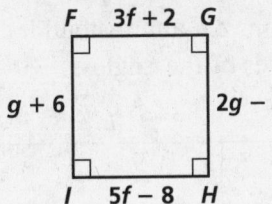

Determine the most precise name for each quadrilateral with the given vertices.

9. $A(1, 4)$, $B(3, 5)$, $C(6, 1)$, $D(4, 0)$ _____

10. $A(-2, 4)$, $B(2, 6)$, $C(6, 4)$, $D(2, -3)$ _____

6-1 • Guided Problem Solving

GPS **Student Page 309, Exercise 25**

Algebra Find the measures of the angles and the lengths of the sides. *DEFG* is an isosceles trapezoid.

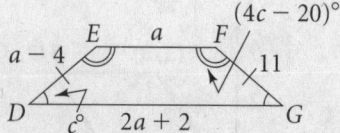

Read and Understand

1. What information is given? _____

2. What are the characteristics of an isosceles trapezoid? _____

3. What are you asked to find? _____

Plan and Solve

4. Write an algebraic expression for $m\angle G$, based on the fact that $m\angle G = m\angle D$. _____

5. Write an equation relating $m\angle G$ and $m\angle F$. _____

6. Solve the equation from Step 5 to find the value of c. _____

7. Substitute the value from Step 6 and find all four angle measures. _____

8. Write an equation based on the fact that $DE = GF$. _____

9. Solve the equation from Step 8 to find the value of a. _____

10. Substitute the value from Step 9 for a and find all four side lengths. _____

Look Back and Check

11. Verify that the sum of the angle measures conforms
    to the Polygon Angle-Sum Theorem (Theorem 3-14). _____

Solve Another Problem

12. Remove the label from $\angle F$ and instead let $m\angle G = 3c - 78$.
    Find the new measures of the angles.

    _____

Practice 6-2

Properties of Parallelograms

Find the value of *x* in each parallelogram.

1. _____

2. _____

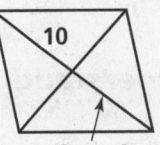

3. _____

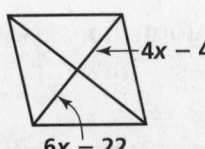

4. _____

$AC = 24$

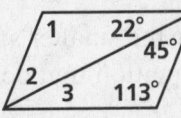

5. _____

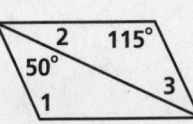

6. _____

$x = EG$

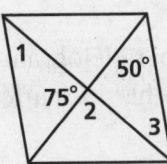

Find the measures of the numbered angles for each parallelogram.

7. _____

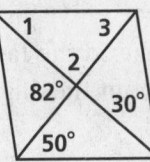

8. _____

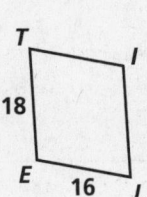

9. _____

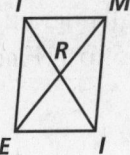

10. _____

11. _____

12. _____

Find the length of $\overline{TI}$ in each parallelogram.

13. _____

14. _____

$OR = \frac{7}{8}IO$

15. _____

$TR = 14, ME = 31$

Name _____ Class _____ Date _____

6-2 • Guided Problem Solving

GPS **Student Page 317, Exercise 41**

Algebra In a parallelogram one angle is 9 times the size of another. Find the measures of the angles.

Read and Understand

1. What information is given? _____

2. What are the characteristics of the angles of a parallelogram? _____

3. Draw a parallelogram and label the given information. Use *x* to represent the measure of one of the angles.

4. What are you asked to find? _____

Plan and Solve

5. Are the two angles described in the problem congruent angles or supplementary angles? Explain. _____

6. Using *x* for the smaller angle measure and 9*x* for the larger angle measure, write an equation that describes the relationship between the two angles. _____

7. Solve the equation from Step 6 to find the two angle measures. _____

Look Back and Check

8. The solution used the fact that the figure is a parallelogram and used properties about the angles. Do the lengths of the sides affect the solution? _____ Explain.

_____

_____

Solve Another Problem

9. Suppose a parallelogram has angle measures with a ratio of 5 to 1. Find the two angle measures. _____

Guided Problem Solving

Practice 6-3

Proving That a Quadrilateral Is a Parallelogram

State whether the information given about quadrilateral *SMTP* is sufficient to prove that it is a parallelogram.

1. $\angle SPT \cong \angle SMT$ _____

2. $\angle SPX \cong \angle TMX$, $\angle TPX \cong \angle SMX$ _____

3. $\overline{SM} \cong \overline{PT}$, $\overline{SP} \cong \overline{MT}$ _____

4. $\overline{SP} \cong \overline{MT}$, $\overline{SP} \parallel \overline{MT}$ _____

Algebra Find the values of *x* and *y* for which the figure must be a parallelogram.

5. $x = $ _____ , $y = $ _____

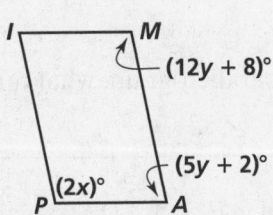

6. $x = $ _____ , $y = $ _____

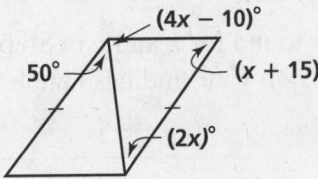

Algebra Find the value of *x*. Then tell whether the figure must be a parallelogram. Explain your answer.

7. _____

_____

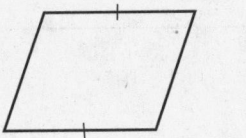

8. _____

_____

Decide whether the quadrilateral is a parallelogram. Explain your answer.

9. _____   **10.** _____   **11.** _____

_____   _____   _____

12. _____   **13.** _____   **14.** _____

_____   _____   _____

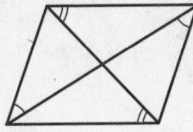

6-3 • Guided Problem Solving

GPS **Student Page 325, Exercise 14**

Algebra Find the values of the variables for which *ABCD* must be a parallelogram.

Read and Understand

1. What information is given? _____

2. What are the characteristics among the angles of a parallelogram? _____

3. What are you asked to do? _____

Plan and Solve

4. If *ABCD* is to be a parallelogram, what must be true of ∠*A* and ∠*D*? Justify your answer.

   _____

5. What must be true of ∠*B* and ∠*D*? Explain. _____

6. Write a system of equations based on the answers to Steps 4 and 5. _____

7. Solve the system for *x* and *y*. _____

Look Back and Check

8. Using the values found for *x* and *y* in Step 7, find the measures of all four angles of *ABCD*. Do your findings match the physical appearance of the figure?

   _____

Solve Another Problem

9. Check for reasonableness: Use an equation to describe the relationship between ∠*A* and ∠*B*. _____

   Did you get the same value for *x*? _____

Guided Problem Solving

Name _____ Class _____ Date _____

Practice 6-4

For each parallelogram, (a) choose the best name, and then (b) find the
measures of the numbered angles.

1. _____

   _____

   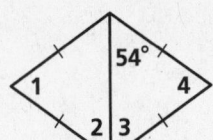

2. _____

   _____

3. _____

   _____

   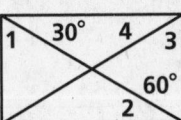

4. _____

   _____

   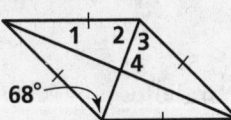

The parallelograms below are not drawn to scale. Can the parallelogram
have the conditions marked? If not, write *impossible*. Explain your answer.

5. _____

   _____

   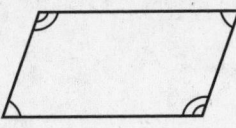

6. _____

   _____

   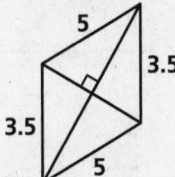

HIJK is a rectangle. Find the value of *x* and the length of each diagonal.

7. $HJ = x$ and $IK = 2x - 7$ _____

8. $HJ = 3x + 7$ and $IK = 6x - 11$ _____

For each rhombus, (a) find the measures of the numbered angles, and then
(b) find the area.

9. _____

   _____

   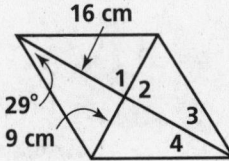

10. _____

    _____

    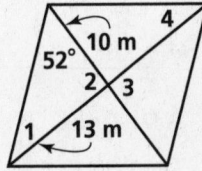

Name_____ Class_____ Date_____

6-4 • Guided Problem Solving

GPS **Student Page 334, Exercise 46**

Algebra Find the values of the variables for parallelogram
$ABCD. BD = 4x = y + 1$.

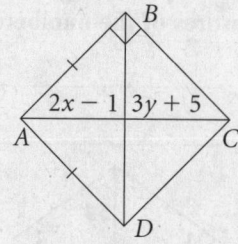

Read and Understand

1. What information is given?_____

2. What kind of line segments are $\overline{AC}$ and $\overline{BD}$?_____

3. What are you asked to do?_____

Plan and Solve

4. What specific type of parallelogram is $ABCD$? Explain._____

_____

5. Because of your answer to Step 4, the diagonals of $ABCD$ are _____

and they _____ each other.

6. Write a system of two equations, based on the results of Step 5._____

7. Solve the system for x and y._____

Look Back and Check

8. Was it necessary to know that $\overline{AB} \cong \overline{AD}$? Was it necessary to know that $m\angle B = 90$? Explain.

_____

Solve Another Problem

9. Suppose $BD = 4x - y + 3$ and the remaining information stays the same.
   Find the length of diagonal $\overline{AC}$.

_____

Practice 6-5

Trapezoids and Kites

Find the measures of the numbered angles in each isosceles trapezoid.

1. _____

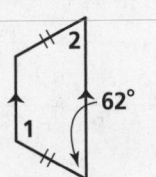

2. _____

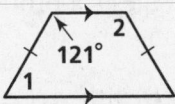

3. _____

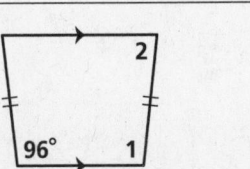

4. _____

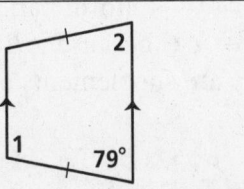

Algebra Find the value of x in each isosceles trapezoid.

5. _____

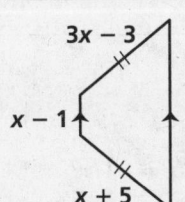

6. _____

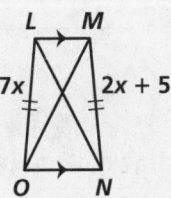

Find the measures of the numbered angles in each kite.

7. _____

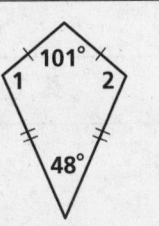

8. _____

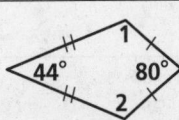

9. _____

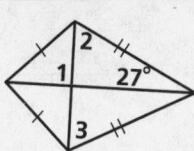

10. _____

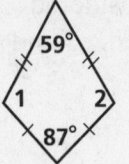

Algebra Find the value of x in each kite.

11. _____

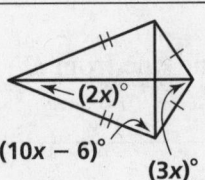

12. _____

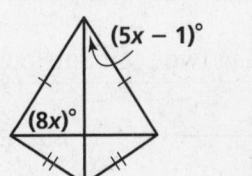

6-5 • Guided Problem Solving

GPS Student Page 340, Exercise 38

Developing Proof The plan suggests a proof of Theorem 6-15.
Write a proof that follows the plan.

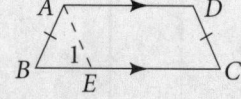

Given: Isosceles trapezoid $ABCD$ with $\overline{AB} \cong \overline{DC}$

Prove: $\angle B \cong \angle C$ and $\angle BAD \cong \angle D$

Plan: Begin by drawing $\overline{AE} \parallel \overline{DC}$ to form parallelogram $AECD$ so
that $\overline{AE} \cong \overline{DC} \cong \overline{AB}$. $\angle B \cong \angle C$ because $\angle B \cong \angle 1$ and $\angle 1 \cong \angle C$. Also,
$\angle BAD \cong \angle D$ because they are supplements of the congruent angles,
$\angle B$ and $\angle C$.

Read and Understand

1. What is given for the proof? _____

2. What are you asked to prove? _____

Plan and Solve

3. With parallelogram $AECD$ drawn, what justifies $\overline{AB} \cong \overline{DC}$, $\overline{DC} \cong \overline{AE}$, and $\overline{AB} \cong \overline{AE}$?

   _____

   _____

4. $\triangle ABE$ is _____, and then $\angle B$ _____ $\angle 1$ because _____.

5. Explain why $\angle 1 \cong \angle C$. _____

   _____

6. Use your results from Steps 4 and 5 to
   describe the relationship between $\angle B$ and $\angle C$. _____

7. Why can $\angle BAD$ and $\angle D$ be considered
   supplements of congruent angles $\angle B$ and $\angle C$? _____

Look Back and Check

8. The drawing shows $AD < BC$. Is our proof still valid if $AD > BC$?

Solve Another Problem

9. Outline a proof involving two segments perpendicular to $\overline{BC}$, one from A and one from D.

   _____

   _____

Practice 6-6

Placing Figures in the Coordinate Plane

Find the coordinates of the midpoint of each segment and find the length of each segment.

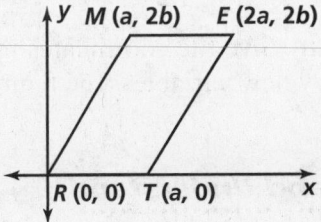

1. $\overline{ME}$ _____

2. $\overline{TR}$ _____

3. $\overline{RM}$ _____

Find the slope of each segment.

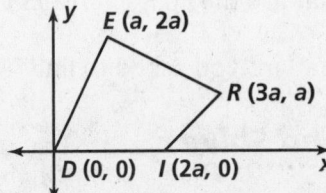

4. $\overline{DI}$ _____

5. $\overline{IR}$ _____

6. $\overline{RE}$ _____

7. $\overline{VE}$ _____

8. $\overline{ER}$ _____

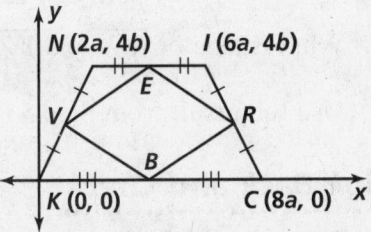

Use the properties of each figure to find the missing coordinates.

9. _____
square

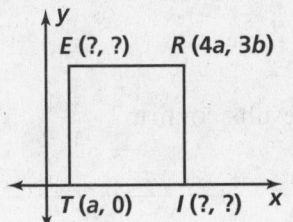

10. _____
parallelogram

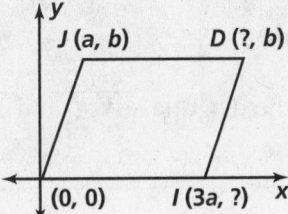

11. _____
isosceles trapezoid

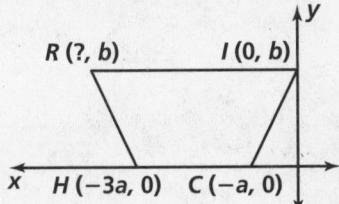

12. _____
kite

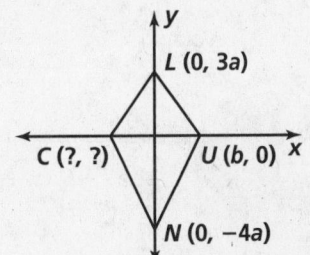

Name _____ Class _____ Date _____

6-6 • Guided Problem Solving

GPS **Student Page 345, Exercise 20**

Algebra Give the coordinates for points W and Z without using any new variables. The figure is a rhombus.

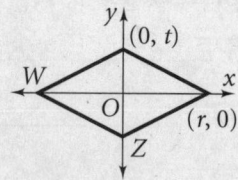

Read and Understand

1. What are you given? _____

2. What are the characteristics of a rhombus? _____

3. What are you asked to find? _____

Plan and Solve

4. Label $(0, 2t)$ point X and label $(2r, 0)$ point Y.
   What is the relation of these segments to the rhombus? _____

5. What is true of $\overline{WX}$ and $\overline{YZ}$ by Theorem 6-3? _____

6. Use the result from Step 5 to write the coordinates of points W and Z. _____

Look Back and Check

7. Suppose, instead of a rhombus, the given figure was a parallelogram.
   Would you still be able to determine the coordinates for points W and Z? _____
   Explain.

   _____

Solve Another Problem

8. Find the slopes of the diagonals $\overline{WX}$ and $\overline{YZ}$. What theorem do the results confirm?

   _____

Practice 6-7

1. Given $\triangle HAL$ with perpendicular bisectors i, b, and m, complete the following to show that i, b, and m intersect in a point.

   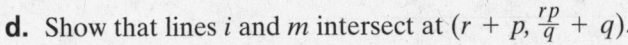

   a. The slope of $\overline{HA}$ is $\frac{-q}{p}$. What is the slope of line i?

   _____

   b. The midpoint of $\overline{HA}$ is (p, q). Show that the equation of line i is $y = \frac{p}{q}x + q - \frac{p^2}{q}$.

   _____

   c. The midpoint of $\overline{HL}$ is $(r + p, 0)$. What is the equation of line m?

   _____

   d. Show that lines i and m intersect at $(r + p, \frac{rp}{q} + q)$.

   _____

   e. The slope of $\overline{AL}$ is $\frac{-q}{r}$. What is the slope of line b?

   _____

   f. What is the midpoint of $\overline{AL}$?

   _____

   g. Show that the equation of line b is $y = \frac{r}{q}x + q - \frac{r^2}{q}$.

   _____

   h. Show that lines b and m intersect at $(r + p, \frac{rp}{q} + q)$.

   _____

   i. Give the coordinates for the point of intersection of i, b, and m.

   _____

Complete Exercise 2 without using any new variables.

2. *RHCP* is a rhombus.

   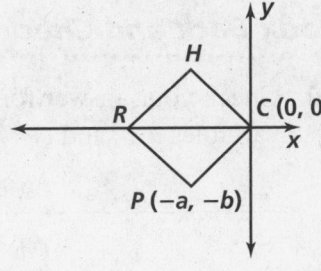

   a. Determine the coordinates of *R*. _____

   b. Determine the coordinates of *H*. _____

   c. Find the midpoint of $\overline{RH}$. _____

   d. Find the slope of $\overline{RH}$. _____

6-7 • Guided Problem Solving

GPS **Student Page 351, Exercise 11**

Prove: The midpoints of the sides of a kite determine a rectangle.

Given: Kite $DEFG$ with $DE = EF$ and $DG = GF$; $K, L, M,$ and N are midpoints of the sides.

Prove: $KLMN$ is a rectangle.

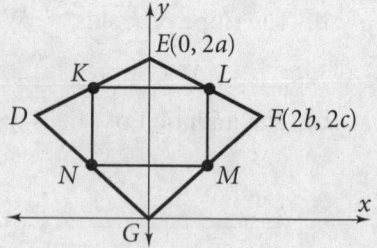

Read and Understand

1. What information is given? _____

2. What are the characteristics of a kite? _____

3. What are you asked to prove? _____

Plan and Solve

4. What are the coordinates of points D and G? _____

5. Use the midpoint formula to find the coordinates of points $L, M, N,$ and K. _____

6. Find the slopes of line segments $\overline{KL}, \overline{NM}, \overline{KN},$ and $\overline{LM}$. _____

7. What can you conclude about the relationships of the pairs of opposite sides of $KLMN$? What does this show about $KLMN$? _____

8. What can you conclude about the pairs of adjacent sides of $KLMN$? _____

9. What kind of angles are $\angle KNM, \angle NML, \angle MLK,$ and $\angle LKN$? _____

Look Back and Check

10. Check your answer for reasonableness by substituting values for the variables $a, b,$ and c.

_____

Solve Another Problem

11. Outline a proof that the diagonals of $DEFG$ are perpendicular. _____

_____

6A: Graphic Organizer

For use before Lesson 6-1

Study Skill When taking notes do not write down everything the teacher is saying. It is impossible to do. Spend time listening and write down the main points and examples. If you are writing fast you cannot listen well.

Write your answers.

1. What is the chapter title? _____

2. Find the Table of Contents page for this chapter at the front of the book.
   Name four topics you will study in this chapter.

   _____   _____

   _____   _____

3. Complete the graphic organizer as you work through the chapter.
   1. Write the title of the chapter in the center oval.
   2. When you begin a lesson, write the name of the lesson in a rectangle.
   3. When you complete that lesson, write a skill or key concept from that lesson in the outer oval linked to that rectangle.
   Continue with steps 2 and 3 clockwise around the graphic organizer.

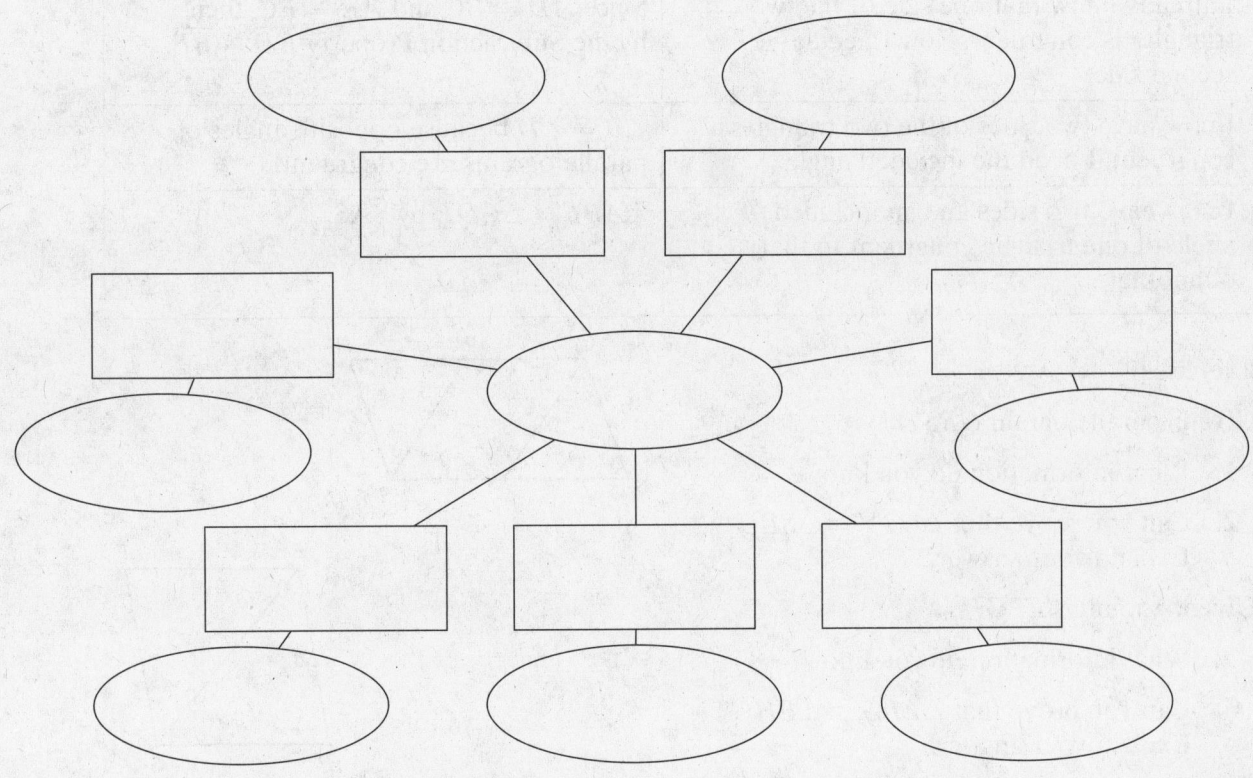

6B: Reading Comprehension

For use after Lesson 6-6

Study Skill As you read a proof, make sure you understand each statement. Look at any diagrams that go along with the proof, or draw a diagram to help you understand each step.

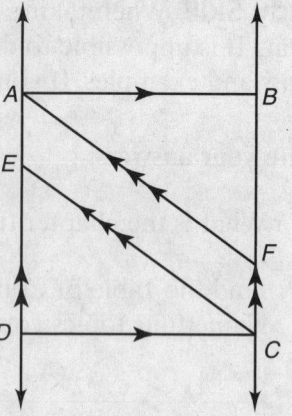

Read the problem and follow along with the thought process and the written steps to complete the proof. Check your understanding by completing the exercise at the bottom of the page.

Given: parallelogram $ABCD$
parallelogram $AECF$

Prove: $\triangle ABF \cong \triangle CDE$

Thought Process	Informal Proof
To prove $\triangle ABF \cong \triangle CDE$, use one of the following theorems; SSS, SAS, ASA, or AAS. It is given that $ABCD$ is a parallelogram, so you know that $\overline{AB} \cong \overline{CD}$ and $\overline{AD} \cong \overline{BC}$.	$\overline{AB} \cong \overline{CD}$ and $\overline{AD} \cong \overline{BC}$ because opposite sides of a parallelogram are congruent.
It is also given that $AECF$ is a parallelogram, so $\overline{AE} \cong \overline{FC}$.	$\overline{AE} \cong \overline{FC}$ because opposite sides of a parallelogram are congruent.
I already know that one side of the two triangles is congruent. Now I need a second side.	Since $\overline{AD} \cong \overline{BC}$ and $\overline{AE} \cong \overline{FC}$, then by the Subtraction Property $\overline{ED} \cong \overline{BF}$.
I now have two sides of the two triangles congruent. I need the included angle.	$\angle B \cong \angle D$ because opposite angles of parallelograms are congruent.
I now have two sides and an included angle of one triangle congruent to that of another.	$\triangle ABF \cong \triangle CDE$ by SAS.

Exercises

Given: parallelogram $QRST$

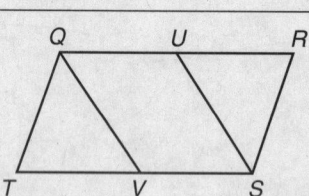

1. What information do you know?

2. Can you prove that $\triangle QTV \cong \triangle SRU$? Explain your answer.

Given: rhombus $EFGH$

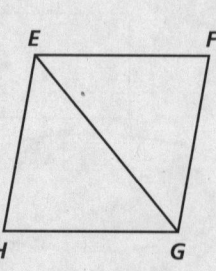

3. What information do you know?

4. Can you prove that $\triangle EFG \cong \triangle EHG$? Explain your answer.

5. **High-Use Academic Words** In Exercise 2, what does *explain* mean for you to do?

   a. simplify   **b.** give reasons for

6C: Reading/Writing Math Symbols
For use after Lesson 6-2

Study Skill Diagrams are handy notetaking tools to help you remember a new concept. When you draw a diagram, label it properly. Without labels, a diagram might be meaningless when you review your notes.

Identify a specific point or segment on the figure for the given terms below. There may be more than one correct response.

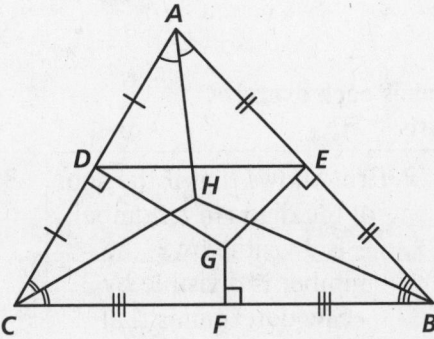

1. angle bisector _____

2. perpendicular bisector _____

3. circumcenter _____

4. midsegment _____

Classify each quadrilateral using the most specific name.

5.

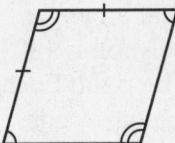

_____

6.

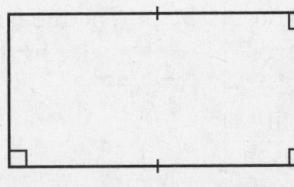

_____

7.

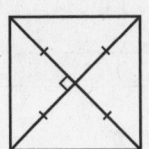

_____

8.

_____

6D: Visual Vocabulary Practice
High-Use Academic Words

For use after Lesson 6-5

Study Skill When interpreting an illustration, notice the information that is given and also notice what is not given. Do not make assumptions.

Concept List

analysis	common	convert
deduce	equivalent	equal
identify	indirect	solve

Write the concept that best describes each exercise.
Choose from the concept list above.

1. $2x + 6 = 40$ $2x = 34$ $x = 17$ _____	**2.** Erin knows that if the sum of the digits in a number is divisible by 3, the number is divisible by 3. She determines that $3 + 4 + 2$ is divisible by 3 and reasons that 342 is divisible by 3. _____	**3.** A conditional statement and its contrapositive. _____
4. Your mother says, "Ann called a few minutes ago." You have two friends named Ann. One is at band practice. You reason that the other Ann must have been the caller. _____	**5.** The measure of the angles in the triangle 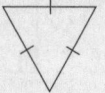 _____	**6.** Miles said that an angle of a regular polygon is 130° but that can't be right. Each angle of a regular n-gon is $\frac{(n-2)180}{n}$. If we let this expression equal 130 and solve for n, we do not get a whole number. _____
7. 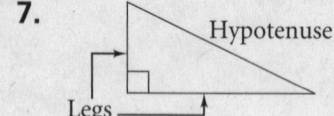 _____	**8.** $1320 \text{ ft} = \frac{1}{4} \text{ mi}$ _____	**9.** 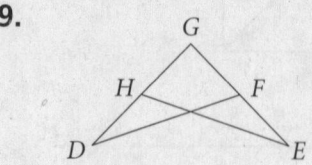 $\angle DGF$ and $\angle EGH$ _____

6E: Vocabulary Check

For use after Lesson 6-4

Study Skill Strengthen your vocabulary. Use these pages and add cues and summaries by applying the Cornell Notetaking style.

Write the definition for each word at the right. To check your work, fold the paper back along the dotted line to see the correct answers.

____________________	Consecutive angles
____________________	Kite
____________________	Parallelogram
____________________	Rhombus
____________________	Trapezoid

6E: Vocabulary Check (continued)

For use after Lesson 6-4

Write the vocabulary word for each definition. To check your work, fold the paper forward along the dotted line to see the correct answers.

Angles of a polygon that share a common side.

_____

A quadrilateral with two pairs of congruent adjacent sides and no opposite sides congruent.

_____

A quadrilateral with two pairs of parallel sides.

_____

A parallelogram with four congruent sides.

_____

A quadrilateral with exactly one pair of parallel sides.

_____

6F: Vocabulary Review Puzzle

For use with Chapter Review

Study Skill Try writing vocabulary words on note cards, with the definitions on the back of the cards. You can then flip through the cards and say the definitions to yourself as you read each word. If you need help remembering the definition, flip the card over.

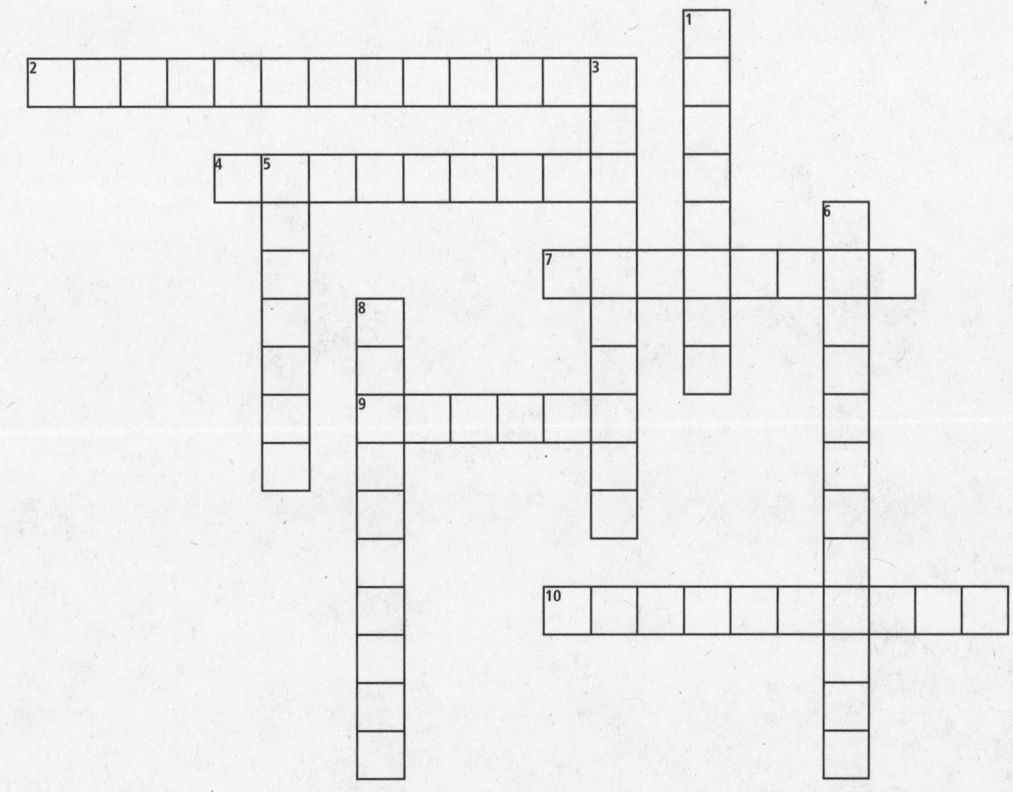

ACROSS	DOWN
2. a quadrilateral with both pairs of opposite sides parallel	**1.** the angle bisectors of a triangle are concurrent at this point
4. a quadrilateral with exactly one pair of sides of parallel sides	**3.** joins the midpoints of the nonparallel a trapezoid
7. the medians of a triangle are concurrent at this point	**5.** quadrilateral with four congruent sides
9. a parallelogram with four congruent sides and are four right angles	**6.** the perpendicular bisectors of a triangle concurrent at this point
10. the side opposite the right angle in a right triangle	**8.** these angles are congruent in an isosceles trapezoid

Practice 7-1

1. The Washington Monument in Washington, D.C., is about 556 ft tall. A three-dimensional puzzle of the Washington Monument is 24 in. tall. What is the ratio of the height of the puzzle to the height of the real monument? _____

Find the actual dimensions of each room.

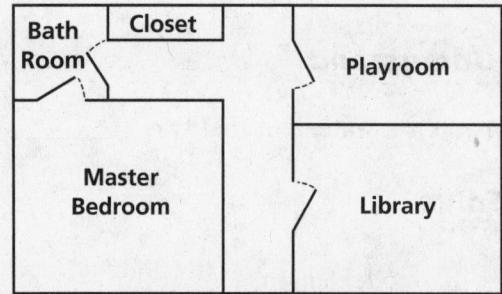

2. playroom _____

3. master bedroom _____

4. closet _____

Scale: 1 in. = 16 ft

Algebra If $\frac{x}{y} = \frac{5}{8}$, are each of the following true or false?

5. $8x = 5y$ _____

6. $5x = 8y$ _____

7. $\frac{x}{5} = \frac{y}{8}$ _____

8. $\frac{x}{8} = \frac{y}{5}$ _____

9. $\frac{x + y}{y} = \frac{13}{8}$ _____

10. $\frac{x}{y} = \frac{10}{16}$ _____

Algebra Solve each proportion for *x*.

11. $\frac{x}{4} = \frac{9}{3}$ _____

12. $\frac{6}{11} = \frac{x}{22}$ _____

13. $\frac{6}{x} = \frac{2}{11}$ _____

14. $\frac{2}{x} = \frac{x}{32}$ _____

15. $\frac{x}{x + 2} = \frac{3}{4}$ _____

16. $\frac{x + 1}{x} = \frac{7}{5}$ _____

For each rectangle, find the ratio of the longer side to the shorter side.

17. _____

25 ft

70 ft

18. _____

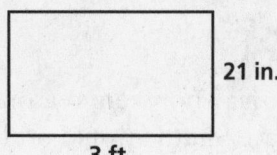

21 in.

3 ft

Complete each of the following.

19. If $3x = 8y$, then $\frac{x}{y} = \frac{?}{?}$. _____

20. If $\frac{a}{7} = \frac{b}{13}$, then $\frac{a}{b} = \frac{?}{?}$. _____

7-1 • Guided Problem Solving

GPS Student Page 370, Exercise 44

Geography Students at the University of Minnesota in Minneapolis built a model globe 42 ft in diameter using a scale of 1 : 1,000,000. About how tall is Mount Everest on the model? (Mount Everest is about 29,000 ft tall.)

Read and Understand

1. A proportion is a statement that two _____ are equal.

Plan and Solve

2. Use the ratio $\frac{\text{model length}}{\text{actual length}}$. First, what is the ratio for the model globe? _____

3. Mount Everest is about 29,000 ft tall. Will this number appear in the numerator or the denominator of the second ratio? _____

4. Let x be the height of Mount Everest on the model globe. Write the proportion. (Since all measurements are in feet, no conversions are necessary.)

   _____

5. What property will you use to eliminate both denominators? _____

   _____

6. Use this property to solve the proportion for x. $x =$ _____ ft

7. Convert your answer to inches. If the model globe has a diameter of 42 feet, how high is Mount Everest in inches? $x =$ _____ in.

Look Back and Check

8. At first, your answer may not seem reasonable. But, on this scale, the Space Shuttle would orbit about 10 in. above the model. Now does your answer seem appropriate? _____

Solve Another Problem

9. The Nile is the longest river on earth at about 4150 miles long. How long (in feet) is the Nile on the model? (Hint: First convert 4150 miles to feet.) _____ ft

Practice 7-2

Similar Polygons

Are the polygons similar? If they are, write a similarity statement, and give the similarity ratio. If they are not, explain.

1. _____

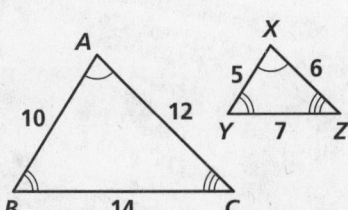

2. _____

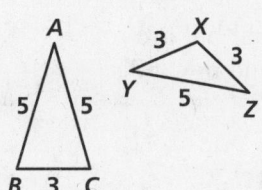

3. _____

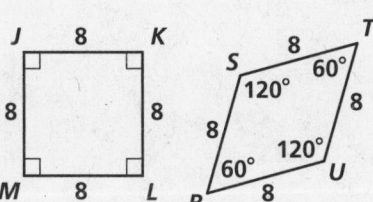

4. _____

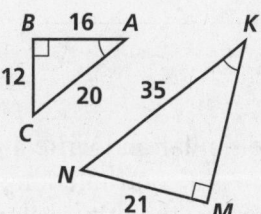

LMNO ~ HIJK. Complete the proportions and congruence statements.

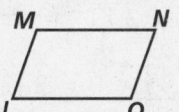

5. $\angle M \cong$? _____

6. $\angle K \cong$? _____

7. $\dfrac{MN}{IJ} = \dfrac{?}{JK}$ _____

8. $\dfrac{HK}{?} = \dfrac{HI}{LM}$ _____

Algebra The polygons are similar. Find the values of the variables.

9. _____

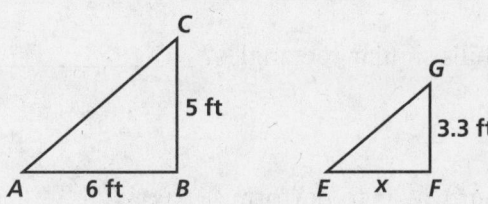

10. _____

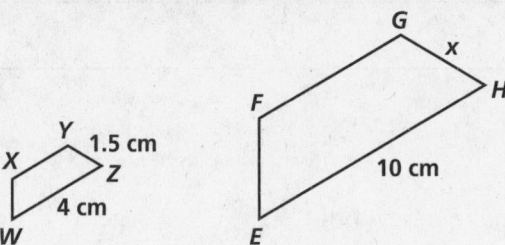

$\triangle WXZ \sim \triangle DFG.$ Use the diagram to find the following.

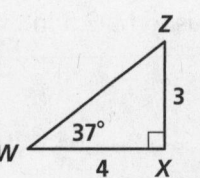
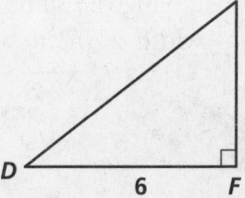

11. the similarity ratio of $\triangle WXZ$ and $\triangle DFG$ _____

12. $m\angle Z$ _____

13. DG _____

14. GF _____

15. $m\angle D$ _____

7-2 • Guided Problem Solving

GPS **Student Page 377, Exercise 48**

Money From 1861 to 1928, U.S. paper currency measured 7.42 in. by 3.13 in. The dimensions of a current bill are shown here. Are the old and new bills similar rectangles?

Read and Understand

1. If the old bill and the new bill are similar rectangles, the ratios of the dimensions must be _____ .

Plan and Solve

Assume the rectangles are similar and write a proportion. If an error occurs in the following steps, there is a contradiction and the assumption was incorrect. If there are no errors, then the rectangles are similar.

$\dfrac{7.42}{3.13} =$ _____

2. Complete the proportion by writing the ratio for the new bill on the right side of the equation.

7.42(_____) = 3.13(_____)

3. Use the Cross-Product Property.

_____ = _____

4. Simplify the products. Do not approximate.

5. Are the two sides of the equation the same? _____

6. Based on your answer in Step 5, are the old and new bills similar rectangles? _____

Look Back and Check

7. There are several ways to solve this problem. One other way is to perform the divisions in the fractions in Step 2. Do so. What values do you obtain? Round the values to four decimal places. _____ and _____

8. Interpret this result. _____

Solve Another Problem

9. Suppose the Department of the Treasury wants to make a new bill having the same ratio of sides as a golden rectangle (1.618 : 1). If the width of the new bill is to be 2.5 in., what will be the length of the new bill? _____ in.

Practice 7-3

Proving Triangles Similar

Explain why the triangles are similar. Write a similarity statement for each pair.

1. _____

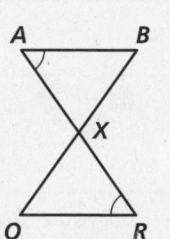

2. _____

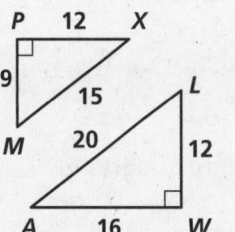

3. _____

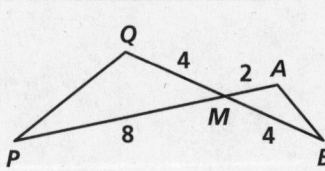

4. _____

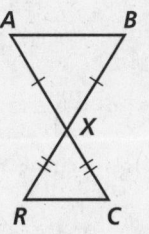

Algebra **Find the value of *x*.**

5. _____

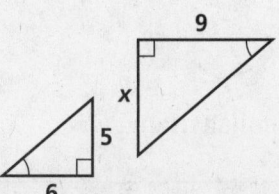

6. _____

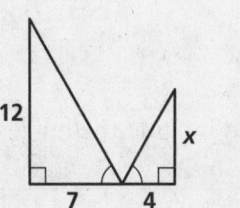

7. _____

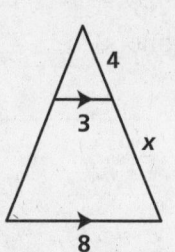

8. _____

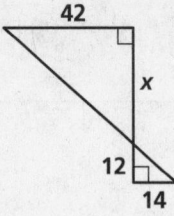

9. Natasha places a mirror on the ground 24 ft from the base of an oak tree. She walks backward until she can see the top of the tree in the middle of the mirror. At that point, Natasha's eyes are 5.5 ft above the ground, and her feet are 4 ft from the image in the mirror. Find the height of the oak tree. _____

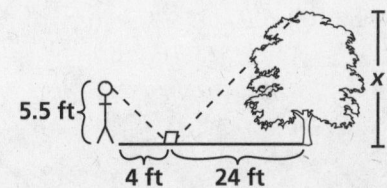

7-3 • Guided Problem Solving

GPS **Student Page 387, Exercise 22**

a. Classify *RSTW*.
b. Must any of the triangles shown be similar? Explain.

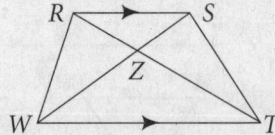

Read and Understand

1. Are any sides of the figure congruent? _____ If so, which ones? _____

2. Are any sides of the figure parallel? _____ If so, which ones? _____

3. Based on your answers to Steps 1 and 2, classify *RSTW*. _____

Plan and Solve

4. How are ∠*RZS* and ∠*WZT* related? _____

5. What do the arrows indicate about sides *RS* and *WT*? _____

6. Therefore, how are ∠*SWT* and ∠*RSW* related? _____

7. Based on your answers to Steps 4 and 6, which triangles are similar? _____

8. What postulate or theorem did you use to justify this result? _____

Look Back and Check

9. △*RSW* and △*TWS* also include the angles given in Step 6. Are they similar triangles? _____
   Why or why not? _____

Solve Another Problem

10. Is the result in Step 7 true for other four-sided figures? _____ If so, which one(s)? _____

_____

Practice 7-4

Similarity in Right Triangles

....

Algebra **Find the geometric mean of each pair of numbers.**

1. 32 and 8 _____

2. 4 and 16 _____

3. 10 and 20 _____

4. 6 and 30 _____

Algebra **Refer to the figure to complete each proportion.**

5. $\dfrac{x}{h} = \dfrac{?}{y}$ _____

6. $\dfrac{a}{b} = \dfrac{?}{h}$ _____

7. $\dfrac{a}{c} = \dfrac{y}{?}$ _____

8. $\dfrac{b}{x} = \dfrac{?}{b}$ _____

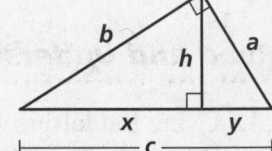

Algebra **Find the values of the variables.**

9. $x =$ _____

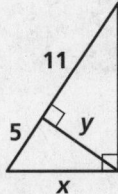

10. $x =$ _____ , $y =$ _____

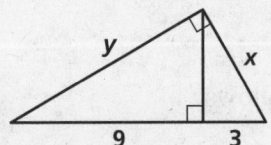

11. $x =$ _____ , $y =$ _____

12. The altitude to the hypotenuse of a right triangle divides the hypotenuse
into segments 6 in. and 10 in. long. Find the length h of the altitude.

....

7-4 • Guided Problem Solving

For a right triangle, denote lengths as follows: ℓ_1 and ℓ_2 the legs, h the hypotenuse, a the altitude, and h_1 and h_2 the hypotenuse segments determined by the altitude. For $h = 2$ and $h_1 = 1$, find the other four measures. Use simplest radical form.

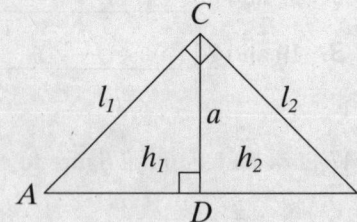

Read and Understand

1. Using the letters A, B, C, and D, label the figure as illustrated. What are the similar triangles you will use to solve this problem? _____

Read and Understand

2. If $h = 2$ and $h_1 = 1$, you can solve for h_2. What is h_2? $h_2 =$ _____

Use $\triangle ACD$ and $\triangle BCD$ to solve for a as follows.

$\dfrac{(\ \ )}{a} = \dfrac{a}{(\ \ )}$ **3.** Write a proportion.

$a^2 =$ _____ **4.** Use the Cross-Product Property.

$a =$ _____ **5.** Take the square root.

To solve for ℓ_1, compare $\triangle ABC$ and $\triangle ACD$.

$\dfrac{l_1}{(\ \ )} = \dfrac{(\ \ )}{l_1}$ **6.** Write a proportion.

$l_1^2 =$ _____ **7.** Use the Cross-Product Property.

$l_1 =$ _____ **8.** Take the square root.

9. Finally, ℓ_2 is found in a similar manner. What is ℓ_2? $\ell_2 =$ _____

Look Back and Check

10. Use a ruler to construct triangles with the dimensions found. Are your answers correct? _____

Solve Another Problem

11. If, instead of h and h_1, values for ℓ_1 and ℓ_2 were given originally, could you solve for the other parts with that information? _____

Practice 7-5

Proportions in Triangles

Use the figure at the right to complete each proportion.

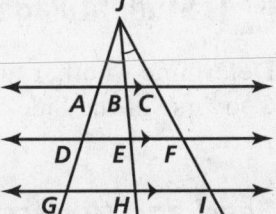

1. $\dfrac{AD}{DG} = \dfrac{?}{EH}$ _____

2. $\dfrac{JA}{JC} = \dfrac{AB}{?}$ _____

3. $\dfrac{JF}{FE} = \dfrac{?}{DE}$ _____

4. $\dfrac{AD}{AG} = \dfrac{?}{BH}$ _____

Algebra Find the values of the variables.

5. $x =$ _____

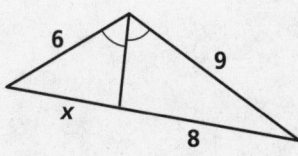

6. $x =$ _____

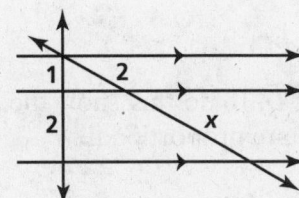

7. $x =$ _____, $y =$ _____

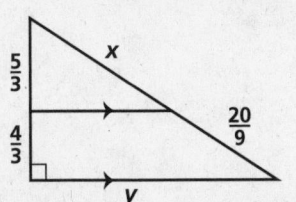

8. $x =$ _____

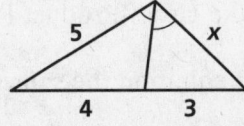

9. $x =$ _____, $y =$ _____

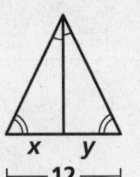

Algebra Solve for *x*.

10. _____

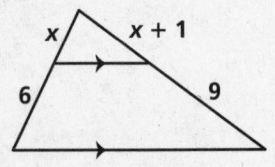

11. _____

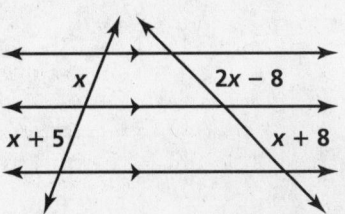

7-5 • Guided Problem Solving

GPS Student Page 402, Exercise 36

Determine whether the segments $\overline{AB}$ and $\overline{CD}$ are parallel. You can use the Converse of the Side-Splitter Theorem.

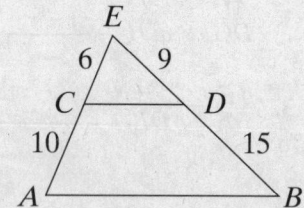

Read and Understand

1. The Converse of the Side-Splitter Theorem states: If a line divides two sides of a triangle proportionally, then it is _____ to the third side.

Plan and Solve

You need to show $\overline{AB}\|\overline{CD}$. To do this, show the corresponding parts divided by the line are proportional.

$\dfrac{AC}{(\ \ )} = \dfrac{(\ \ )}{DE}$ **2.** Write a proportion.

$\dfrac{10}{(\ \ )} = \dfrac{(\ \ )}{9}$ **3.** Substitute.

$90 = $ _____   **4.** Use the Cross-Product Property.

5. Are the two sides of the equation the same? _____

6. Therefore, are $\overline{AB}$ and $\overline{CD}$ parallel? _____

Look Back and Check

7. If your answer to Step 5 were different, how would that change your answer to Step 6? _____

_____

Solve Another Problem

8. Based on your answer to Step 6, how are $\triangle AEB$ and $\triangle CED$ related? _____

7A: Graphic Organizer

For use before Lesson 7-1

Study Skill When taking notes, write down everything written on the chalkboard or overhead. What you write down may be a clue as to what might be on an exam or test.

Write your answers.

1. What is the chapter title? _____

2. Find the Table of Contents page for this chapter at the front of the book. Name four topics you will study in this chapter.

   _____   _____

   _____   _____

3. Complete the graphic organizer as you work through the chapter.
   1. Write the title of the chapter in the center oval.
   2. When you begin a lesson, write the name of the lesson in a rectangle.
   3. When you complete that lesson, write a skill or key concept from that lesson in the outer oval linked to that rectangle.
   Continue with steps 2 and 3 clockwise around the graphic organizer.

7B: Reading Comprehension

Study Skill When you are reading to solve a problem, you may be required to remember a concept or skill that you learned earlier in a course to solve the problem. That is why it is a good idea to record important ideas or concepts in a notebook. The act of writing these concepts will help you remember them, and they will be in your notebook for you to study at a later date.

Read through the problem and study the diagram. Then answer the questions below to help you solve the problem.

Jaime wants to find the height of a building, but he does not have a way to measure it directly. From a point A, 100 ft from the base of the building B, the angle to a point C, 50 ft above the base of the building measures 27°. Locate the point on the ground, D at which the angle to the top of the building, H also measures 27°. You can now use the similarity of these two triangles to calculate the height of the building.

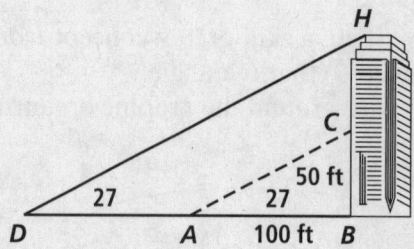

1. Which two triangles are similar? _____

2. Why are the two triangles similar? _____

3. What is the ratio of $CB : AB$? _____

4. What is the ratio of $HB : DB$? _____

5. State a proportion that compares corresponding sides of similar triangles and would allow you to find HB. _____

6. If $DB = 500$ ft, what is the height of the building? _____

7. **High-Use Academic Words** In the word problem, what does *locate* mean for you to do?

   a. determine the location of
   b. label

7C: Reading/Writing Math Symbols

For use after Lesson 7-2

Study Skill In mathematics, you will often be asked to compare diagrams, looking for similarity or congruence. In doing so, you must pay close attention to the symbols on the diagrams.

Determine whether each of the following expressions is equivalent to the ratio *a* to *b*.

1. $a + b$

2. $2ab$

3. $\dfrac{a}{b}$

4. $a - b$

5. $a : b$

6. $\dfrac{b}{a}$

State the postulate or theorem you can use to prove the triangles congruent. If the triangles *cannot* be proven congruent, write *not possible*.

7.

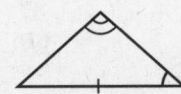

8.

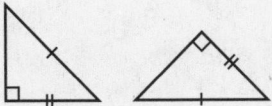

9.

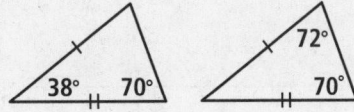

10.

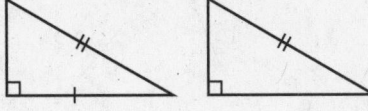

Name_____ Class_____ Date_____

7D: Visual Vocabulary Practice

For use after Lesson 7-4

Study Skill Making sense of mathematical symbols is like reading a foreign language that uses different letters.

Concept List

Angle-Angle Similarity Postulate	Cross-Product Property	geometric mean
Side-Side-Side Similarity Theorem	golden rectangle	scale
Side-Angle-Side Similarity Theorem	golden ratio	simplest radical form

**Write the concept that best describes each exercise.
Choose from the concept list above.**

1. 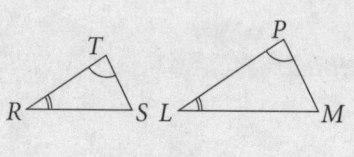 $\triangle RTS \sim \triangle LPM$ _____	**2.** about $1.618 : 1$ _____	**3.** 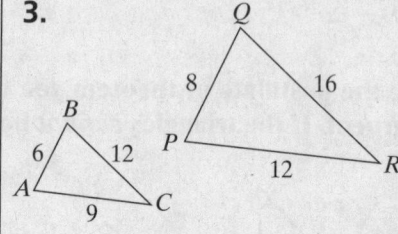 $\triangle ABC \sim \triangle PQR$ _____
4. $\dfrac{6}{x} = \dfrac{x}{24}$ $x^2 = 144$ $x = 12$ _____	**5.** $1 \text{ cm} : 0.75 \text{ km}$ _____	**6.** $\dfrac{a}{b} = \dfrac{c}{d}$ $ad = bc$ _____
7. 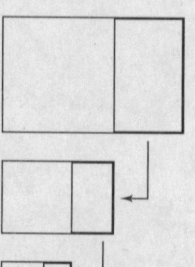 _____	**8.** $h = \sqrt{50} = 5\sqrt{2}$ _____	**9.** 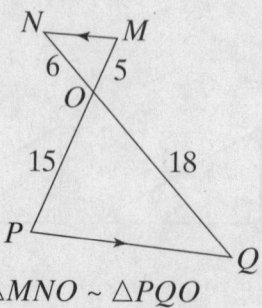 $\triangle MNO \sim \triangle PQO$ _____

Vocabulary and Study Skills

7E: Vocabulary Check

For use after Lesson 7-3

Study Skill Strengthen your vocabulary. Use these pages and add cues and summaries by applying the Cornell Notetaking style.

Write the definition for each word at the right. To check your work, fold the paper back along the dotted line to see the correct answers.

_____

_____

_____

_____

_____

_____

_____

_____

_____

_____

_____

_____

Similarity ratio

Cross-Product Property

Ratio

Golden rectangle

Scale

Vocabulary and Study Skills

7E: Vocabulary Check (continued)   For use after Lesson 7-3

Write the vocabulary word for each definition. To check your work, fold the paper forward along the dotted line to see the correct answers.

The ratio of lengths of corresponding sides of similar polygons.

_____

The product of the extremes of a proportion is equal to the product of the means.

_____

A comparison of two quantities by division.

_____

A rectangle that can be divided into a square and a rectangle that is similar to the original rectangle.

_____

The ratio of any length in a scale drawing to the corresponding actual length.

_____

Name _____ Class _____ Date _____

7F: Vocabulary Review

For use with Chapter Review

Study Skill In any course when you learn a large number of vocabulary terms, it is good to once in a while take the time to go back and review some of the terms from previous chapters.

Match each term in Column A with its definition in Column B by drawing a line between them.

Column A

1. similar polygons
2. central angle
3. segment of a circle
4. geometric mean
5. sector of a circle
6. adjacent arcs
7. polygon
8. arc length
9. circle
10. ratio
11. centroid
12. proportion
13. hypotenuse
14. scalene triangle
15. alternate interior angles

Column B

A. positive number such that the product of the extremes equals the square of the number
B. triangle with no sides congruent
C. closed figure with at least three sides
D. fraction of the circle's circumference
E. angle whose vertex is the center of the circle
F. nonadjacent interior angles on opposite sides of the transversal
G. set of all points in a plane equidistant from one point
H. side opposite the right angle in a triangle
I. part of a circle bounded by an arc and the segment adjoining its endpoints
J. region bounded by two radii and their intercepted arc
K. arcs on the same circle with exactly one point in common
L. congruent corresponding angles and proportional corresponding sides
M. statement that two ratios are equal
N. the medians of a triangle are concurrent at this point
O. comparison of two quantities by division

Practice 8-1

The Pythagorean Theorem and Its Converse

Find the value of each variable. Leave your answers in simplest radical form.

1. _____

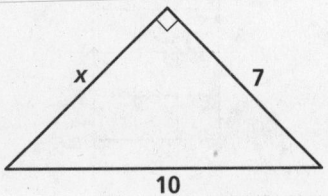

2. _____

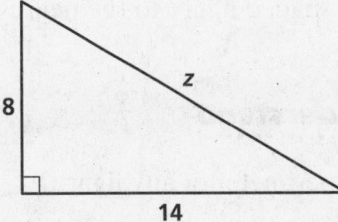

3. _____

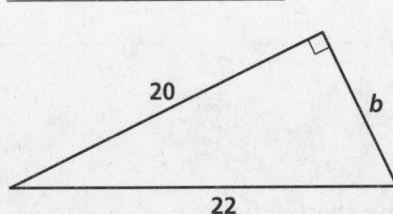

4. _____

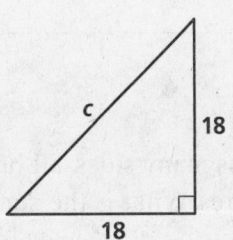

Find the length of each hypotenuse. Use your calculator, and round your answers to the nearest whole number.

5. _____

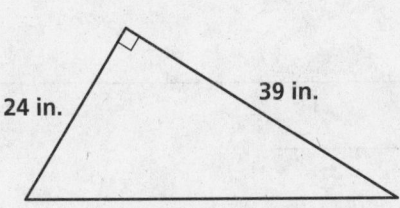

6. _____

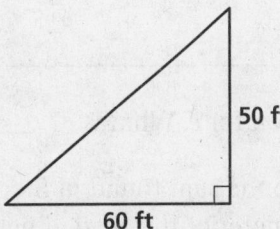

7. _____

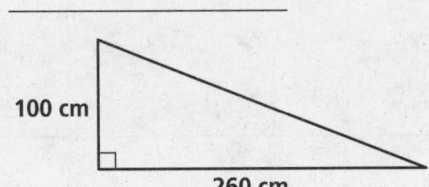

8. _____

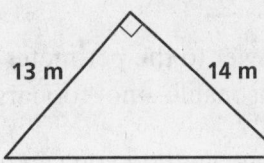

The numbers represent the lengths of the sides of a triangle. Classify each triangle as *acute, obtuse,* or *right*.

9. 6, 9, 10 _____

10. 20, 100, 110 _____

11. 7, 24, 25 _____

8-1 • Guided Problem Solving

GPS **Student Page 422, Exercise 50**

The figure to the right is drawn on centimeter grid paper. Find the perimeter of the shaded figure to the nearest tenth.

Read and Understand

1. What is the perimeter of any figure? _____

2. What theorem will be used to solve for the perimeter of the given figure?

_____

Plan and Solve

3. The shaded figure has many sides, all but one of which are sides of
   one-centimeter squares. What is the sum of these lengths for the shaded figure? _____

4. The remaining side, the longest one, is the diagonal of
   a rectangle. What are the dimensions of this rectangle? _____

5. Let c be the length of the diagonal (in cm) and write c^2 in terms of the
   known sides. Use the answer to Step 2 to do this.

_____

6. Solve this equation for c. What is c? _____

7. Add this value to the sum found in Step 3.
   What is the perimeter of the shaded figure? _____

Look Back and Check

8. Compare your answer to the perimeter of the entire rectangle.
   Is your answer reasonable—not too large or too small? _____

9. Describe at least one method you can use to approximate the answer. _____

_____

Solve Another Problem

10. Find the sum of the perimeters of the two non-shaded figures in the same drawing. _____

Practice 8-2

Special Right Triangles

Find the value of each variable. Leave your answers in simplest radical form.

1. $x =$ _____, $y =$ _____

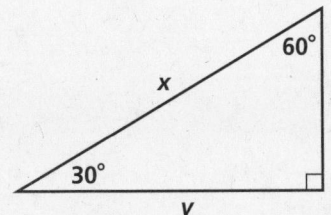

2. $x =$ _____

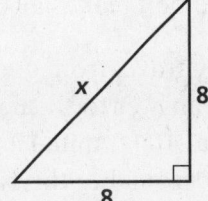

3. $y =$ _____

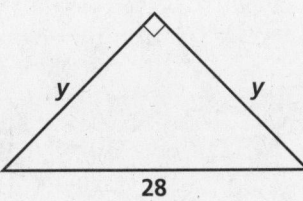

4. $z =$ _____

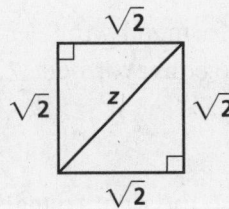

5. $x =$ _____, $y =$ _____

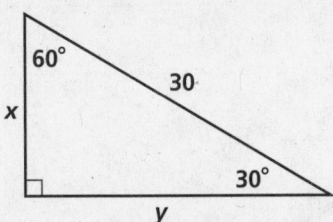

6. $s =$ _____

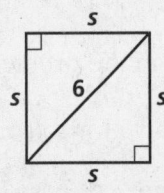

7. Find the length to the nearest centimeter of the diagonal of a square 30 cm on a side.

_____

8. In a 30°-60°-90° triangle, the shorter leg is 6 ft long. Find the length to the nearest tenth of a foot of the other two sides.

_____

Algebra Find the value of each variable. Leave your answers in simplest radical form.

9. $a =$ _____, $b =$ _____

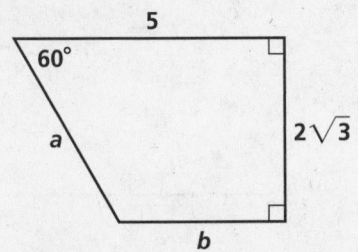

10. $p =$ _____, $q =$ _____, $r =$ _____, $s =$ _____

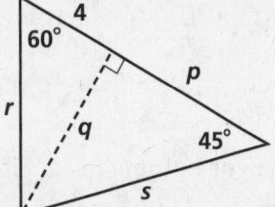

Geometry Lesson 8-2 **315**

8-2 • Guided Problem Solving

• •

GPS **Student Page 429, Exercise 25**

Farming A conveyor belt carries bales of hay from the ground to the barn loft 24 ft above the ground. The belt makes a 60° angle with the ground.

a. How far does a bale of hay travel from one end of the conveyor belt to the other? Round your answer to the nearest foot.

b. The conveyor belt moves at 100 ft/min. How long does it take for a bale of hay to go from the ground to the barn loft?

Read and Understand

1. What kind of triangle is formed by the
   ground, the barn, and the conveyor belt? _____

Plan and Solve

To assist you in your work, use the right triangle given to the right where s, l, and h are the lengths of the shorter side, the longer side, and the hypotenuse, respectively.

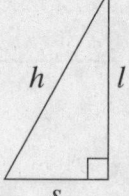

2. Does the 24-ft distance given in the problem correspond to s, l, or h? _____

3. In part (a), are we asked to solve for s, l, or h? _____

4. Complete the equation for a 30°-60°-90° triangle: $l =$ _____ $\cdot s$.

5. Use the value given in the problem and solve for s. Do not approximate yet. $s =$ _____

6. Complete the equation for a 30°-60°-90° triangle: $h =$ _____ $\cdot s$.

7. Use the answer to Step 5 to solve for h. Do not simplify or approximate yet. $h =$ _____

8. Round to the nearest foot and answer the question in part (a). _____

9. For part (b) use the equation **distance = rate × time.** What is the answer to part (b)? _____

Look Back and Check

10. Sketch a triangle with the values expressed in mm rather than feet. Do the values form a 30°-60°-90° triangle? _____

Solve Another Problem

11. Answer part (a) if the conveyor belt makes a 45° angle with the ground. _____

Practice 8-3

The Tangent Ratio

Write the tangent ratios for ∠E and ∠F.

1. _____

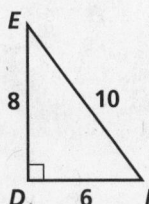

2. _____

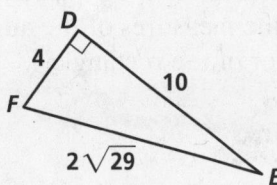

Find each missing value. Round your answers to the nearest tenth.

3. $\tan 46° = \dfrac{?}{12}$

4. $\tan \underline{\ ?\ } = \dfrac{3}{5}$

Find the value of x. Round your answers to the nearest tenth.

5. _____

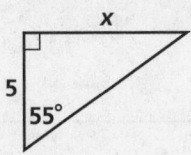

6. _____

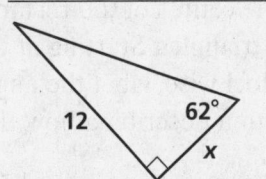

To the nearest tenth, find the measure of the acute angle that the given line forms with a horizontal line.

7. $y = \dfrac{1}{2}x + 4$

8. $y = 3x - 6$

Find the value of x. Round your answers to the nearest degree.

9. _____

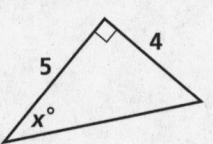

10. _____

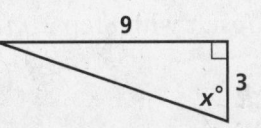

11. _____

12. _____

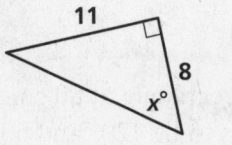

8-3 • Guided Problem Solving

GPS **Student Page 435, Exercise 26**

Reasoning A rectangle is 80 cm long and 20 cm wide. To the nearest degree, find the measures of the angles formed by the diagonals at the center of the rectangle.

Read and Understand

1. Draw a picture of the rectangle with its diagonals. Let the bottom and top be 80 cm and the sides be 20 cm. The diagonals form 4 angles. Label the angle on top A and the angle on the right B.

2. What is $m\angle A + m\angle B$? _____°

Plan and Solve

3. There are several ways to find the answers. We will use a right triangle that we created on the bottom left corner of the rectangle. Draw a perpendicular from the center of the rectangle to the bottom side. This line creates two right triangles. Starting at the top of the left triangle and moving counterclockwise, label the angles of this triangle X, Y, and Z. Write an equation describing how the $m\angle A$ relates to the $m\angle X$. _____

4. Using the angles in your figure, $m\angle X + m\angle Y =$ _____°.

5. What are the lengths of the legs of the triangle? _____

6. Complete the equation: $\tan X =$ _____

7. Therefore, $X = \tan^{-1}$ _____.

8. Rounding to the nearest degree, $m\angle X =$ _____°.

9. Recall from Step 3 that $m\angle A$ is related to $m\angle X$, so $m\angle A =$ _____°.

10. Finally, combine this result with Step 2, $m\angle B =$ _____°.

Look Back and Check

11. Do the values you found for the angles appear to approximate the angles in the figure? _____

Solve Another Problem

12. Keep the length of the rectangle at 80 cm. Suppose you want the angles formed by the diagonals to be 120° and 60°. What is the width of the rectangle? _____ cm

Guided Problem Solving

Practice 8-4

Write the ratios for sin *P* and cos *P*.

1. _____

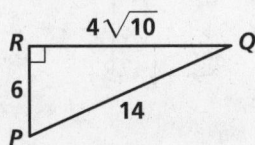

2. _____

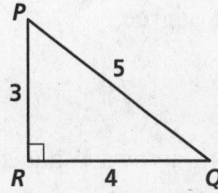

3. _____

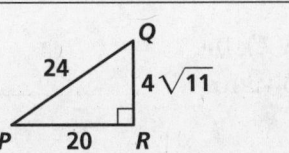

4. _____

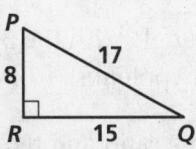

Find the value of *x*. Round lengths of segments to the nearest tenth and angle measures to the nearest degree.

5. _____

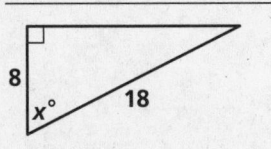

6. _____

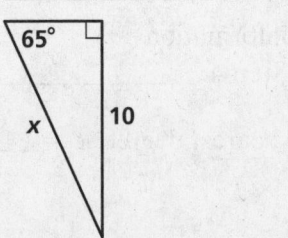

7. _____

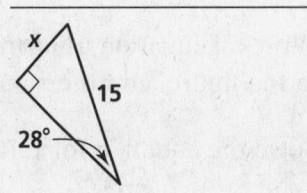

8. _____

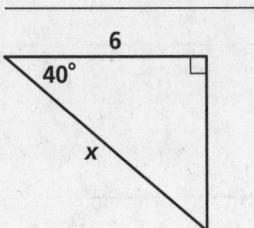

9. _____

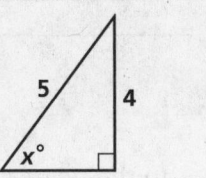

10. _____

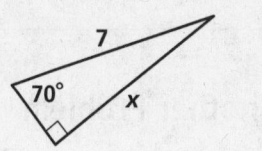

11. _____

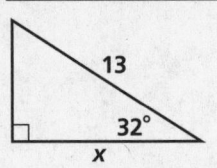

12. _____

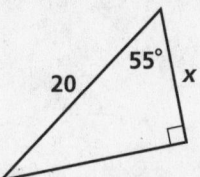

8-4 • Guided Problem Solving

GPS **Student Page 442, Exercise 22**

Find the values of w and then x. Round lengths to the nearest tenth and angle measures to the nearest degree.

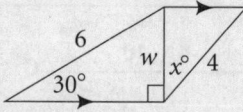

Read and Understand

1. Two sides are marked with arrows. What does that indicate? _____

Plan and Solve

2. First, examine the right triangle with the $30°$ angle. Given an angle ($30°$), the side opposite (w), and the hypotenuse (6), what ratio can be used to solve for w? _____

3. Write an equation using this ratio and the information in the figure. _____

4. Solve the equation for w. Round to the nearest tenth. $w =$ _____

5. Now, look at the other triangle with the angle $x°$. Is this also a right triangle? _____

6. Given an angle ($x°$), the side adjacent (w), and the hypotenuse (4), what ratio can be used to solve for x? _____

7. Write an equation using this ratio, the information in the figure, and the value found in Step 4. _____

8. Solve the equation for x. Round to the nearest degree. $x =$ _____°

Look Back and Check

9. The answers can be checked using other ratios. Explain one method. _____

_____

Solve Another Problem

10. What are the lengths of the two parallel sides, to the nearest tenth? _____

Practice 8-5

Angles of Elevation and Depression

1. Describe each angle as it relates to the diagram.

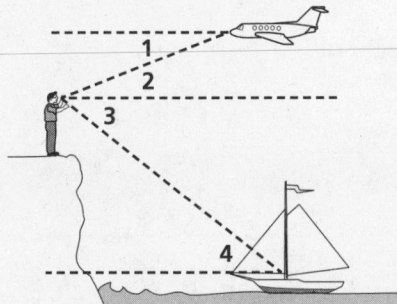

a. ∠1 _____

b. ∠2 _____

c. ∠3 _____

d. ∠4 _____

Find the value of *x*. Round the lengths to the nearest tenth.

2. _____

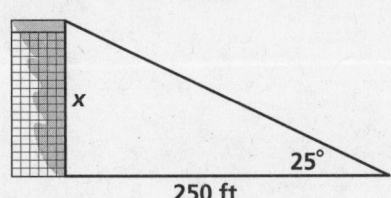

3. _____

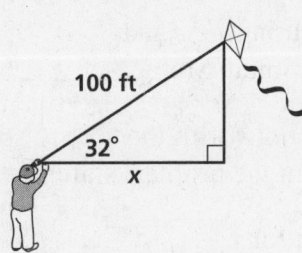

4. _____

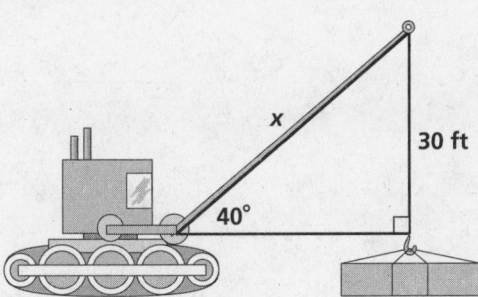

5. _____

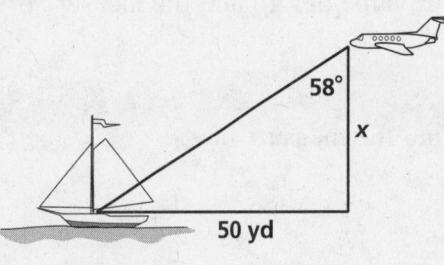

6. A person standing 30 ft from a flagpole can see the top of the pole at a 35° angle of elevation.

a. Draw a diagram.

b. The person's eye level is 5 ft from the ground. Find the height of the flagpole to the nearest foot.

_____

8-5 • Guided Problem Solving

GPS **Student Page 448, Exercise 19**

Algebra The angle of elevation e from A to B is $(7x - 5)°$ and the angle of depression d from B to A is $4(x + 7)°$. Find the measure of each angle.

Read and Understand

1. Identify (by number) angles e and d in the figure at the right.
   $\angle e =$ _____, $\angle d =$ _____

2. In this exercise, the angle of elevation e from A to B and the angle of depression d from B to A are _____ (congruent, complementary, or supplementary).

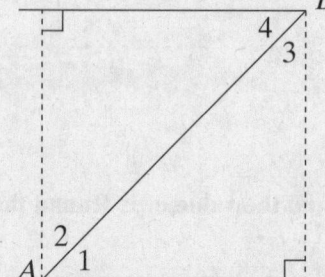

Plan and Solve

3. Write an equation using $m\angle e$ and $m\angle d$ and the relation in Step 2. _____

4. Replace $m\angle e$ and $m\angle d$ with the expressions given in the problem statement. _____

5. Solve the equation for x.

   $x =$ _____

6. Use this value of x to find the measure of $\angle e$.

   $m\angle e =$ _____ °

7. Now find the measure of $\angle d$.

   $m\angle d =$ _____ °

Look Back and Check

8. Do your answers appear to be reasonable? _____

Solve Another Problem

9. Suppose the surveyor realized she had made an error when she recorded the information for the angle of depression d from B to A. Instead of $d: 4(x + 7)°$, she realized later she should have written $d: 4(x + 4)°$. The angle of elevation e was recorded correctly. Find the measures of angles e and d using the corrected information. $m\angle e =$ _____ ° and $m\angle d =$ _____ °

Practice 8-6

Vectors

· ·

Describe each vector as an ordered pair. Give the coordinates to the nearest tenth.

1. _____

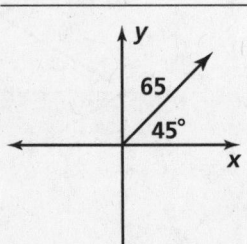

2. _____

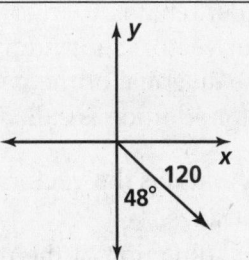

Find the magnitude and direction of each vector. Round your answers to the nearest tenth.

3. _____

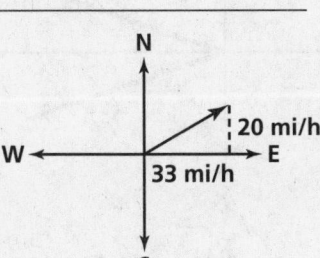

4. _____

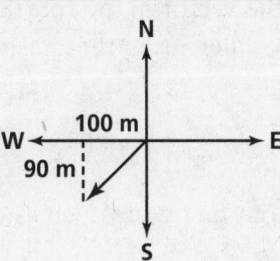

Use compass directions to describe the direction of each vector.

5. _____

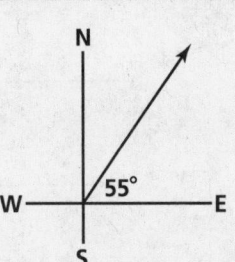

6. _____

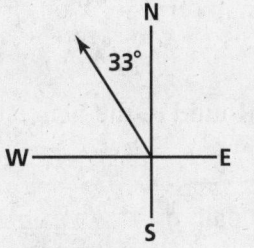

For Exercises 7–8, (a) write the resultant as an ordered pair, and (b) draw the resultant.

7. _____

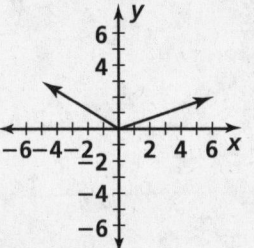

8. _____

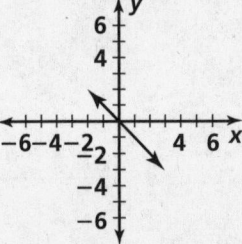

9. Sketch a vector that has the direction 48° south of east.

· ·

8-6 • Guided Problem Solving

Student Page 457, Exercise 31

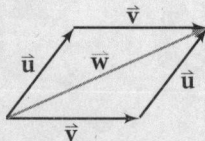

The diagram at the left shows that you can add vectors in any order. That is, $\vec{u} + \vec{v} = \vec{v} + \vec{u}$. Notice also that the four vectors shown form a parallelogram. The resultant $\vec{w}$ is the diagonal of the parallelogram. This representation of vector addition is called *The Parallelogram Rule*.

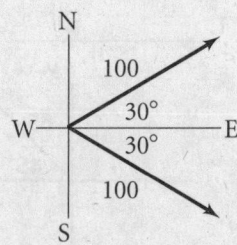

a. Draw a parallelogram that has the vectors in the figure at the right as adjacent sides.

b. Find the magnitude and direction of the resultant.

Read and Understand

1. In the figure at the right, label the vector in the first quadrant as $\vec{u}$ and the vector in the fourth quadrant as $\vec{v}$. Then draw a parallelogram that has vectors $\vec{u}$ and $\vec{v}$ as adjacent sides.

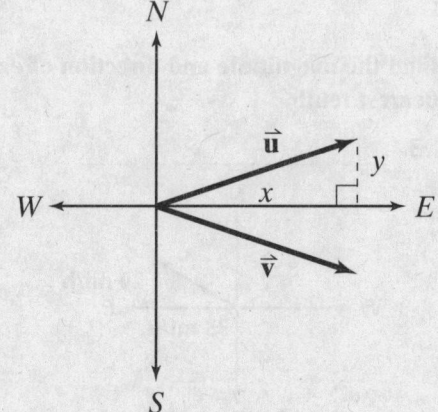

Plan and Solve

In order to add the vectors, first write each as an ordered pair. Begin with vector $\vec{u}$.

2. Complete each equation in terms of x or y.

   cos 30° = _____   sin 30° = _____

3. Rewrite each equation in terms of x or y.

   $x = $ _____ $y = $ _____

4. Solve each equation. Round to the nearest tenth.

   $x \approx $ _____ $y \approx $ _____

5. Write $\vec{u}$ as an ordered pair. $\vec{u} = \langle$ ____ , ____ $\rangle$

6. Similarly, write $\vec{v}$ as an ordered pair. $\vec{v} = \langle$ ____ , ____ $\rangle$

7. Now find the resultant. $\vec{u} + \vec{v} = \langle$ ____ , ____ $\rangle$

8. Find the magnitude and direction of the resultant. mag: _____ ; dir: _____

Look Back and Check

9. Do your answers appear reasonable? _____

Solve Another Problem

10. Change the angles for both vectors $\vec{u}$ and $\vec{v}$ from 30° to 60° and answer part (b) again. magnitude: _____ ; direction: _____

8A: Graphic Organizer

For use before Lesson 8-1

Study Skill When taking notes make your original notes as easy to read as possible. Use abbreviations of your own invention when possible. The amount of time needed to recopy messy notes would be better spent rereading and thinking about them.

Write your answers.

1. What is the chapter title? _____

2. Find the Table of Contents page for this chapter at the front of the book. Name four topics you will study in this chapter.

   _____   _____

   _____   _____

3. Complete the graphic organizer as you work through the chapter.
   1. Write the title of the chapter in the center oval.
   2. When you begin a lesson, write the name of the lesson in a rectangle.
   3. When you complete that lesson, write a skill or key concept from that lesson in the outer oval linked to that rectangle.
   Continue with steps 2 and 3 clockwise around the graphic organizer.

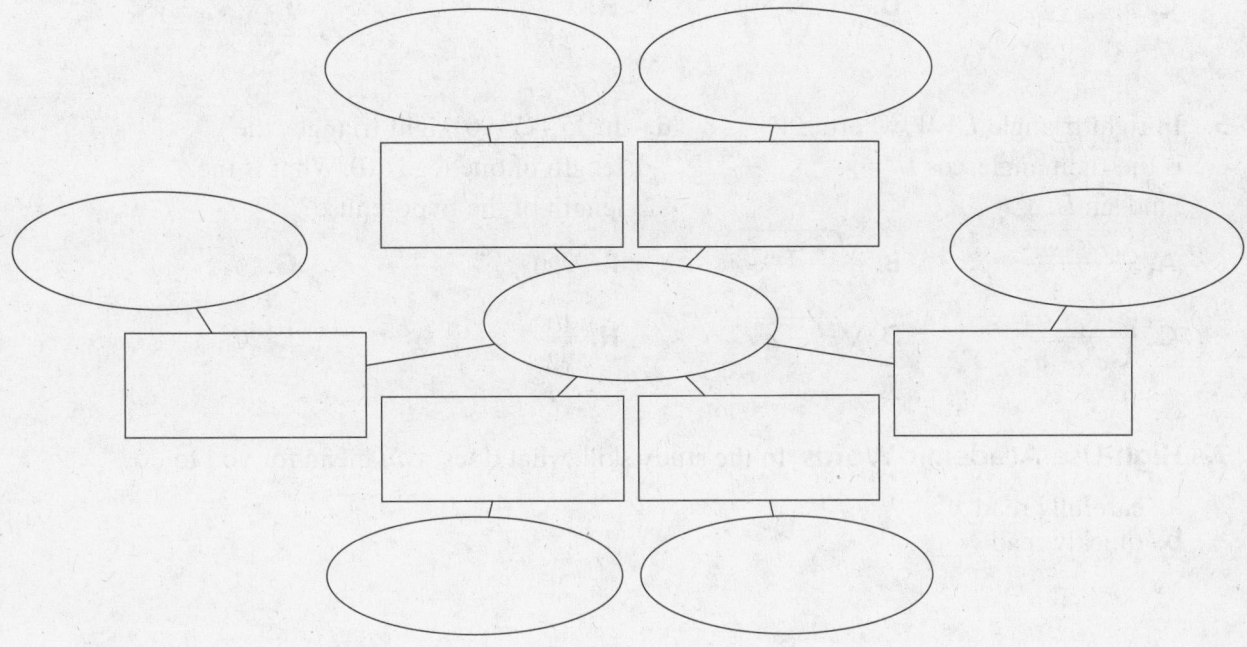

8B: Reading Comprehension

Study Skill When you are taking a test, read over the directions and scan the problems of each section. If you see that you will need to use a particular concept that you sometimes have difficulty recalling, take a minute to write down the concept. You can then use those notes to answer the questions.

Read each description of a right triangle and answer the question that follows.

1. In right triangle ZYX, where $\angle Y$ is the right angle, $\tan Z = \frac{18}{x}$. Find $\tan X$.

   A. $\frac{x}{18}$ **B.** $\frac{18}{x}$

   C. 18 **D.** x^2

2. In $\triangle MNO$ where $\angle N$ is the right angle, $\cos M = \frac{6}{n}$. Which is the only possible value for $\sin M$?

   F. $\frac{n}{6}$ **G.** 6

   H. n **J.** $\frac{3}{n}$

3. For angle of elevation R, $\tan R = \frac{3}{4}$. What is the cosine of R?

   A. $\frac{4}{3}$ **B.** $\frac{4}{5}$

   C. 5 **D.** $\frac{3}{5}$

4. In $\triangle EFG$, where $\angle F$ is the right angle, $\sin G = \frac{y}{x}$. What is the length of the other leg?

   F. $\sqrt{x^2 + y^2}$ **G.** x

   H. y **J.** $\sqrt{x^2 - y^2}$

5. In right triangle UVW, where $\angle V$ is the right angle, $\cos U = \frac{a}{c}$. Find $\sin U$.

   A. $\frac{\sqrt{c^2 - a^2}}{a}$ **B.** $\frac{\sqrt{c^2 - a^2}}{c}$

   C. $\frac{c}{\sqrt{c^2 - a^2}}$ **D.** $\sqrt{c^2 - a^2}$

6. In 45°-45°-90° right triangle, the length of one leg is 10. What is the length of the hypotenuse?

   F. $\sqrt{20}$ **G.** $10\sqrt{2}$

   H. $\frac{10}{\sqrt{2}}$ **J.** 20

7. **High-Use Academic Words** In the study skill, what does *scan* mean for you to do?

   a. carefully read
   b. quickly read

8C: Reading/Writing Math Symbols

For use after Lesson 8-4

Study Skill Sometimes there is more than one way to express an idea or concept with symbols. For example, the reciprocal of x can be expressed as $\frac{1}{x}$ or x^{-1}. Be sure you know all of the symbols for ideas or concepts that can be expressed in more than one way.

Match the math expression in Column A with its meaning in Column B by drawing a line between them.

Column A

1. $\sin Q$
2. $\tan^{-1}(0.5)$
3. $90 - x$
4. $r \approx 2$
5. $\cos T$
6. $180 - x$
7. $\triangle ABC \sim \triangle EFG$
8. $\tan S$

Column B

A. r is approximately equal to 2.

B. supplement of an angle whose measure is x

C. in a right triangle, side adjacent to $\angle T$ divided by the hypotenuse

D. complement of an angle whose measure is x

E. in a right triangle, side opposite $\angle S$ divided by the side adjacent to $\angle S$

F. in a right triangle, side opposite $\angle Q$ divided by the hypotenuse

G. inverse tangent of 0.5

H. Triangle ABC is similar to triangle EFG.

Write the following expressions using math symbols.

9. The inverse of the sine of $\angle A$ is equal to $\frac{5}{12}$. _____

10. Triangle ABC is similar to triangle XYZ. _____

11. The measure of angle A is approximately 52 degrees. _____

12. The tangent of angle Z is seven divided by 24. _____

8D: Visual Vocabulary Practice

For use after Lesson 8-2

Study Skill When learning a new concept, try to draw a picture to illustrate it.

Concept List

30°-60°-90° triangle	45°-45°-90° triangle	congruent sides
hypotenuse	inverse of tangent	obtuse triangle
Pythagorean Theorem	Pythagorean triple	tangent

Write the concept that best describes each exercise.
Choose from the concept list above.

1. 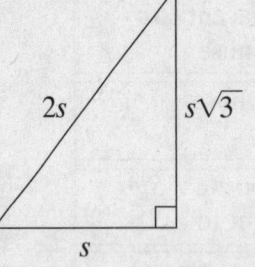 _____	**2.** $\tan^{-1}$ _____	**3.** 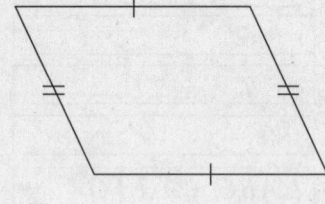 _____
4. $\dfrac{\text{leg opposite angle}}{\text{leg adjacent to angle}}$ _____	**5.** A right triangle has legs of length 40 and 9 and a hypotenuse of length 41. It must be true that $40^2 + 9^2 = 41^2$. _____	**6.** 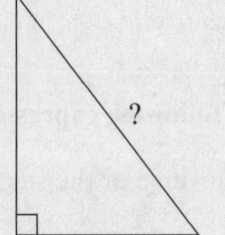 _____
7. 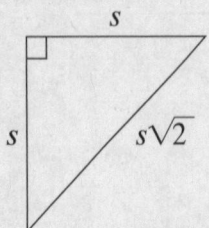 _____	**8.** 5, 12, 13 or 7, 24, 25 _____	**9.** $c^2 > a^2 + b^2$ _____

Name ______________________ Class ______________ Date ______________

8E: Vocabulary Check

For use after Lesson 8-3

Study Skill Strengthen your vocabulary. Use these pages and add cues and summaries by applying the Cornell Notetaking style.

Vocabulary and Study Skills

Write the definition for each word at the right. To check your work, fold the paper back along the dotted line to see the correct answers.

______________________ ______________________ ______________________	Obtuse triangle
______________________ ______________________ ______________________	Isosceles triangle
______________________ ______________________ ______________________	Hypotenuse
______________________ ______________________ ______________________	Right triangle
______________________ ______________________ ______________________	Pythagorean triple

8E: Vocabulary Check (continued)

For use after Lesson 8-3

Write the vocabulary word for each definition. To check your work, fold the
paper forward along the dotted line to see the correct answers.

A triangle with one angle
whose measure is between
90 and 180.

_____

A triangle that has at least
two congruent sides.

_____

The side opposite the right
angle in a right triangle.

_____

A triangle that contains
one right angle.

_____

A set of three nonzero
whole numbers a, b, and c
that satisfies the equation
$a^2 + b^2 = c^2$.

_____

Vocabulary and Study Skills

Name_____ Class_____ Date_____

8F: Vocabulary Review Puzzle

For use with Chapter Review

Study Skill Most math exams do not have a vocabulary section, only problems to be solved. However, in order to solve the problems you must understand the vocabulary being used in the questions. The next time you study for a math test, spend some time studying the vocabulary of the chapter.

Complete the word search.

angle of depression	angle of elevation	congruent
cosine	identity	inverse tangent
hypotenuse	measurement	opposite
resultant	proportion	Pythagorean
sine	tangent	vector

```
J  A  T  N  A  T  L  U  S  E  R  Y  G  D  H  P  G
H  S  N  L  P  U  R  F  S  I  M  E  E  M  Q  O  I
I  Y  H  G  E  A  K  U  R  R  E  L  O  F  L  S  B
T  N  T  N  L  O  N  Q  G  M  A  M  M  D  M  T  P
B  K  V  I  X  E  X  X  E  C  S  Q  E  A  L  V  Y
D  W  M  E  T  D  O  T  S  B  U  N  T  P  X  L  T
Z  I  T  O  R  N  I  F  A  D  R  Y  R  L  P  A  H
S  R  P  S  Z  S  E  O  E  E  E  J  I  I  M  T  A
H  Y  M  C  O  N  E  D  C  L  M  Z  C  R  D  E  G
H  E  D  P  I  L  U  T  I  N  E  B  M  J  C  V  O
R  F  P  S  U  T  A  B  A  F  N  V  E  C  T  O  R
Y  O  O  R  I  N  I  V  G  N  T  M  A  D  D  K  E
B  C  O  N  G  R  U  E  N  T  G  H  N  T  B  R  A
A  N  G  L  E  O  F  D  E  P  R  E  S  S  I  O  N
R  A  E  U  A  R  A  X  L  L  Y  T  N  E  J  O  B
M  C  O  O  V  Z  L  P  R  O  P  O  R  T  I  O  N
```

Name _____ Class _____ Date _____

Practice 9-1

Translations

State whether each transformation appears to be an isometry. Explain.

1. _____

_____

2. _____

_____

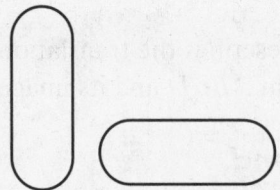

3. In the diagram, $C'D'E'F'$ is the image of $CDEF$.

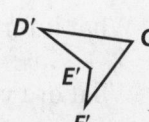

a. Name the images of $\angle C$ _____ and
   $\angle F$. _____

b. List the pairs of corresponding sides. _____

Find the rule that describes the given translation.

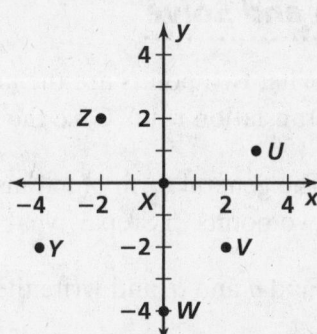

4. $Z \to Y$ _____

5. $Y \to W$ _____

6. $W \to V$ _____

Find the image of each figure under the given translation.

7. translation
   $(x, y) \to (x + 2, y + 4)$

_____

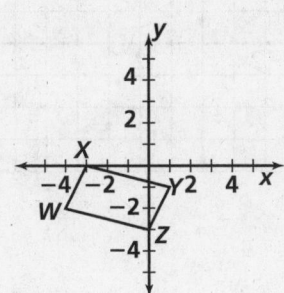

8. translation
   $(x, y) \to (x - 2, y + 1)$

_____

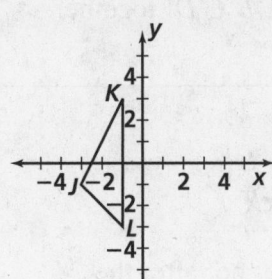

Find a single translation that has the same effect as each composition of translations.

9. $(x, y) \to (x + 4, y - 8)$ followed by $(x, y) \to (x + 9, y - 5)$ _____

10. $(x, y) \to (x + 1, y + 2)$ followed by $(x, y) \to (x + 2, y + 1)$ _____

11. $\triangle PNQ$ has vertices $P(2, 5)$, $N(-3, -1)$, and $Q(4, 0)$.

a. Determine the image of P under the translation $(x, y) \to (x - 5, y - 6)$. _____

b. Use matrices to find the image of $\triangle PNQ$ under the translation $(x, y) \to (x - 2, y + 3)$.

_____

9-1 • Guided Problem Solving

GPS **Student Page 475, Exercise 26**

Coordinate Geometry Parallelogram $ABCD$ has vertices $A(3, 6)$, $B(5, 5)$, $C(4, 2)$, and $D(2, 3)$. The figure is translated so that the image of point C is at the origin.

   a. Find the rule that describes the translation.
   b. Graph parallelogram $ABCD$ and its image.

Read and Understand

   1. What information is given? _____

   2. What are you asked to do?_____

Plan and Solve

   3. What two points are the key to finding the
      translation rule? Give the coordinates for each. _____

   4. The general form of a translation rule is $(x, y) \rightarrow (x + a, y + b)$. For the
      two points in Step 3, what is x? What is y? What are $x + a$ and $y + b$? _____

   5. Find a and b, and write the translation rule. _____

   6. Use the translation rule to find image points A', B', and D'.

      _____

   7. Graph $ABCD$ and $A'B'C'D'$ together.

      _____

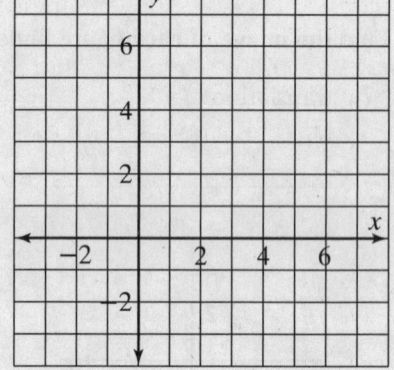

Look Back and Check

   8. Since translation does not alter the
      size or shape of a figure, $ABCD$ and
      $A'B'C'D'$ should be congruent. Are they? _____

Solve Another Problem

   9. Suppose that instead of being translated to the origin, point C had been
      translated to point $(5, -1)$. What would the translation rule have been?
      What would the coordinates of points A', B', and D' have been?

_____

Practice 9-2

Reflections

. . . .

Each point is reflected across the line indicated. Find the coordinates of the images.

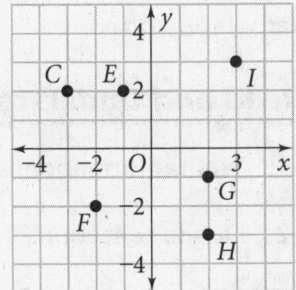

1. *C* across the *x*-axis _____

2. *H* across the *y*-axis _____

3. *E* across *y* = −1 _____

4. *F* across *x* = 1 _____

5. *G* across *x* = 3 _____

6. *I* across *y* = −0.5 _____

7. For figure *WXYZ*, draw its reflection image across each line.

    a. *x*-axis

    b. *y*-axis

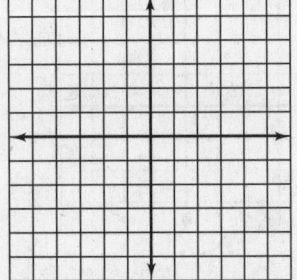

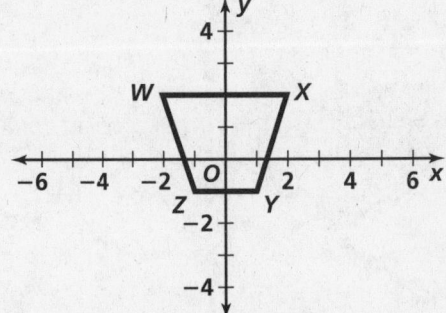

Given points $T(2, 4)$**,** $A(-3, -4)$**, and** $B(0, -4)$**, draw** $\triangle TAB$ **and its reflection image across each line.**

8. *x*-axis

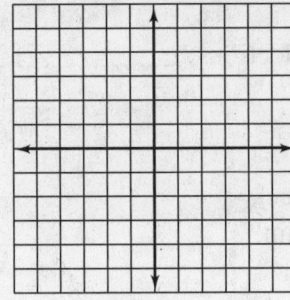

9. *y*-axis

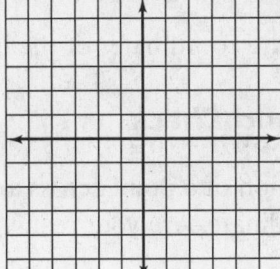

Find the image of $O(0, 0)$ **after two reflections, first across** l_1**, and then across** l_2**.**

10. l_1: $y = 2$; l_2: $x = -3$ _____

9-2 • Guided Problem Solving

GPS **Student Page 481, Exercise 28**

Find the image of $O(0, 0)$ after two reflections, first across $y = 3$ and then across the x-axis.

Read and Understand

1. What information is given? _____

2. Define reflection. _____

3. What are you asked to find? _____

Plan and Solve

4. Draw point $O(0, 0)$ and both reflection lines.

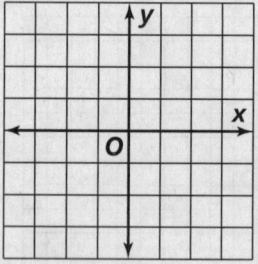

5. Reflect point O across $y = 3$ to obtain O'. Graph the point.

6. Reflect point O' across the x-axis (the line $y = 0$) to obtain O''. Graph the point.

7. What are the coordinates of the image of O after the two reflections? _____

Look Back and Check

8. The reflection of a point across a horizontal line does not affect the x-coordinate. Are your results consistent with this? Explain. _____

_____

Solve Another Problem

9. What would the result be if the order of reflections were reversed—first across the x-axis and then across $y = 3$? _____

Name _____ Class _____ Date _____

Practice 9-3

Rotations

Regular octagon *EIGHTSUP* is divided into eight congruent triangles.
Find the image of each point or segment for the given rotation.

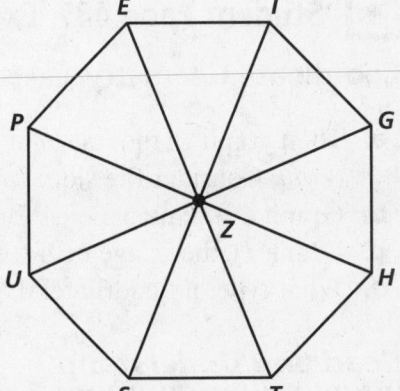

1. 45° rotation of *G* about *Z* _____

2. 225° rotation of *U* about *Z* _____

3. 315° rotation of *E* about *Z* _____

4. 270° rotation of $\overline{EI}$ about *Z* _____

5. 135° rotation of *S* about *Z* _____

6. 360° rotation of $\overline{ST}$ about *Z* _____

Copy each figure and point *P*. Draw the image of each figure for the given
rotation about *P*. Label the vertices of each image.

7. 50°

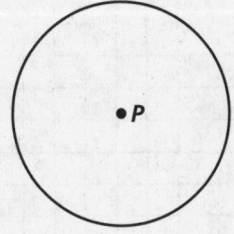

8. 90°

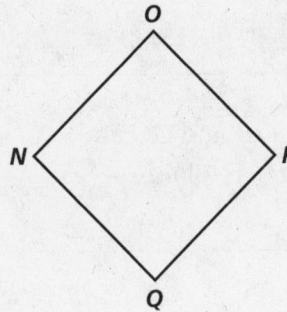

Copy △*PQR* and point *S*. Then draw the image for the given composition
of rotations about point *S*.

9. 20° and then 70°

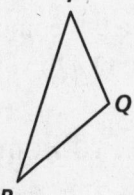

9-3 • Guided Problem Solving

GPS **Student Page 487, Exercise 31**

Coordinate Geometry Graph $A(5, 2)$.

a. Then graph B, the image of A, for a 90° rotation about the origin O.
   (*Hint:* Consider the slope of $\overline{OA}$.)

b. Graph C, the image of A for a 180° rotation about O.

c. Graph D, the image of A for a 270° rotation about O.

d. What type of quadrilateral is $ABCD$? Explain.

Read and Understand

1. What information is given? What is assumed since nothing is stated?

   _____

2. What types of special quadrilaterals might
   describe $ABCD$ once you locate the vertices? _____

   _____

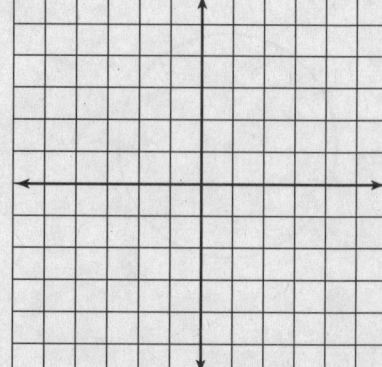

Plan and Solve

3. Plot point $A(5, 2)$. What is the slope of segment $\overline{OA}$?

   _____

4. Graph points B, C, and D so that segments $\overline{OB}$, $\overline{OC}$, and $\overline{OD}$
   are all the same length as $\overline{OA}$.

   _____

   _____

5. The angle between $\overline{OA}$ and $\overline{OB}$ measures 90°, as do the angle between $\overline{OB}$ and $\overline{OC}$ and
   the angle between $\overline{OC}$ and $\overline{OD}$. What are the slopes of $\overline{OB}$, $\overline{OC}$, and $\overline{OD}$? Explain.

   _____

   _____

6. Draw the quadrilateral $ABCD$. Using the results from
   Steps 4 and 5, what type of quadrilateral best describes $ABCD$? _____

Look Back and Check

7. The rule for a 90° counterclockwise rotation is
   $(x, y) \rightarrow (-y, x)$. Do your results confirm this? _____

Solve Another Problem

8. For point $A(-7, 2)$, find images B, C, and D under
   clockwise rotations of 90°, 180°, and 270°, respectively. _____

Practice 9-4

Symmetry

Tell whether each three-dimensional object has rotational symmetry about a line and/or reflectional symmetry in a plane.

1. _____

2. _____

3. _____

Draw all lines of symmetry for each figure.

4.

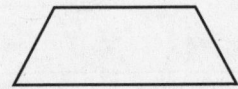

5.

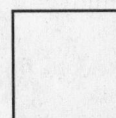

Judging from appearance, tell what type(s) of symmetry each figure has. If it has line symmetry, sketch the figure and the line(s) of symmetry. If it has rotational symmetry, state the angle of rotation.

6. _____

7. _____

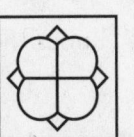

8. _____

9. _____

BOOK

10. _____

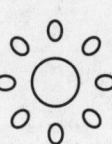

11. _____

Each diagram shows a figure folded along a line of symmetry. Sketch the unfolded figure.

12.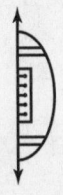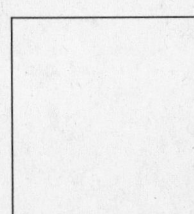

13. COOK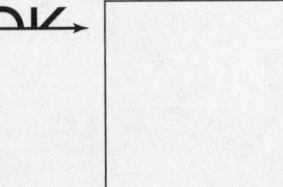

14.

9-4 • Guided Problem Solving

GPS **Student Page 495, Exercise 37**

Coordinate Geometry A figure has a vertex at $(3, 4)$. If the figure has line symmetry about the y-axis, state the coordinates of another vertex of the figure.

Read and Understand

1. What information is given? _____

2. What is line symmetry? _____

3. What are you asked to find? _____

Plan and Solve

4. In this kind of exercise, the two vertices are _____ of each other, under the isometry associated with the given type of symmetry.

5. What isometry is associated with symmetry about the y-axis? _____

6. What is the image of point $(3, 4)$ under the isometry found in Step 5? _____

Look Back and Check

7. Is $(3, 4)$ the image, under reflection across the y-axis, of the point found in Step 6? _____

Solve Another Problem

8. A figure has a vertex at $(6, -7)$. If the figure has point symmetry about the origin, state the coordinates of another vertex of the figure. _____

Practice 9-5

Dilations

Find the scale factor for the dilation that maps the solid-line figure onto the dashed-line figure.

1. _____

2. _____

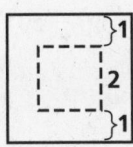

3. _____

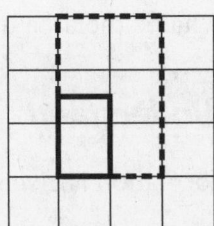

For each pair of figures, determine whether one figure is a dilation of the other.

4. _____

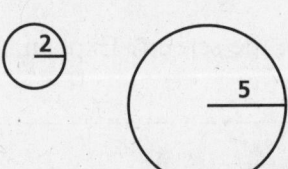

5. _____

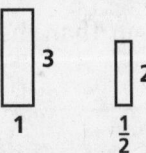

6. _____

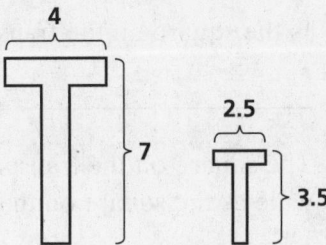

Draw $\triangle A'R'T'$ under the dilation with the given center and scale factor.

7. center T, scale factor $\frac{1}{2}$

8. center O, scale factor 2

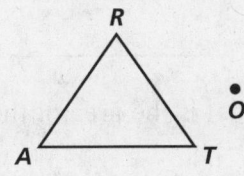

Find the image of $\triangle PQR$ for a dilation with center $(0, 0)$ and the given scale factor.

9. $P(-6, 6), Q(-3, 0), R(0, -3)$ _____

scale factor 2

10. $P(-10, 5), Q(-5, 0), R(0, 5)$ _____

scale factor $\frac{1}{5}$

9-5 • Guided Problem Solving

GPS **Student Page 502, Exercise 56**

Overhead Projection An overhead projector can dilate figures on transparencies. The area of a square on the screen is 3 ft^2. The scale factor is 16. What is the area of the square on the transparency?

Read and Understand

1. What information is given? _____

2. What is a scale factor? _____

3. What are you asked to find? _____

Plan and Solve

4. Is the square on the transparency smaller or larger than the square on the screen? Explain.

   _____

5. The square on the transparency is _____ as tall and _____ as wide as the square on the screen.

6. Based on the answer to Step 5, the area of the square on the transparency is _____

   as great as the area of the square on the screen. Why? _____

   _____

7. What is the area of the square on the transparency? _____

Look Back and Check

8. Does it matter whether the figure being projected is a square? Would the result be the same if the shape were a circle or a triangle with an area of 3 ft^2 on the screen? Explain. _____

   _____

Solve Another Problem

9. An architectural drawing of a house foundation is rendered with a scale factor of $\frac{1}{30}$. If the area of the foundation in the drawing is 2.8 ft^2, what is the area of the actual foundation planned to be? _____

Guided Problem Solving

Practice 9-6

Compositions of Reflections

Match each image of the figure at the left with one of the following isometries:
A. reflection   B. rotation   C. translation   D. glide reflection.

I. _____ II. _____ III. _____ IV. _____

1. PUSH→

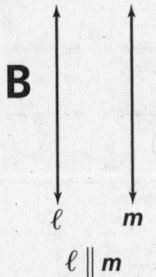

PUSH→

PUSH→

←HSUP

Find the image of each letter through a reflection across line ℓ and then
a reflection across line *m*. Describe the resulting translation.

2.

B

ℓ   m

ℓ ∥ m

3.

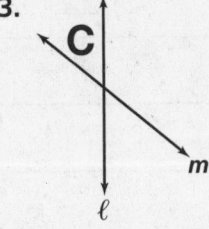

C

m

ℓ

4.

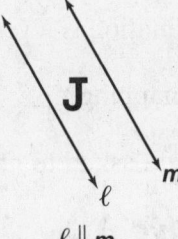

J

ℓ   *m*

ℓ ∥ m

Find the glide reflection image of △*BEST* for the given glide and
reflection line.

5. $(x, y) \rightarrow (x - 2, y)$ and $x = 0$

6. $(x, y) \rightarrow (x - 1, y + 1)$ and $y = 0$

State whether each mapping is a reflection, rotation, translation,
or glide reflection.

7. △*ABCD* → △*GHCD* _____

8. △*HGJI* → △*LMJK* _____

9. △*GFED* → △*RQOP* _____

10. △*MNOP* → △*ABCD* _____

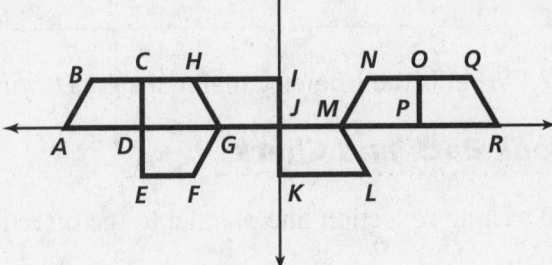

9-6 • Guided Problem Solving

GPS **Student Page 511, Exercise 36**

Is the mapping $\triangle EDC \rightarrow \triangle PQM$ a reflection,
translation, rotation, or glide reflection?
Find the reflection line, translation rule,
center and angle of rotation, or glide
translation and reflection line.

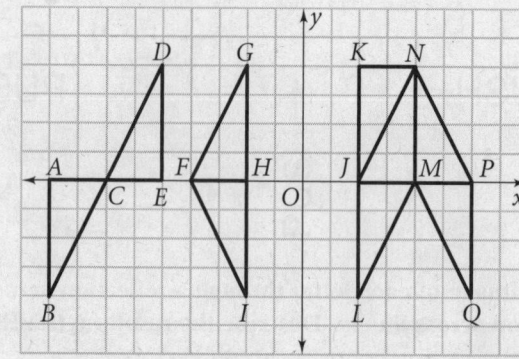

Read and Understand

1. What information is given? _____

2. What is a mapping? _____

3. What are you asked to find? _____

Plan and Solve

4. Are $\triangle EDC$ and $\triangle PQM$ congruent? Explain why this is important and
   state the correspondence of vertices.

   _____

   _____

5. Does the sequence of vertices *E-D-C* go clockwise or counterclockwise

   around $\triangle EDC$? _____ What about *P-Q-M* around

   $\triangle PQM$? _____ What does this information tell you? _____

   _____

6. Can $\triangle EDC$ be mapped onto $\triangle PQM$ by a simple reflection? If yes, what is the reflection line?

   _____

7. What is the isometry that maps $\triangle EDC$ onto $\triangle PQM$? _____

Look Back and Check

8. Is the reflection line parallel to the direction of translation? _____

Solve Another Problem

9. Describe the isometry that maps $\triangle ABC$ onto $\triangle MNJ$. _____

   _____

Practice 9-7

Describe the symmetries of each tessellation. Copy a portion of the tessellation, and draw any centers of rotational symmetry or lines of symmetry.

1. _____

2. _____

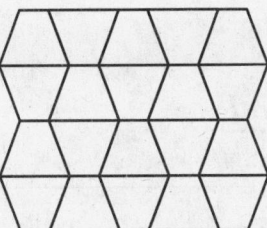

3. _____

4. _____

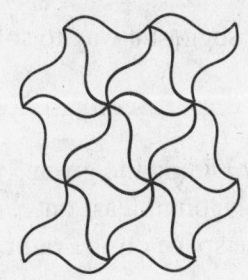

Use each figure to create a tessellation on dot paper.

5.

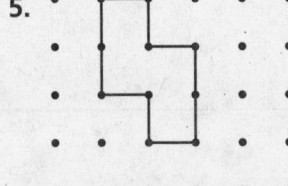

6.

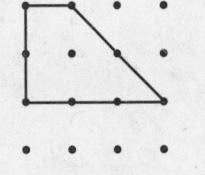

Determine whether each figure will tessellate a plane.

7. rhombus _____

8. regular decagon _____

9. regular hexagon _____

9-7 • Guided Problem Solving

●●

GPS **Student Page 519, Exercise 26**

Can the set of polygons shown at the right be used to create a tessellation? If so, draw a sketch.

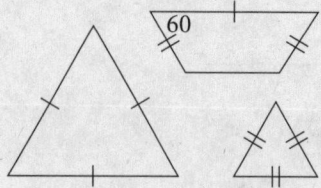

Read and Understand

1. What are you given? _____

2. What are the characteristics of a tessellation? _____

Plan and Solve

3. How does Theorem 9-7 suggest a way to solve the problem? _____

   _____

4. Form a quadrilateral by joining the given polygons, using each polygon at least once. Sketch your result in the space on the right.

5. Extend the sketch from Step 4 to create a tessellation.

Look Back and Check

6. List the symmetries in the tessellation you created. _____

Solve Another Problem

7. Can a tessellation be created using just the trapezoid

   and the large triangle? _____ If so, draw a sketch.

9A: Graphic Organizer

For use before Lesson 9-1

Study Skill Keep notes as you work through each chapter to help you organize your thinking and to make it easier to review the material when you complete the chapter.

Write your answers.

1. What is the chapter title? _____

2. Find the Table of Contents page for this chapter at the front of the book.
   Name four topics you will study in this chapter.

   _____   _____

   _____   _____

3. Complete the graphic organizer as you work through the chapter.
   1. Write the title of the chapter in the center oval.
   2. When you begin a lesson, write the name of the lesson in a
      rectangle.
   3. When you complete that lesson, write a skill or key concept from
      that lesson in the outer oval linked to that rectangle.
   Continue with steps 2 and 3 clockwise around the graphic organizer.

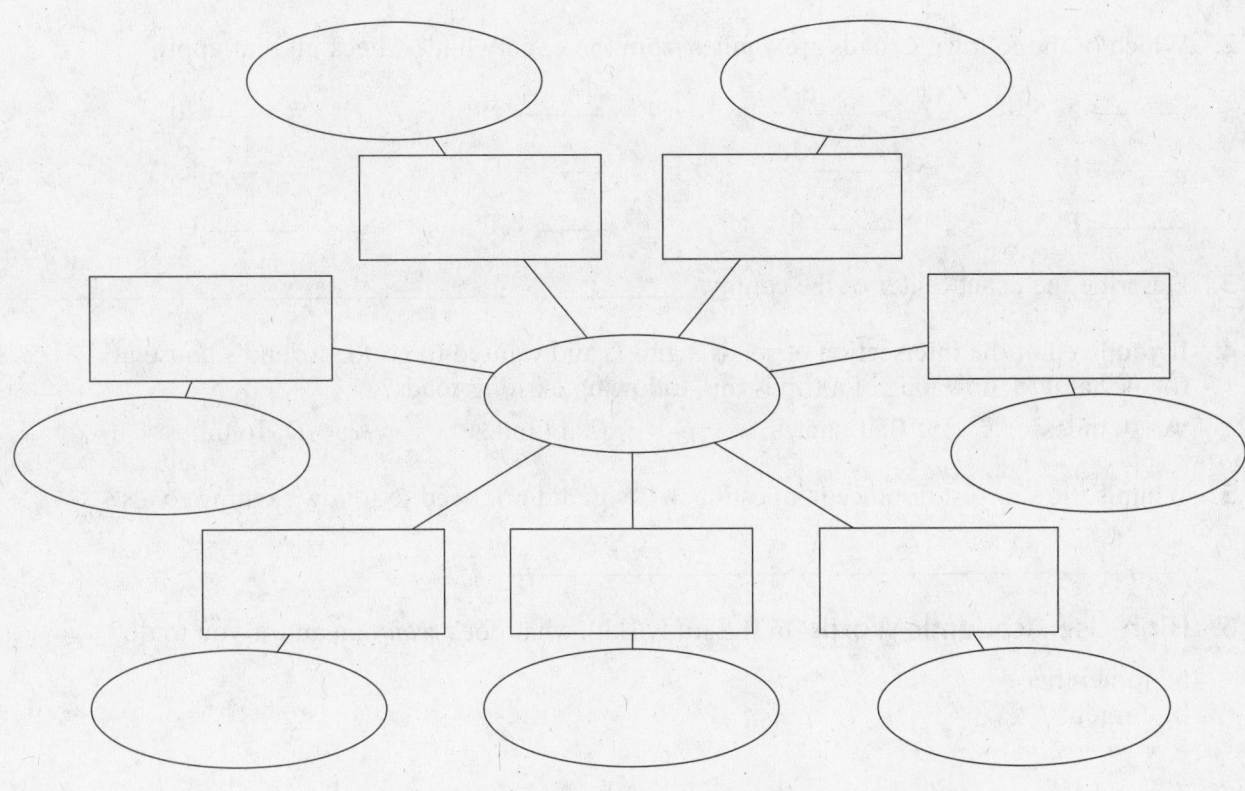

Name _____ Class _____ Date _____

9B: Reading Comprehension

For use after Lesson 9-3

Study Skill If you read while you are distracted, you will not retain the information you read. Try reading somewhere quiet without distractions. If you still cannot concentrate on what you are reading, take a break and try reading again later.

Read the following passage and answer the questions that follow.

> Fulton County has laid its roads out in a rectangular grid. The roads are named with letters and numbers. The roads named with letters (A, B, C, etc.) run east and west. The roads named with counting numbers (1, 2, 3, etc.) run north and south. The county lines are roads A and 1 in one corner and roads V and 24 in the opposite corner. The distance between any two consecutive letter roads or any two consecutive number roads is one mile.

1. What are the dimensions of the county?
   A. 2 miles by 3 miles
   B. 20 miles by 20 miles
   C. 22 miles by 24 miles
   D. 21 miles by 23 miles

2. Which of the following roads are 4 miles from the county line? Check all that apply.

   _____ 5   _____ 6   _____ 19   _____ 20

   _____ B   _____ C   _____ D   _____ E

   _____ R   _____ S   _____ T   _____ U

3. Describe the exact center of the county. _____

4. If you lived at the intersection of roads 3 and E and wanted to go to a friend's house at roads 9 and M, how long of a trip is this, following existing roads?
   A. 10 miles   **B.** 12 miles   **C.** 14 miles   **D.** 16 miles

5. What is the shortest distance in question 4, if you did not need to follow existing roads?

   _____

6. **High-Use Academic Words** In the study skill, what does *retain* mean for you to do?
   a. remember
   b. forget

9C: Reading/Writing Math Symbols

For use after Lesson 9-6

Study Skill When you are reading an extensive word problem consider writing a summary of the information to help you evaluate what the problem says.

Classify the isometries shown. Then tell whether the orientations are the same or opposite.

1.

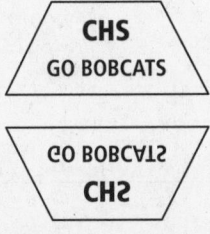

2.

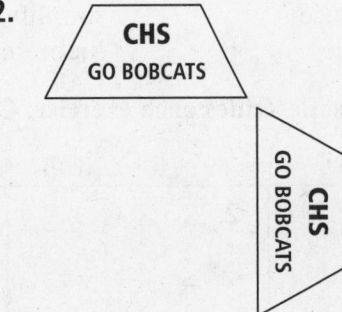

3.

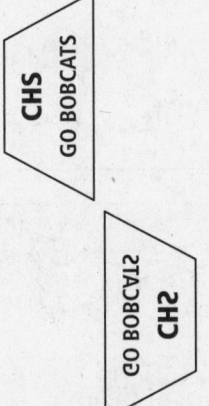

4.

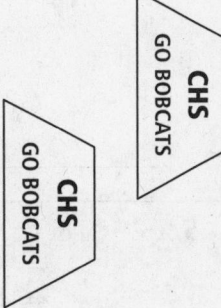

5.

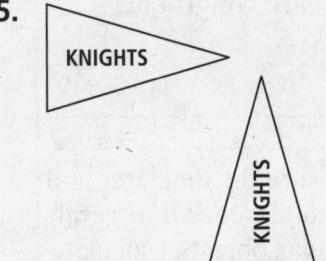

6.

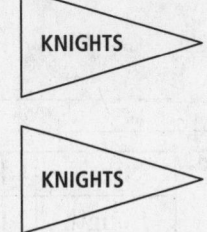

9D: Visual Vocabulary Practice
High-Use Academic Words

For use after Lesson 9-5

Study Skill When making a sketch, make it simple but make it complete. Also, remember that often there is more than one right way to sketch something.

Concept List

application	characteristic	explain
investigate	reduce	simplify
symbols	table	theorem

Write the concept that best describes each exercise. Choose from the concept list above.

1. 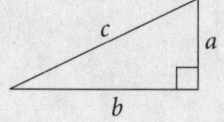 $a^2 + b^2 = c^2$ _____	**2.** 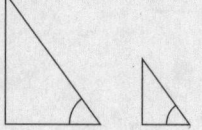 _____	**3.** _____
4. 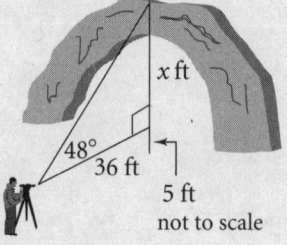 _____	**5.** $\sqrt{2} \cdot \sqrt{8} = \sqrt{2 \cdot 8}$ $\qquad = \sqrt{16}$ $\qquad = 4$ _____	**6.** 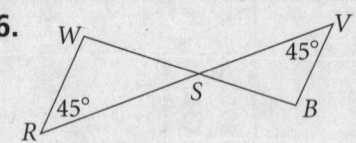 $\angle RSW \cong \angle VSB$ because vertical angles are congruent. _____
7. A trapezoid has exactly one pair of parallel lines. _____	**8.** Stage | 1 | 2 | 3 Length | 1 | 4 | 16 _____	**9.** Measure the diameter and circumference of several circular objects. Calculate the ratio of the circumference and diameter. What do you notice? _____

For item 8, the table:

Stage	1	2	3
Length	1	4	16

Name ______________________ Class ______________ Date ______________

9E: Vocabulary Check

For use after Lesson 9-4

Study Skill Strengthen your vocabulary. Use these pages and add cues and summaries by applying the Cornell Notetaking style.

Write the definition for each word at the right. To check your work, fold the paper back along the dotted line to see the correct answers.

______________________	Transformation
______________________	Preimage
______________________	Image
______________________	Isometry
______________________	Composition

Name ______________________ Class ______________ Date ______________

9E: Vocabulary Check (continued)

For use after Lesson 9-4

Write the vocabulary word for each definition. To check your work, fold the paper forward along the dotted line to see the correct answers.

A change in the position, size, or shape of a geometric figure. ______________________

The given figure before a transformation is applied. ______________________

The resulting figure after a transformation is applied. ______________________

A transformation in which an original figure and its image are congruent. ______________________

A transformation in which a second transformation is performed on the image of a first transformation. ______________________

9F: Vocabulary Review Puzzle

For use with Chapter Review

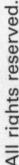
Study Skill When reviewing information for a quiz or test, break the information into small sections. Practice recalling the information in each section until you are confident of your knowledge of the section before you move on to a new section.

ACROSS

2. three-dimensional figure whose surfaces are polygons
3. a figure in which an isometry maps the figure onto itself
4. angle whose measure is between 90 and 180
6. transformation in which the preimage and its image are congruent
8. comparison of two quantities by division
12. transformation that proportionally reduces or enlarges a figure
13. isometry that maps all points of a figure the same distance in the same direction
14. set of all points that meet a stated condition
15. segment of a triangle joining a vertex and the midpoint of the side opposite the vertex
16. like a pyramid but its base is a circle
18. a triangle in which no sides have the same length

DOWN

1. translation followed by a reflection in a line parallel to the translation vector
5. repeating pattern of figures that covers a plane without gaps or overlaps
7. segment with endpoints on a circle
9. perpendicular segment that joins the planes of the bases in a prism
10. isometry that does not change orientation
11. change in position, shape or size of a figure
14. series of points that extend in two opposite directions without end
17. point where three or more edges meet

Practice 10-1

Areas of Parallelograms and Triangles

Find the area of each triangle, given the base *b* and the height *h*.

1. $b = 4$, $h = 4$ _____

2. $b = 20$, $h = 6$ _____

3. $b = 4.8$, $h = 0.8$ _____

4. $b = 3\frac{1}{4}$, $h = \frac{1}{2}$ _____

5. $b = 8$, $h = 2\frac{1}{4}$ _____

6. $b = 100$, $h = 30$ _____

Find the value of *h* in each parallelogram.

7. _____

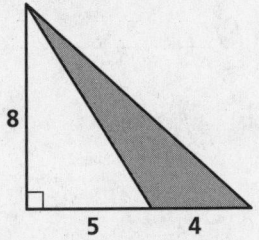

8. _____

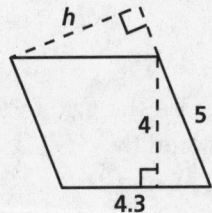

9. What is the area of $\triangle DEF$ with vertices $D(-1, -5)$, $E(4, -5)$, and $F(4, 7)$? _____

Find the area of the shaded region.

10. _____

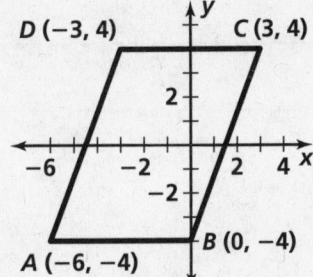

11. _____

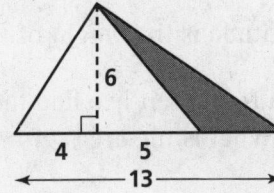

Find the area of each parallelogram.

12. _____

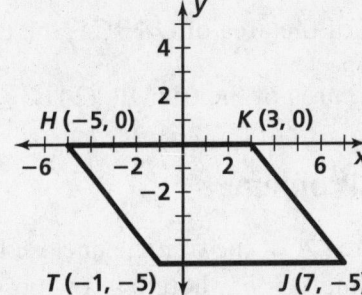

13. _____

10-1 • Guided Problem Solving

GPS Student Page 538, Exercise 24

Given $y = x, x = 0, y = 7$:

a. graph the lines
b. find the area of the triangle enclosed by the lines.

Read and Understand

1. What is the formula for the area of a triangle with base b and height h? $A =$ _____

Plan and Solve

2. Draw the three given lines on the grid to the right.
   The three vertices determined by
   the lines are $O(0, 0), A(0, 7)$, and B _____.

3. What kind of angle is $\angle A$? _____

4. Since the base can be any side, select
   $\overleftrightarrow{AB}$ as the base. What is the
   length b of the base $\overleftrightarrow{AB}$? $b =$ _____

5. If $\overleftrightarrow{AB}$ is the base, what is the altitude of the triangle? _____

6. The length of the altitude is the height of the triangle. What is the height h? _____

7. Now use the formula from Step 1 to find the
   area of the triangle. What is the area? $A =$ _____

Look Back and Check

8. Draw a line from point B perpendicular to the x-axis,
   intersecting the x-axis at $C(7, 0)$. What kind of figure is $OABC$? _____

9. What is the area of $OABC$? _____

10. What portion of the area of $OABC$ is the triangle OAB? _____

11. So, what is the area of the triangle OAB? _____

Solve Another Problem

12. What is the area A of the triangle enclosed by the lines
    $y = x, x = 0$, and $y = b$, where b is any positive number? $A =$ _____

Name _____ Class _____ Date _____

Practice 10-2

Areas of Trapezoids, Rhombuses, and Kites

Find the area of each trapezoid.

1. _____

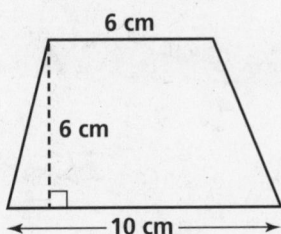

2. _____

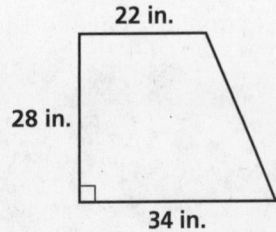

Find the area of each rhombus.

3. _____

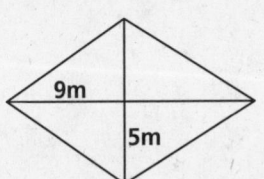

4. _____

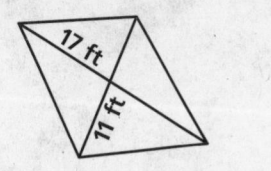

Find the area of each kite.

5. _____

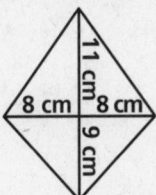

6. _____

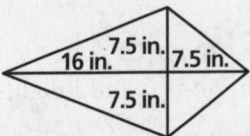

Find the area of each trapezoid to the nearest tenth.

7. _____

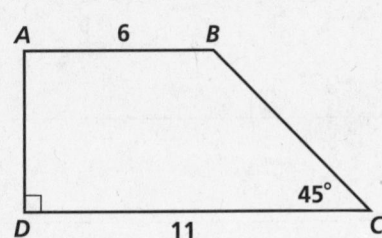

8. _____

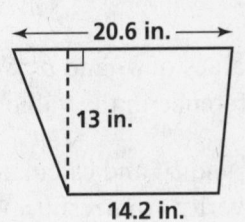

10-2 • Guided Problem Solving

GPS **Student Page 543, Exercise 20**

Gold Bars Find the area of each trapezoidal end face of the gold bars if the bases are 4 cm and 2 cm and the height is 3 cm.

Read and Understand

1. What is the formula for the area A of a trapezoid with bases b_1 and b_2 and height h? $A =$ _____

Plan and Solve

2. Substitute the given values for the variables. $h =$ _____, $b_1 =$ _____, $b_2 =$ _____

3. Find the area of the trapezoidal end face. $A =$ _____

Look Back and Check

4. In Step 2, what if the values of b_1 and b_2 were reversed? Would that make a difference in the value for the area A? _____

5. Switch the values of b_1 and b_2 and calculate the area A of the trapezoid again to verify your results. Were you correct? _____

Solve Another Problem

6. Suppose that, instead of a trapezoid, the end face was a square. For the area of the end face to be the same as before, how long would the side s of the square have to be? $s =$ _____

Guided Problem Solving

Practice 10-3

Areas of Regular Polygons

Find the values of the variables for each regular hexagon. Leave your answers in simplest radical form.

1. $x =$ _____, $y =$ _____

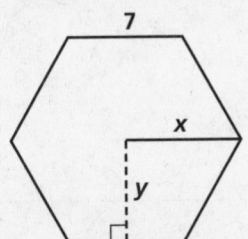

2. $x =$ _____, $p =$ _____, $q =$ _____

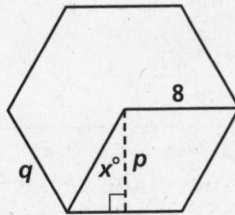

Each regular polygon has radii and an apothem as shown. Find the measure of each numbered angle.

3. $m\angle 1 =$ _____, $m\angle 2 =$ _____,

$m\angle 3 =$ _____, $m\angle 4 =$ _____

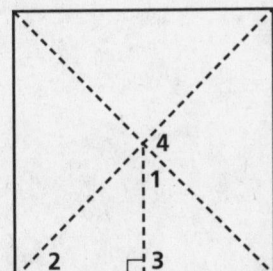

4. $m\angle 5 =$ _____, $m\angle 6 =$ _____,

$m\angle 7 =$ _____

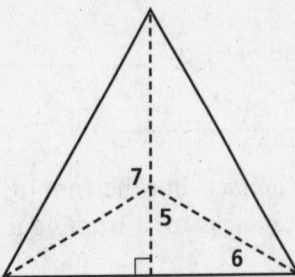

Find the area of each regular polygon to the nearest square inch.

5. _____

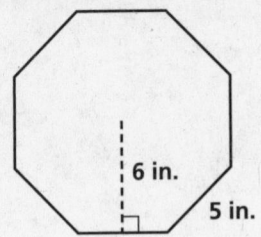

6. _____

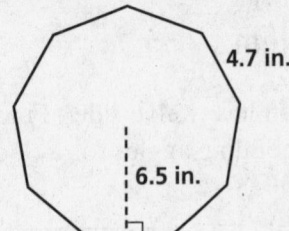

10-3 • Guided Problem Solving

GPS **Student Page 549, Exercise 26**

A portion of a regular decagon has radii and an apothem drawn. Find the measure of each numbered angle.

Read and Understand

1. A regular decagon has _____ sides.

2. What are the characteristics of the angles and sides of a regular polygon? _____

Plan and Solve

3. To find $m\angle 1$, divide _____ by the number in Step 1.

4. $m\angle 1 = $ _____

5. The apothem _____ the vertex angle of the isosceles triangle formed by the radii.

6. To find $m\angle 2$, divide $m\angle 1$ by _____.

7. $m\angle 2 = $ _____

8. To find $m\angle 3$, use the fact that the sum of the measures of the angles of a triangle is _____.

9. $m\angle 3 = $ _____

Look Back and Check

10. One way to check your answers is to add the angles of the isosceles triangle formed by the radii—that is, $m\angle 1 + 2m\angle 3$. What is the result? _____

Solve Another Problem

11. A regular dodecagon has twelve sides. Find the measures of the three corresponding angles for a dodecagon.

    $m\angle 1 = $ _____, $m\angle 2 = $ _____, $m\angle 3 = $ _____

Guided Problem Solving

Name _____ Class _____ Date _____

Practice 10-4

Perimeters and Areas of Similar Figures

For each pair of similar figures, find the ratio of the perimeters and the ratio of the areas.

1. _____

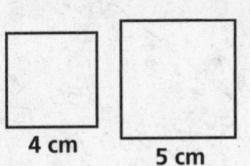

4 cm   5 cm

2. _____

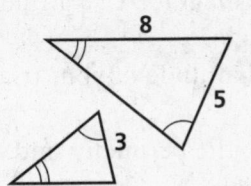

8
5
3

Find the similarity ratio of each pair of similar figures.

3. two regular hexagons with areas 8 in.^{2} and 32 in.^{2} _____

4. two circles with areas 128π cm^2 and 18π cm^2 _____

For each pair of similar figures, the area of the smaller figure is given. Find the area of the larger figure.

5. _____

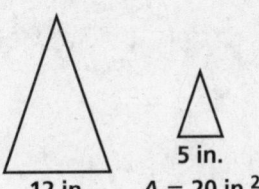

12 in.   5 in. $A = 20$ in.^{2}

6. _____

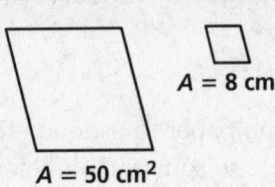

7 cm
$A = 84$ cm^2

15 cm

For each pair of similar figures, find the ratio of the perimeters.

7. _____

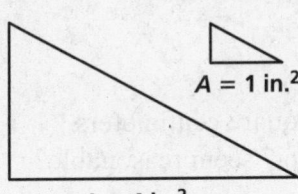

$A = 1$ in.^{2}

$A = 4$ in.^{2}

8. _____

$A = 8$ cm^2

$A = 50$ cm^2

9. The shorter sides of a rectangle are 6 ft. The shorter sides of a similar rectangle are 9 ft. The area of the smaller rectangle is 48 ft^2. What is the area of the larger rectangle? _____

10-4 • Guided Problem Solving

GPS **Student Page 557, Exercise 39**

a. **Surveying** A surveyor measured one side and two angles of a field as shown in the diagram. Use a ruler and a protractor to draw a similar triangle.

b. Measure the sides and altitude of your triangle and find its perimeter and area.

c. **Estimation** Estimate the perimeter and area of the field.

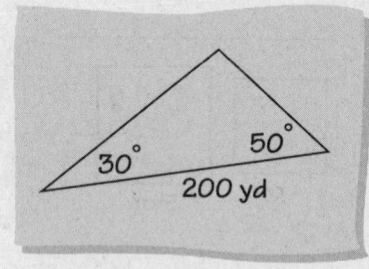

Read and Understand

1. The figure you draw will not have a side measuring 200 yd. Instead, you are making a _____ drawing.

Plan and Solve

2. Use a ruler and protractor to draw a triangle, in the area to the right, similar to the one shown.

3. Measure the sides of your triangle using millimeters. What are the values?

_____ , _____ , _____

4. Find the ratio of corresponding sides of the actual triangle and your scaled drawing. _____

5. What is the perimeter p of your triangle? $p =$ _____

6. What is the altitude a of your triangle? $a =$ _____

7. What is the area A of your triangle? $A =$ _____

8. Based on your answers to Steps 4 and 5, estimate the perimeter of the field measured by the surveyor. perimeter = _____ yd

9. Based on your answers to Steps 4 and 7, estimate the area of the field measured by the surveyor. area = _____ yd^2

Look Back and Check

10. Use centimeter graph paper to estimate the area of your triangle in square centimeters. Convert this estimate to square millimeters. Does your answer to Step 7 seem reasonable?

_____

Solve Another Problem

11. Reflect the triangle across the 200 yd side to form a kite. Find the area A of the kite using the formula $A = \frac{1}{2}d_1d_2$. $A =$ _____ yd^2

Practice 10-5

Find the area of each polygon. Round your answers to the nearest tenth.

1. an equilateral triangle with apothem 5.8 cm _____

2. a square with radius 17 ft _____

3. a regular hexagon with apothem 19 mm _____

4. a regular octagon with radius 20 in. _____

Find the area of each triangle. Round your answers to the nearest tenth.

5. _____
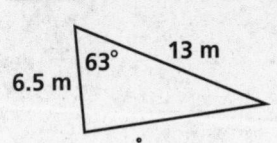

6. _____
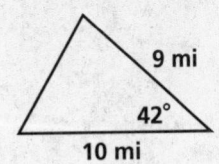

7. _____
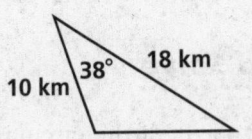

8. _____
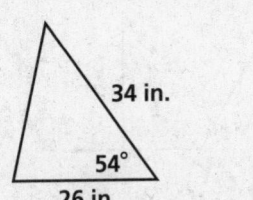

9. _____
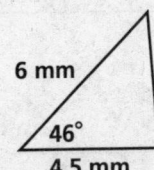

10. _____
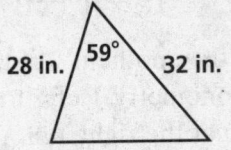

Find the area of each regular polygon to the nearest tenth.

11. a triangular dog pen with apothem 4 m _____

12. a hexagonal swimming pool cover with radius 5 ft _____

13. an octagonal floor of a gazebo with apothem 6 ft _____

14. a square deck with radius 2 m _____

10-5 • Guided Problem Solving

GPS **Student Page 562, Exercise 18**

Industrial Design Refer to the diagram of the regular hexagonal nut. Round each answer to the nearest unit.

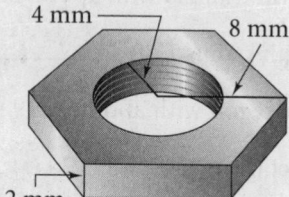

  a. Find the area of the circular hole in the hexagonal nut.
  b. Find the area of the hexagonal face.

Read and Understand

1. To find the area of the hexagonal face A_f, find the area of the hexagon A_h and _____ the area of the circular hole A_c.

Plan and Solve

2. The area A_c of the circular hole is _____ mm^2.

3. The area of a regular polygon with apothem a and perimeter p is $A =$ _____.

4. To find the apothem a of the hexagon, use trigonometry. Refer to the diagram at the right. $m\angle XCY =$ _____.

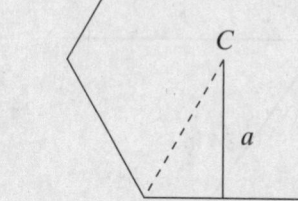

  $\tan(m\angle XCY) = \dfrac{(\quad)}{a}$ **5.** Use tangent ratio.

  $a =$ _____   **6.** Solve for a.

7. Use this value of a and the formula in Step 3 to find the area A_h of the hexagon. $A_h =$ _____ mm^2

8. The area A_f of the hexagonal face is _____ mm^2.

Look Back and Check

9. Notice that the areas should be related by $A_c \leq A_f \leq A_h$. Is your answer reasonable? _____

Solve Another Problem

10. The nut is used with a washer with outside radius 8 mm and inside radius 4 mm. What is the area of the face of the washer? _____ mm^2

Practice 10-6

Circles and Arcs

Find the circumference of each circle. Leave your answers in terms of π.

1. _____

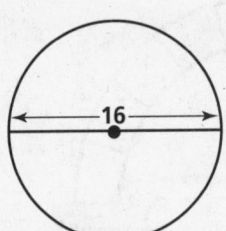

2. _____

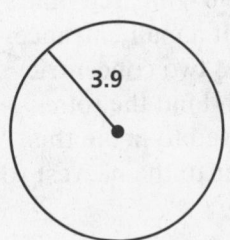

In ⊙C, $\overline{EA}$ and $\overline{FB}$ are diameters. Identify the following.

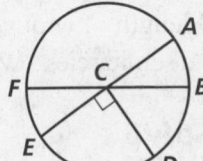

3. two major arcs _____

4. two minor arcs _____

5. a pair of adjacent arcs _____

A market research survey found that adults' favorite vegetables are as shown below. Find the measure of the central angle for each of the following vegetables. Give your answers to the nearest degree.

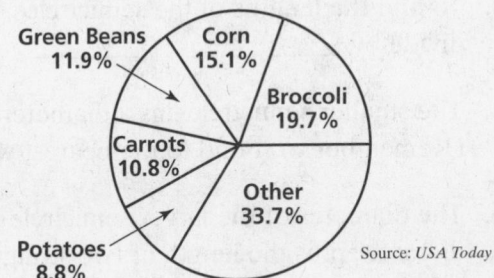

6. potatoes _____

7. corn _____

8. broccoli _____

Find the measure of each arc in ⊙C.

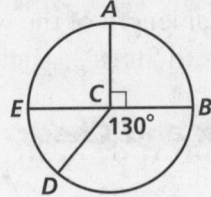

9. $\overset{\frown}{ED}$ _____ 10. $\overset{\frown}{AED}$ _____

11. $\overset{\frown}{ABD}$ _____ 12. $\overset{\frown}{BD}$ _____

Find the length of each arc. Leave your answers in terms of π.

13. _____

$\overset{\frown}{AB}$

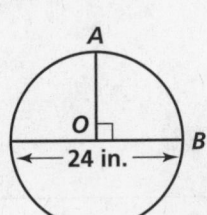

14. _____

$\overset{\frown}{CDE}$

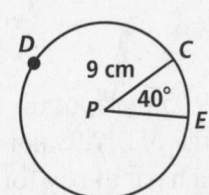

10-6 • Guided Problem Solving

GPS **Student Page 571, Exercise 59**

Metalworking Nina designed an arch made of wrought iron for the top of a mall entrance. The 11 segments between the two concentric semicircles are each 3 ft long. Find the total length of the wrought iron used to make this structure. Round your answer to the nearest foot.

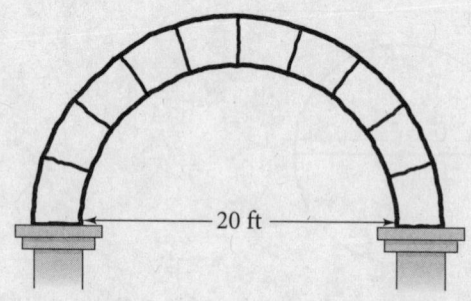

20 ft

Read and Understand

1. The total length of wrought iron is the sum of the _____ straight segments and _____ concentric semicircles. (Write how many of each.)

Plan and Solve

2. The length of the straight segments is _____ × _____ ft = _____ ft.

3. To find the lengths of the semicircles, we use the formula for the _____ of a circle and divide by _____.

4. The smaller semicircle has a diameter of 20 ft. Therefore, its length is $\frac{1}{2}\pi d$ = _____ ft. (Remember to round to the nearest whole foot.)

5. The diameter of the larger semicircle is the smaller diameter plus the length of two straight sections, or a total of _____ ft.

6. So, the length of the larger semicircle is _____ ft.

7. The total length of the wrought iron is the sum of your answers to Steps 2, 4, and 6. What is the total length? _____ ft

Look Back and Check

8. To check your answer, use 3 to approximate π. The length of the smaller semicircle would then be about $\frac{1}{2}(3)(20)$, or about 30 ft.

   Approximate the other lengths and add the values. What is your result? _____ ft

Solve Another Problem

9. Nina's supplier charges $19.95 per foot for the wrought iron. There is an additional charge of $12.95 per foot for shaping the two semicircles. What will Nina have to pay for the materials for the arch? $_____

Practice 10-7

Areas of Circles and Sectors

The radius of ⊙O is 7. Find the area of each of the following. Leave
your answers in terms of π.

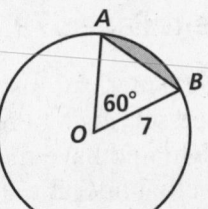

1. ⊙O _____

2. △AOB _____

3. sector AOB _____

4. the shaded segment _____

Find the area of each shaded sector of a circle. Leave your answers in
terms of π.

5. _____

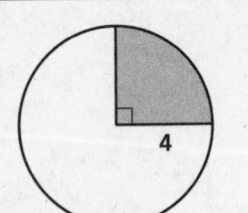

6. _____

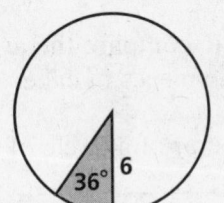

7. _____

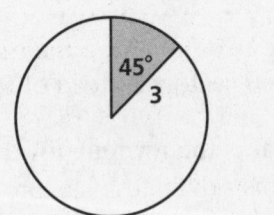

8. _____

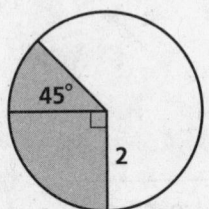

9. _____

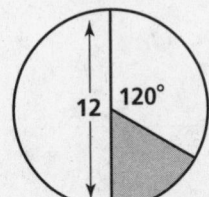

10. _____

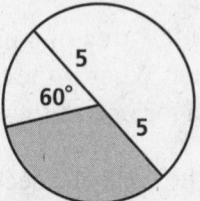

Find the area of each shaded segment of a circle. Round your answers to the
nearest whole number.

11. _____

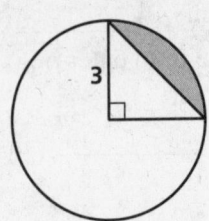

12. _____

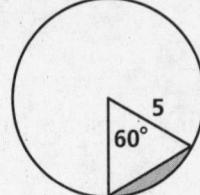

10-7 • Guided Problem Solving

Student Page 579, Exercise 29

Writing The American Institute of Baking suggests a technique for cutting and serving a tiered cake. The tiers of a cake have the same height and have radii 8 in. and 13 in. The top tier and the cake directly under it are each cut into 8 wedges as shown. The outer ring of the 13-inch tier is cut into 12 pieces. Which would be larger, a piece from the top or a piece from the outer ring? Explain.

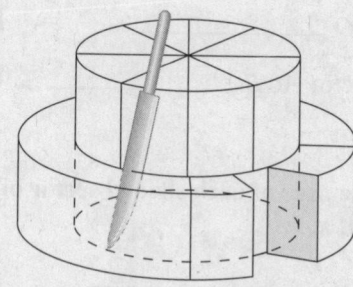

Read and Understand

Since the two tiers have the same height, we can compare the areas of the circles and sectors instead of the volumes of the pieces of cake.

1. What is the formula for the area A of a sector of a circle of radius r defined by an arc $\overset{\frown}{AB}$? $A =$ _____

Plan and Solve

2. First, find the area of a piece from the top tier. What is the measure of the arc for one of these pieces? _____

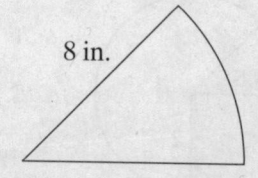

8 in.

Piece from top tier

3. What is the area of a sector of one of the 8 top pieces? Round your answer to the nearest square in. _____ in.²

4. One of the 12 pieces from the outer ring is the difference of sectors of an 8-in. circle and a 13-in. circle. What is the measure of the arc for one of these 12 pieces?

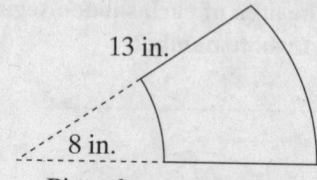

13 in.

8 in.

Piece from outer ring

_____

5. What is the area of one of the 12 pieces from the outer ring? _____ in.²

6. Which piece is larger? _____

Look Back and Check

7. Does your answer seem reasonable? _____

Solve Another Problem

8. Suppose the bottom tier has a 12-inch radius instead of 13 inches. Which would be larger now, a piece from the top tier or a piece from the outer ring? _____

Practice 10-8

Use the dartboard at the right for Exercises 1–3.

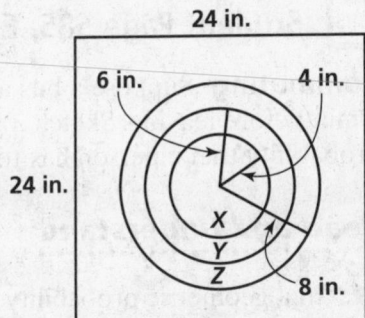

24 in.

6 in.   4 in.

24 in.

X
Y
Z

8 in.

1. If a dart hits the board, find the probability that it will land in region *X*. _____

2. If a dart hits the board, find the probability that it will land in region *Y*. _____

3. If a dart hits the board, find the probability that it will land in region *Z*. _____

Find the probability that a point chosen at random from $\overline{AK}$ is on the given segment.

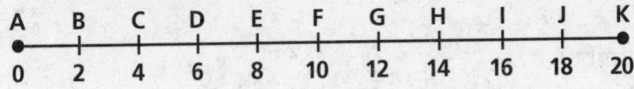

A   B   C   D   E   F   G   H   I   J   K
0   2   4   6   8   10 12 14 16 18 20

4. $\overline{CF}$ _____   5. $\overline{GK}$ _____   6. $\overline{AK}$ _____

7. The state of Connecticut is approximated by a rectangle 100 mi by 50 mi. Hartford is approximately at the center of Connecticut. If a meteor hit the earth within 200 mi of Hartford, find the probability that the meteor landed in Connecticut. _____

8. A stoplight at an intersection stays red for 60 seconds, changes to green for 45 seconds, and then turns yellow for 15 seconds. If Jamal arrives at the intersection at a random time, what is the probability that he will have to wait at a red light for more than 15 seconds?

_____

In each figure, a point between *A* and *B* on the number line is chosen at random. What is the probability that the point is between *C* and *D*?

9. _____

A   C D   B
-2   0   2   4

10. _____

A C   D   B
-10 0   10   20

11. _____

A   C   D B
-2   0   2 4

12. _____

A   C   D   B
-3   0   3   6

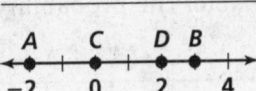

10-8 • Guided Problem Solving

GPS Student Page 585, Exercise 28

Commuting Suppose a bus arrives at a bus stop every 25 min and waits 5 min before leaving. Sketch a geometric model. Use it to find the probability that a person has to wait more than 10 min for a bus to leave.

Read and Understand

1. In a geometric probability model, points represent _____.

2. If points of segments represent outcomes, then $\dfrac{\text{length of favorable segment}}{\text{length of entire segment}} = P($_____$)$.

Plan and Solve

Refer to the segment model to the right. Let the number below each point represent the number of minutes.

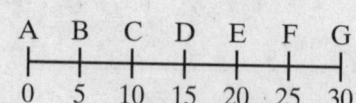

3. What is the segment corresponding to the event "a bus arrives every 25 minutes"? _____

4. What segment corresponds to "the bus waits five minutes after arriving"? _____

5. If a person arrives in the last 10 minutes before the bus leaves, the waiting time is 10 minutes or less. What segment corresponds to this event? _____

6. So, what segment corresponds to a person having to wait more than 10 min for a bus to leave?

_____ Shade this segment on the figure.

7. Now use the formula in Step 2 to find the probability.
   P(a person has to wait more than 10 min for a bus to leave) = _____

Look Back and Check

8. Another way to solve this problem is by using a clock face. The segment $\overline{AG}$ will correspond to the minute hand moving from 12 to 6 on the clock face, $\overline{AE}$ from 12 to 4, etc. The probability would be interpreted in terms of sector areas: $P(event) = \dfrac{\frac{4}{12}\pi r^2}{\frac{6}{12}\pi r^2} = $ _____.

   Are the answers the same? _____

Solve Another Problem

9. Suppose a bus arrives every 20 min and again waits 5 min. Determine the given probability. P(a person has to wait more than 10 min for a bus to leave) = _____

10A: Graphic Organizer

For use before Lesson 10-1

Study Skill When taking notes make your original notes as easy to read as possible. Use abbreviations of your own invention when possible. The amount of time needed to recopy messy notes would be better spent rereading and thinking about them.

Write your answers.

1. What is the chapter title? _____

2. Find the Table of Contents page for this chapter at the front of the book. Name four topics you will study in this chapter.

_____   _____

_____   _____

3. Complete the graphic organizer as you work through the chapter.
   1. Write the title of the chapter in the center oval.
   2. When you begin a lesson, write the name of the lesson in a rectangle.
   3. When you complete that lesson, write a skill or key concept from that lesson in the outer oval linked to that rectangle.
   Continue with steps 2 and 3 clockwise around the graphic organizer.

10B: Reading Comprehension

For use after Lesson 10-7

Study Skill To be successful in mathematics you need to be able to read and understand mathematical symbols. These symbols will help you determine relationships in figures and diagrams.

Match the symbol on the left with its appropriate meaning on the right by drawing a line between them.

1.	$m\angle A$	A.	parallelogram $WXYZ$
2.	$62°$	B.	product of the diagonals d_1 and d_2
3.	$d_1 d_2$	C.	a squared
4.	$\sqrt{x}$	D.	arc EF
5.	$\square WXYZ$	E.	measure of angle A
6.	n-gon	F.	measure of arc QR
7.	$\overset{\frown}{EF}$	G.	square root of x
8.	a^2	H.	pi
9.	π	I.	many-sided polygon
10.	$m\overset{\frown}{QR}$	J.	62 degrees

Write the descriptions as mathematical expressions using appropriate symbols.

11. a squared plus b squared equals c squared. _____

12. The measure of arc AC is 105 degrees. _____

13. Line MN is parallel to line RS. _____

14. The square root of 225 is 15. _____

15. triangle JKL _____

16. Arc XY is congruent to arc PQ. _____

17. parallelogram $ABCD$ _____

18. Four squared equals sixteen. _____

19. **High-Use Academic Words** In the study skill, what does *determine* mean for you to do?

   a. sketch
   b. figure out

10C: Reading/Writing Math Symbols   For use after Lesson 10-7

Study Skill When you read a mathematics problem, be sure you highlight or take notes on the important information in the problem. Do not forget to study any diagrams or figures that accompany the problem. Then when you are solving the problem, look at your highlighted information or notes for the values you will need to solve the problem.

Use the following description and diagram to answer the questions.

The shape of a roof as viewed from above is shown in the diagram. The building owner is installing new shingles on the roof. Three bundles of shingles are called a *square* and cover 100 square feet. Bundles of shingles cost $9 each. An experienced roofer can lay a bundle of shingles in an average of 15 minutes.

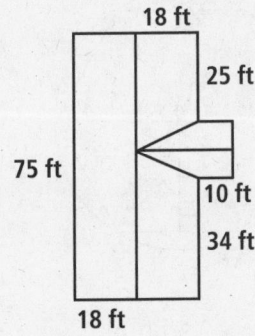

1. What is the area of the roof? _____

2. How many square feet does a bundle of shingles cover? _____

3. How many bundles of shingles are needed? _____

4. How many squares of shingles are needed? _____

5. What is the cost of a bundle of shingles? _____

6. What is the cost of a square of shingles? _____

7. How long will it take an experienced roofer to lay a square of shingles? _____

8. How long will it take an experienced roofer to complete the entire job? _____

9. If the roofer gets paid $30 per hour, how much will she earn for the job? _____

10. What is the total cost of the job? _____

10D: Visual Vocabulary Practice

For use after Lesson 10-3

Study Skill When learning a term that can be illustrated, draw a picture of the most general term. For instance, if you were learning the term *triangle,* draw a triangle that has no special features such as all sides being equal.

Concept List

altitude of a parallelogram	apothem	area of a kite or rhombus
area of a trapezoid	area of a triangle	height of a triangle
perimeter (of an octagon)	radius	similarity ratio

Write the concept that best describes each exercise.
Choose from the concept list above.

1. 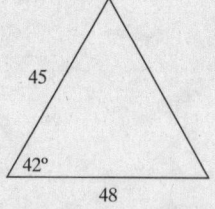 $\frac{1}{2} \cdot 48 \cdot 45 \cdot \sin 42°$ _____	**2.** 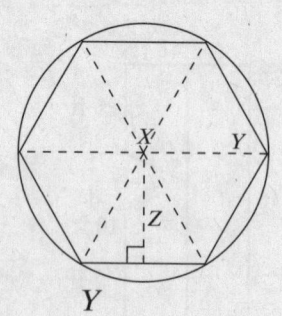 _____	**3.** 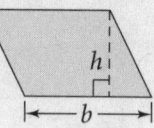 _____
4. $\frac{1}{2}(17)(23 + 19)$ _____	**5.** 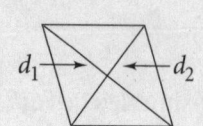 $\frac{1}{2}d_1 d_2$ _____	**6.** $\frac{a}{b} = \frac{3}{8}$ _____
7. 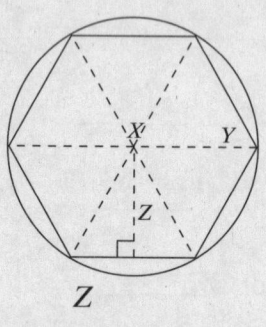 _____	**8.** $ns = 8 \cdot 3 = 24$ _____	**9.** 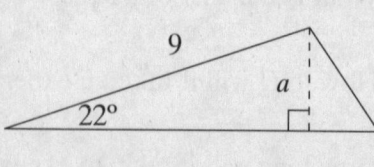 $a = 9 \sin 22° \approx 3.4$ _____

Name ______________________ Class ______________ Date ______________

10E: Vocabulary Check

For use after Lesson 10-6

Study Skill Strengthen your vocabulary. Use these pages and add cues and summaries by applying the Cornell Notetaking style.

Write the definition for each word at the right. To check your work, fold the paper back along the dotted line to see the correct answers.

______________________ ______________________ ______________________	Semicircle
______________________ ______________________ ______________________	Adjacent arcs
______________________ ______________________ ______________________	Apothem
______________________ ______________________ ______________________	Circumference
______________________ ______________________ ______________________	Concentric circles

Vocabulary and Study Skills

Name ______________________ Class ______________ Date ______________

10E: Vocabulary Check (continued)

For use after Lesson 10-6

Write the vocabulary word for each definition. To check your work, fold the paper forward along the dotted line to see the correct answers.

Half a circle. ______________________

Arcs on the same circle with exactly one point in common. ______________________

The distance from the center to the side of a regular polygon. ______________________

The distance around a circle. ______________________

Circles that lie on the same plane and have the same center. ______________________

10F: Vocabulary Review Puzzle

For use with Chapter Review

Study Skill Mathematics has its own vocabulary, often with many new terms in each chapter. Some mathematics vocabulary terms may have different meanings in everyday language. Make sure you understand the different meanings of such words.

Fill in the blanks in each sentence. Copy the letters in the numbered blanks to the boxes with the same number at the bottom of the page to find a famous saying by Euclid.

1. $\underset{25}{\_}\ \underset{26}{\_}\ \_\ \_\ \_\ \_\ \_\ \_\quad \_\ \_\ \_\ \underset{7}{\_}$ have exactly one point in common.

2. Half a circle is known as a $\_\ \_\ \_\ \_\ \_\ \_\ \_\ \underset{18}{\_}\ \_\ \_$.

3. The point from which all points on the circumference of a circle are equidistant is the $\_\ \_\ \_\ \_\ \underset{27}{\_}\ \underset{11}{\_}\ \_$.

4. A fraction of a circle's circumference is known as the $\_\ \_\ \_\quad \_\ \_\ \_\ \_\ \_\ \underset{1}{\_}$.

5. The area of a rectangle is the product of its $\_\ \_\ \underset{15}{\_}\ \_$ and height.

6. A $\_\ \underset{14}{\_}\ \_\ \_\ \_\ \_$ is the set of all points in a plane equidistant from a given point.

7. An angle formed by two radii of a circle is called a $\_\ \_\ \underset{16}{\_}\ \_\ \_\ \_\ \_$ $\_\ \_\ \_\ \_$.

8. $\_\ \underset{19}{\_}\ \_\ \_\ \_\ \_\ \_\ \_\quad \_\ \_\ \_\ \underset{8}{\_}$ have the same measure and are in the same circle or congruent circles.

9. The $\_\ \_\ \_\ \_\ \underset{13}{\_}\ \_\ \_\ \_$ of a circle is equal to two times the radius.

10. In a circle, a $\_\ \_\ \_\ \underset{17}{\_}\ \_\quad \_\ \_\ \_\ \_$ is greater than a semicircle.

11. $\_\ \underset{24}{\_}\ \_\ \_\ \_\ \_\ \_\ \underset{2}{\_}\ \_\quad \_\ \_\ \_\ \_\ \underset{22}{\_}\ \_\ \_$ have a common center.

12. A $\_\ \_\ \underset{5}{\_}\ \underset{28}{\_}\ \_\quad \_\ \_\ \_$ is smaller than a semicircle.

13. The numbers 3, 4, and 5 are known as a $\_\ \underset{20}{\_}\ \_\ \underset{10}{\_}\ \_\ \underset{3}{\_}\ \underset{31}{\_}\ \underset{35}{\_}\ \_\ \_$ $\_\ \underset{23}{\_}\ \_\ \_\ \_$.

14. Half of a diameter is a $\_\ \underset{21}{\_}\ \_\ \_\ \_$.

15. The $\_\ \_\ \_\ \underset{34}{\_}\ \underset{4}{\_}\ \underset{33}{\_}\ \underset{32}{\_}$ of a regular polygon is the perpendicular distance from the center to a side.

16. A $\_\ \underset{6}{\_}\ \_\ \_\ \_\ \_$ of a circle, formed by two radii and their intecepted arc, looks like a slice of pizza.

17. The $\_\ \underset{30}{\_}\ \_\ \underset{29}{\_}\ \_\ \underset{9}{\_}$ of a trapezoid is the perpendicular distance between the bases.

18. $\_\ \_\ \underset{12}{\_}\ \_\ \_\ \_\ \_\ \_\ \_\ \_\ \_\ \_\ \_$ is the distance around a circle.

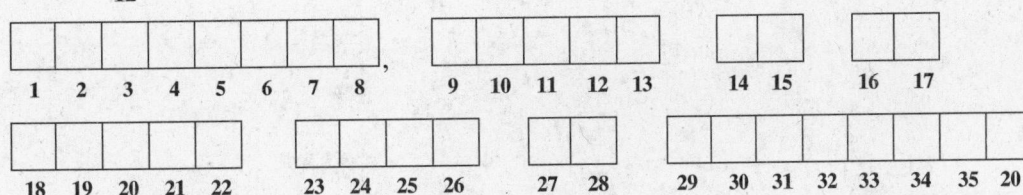

377

Geometry Chapter 10

Name _____ Class _____ Date _____

Practice 11-1

Space Figures and Cross Sections

Use Euler's Formula to find the missing number for each polyhedron.

1. Faces: 5
Edges: _____
Vertices: 5

2. Faces: _____
Edges: 9
Vertices: 6

3. Faces: 8
Edges: 18
Vertices: _____

Match each three-dimensional figure with its net.

4. _____

5. _____

6. _____

7. _____

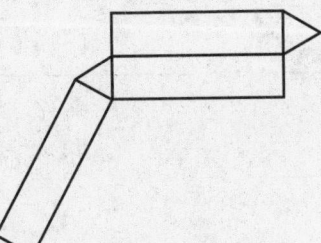 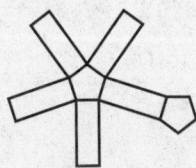 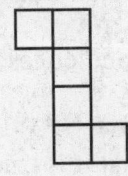 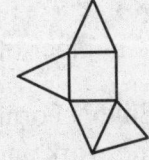

A.

B.

C.

D.

Describe the cross section in each diagram.

8. _____

9. _____

10. _____

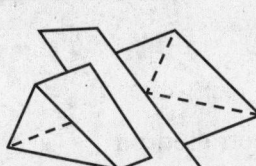 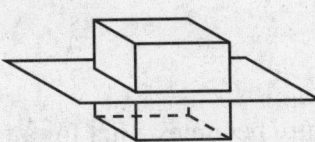 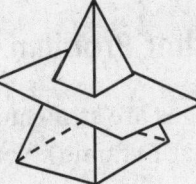

11-1 • Guided Problem Solving

GPS Student Page 602, Exercise 32

Euler's Formula $F + V = E + 1$ applies to any two-dimensional network where F is the number of regions formed by V vertices linked by E edges (or paths). Verify Euler's Formula for the network shown.

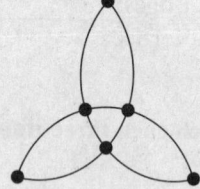

Read and Understand

1. What information is given? _____

2. What are you asked to do? _____

Plan and Solve

3. Find the number of regions bounded by the network (not counting the region outside the figure). $F =$ _____

4. Find the number of vertices and edges (paths). $V =$ _____; $E =$ _____

5. Write Euler's Formula, $F + V = E + 1$, for the network and verify that it is true. _____

Look Back and Check

6. What happens to F, V, and E if one of the edges is removed? Then verify that Euler's Formula is still true.

_____

Solve Another Problem

7. If the edges are straightened, the figure becomes a net for a tall, skinny tetrahedron (triangular pyramid). Verify Euler's Formula ($F + V = E + 2$) for this solid.

_____

Practice 11-2

Surface Areas of Prisms and Cylinders

Find the lateral area of each cylinder to the nearest tenth.

1. _____

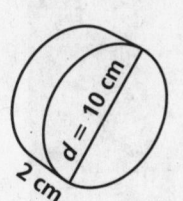

2. _____

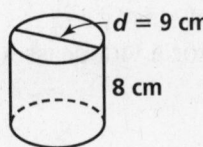

3. _____

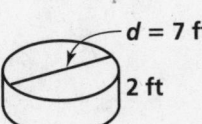

4. _____

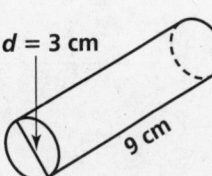

Find (a) the lateral area and (b) the surface area of each prism. Round your answers to the nearest whole number.

5. _____

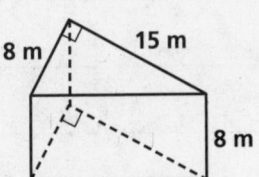

6. _____

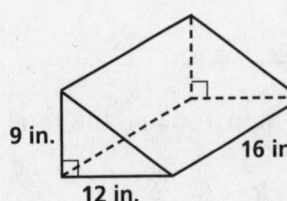

7. _____

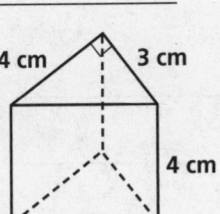

8. _____

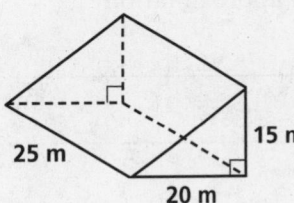

Find the surface area of each cylinder in terms of π.

9. _____

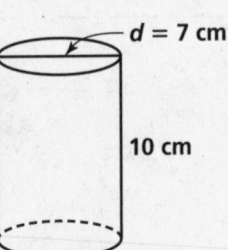

10. _____

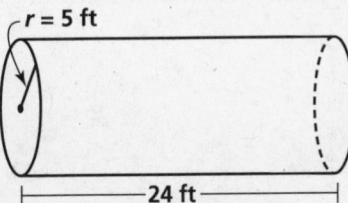

11-2 • Guided Problem Solving

Student Page 613, Exercise 24

Packaging A typical box for a videocassette tape is open on one side as pictured at the right. How many square inches of cardboard are in a typical box for a videocassette tape?

1 in.

SUPER VHS
VIDEOCASSETTE

$7\frac{1}{2}$ in.

2 HOURS
ST-120

4 in.

Read and Understand

1. What information is given? _____

2. What are you asked to find? _____

Plan and Solve

3. Treating each side of the box as a rectangle, list the sides and the dimensions of each.

_____

4. Find the area of each side listed in Step 3. _____

_____

5. Add the areas from Step 4 to find the total area of cardboard. _____

Look Back and Check

6. Is the answer in Step 5 reasonable? Why should this answer be considered only an approximation?

_____

_____

Solve Another Problem

7. Some videocassette boxes have the opening at the bottom instead of on the side. How many *more* square inches of cardboard are in a typical open-bottom box than an open-side box ? _____

Practice 11-3

Surface Areas of Pyramids and Cones

Find the lateral area of each cone to the nearest whole number.

1. _____

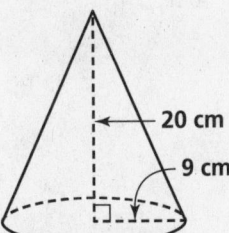

2. _____

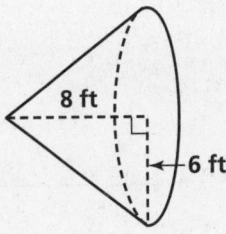

Find the surface area of each cone in terms of π.

3. _____

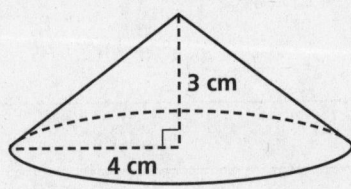

4. _____

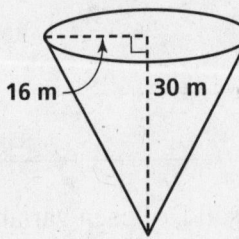

Find the lateral area of each regular pyramid to the nearest tenth.

5. _____

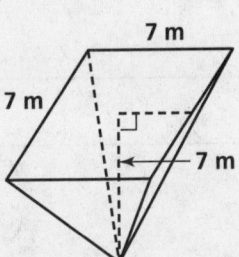

6. _____

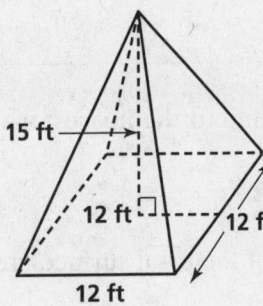

Find the surface area of each regular pyramid to the nearest tenth.

7. _____

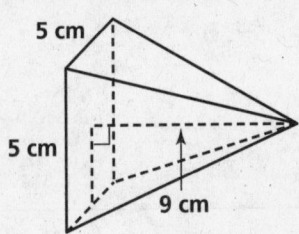

8. _____

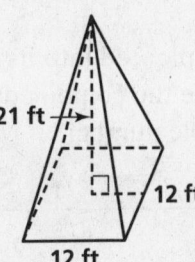

11-3 • Guided Problem Solving

Student Page 622, Exercise 29

Find the surface area to the nearest whole number.

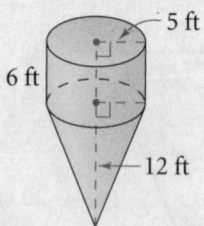

Read and Understand

1. What information is given? _____

2. What are you asked to find? _____

Plan and Solve

3. Identify the surfaces of the solid, and give the general formula for the area of each.

   _____

   _____

4. Find the value, for this solid, of each variable in the formulas you gave in Step 3. Where a calculation was necessary, describe it. _____

   _____

5. Find the area of each surface of the solid, to the nearest tenth.

   _____

6. Add the areas and round to the nearest whole number. _____

Look Back and Check

7. About what fraction of the total surface area comes from the cone? Does this seem right?

   _____

Solve Another Problem

8. Suppose the solid were separated into its two parts, a cylinder and a cone. What would be the combined area of the two parts? Round to the nearest whole number.

   _____

Practice 11-4

Volumes of Prisms and Cylinders

Find the volume of each cylinder to the nearest tenth.

1. _____

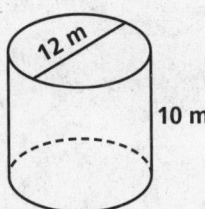

2. _____

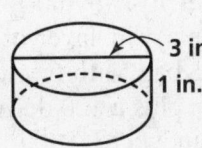

3. _____

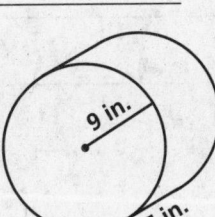

4. _____

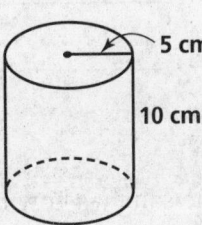

Find the volume of each prism to the nearest whole number.

5. _____

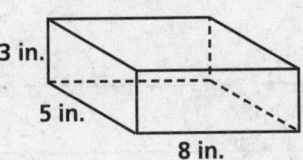

6. _____

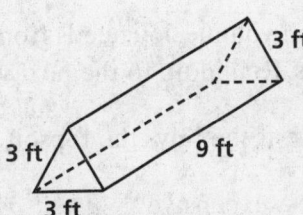

7. _____

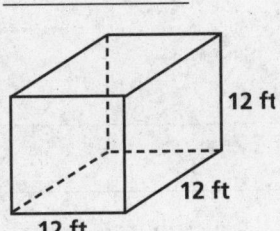

8. _____

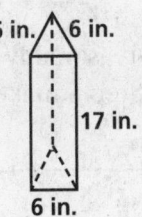

Find the volume of each composite figure.

9. _____

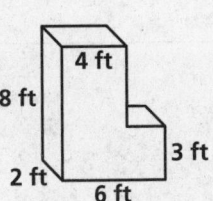

10. _____

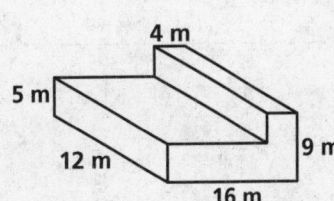

11-4 • Guided Problem Solving

GPS **Student Page 629, Exercise 29**

Landscaping To landscape her 70-ft-by-60-ft rectangular backyard, Joy is planning first to put down a 4-in. layer of topsoil. She can buy bags of topsoil at $2.50 per 3-ft^3 bag, with free delivery. Or she can buy bulk topsoil for $22.00/yd^3 , plus a $20 delivery fee. Which option is less expensive? Explain.

Read and Understand

1. What information is given? _____

2. What are you asked to find? _____

Plan and Solve

3. Four inches of topsoil is the same as how many feet of topsoil? _____

4. Consider the topsoil to be laid down as a
   rectangular prism. What is its volume in cubic feet? _____

5. How many 3-ft^3 bags would Joy need to buy, and what would that cost? _____

6. Convert the topsoil volume Joy needs from cubic
   feet to cubic yards. Round up to the next whole number. _____

7. Compute Joy's cost if she buys the topsoil by the cubic yard. _____

8. Which option is less expensive? _____

Look Back and Check

9. Do the two options come out reasonably close to one
   another? Does the answer in Step 8 make sense? Explain. _____

   _____

Solve Another Problem

10. Suppose Joy's backyard were much smaller—60 ft by 20 ft. Which
    way of buying topsoil would be less expensive? Justify your answer.

    _____

Guided Problem Solving

Practice 11-5

Volumes of Pyramids and Cones

Find the volume of each pyramid.

1. _____

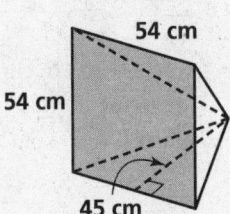

54 cm
54 cm
45 cm

2. _____

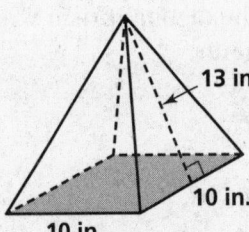

13 in.
10 in.
10 in.

3. _____

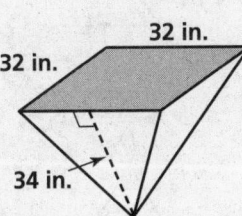

32 in.
32 in.
34 in.

4. _____

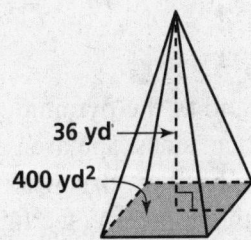

36 yd
400 yd²

Find the volume of each cone. Round your answers to the nearest tenth.

5. _____

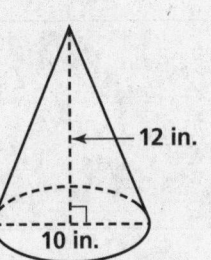

12 in.
10 in.

6. _____

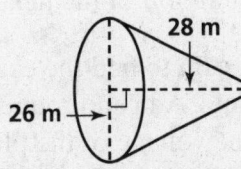

28 m
26 m

7. _____

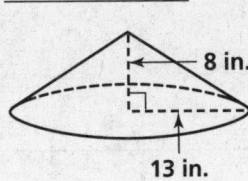

8 in.
13 in.

8. _____

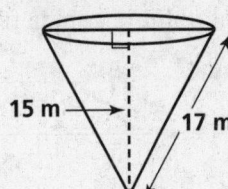

15 m
17 m

***Algebra* Find the value of the variable in each figure.**

9. _____

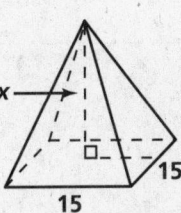

x
15
15
Volume = 1500

10. _____

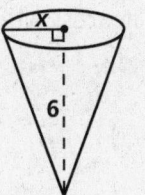

x
6
Volume = 8π

L1 Practice

Geometry Lesson 11-5

11-5 • Guided Problem Solving

GPS **Student Page 635, Exercise 24**

Hardware Builders use a plumb bob to find a vertical line. The plumb bob shown combines a regular hexagonal prism with a pyramid. Find its volume to the nearest cubic centimeter.

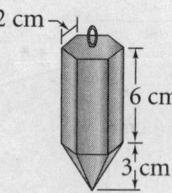

Read and Understand

1. What information is given? _____

2. What are you asked to find? _____

Plan and Solve

3. The base of the prism, and of the pyramid, is a regular hexagon with 2-cm sides. The area of a regular polygon is given by $A = \frac{1}{2}ap$, where p is the perimeter and a is the apothem (see figure). What type of triangle is $\triangle DEF$? What is the length EF? _____

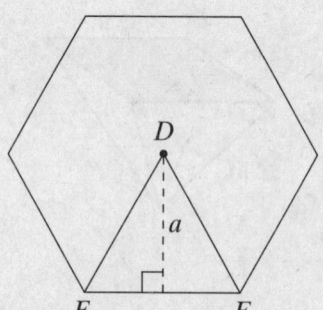

4. Use the Pythagorean Theorem to find the exact value of a. Then find the exact area B of the hexagonal base. _____

5. Use $V_1 = Bh$ and $V_2 = \frac{1}{3}Bh$ to find the exact volumes of the prism and the pyramid. Add and round to the nearest whole number to find the volume of the plumb bob.

_____

Look Back and Check

6. What fraction of the total volume comes from the hexagonal prism? Does this seem reasonable?

_____

Solve Another Problem

7. Suppose the hexagonal prism were reduced in length to 3 cm. What would be the new volume of the plumb bob? Round to the nearest whole number. _____

Name _____ Class _____ Date _____

Practice 11-6

Surface Areas and Volumes of Spheres

Find the surface area of each sphere. Round your answers to the nearest tenth.

1. _____

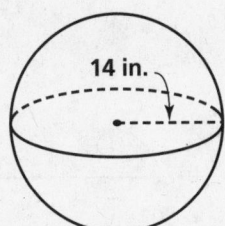

2. _____

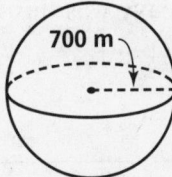

3. _____

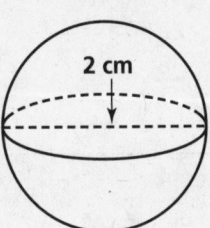

4. _____

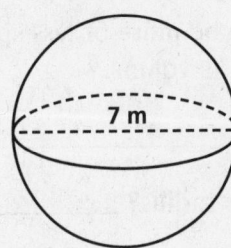

Find the volume of each sphere. Round your answers to the nearest tenth.

5. _____

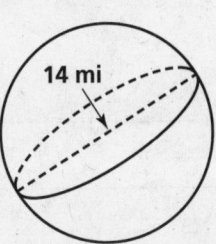

6. _____

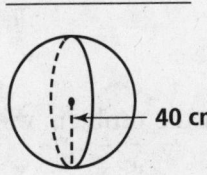

7. _____

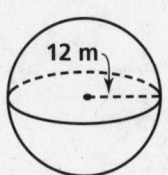

8. _____

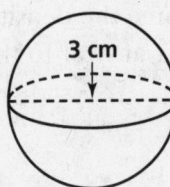

Use the given circumference to approximate the volume of each object. Round your answers to the nearest whole number.

9. a volleyball with $C = 69$ cm _____

10. a golf ball with $C = 13.5$ cm _____

L1 Practice

Geometry Lesson 11-6

389

11-6 • Guided Problem Solving

Meteorology On Sept. 3, 1970, a hailstone with diameter 5.6 in. fell at Coffeyville, Kansas. It weighed about 0.018 lb/in.^{3} compared to the normal 0.033 lb/in.^{3} for ice. About how heavy was this Kansas hailstone?

Read and Understand

1. What information is given? _____

2. What are you asked to find? _____

Plan and Solve

3. Assume the hailstone to be more or less spherical. What is the formula for its volume?

   _____

4. What is r, the hailstone's radius? _____

5. Find the hailstone's volume to the nearest hundredth. _____

6. Multiply by the hailstone's density to find the hailstone's weight. Round to the nearest tenth. _____

Look Back and Check

7. What information given in the problem was not used? Why not? _____

   _____

Solve Another Problem

8. Find the weight, in ounces, of a more typical hailstone with a diameter of 0.4 in. (1 lb = 16 oz). Assume the density to be the same as for the large one. Round your answer to the nearest hundredth. _____

Practice 11-7

Areas and Volumes of Similar Solids

The figures in each pair are similar. Use the given information to find the similarity ratio of the smaller figure to the larger figure.

1. _____

S.A. = 49 cm^2 S.A. = 81 cm^2

2. _____

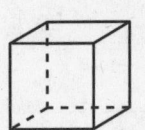

V = 125 in.^{3} V = 512 in.^{3}

Are the two solids in each pair similar? If so, give the similarity ratio. If not, write *not similar*.

3. _____

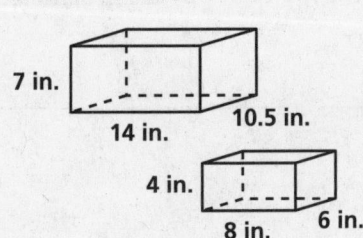

7 in.   14 in.   10.5 in.

4 in.   8 in.   6 in.

4. _____

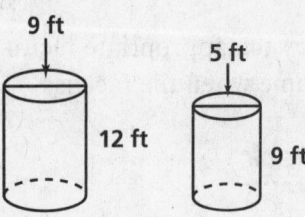

9 ft   12 ft   5 ft   9 ft

The surface areas of two similar figures are given. The volume of the larger figure is given. Find the volume of the smaller figure.

5. _____

S.A. = 25 cm^2
S.A. = 36 cm^2
V = 216 cm^3

6. _____

S.A. = 16 in.^{2}
S.A. = 25 in.^{2}
V = 500 in.^{3}

The volumes of two similar figures are given. The surface area of the smaller figure is given. Find the surface area of the larger figure.

7. _____

V = 8 ft^3
V = 125 ft^3
S.A. = 4 ft^2

8. _____

V = 125 cm^3
V = 1000 cm^3
S.A. = 150 cm^2

11-7 • Guided Problem Solving

GPS **Student Page 650, Exercise 29**

A clown's face on a balloon is 4 in. high when the balloon holds 108 in.^{3} of air. How much air must the balloon hold for the face to be 8 in. high?

Read and Understand

1. What information is given? _____

2. What are you asked to find? _____

Plan and Solve

3. What is the similarity ratio of the two balloon sizes? Explain. _____

4. What, by Theorem 11-12, is the corresponding ratio of air volumes for the balloon? _____

5. Multiply 108 in.^{3} by the appropriate factor to obtain the air volume when the face is 8 in. high. _____

Look Back and Check

6. The similarity ratio of two solids should be a ratio of lengths (not of areas or volumes). Is that what you used? Explain.

   _____

Solve Another Problem

7. A star on a balloon has an area of 4 cm^2 when the balloon holds 104 cm^3 of air. How much air must the balloon hold for the star to have an area of 9 cm^2? _____

11A: Graphic Organizer

For use before Lesson 11-1

Study Skill To help remember formulas and other important information, use a mnemonic. A mnemonic is a memory device to help us associate new information with something familiar. For example, to remember a formula or equation change it into something meaningful. To remember the metric terms *kilo, hecto, deka meter, deci, centi, milli,* in order, use the first letter of each metric term to represent a word, such as, *k*angaroo *h*ops *d*own *m*ountain *d*rinking *c*hocolate *m*ilk. The key is to create your own; then you won't forget them.

Write your answers.

1. What is the chapter title? _____

2. Find the Table of Contents page for this chapter at the front of the book. Name four topics you will study in this chapter.

   _____   _____

   _____   _____

3. Complete the graphic organizer as you work through the chapter.
   1. Write the title of the chapter in the center oval.
   2. When you begin a lesson, write the name of the lesson in a rectangle.
   3. When you complete that lesson, write a skill or key concept from that lesson in the outer oval linked to that rectangle.
   Continue with steps 2 and 3 clockwise around the graphic organizer.

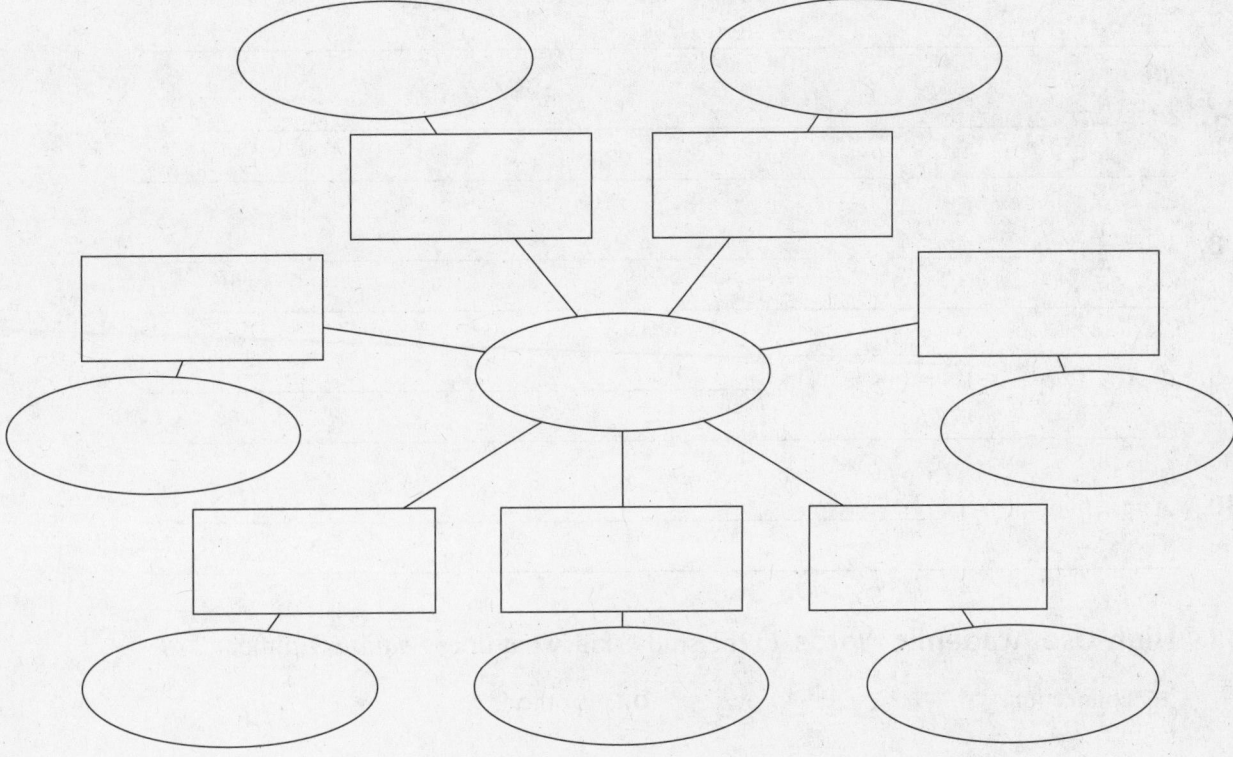

11B: Reading Comprehension

For use after Lesson 11-6

Study Skill Formulas describe the mathematical relationship between variables. If you know the values for all but one of the variables in a formula, then you can use the formula to find the unknown variable.

For each formula, write out what it means and write what it is used to calculate.

1. $A = \frac{1}{2}bh$ _____

_____

2. $m = \frac{y_2 - y_1}{x_2 - x_1}$ _____

_____

3. $a^2 + b^2 = c^2$ _____

_____

4. $A = \pi r^2$ _____

_____

5. $V = \pi r^2 h$ _____

_____

6. $\left(\frac{x_1 + x_2}{2}, \frac{y_1 + y_2}{2} \right)$ _____

_____

7. $C = 2\pi r$ _____

_____

8. $V = \frac{1}{3}\pi r^2 h$ _____

_____

9. $d = \sqrt{(x_1 - x_2)^2 + (y_2 - y_1)^2}$ _____

_____

10. $A = \frac{1}{2}h(b_1 + b_2)$ _____

_____

11. **High-Use Academic Words** In the study skill, what does *relationship* mean?

    a. connections   **b.** hypothesis

11C: Reading/Writing Math Symbols

For use after Lesson 11-2

Study Skill When you read math problems, look for key words that indicate important information. In geometry, these key words are often words that describe the dimensions of a figure. *Height, width, length, radius, diameter,* and *volume* are just a few examples of key words.

Read through the following example and then answer the questions that follow.

Find the surface area of a cylinder that has a radius of 3 inches, and a height of 5 inches.

Think: Sketch the cylinder that is described. Find the area of the top and bottom.

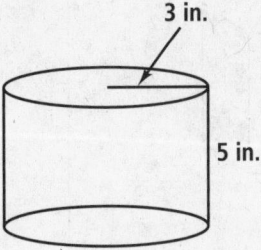

The top is a circle.
$A = \pi r^2$
$A = \pi \cdot (3)^2$
$A = \pi \cdot 9$
$A = 9\pi \approx 28.3 \text{ in.}^2$

Think: Find the area of the lateral surface. Sketch the rectangle.

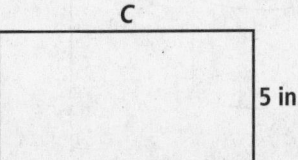

$A = bh = C \cdot 5$
The formula for the circumference is $C = 2\pi r$.
$C = 2\pi r$
$C = 2\pi \cdot 3$
$C = 6\pi$
$A = 6\pi \cdot 5$
$A = 30\pi \approx 94.2 \text{ in.}^2$

Think: Add the areas of the top, bottom, and lateral surfaces.
$S.A. = 9\pi + 9\pi + 30\pi$
$S.A. = 48\pi \approx 150.8 \text{ in.}^2$

1. Find the surface area of a cylinder with a height of 8 inches and a radius of 6 inches to the nearest tenth.

2. Find the surface area of the prism.

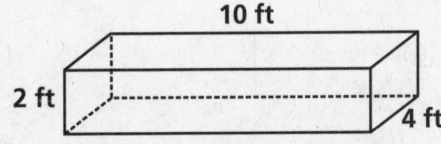

11D: Visual Vocabulary Practice

For use after Lesson 11-5

Study Skill Mathematics can be like learning a sport, where you have to be able to visualize.

Concept List

altitude	base	cone
cross section	cylinder	polyhedron
prism	pyramid	sphere

Write the concept that best describes each exercise.
Choose from the concept list above.

<table>
<tr>
<td>

1.
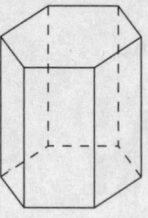

_____
</td>
<td>

2.
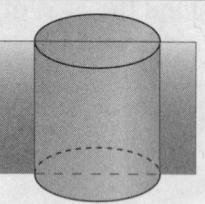

_____
</td>
<td>

3.
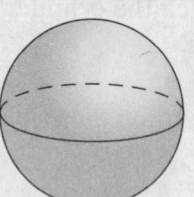

_____
</td>
</tr>
<tr>
<td>

4.
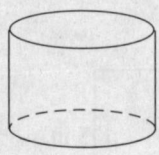

_____
</td>
<td>

5.
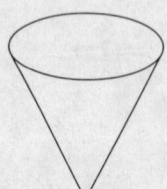

_____
</td>
<td>

6.
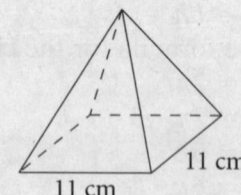

11 cm
11 cm

_____
</td>
</tr>
<tr>
<td>

7.

_____
</td>
<td>

8.

h

_____
</td>
<td>

9.
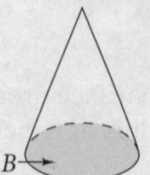

B

_____
</td>
</tr>
</table>

11E: Vocabulary Check

Study Skill Strengthen your vocabulary. Use these pages and add cues and summaries by applying the Cornell Notetaking style.

Write the definition for each word at the right. To check your work, fold the paper back along the dotted line to see the correct answers.

_____

_____

_____   Face

_____

_____   Edge

_____

_____

_____   Altitude (of a prism or cylinder)

_____

_____

_____   Surface area (of a prism, cylinder, pyramid, or cone)

_____

_____

_____   Volume

_____

_____

_____

11E: Vocabulary Check (continued)

**Write the vocabulary word for each definition. To check your work, fold the
paper forward along the dotted line to see the correct answers.**

A surface of a polyhedron.

_____

An intersection of two
faces of a polyhedron.

_____

A perpendicular segment
that joins the planes of
the bases.

_____

The sum of the lateral area
and the areas of the bases.

_____

A measure of the space a
figure occupies.

_____

11F: Vocabulary Review

Study Skill Consider working with a partner to learn new vocabulary terms. Drill each other by saying the term and having your partner repeat the definition to you. You may also wish to make flash cards.

Fill in the blanks with the appropriate word.

1. A(n) _____ is a three-dimensional figure whose surfaces are polygons.

2. A(n) _____ is a segment that is formed by the intersection of two faces.

3. Three or more edges meet at a point called a _____.

4. The intersection of a solid and a plane is a _____.

5. A(n) _____ is a polyhedron with two congruent parallel bases.

6. A(n) _____ is a perpendicular segment that joins the planes of the bases in a prism.

7. A(n) _____ has lateral faces that are rectangles and a lateral edge is an altitude.

8. The length of the altitude of a lateral face of a pyramid is a(n) _____.

9. A(n) _____ is like a pyramid but its base is a circle.

10. _____ is the space a figure occupies.

11. A(n) _____ is the set of all points in space equidistant from a given point.

12. A great circle divides a sphere into two _____.

13. _____ have the same shape, and all corresponding dimensions are in proportion.

14. In a right triangle, the _____ is the side opposite the right angle.

Practice 12-1

Tangent Lines

Assume that lines that appear to be tangent are tangent. *C* is the center of
each circle. Find the value of *x*.

1. _____

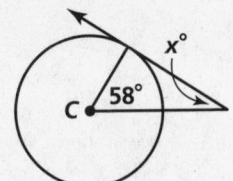

2. _____

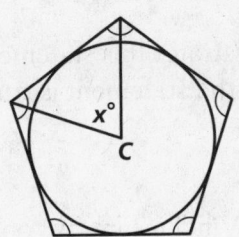

In each diagram, $\overrightarrow{AB}$ is tangent to $\odot C$ at *B*. Find the value of *x*.

3. _____

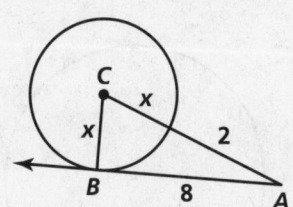

4. _____

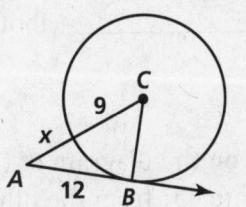

In each diagram, $\overleftrightarrow{ZY}$ is tangent to circles *O* and *P*. Find the value of *x*.

5. _____

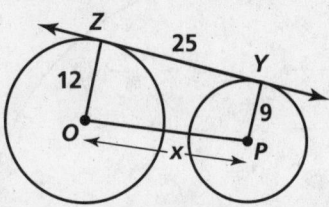

6. _____

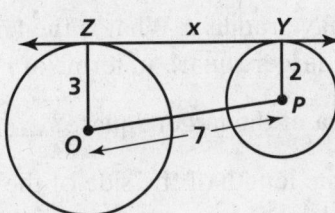

Tell whether each polygon is inscribed in or circumscribed about the circle.

7. _____

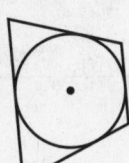

8. _____

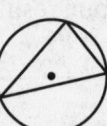

9. _____

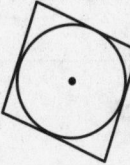

12-1 • Guided Problem Solving

GPS **Student Page 666, Exercise 21**

History Leonardo da Vinci wrote, "When each of two squares touch the same circle at four points, one is double the other."

a. Sketch a figure that illustrates this statement.

b. **Writing** Explain why the statement is true.

Read and Understand

1. What do you think da Vinci meant by "one is double the other"? _____

_____

2. One square is _____ in the circle

and one square is _____ about the circle.

Plan and Solve

3. Draw the two squares on the diagram of the circle to the right. (*Hint:* Rotate one square 45° from the other.)

4. To help solve the problem, enlarge one quarter of the circle. Use the space to the right and add the portions of the squares tangent to the circle in that quarter.

5. Let the circle have radius *r*. What is the length of a side of the larger square in terms of *r*? _____

6. What is the area of the larger square? _____

7. To determine the length of the side of the smaller square, use right triangle trigonometry or special triangle trigonometry. What is the length of a side of the smaller square? _____

8. What is the area of the smaller square? _____

9. How do you interpret da Vinci's words in terms of your results?

_____

Look Back and Check

10. Does your answer seem reasonable? _____

Solve Another Problem

11. Suppose two circles touch a square at four points. How do the circles compare? _____

_____

Guided Problem Solving

Practice 12-2

Find the radius and $m\widehat{AB}$.

1. _____

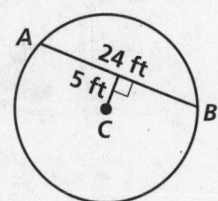

2. _____

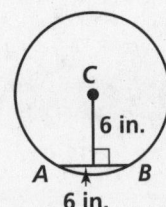

Find the value of x to the nearest tenth.

3. _____

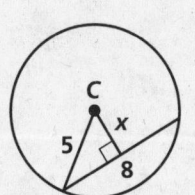

4. _____

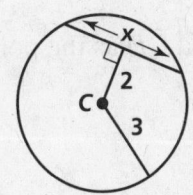

5. _____

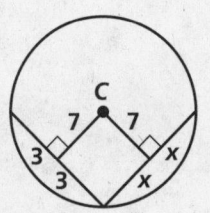

6. _____

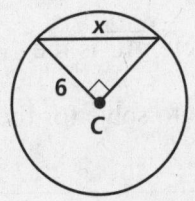

List what you can conclude from each diagram.

7. _____

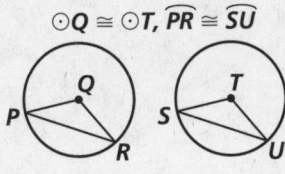

$\odot Q \cong \odot T$, $\widehat{PR} \cong \widehat{SU}$

8. _____

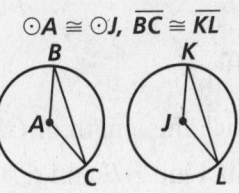

$\odot A \cong \odot J$, $\overline{BC} \cong \overline{KL}$

Write a two-column proof, a paragraph proof, or a flow proof.

9. Given: $\odot O$ with $m\widehat{AB} = m\widehat{BC} = m\widehat{CA}$
   Prove: $m\angle ABC = m\angle BCA = m\angle CAB$

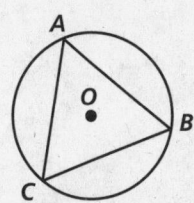

12-2 • Guided Problem Solving

GPS Student Page 675, Exercise 30

$\odot A$ and $\odot B$ are congruent. $\overline{CD}$ is a chord of both circles. $AB = 8$ in. and $CD = 6$ in. How long is a radius?

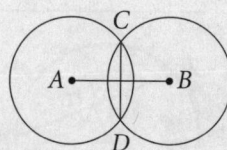

Read and Understand

1. $\overline{AB}$ is _____ to $\overline{CD}$.

2. By Theorem 12-6, the diameter $\overline{AB}$ _____ the chord $\overline{CD}$.

Plan and Solve

Label the intersection of $\overline{AB}$ and $\overline{CD}$ as the point E.

3. If $AB = 8$ in., then $AE = $ _____ in.

   And if $CD = 6$ in., then $CE = $ _____ in.

4. Draw the segment $\overline{AC}$. $\triangle ACE$ is a _____ triangle.

5. In terms of parts of the circle, $\overline{AC}$ is the _____.

6. What theorem can you use to solve for the radius? _____

7. How long is a radius? _____ in.

Look Back and Check

8. Is your answer reasonable? _____

Solve Another Problem

9. Suppose that AB is twice the length of CD and the radius is $2\sqrt{5}$ in. Find AB and CD. $AB = $ _____ in., $CD = $ _____ in.

Practice 12-3

Inscribed Angles

For each diagram, indicate a pair of congruent inscribed angles.

1. _____

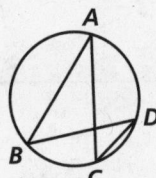

2. _____

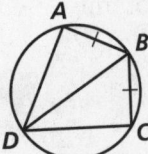

Find the value of each variable.

3. _____

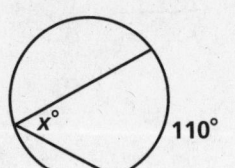

4. _____

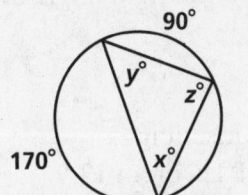

5. _____

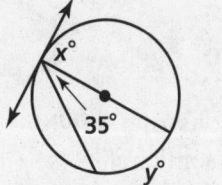

6. _____

7. _____

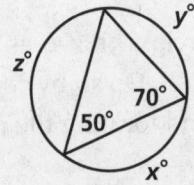

8. _____

9. **Find each indicated measure for ⊙O.**

a. $m\angle A$ _____

b. $m\angle B$ _____

c. $m\angle C$ _____

d. $m\angle D$ _____

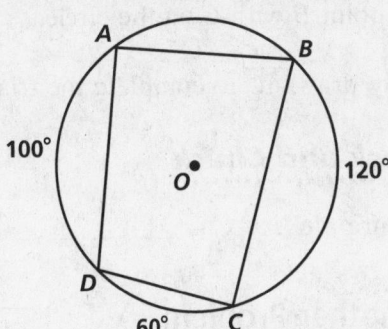

12-3 • Guided Problem Solving

GPS **Student Page 683, Exercise 35**

Constructions Use Corollary 2 of Theorem 12-9 to construct a right triangle given one leg and the hypotenuse.

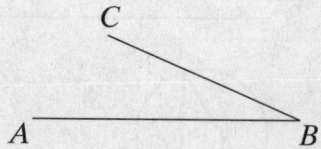

Read and Understand

Let the hypotenuse and leg be as given in the figure with the understanding that $\angle B$ will vary depending on the placement of the second leg. Label the figure as illustrated.

1. If $\overline{AB}$ is the hypotenuse, which angle will be the right angle of the triangle? $\angle$ _____

Plan and Solve

2. One way to construct a right triangle is by inscribing the sides in a semicircle. Use Corollary 2 of Theorem 12-9 to find the measure of $\overarc{AB}$ intercepted by $\angle C$. $m\overarc{AB}$ = _____

3. According to this result, what part of the circle is $\overline{AB}$? _____

4. To construct a circle with $\overline{AB}$ as a diameter, you need to locate the center O of $\overline{AB}$. Do so by constructing the perpendicular bisector of $\overline{AB}$ and locating the point O of intersection.

5. Now use a compass to draw $\odot O$ with $\overline{AB}$ as a diameter.

6. Add the given leg $\overline{BC}$ using a compass to measure the distance from point B with C on the circle.

7. Finally, draw $\overline{AC}$ to complete the triangle.

Look Back and Check

8. Measure $\angle C$. $m\angle C$ = _____

Solve Another Problem

9. Use a Pythagorean triple to construct a triangle using the method above. Measure the second leg and check that $a^2 + b^2 = c^2$.

Practice 12-4

Angle Measures and Segment Lengths

Find the value of *x*.

1. _____

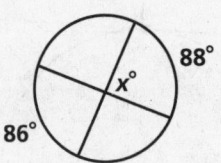

2. _____

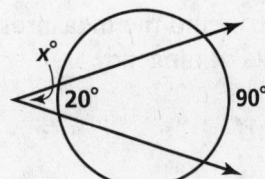

3. _____

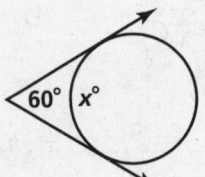

4. _____

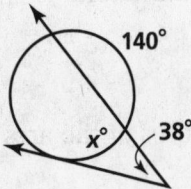

Algebra Find the value of each variable using the given chords, secants, and tangents. If your answer is not a whole number, round it to the nearest tenth.

5. _____

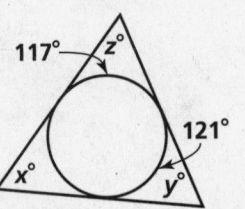

6. _____

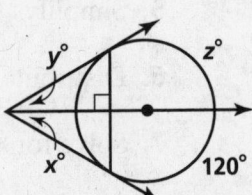

7. _____

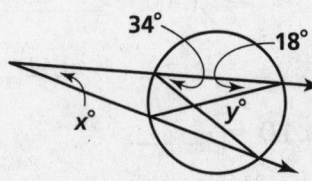

8. _____

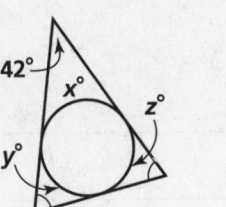

9. _____

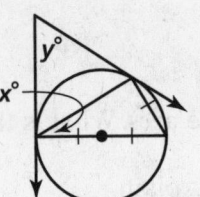

10. _____

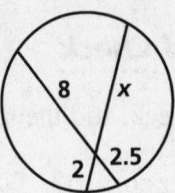

11. _____

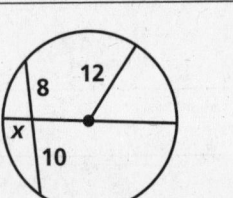

12. _____

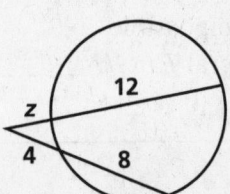

13. _____

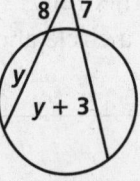

12-4 • Guided Problem Solving

GPS **Student Page 692, Exercise 27**

A circle is inscribed in a quadrilateral whose four angles have measures 85, 76, 94, and 105. Find the measures of the four arcs between consecutive points of tangency.

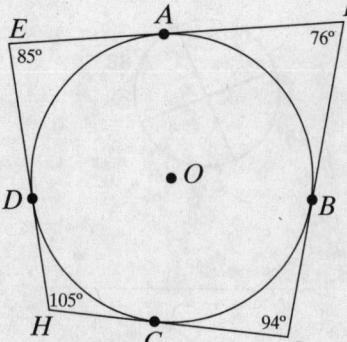

Read and Understand

One possible quadrilateral and circle is illustrated at the right.

1. Since the circle is inscribed inside the quadrilateral, each of the sides of the quadrilateral is _____ to $\odot O$.

Plan and Solve

2. Since the sum of the measures of the arcs of a circle is 360, $\overset{\frown}{ABCD}$ = _____ − $m\overset{\frown}{AD}$.

   Complete each of the following steps to find $m\overset{\frown}{AD}$.

   $m\angle E =$ _____ $\left(m\overset{\frown}{ABCD} - m\overset{\frown}{AD} \right)$ **3.** Theorem 12-11(2)

   _____ $= \frac{1}{2}\left(\left(360 - m\overset{\frown}{AD} \right) - m\overset{\frown}{AD} \right)$ **4.** Substitute.

   $= \frac{1}{2}\left(360 - \underline{\hspace{1cm}} m\overset{\frown}{AD} \right)$ **5.** Simplify.

   $=$ _____ $- m\overset{\frown}{AD}$ **6.** Distribute.

   $m\overset{\frown}{AD} =$ _____   **7.** Solve for $m\overset{\frown}{AD}$.

8. Notice the shortcut implied in Step 6: $m\overset{\frown}{AD} = 180 - m\angle E$.
   Use this method to solve for the remaining arc measures. $m\overset{\frown}{AB} =$ _____,
   $m\overset{\frown}{BC} =$ _____, $m\overset{\frown}{CD} =$ _____

Look Back and Check

9. As a quick check, add the measures of the arcs. What is the sum? _____

10. Is your answer correct? _____ Explain. _____

Solve Another Problem

11. Explain, using Theorem 12-9, why it is impossible to circumscribe a circle about quadrilateral *EFGH*. _____

_____

_____

Practice 12-5

Circles in the Coordinate Plane

· ·

Find the center and radius of each circle.

1. $x^2 + y^2 = 36$ _____

2. $(x + 1)^2 + (y + 6)^2 = 16$ _____

Write the standard equation of each circle.

3. center $(0, 0)$; $r = 7$ _____

4. center $(5, 3)$; $r = 2$ _____

5. center $(-5, 4)$; $r = \frac{1}{2}$ _____

6. center $(-2, -5)$; $r = \sqrt{2}$ _____

Write an equation for each circle.

7. _____

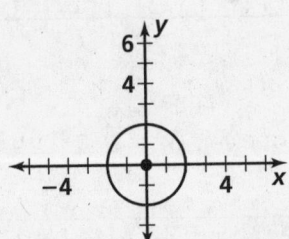

8. _____

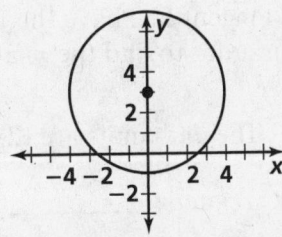

9. _____

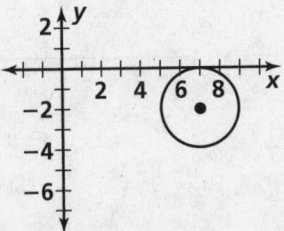

10. _____

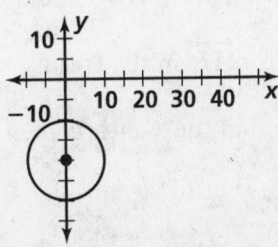

Graph each circle. Label its center, and state its radius.

11. $x^2 + y^2 = 25$

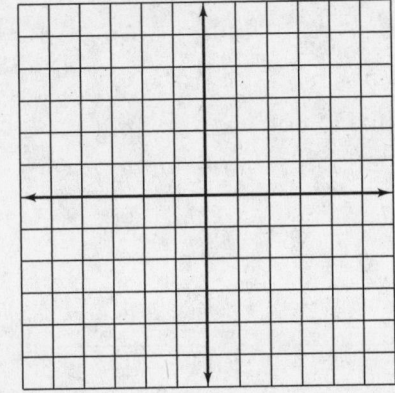

12. $(x - 3)^2 + (y - 5)^2 = 9$

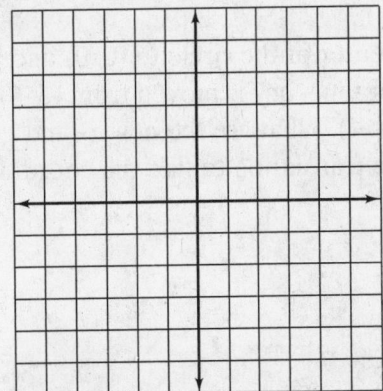

12-5 • Guided Problem Solving

GPS **Student Page 698, Exercise 47**

What are the x- and y-intercepts of the line tangent to the circle $(x - 2)^2 + (y - 2)^2 = 5^2$ at the point $(5, 6)$?

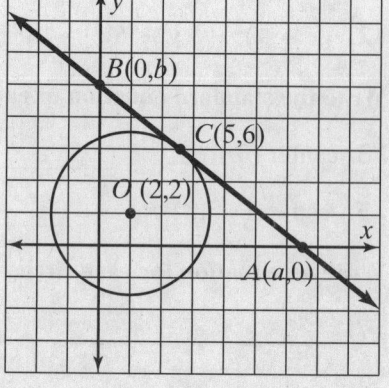

Read and Understand

1. Refer to the diagram at the right with the x-intercept at $A(a, 0)$ and the y-intercept at $B(0, b)$. What is the center of $\odot O$? _____ What is the radius? _____

Plan and Solve

Let the equation for the tangent line have the form $y = mx + b$. You must find m and b in order to find the x- and y-intercepts.

2. Draw the radius $\overline{OC}$. The endpoints are $(2, 2)$ and $(5, 6)$. What is the slope M? $M = $ _____

3. How are $\overleftrightarrow{AB}$ and $\overline{OC}$ related? _____

4. Therefore, what is the slope m of $\overleftrightarrow{AB}$? $m = $ _____

5. Use m and the point $(5, 6)$ on $\overleftrightarrow{AB}$ to find the y-intercept b. What is b? $b = $ _____

6. Write the equation for $\overleftrightarrow{AB}$ in the form $y = mx + b$. _____

7. Use the equation to find the x-intercept, a. What is a? $a = $ _____

Look Back and Check

8. Find the equation of the line through the x- and y-intercepts just found. _____
    Is this the same as the equation in Step 6? _____

Solve Another Problem

9. Move the center of the circle to $(0, 0)$ and keep the radius as 5. The point of tangency is moved from $(5, 6)$ to $(3, 4)$ (since $5 - 2 = 3$ and $6 - 2 = 4$). What are the new x- and y-intercepts? (Careful: Do not use a simple translation to find the coordinates.)

Practice 12-6

Locus: A Set of Points

Draw each locus of points in a plane.

1. 1.5 cm from point T • T

2. equidistant from the endpoints of $\overline{AB}$

Draw the locus of points in a plane that satisfy the given conditions.

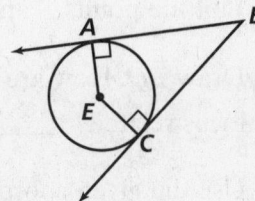

3. equidistant from points X and Y and on a circle with center at point X and radius $= \frac{1}{2}XY$

4. equidistant from the sides of $\angle ABC$ and on $\odot E$

Describe each locus.

5. the set of points in a plane equidistant from two parallel lines _____

_____

6. the set of points in space a given distance from a point _____

_____

7. the set of points in a plane less than 1 in. from a given point _____

_____

8. Sketch and label the locus of all points in a plane 0.75 in. from a line $\overleftrightarrow{RS}$.

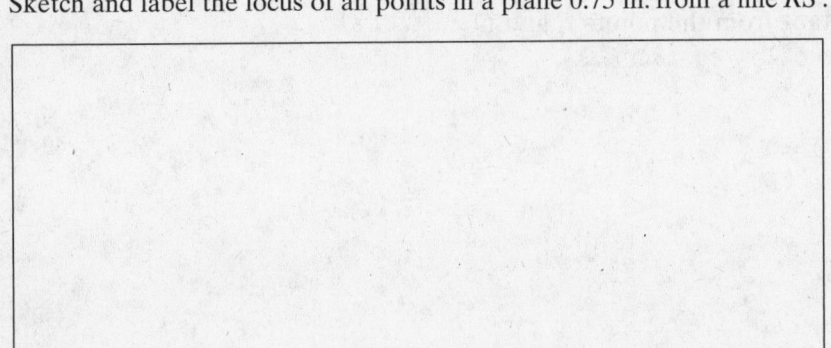

12-6 • Guided Problem Solving

GPS **Student Page 703, Exercise 24**

Coordinate Geometry Write an equation for the locus: In the plane, the points equidistant from the points $P(1, 3)$ and $Q(5, 1)$.

Read and Understand

1. What kind of geometric object will the locus of points be? _____

Plan and Solve

2. Plot the points P and Q on the grid to the right.

3. Draw $\overline{PQ}$. How are the slope of $\overline{PQ}$ and the slope of the locus related? _____

4. Use the given coordinates to find the slope M of $\overline{PQ}$. $M =$ _____

5. Therefore, what is the slope m of the locus? $m =$ _____

6. What is one point on the locus? That is, what is one obvious point equidistant from P and Q? _____

7. What are the coordinates of this point? _____

8. Use the coordinates and the value of m to find the y-intercept b of the locus. $b =$ _____

9. Write the equation of the locus in the form $y = mx + b$. _____

Look Back and Check

10. Locate the x-intercept of the locus given in Step 8. _____

    Is it equidistant from the two points given in the problem statement? _____

Solve Another Problem

11. Reverse the coordinates—$P(3, 1)$ and $Q(1, 5)$. Write the equation of the locus of points equidistant from the points P and Q.

12A: Graphic Organizer

For use before Lesson 12-1

Study Skill After reading a section, recall the information. Ask yourself questions about the section. If you cannot recall enough information, reread portions you had trouble remembering. The more time you spend studying the more you can recall.

Write your answers.

1. What is the chapter title? _____

2. Find the Table of Contents page for this chapter at the front of the book. Name four topics you will study in this chapter.

_____   _____

_____   _____

3. Complete the graphic organizer as you work through the chapter.
   1. Write the title of the chapter in the center oval.
   2. When you begin a lesson, write the name of the lesson in a rectangle.
   3. When you complete that lesson, write a skill or key concept from that lesson in the outer oval linked to that rectangle.
   Continue with steps 2 and 3 clockwise around the graphic organizer.

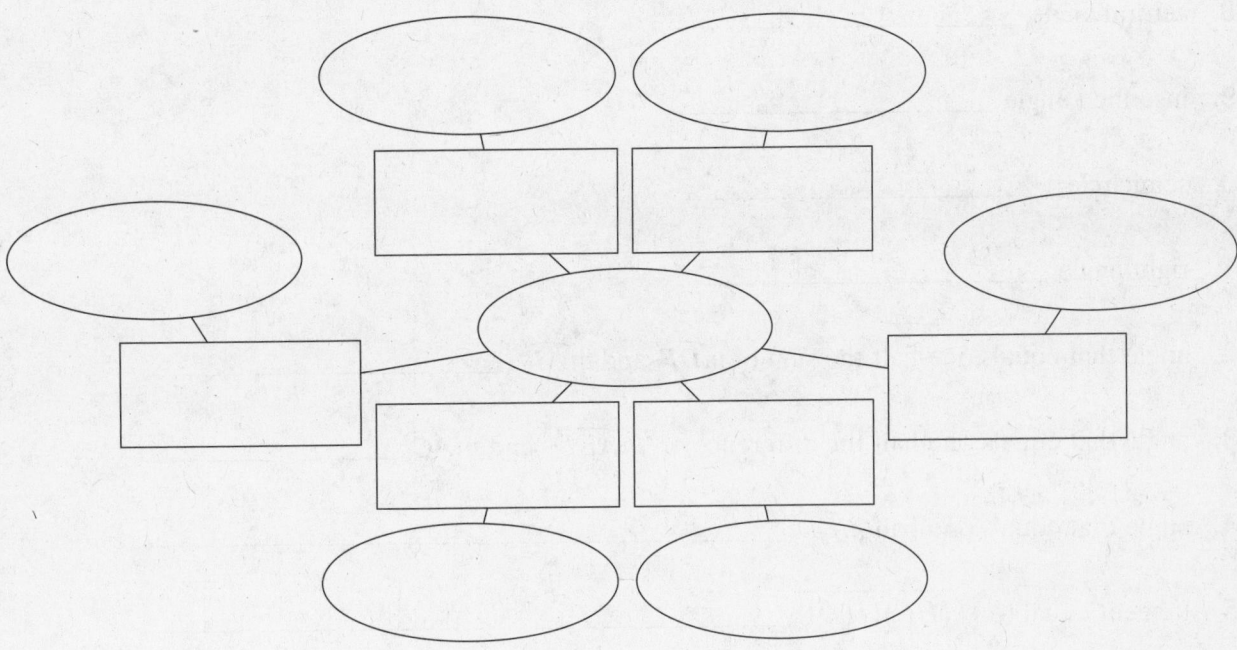

12B: Reading Comprehension

For use after Lesson 12-5

Study Skill Sometimes it is hard to understand mathematical definitions that you read unless you can also see a diagram. When you think you will have trouble remembering definitions, draw and label a diagram.

Refer to the diagram to identify the items in the following list.

1. 2 diameters _____

2. 3 chords _____

3. secant segment _____

4. tangent segment _____

5. 3 minor arcs _____

6. 3 major arcs _____

7. 2 congruent arcs _____

8. central angle _____

9. inscribed angle _____

10. semicircle _____

11. right angle _____

12. angle that equals one-half the sum of $m\widehat{DF}$ and $m\widehat{AB}$ _____

13. angle that equals one-half the difference of $m\widehat{AED}$ and $m\widehat{AC}$ _____

14. angle that equals one-half $m\widehat{ED}$ _____

15. tangent equal to $\sqrt{(HC)(HD)}$ _____

16. High-Use Academic Words In the direction line, what does *refer to* mean for you to do?

    a. get information from
    b. make measurements of

Name _____ Class _____ Date _____

12C: Reading/Writing Math Symbols

For use after Lesson 12-3

Study Skill When you are reading, use the context to help you decide which of several meanings a word has. Clues from the context can sometimes also help you decide the meanings of unfamiliar terms.

Use symbols to describe the relationships described below.

1. $\overleftrightarrow{BC}$ is tangent to the circle. What do you know about $\overleftrightarrow{BC}$ and the radius?

   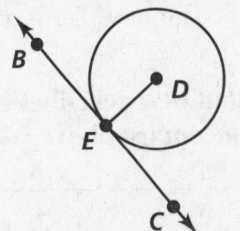

   _____

2. In $\odot G$, $\overleftrightarrow{EF}$ is perpendicular to $\overline{GH}$. What do you know about the line and the circle?

   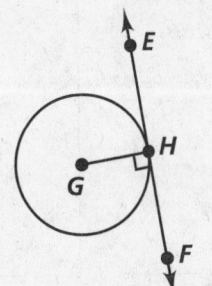

   _____

3. If $\overline{WX}$ and $\overline{ZX}$ are tangent to the circle at W and Z, what do you know about the two segments?

   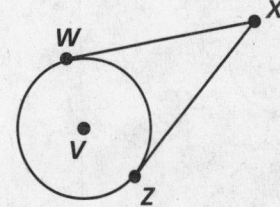

   _____

4. If $\overline{AB}$ is a diameter and bisects $\overline{XY}$, and Z is the center of the circle, what do you know about $\overline{AB}$ and $\overline{XY}$?

   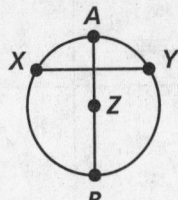

   _____

5. $\overline{JH}$ is a diameter and bisects $\overline{KL}$ and G is the center of the circle. If $LH = 5$ and $ML = 3$, what is the length of $\overline{HM}$?

   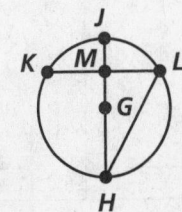

   _____

12D: Visual Vocabulary Practice

For use after Lesson 12-6

Study Skill You know that you have mastered a new term when you are able to apply it.

Concept List

chord	circumscribed about	inscribed angle
inscribed in	intercepted arc	locus
secant	standard form of an equation of a circle	tangent to a circle

Write the concept that best describes each exercise.
Choose from the concept list above.

1. 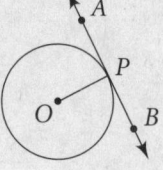 _____	**2.** $(x + 3)^2 + (y - 1)^2 = 5^2$ _____	**3.** 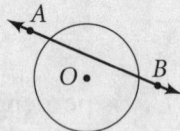 _____
4. 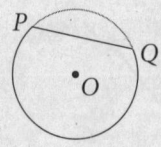 _____	**5.** 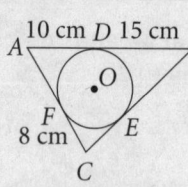 $\triangle ABC$ _____	**6.** 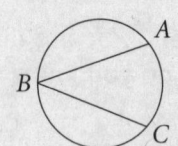 $\widehat{AC}$ _____
7. 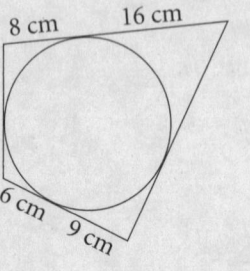 _____	**8.** $m\angle ABC = \frac{1}{2}m\widehat{AC}$ _____	**9.** 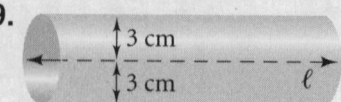 points that are 3 cm from a line ℓ _____

12E: Vocabulary Check

Study Skill Strengthen your vocabulary. Use these pages and add cues and summaries by applying the Cornell Notetaking style.

Write the definition for each word at the right. To check your work, fold the paper back along the dotted line to see the correct answers.

_____

_____

Inscribed in

_____

_____

Chord

_____

_____

Point of tangency

_____

_____

Tangent to a circle

_____

_____

Circumscribed about

_____

_____

12E: Vocabulary Check (continued)   For use after Lesson 12-4

Write the vocabulary word for each definition. To check your work, fold the
paper forward along the dotted line to see the correct answers.

A circle inside a polygon
with the sides of the
polygon tangent to the
circle.   _____

A segment whose
endpoints are on a circle.   _____

The single point of
intersection of a tangent
line and a circle.   _____

A line, segment, or ray in
the plane of a circle that
intersects the circle in
exactly one point.   _____

A circle outside a
polygon with the vertices
of the polygon on the
circle.   _____

12F: Vocabulary Review

For use with Chapter Review

Study Skill Make sure you are alert when you are learning a new concept or new vocabulary words. If your mind is wandering as you read or as you listen to a lecture, the concepts you read or hear may not become entrenched in your memory.

Match each term in Column A with its definition in Column B by drawing a line between them.

Column A		Column B
1. chord	A.	sum of two vectors
2. standard form of an equation of a circle	B.	any quantity that has magnitude and direction
3. locus	C.	line perpendicular to the radius of a circle at the endpoint of the radius
4. resultant	D.	a segment whose endpoints are on a circle
5. tangent	E.	$a^2 + b^2 = c^2$
6. vector	F.	$(x - h)^2 + (y - k)^2 = r^2$
7. Pythagorean Theorem	G.	set of all points that meet a stated condition

Match each term in Column C with its definition in Column D by drawing a line between them.

Column C		Column D
8. secant	H.	angle of measurement above a horizontal line
9. inscribed triangle	I.	a triangle with all the vertices lying on a circle
10. angle of depression	J.	formed by the intersection of a solid and a plane
11. polyhedron	K.	segment formed by the intersection of two faces of a polyhedron
12. angle of elevation	L.	angle of measurement below a horizontal line
13. edge	M.	line that intersects a circle at two points
14. cross section	N.	a three-dimensional figure whose surfaces are polygons